The Princess of Albemarle

The American South Series

Elizabeth R. Varon and Orville Vernon Burton, Editors

JANE TURNER CENSER

The Princess
of Albemarle

AMÉLIE RIVES, AUTHOR AND CELEBRITY
AT THE FIN DE SIÈCLE

UNIVERSITY OF VIRGINIA PRESS
Charlottesville and London

University of Virginia Press
© 2022 by the Rector and Visitors of the University of Virginia
All rights reserved
Printed in the United States of America on acid-free paper

First published 2022

1 3 5 7 9 8 6 4 2

Library of Congress Cataloging-in-Publication Data

Names: Censer, Jane Turner, author.
Title: The princess of Albemarle : Amélie Rives, author and
celebrity at the fin de siècle / Jane Turner Censer.
Description: Charlottesville : University of Virginia Press, 2022. | Series:
The American South series | Includes bibliographical references and index.
Identifiers: LCCN 2021042974 (print) | LCCN 2021042975 (ebook) |
ISBN 9780813948195 (hardcover) | ISBN 9780813948201 (ebook)
Subjects: LCSH: Rives, Amélie, 1863–1945. | Novelists, American—19th century—
Biography. | Women and literature—United States—History—20th century. |
Women, White—Southern States—History—20th century. | Upper class women—
Southern States—History—20th century.
Classification: LCC PS3093 .C46 2022 (print) | LCC PS3093 (ebook) |
DDC 813/.4 [B]—dc23/eng/20211013
LC record available at https://lccn.loc.gov/2021042974
LC ebook record available at https://lccn.loc.gov/2021042975

Cover photo: Amélie Rives with flowers in her hair.
(Amélie Rives Troubetzkoy Collection, The Valentine)

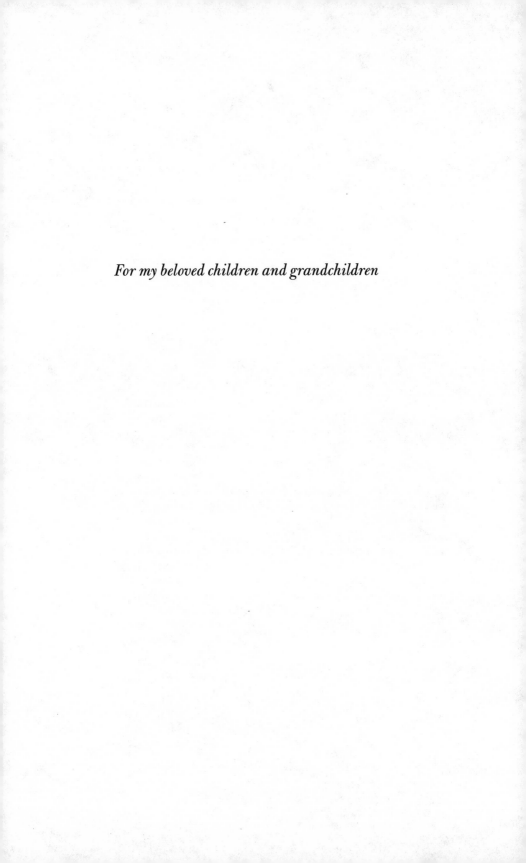

For my beloved children and grandchildren

Contents

Contents

Illustrations

Acknowledgments

Even though writing may seem a solitary endeavor, producing a research-based book means asking for and receiving the help of many. With this manuscript as so many others since our graduate school years together, J. William Harris helped me sharpen both my argument and my prose. Kate Grauvogel, Cynthia Kierner, and Elizabeth Varon also read all the chapters and from their different expertises provided valuable suggestions. In the scholarly community, I appreciate the help of Leila Christenbury, Lisa Francavilla, and Sandra Treadway. Among the numerous friends and colleagues at George Mason University who provided aid are Sheila ffolliott, Rosemary Jann, Deborah Kaplan, Peter Stearns, George Oberle, Jennifer Ritterhouse, Ellen Todd, and Rosemarie Zagarri. I also would like to thank George Mason University and the Department of History and Art History for research and sabbatical support.

The hospitality I received made my research trips enjoyable and much more productive. I am grateful to Cheryl and John Lang in Raleigh, Carol and Jim Hoopes and Terry Rockefeller and J. William Harris in Boston, and my cousins Jane and Paul Kingston in Charlottesville for being such gracious hosts. J. Winthrop Aldrich was kind enough to share the Rokeby letters that remain with the descendants of the Chanler family; I very much appreciate his willingness to open up the family archive to me.

Librarians and archivists are essential supports of research, and I am deeply indebted to a score of talented professionals, who often went to extraordinary lengths to help me find important documents. I am grateful to the staffs of the Rare Book and Manuscript Library, Columbia University; the David M. Rubenstein Rare Book and Manuscript Library, Duke University; Houghton Library, Harvard University; the Library of Congress;

the Southern Historical Collection, University of North Carolina; and the Virginia Historical Society. I want especially to thank Steven Smith at the Historical Society of Pennsylvania; Meredith Mann at the Brooke Russell Astor Reading Room in the New York Public Library; Charles Doran at Special Collections in Firestone Library, Princeton University; Regina Rush and Anne Causey at the Albert and Shirley Small Special Collections Library, University of Virginia; and June Can and Ingrid Lennon-Pressey at the Beinecke Library, Yale University.

Because Amélie Rives was so frequently photographed, I wished the book's illustrations to show how the public recognized and evaluated her image. Securing these pictures during the pandemic with its closed libraries and reading rooms posed special problems. I am deeply indebted to Anne P. Causey at the Albert and Shirley Small Special Collections Library, University of Virginia; Diana Carey at the Schlesinger Library, Radcliffe Institute, Harvard University; Edward Copenhagen at the Harvard University Archives; and Andrew Foster and Troy Wilkinson at the Virginia Historical Society of the Virginia Museum of History and Culture. Dana Puga at the Library of Virginia went the extra mile in assisting me to find replacement images. Kelly Kerny and Meg Hughes also were of enormous help in accessing the extraordinary riches of the Amélie Rives Troubetzkoy Collection at the Valentine Museum in Richmond.

Portions of chapters 2, 3, 7, and 8 appeared in "The Southern Lady and the Northern Publishers: A Tumultuous Relationship," *Journal of Southern History* 85 (February 2019): 7–32; and "The Gift of Friendship: Ellen Glasgow and Amélie Rives, Virginia Writers," *Virginia Magazine of History and Biography* 124 (2016): 99–133.

I should also note the hard work expended on this book at the University of Virginia Press. My editor Nadine Zimmerli was extraordinarily helpful at every step of the way, from expertly shepherding the manuscript through the review process to providing important editorial advice. Ellen Satrom has been a constant source of good advice, and Ceci Sorochin kindly helped me with some of the more technical issues of illustrations. Ruth Melville's expert copyediting saved me from the many infelicities and glitches that had crept in over time.

Finally, in all this work my family has been a source of inspiration as well as invaluable assistance. Over the years my husband, Jack R. Censer, has read, discussed, and improved my writings; I think he knows how crucial his support has been to all my endeavors, scholarly and otherwise. My daughter, Marjorie, and my son, Joel, grew up arguing over history, and their spouses, Thomas Gaultney and Jennifer Spector, have learned tolerance for the family obsession with the past. It remains to be seen if my granddaughters, Alexandra Jane Gaultney, Remy Pearl Censer, and Marigold Diane Censer, will follow that tradition.

The Princess of Albemarle

Introduction

In 1890 Amélie Rives was one of the most famous women in America. Only two years earlier she had published a magazine story, "The Quick or the Dead?," whose heroine's waffling between loyalty to her dead husband and her attraction to his very alive and lively cousin entranced thousands of readers but outraged ministers and other guardians of public virtue. A decade before author Kate Chopin wrote about female passion, Rives had created a heroine aware of sexual attraction and seemingly ready to act on it. Her story became a best-selling novella, which featured its beautiful golden-haired author on the frontispiece. Such billing, along with newspaper accounts from Maine to Oregon that touted her as "one of the most remarkably beautiful" women of the day, emblazoned her name and likeness on the national mind.[1]

Americans more attuned to newspapers than to the literary world might have pointed in 1890 to the numerous jokes and anecdotes circulating about Rives's beauty and headstrong actions. Her precipitant wedding in 1888 to Archie Chanler, great-great-grandson of John Jacob Astor and heir to an enormous fortune, added to her celebrity status—a status further stamped by visits to Europe to improve her painting and drawing. Moreover, reports that a fellow art student had committed suicide, allegedly because of an obsession with her, added scandal to the many stories of her beauty and unconventional behavior.

As the 1890s began, Rives appeared to be a new kind of celebrity. She seemed poised to become an important figure in popular culture as well as a literary phenomenon. An 1891 article on authors in the postwar South in *Lippincott's Magazine* referred to Amélie Rives as "the most noted of the younger writers not only of the South but of America."[2] Turning out a raft of historical dramas, local color stories, and poetry, Rives was beginning what promised to be a highly productive literary career as well as emerging as a favorite subject of newspapers and magazines. Yet over the next decade, Rives's career ran aground on the shoals created by her unhappy marriage to an extremely wealthy man. Extensive luxurious travel, life with a husband who preferred her not to write, and her own physical ailments led to an addiction to morphine and cocaine. All this sapped literary productivity. Even as she wrote less, her stories continued to tout their heroines' beauty, outspokenness, and passionate natures. Seven years into her marriage, Amélie filed for divorce. Less than six months later she married Pierre Troubetzkoy, a Russian prince and portrait painter—news that the media splashed across America.

Rives continued to write novels, short stories, plays, and poems well into the twentieth century, but by her death in 1945 the public no longer clamored for works by or about her. Showing that she had been slipping from the public eye, the *New York Times* obituary called her a "popular novelist of the Nineties" and felt obliged to remind readers of the "the literary furor" caused by her first novella "because of its frank treatment of subjects then regarded as taboo in any book."[3]

Rives disappeared from popular culture even after she had managed to claw her way back into literary life. In the early decades of the twentieth century, she reclaimed a reputation in literary circles as she changed her celebrity from resting on beauty and outlandish behavior to the more demure stance of an aristocratic author who held both European and American ties. In part, she relied on carefully staged interviews to burnish her image. And in terms of her wider public, Rives took even greater control. She destroyed her correspondence—from the letters of her youthful swains to those of more famous admirers such as Britain's Lord Curzon. Not a single letter between Amélie Rives and her second husband can be found, even though the couple frequently lived apart. Yet despite her destruction of documents that came into her possession, Rives wrote such vivid letters that many of her correspondents retained them. These form one of the pillars of this book.

In the almost eighty years that have elapsed since Rives's death, she has further receded from common knowledge. To be sure, scholars, especially those interested in Virginia writers, have not totally overlooked her. Welford Dunaway Taylor investigated her literary career in his 1973 volume on her life, as did George C. Longest, who wrote a doctoral dissertation on her writings and compiled a bibliography of publications about her. More recently, Donna Lucey penned a joint biography of Rives and her wealthy, eccentric first husband. Lucey's title, *Archie and Amélie: Love and Madness in the Gilded Age,* indicates her focus on the couple's relationship and aberrant behavior.[4]

A further examination of Rives's career is in order, because her writings and her self-fashioning provide an excellent window on transformations in southern and American culture for women, including elite women, as the nineteenth century turned into the twentieth. Even though Rives should not and cannot be called a typical person, many aspects of her life, like her fiction, cast light on the boundaries of acceptable thought and proper behavior. Not only did her life touch on the important alterations in gender relations and representations of female beauty and behavior that were taking place, Rives and her career also cast revealing angles on the growing cult of celebrity and the changing world of literary endeavor. Like others living in the glare of publicity, she found celebrity to be a burden as well as a means to merchandise her talents.

How an ambitious, privileged woman circumnavigated the challenging social and literary currents of the day inspired my study. Each chapter of the book illuminates Rives's adventures in self-fashioning and the pitfalls that she encountered as she became a published author and a celebrated beauty. Her long relationship with the press prefigured the love-hate bond common among modern celebrities—even though Rives influenced the coverage, she nevertheless was also criticized and lampooned. She also exemplified changes in the representations of female activity and beauty as well as gender relations. While her story could be interpreted as the triumph of the brainy belle through marriage to northern money, contemporaries would have read presentations of her illnesses and breakdowns as indications of the life led by a nervous and overwrought "authoress."

In my account, the reader sees how Rives confronted the misery of her first marriage and remade her life—choosing a divorce and remarriage to Pierre Troubetzkoy, a handsome Italian-born portrait painter. That he was descended from Russian princes gave her the opportunity to refashion her identity as well as to achieve marital happiness. She resumed her fiction writing but presented herself as an aristocrat—she was an author who lived secluded on an estate in Virginia and summered on Lake Maggiore in Italy. After writing two well-received books in blank verse, she turned to novels that would find a wide audience and provide much needed financial support. In the twentieth century she experimented with writing for the stage and screen and achieved a measure of success there as well. Supporting fellow authors in the face of censorship, Rives voiced her approval of woman's rights and antilynching legislation. She also provided companionship and encouragement to fellow writers such as Ellen Glasgow, Louis Auchincloss, Julian Meade, and Emily Clark. Overall, her career and its decline in American literary and cultural memory provide insights into how celebrity and reputation ebb and flow over time.

Important to her writing career, Rives always considered herself more a Virginian than a southerner. From early childhood, she cared deeply about Castle Hill, the family plantation in Albemarle, as well as the hills and streams of the Piedmont, and she made Castle Hill her permanent home after her first marriage dissolved. While often using Virginia backdrops for her novels, after the turn of the century she moved away from southern themes and thus dropped out of those grouped under the rubric of southern writers. Instead, her books came from an author who presented herself as part of cosmopolitan culture; she advocated a more tolerant South but was not an activist, and she herself had not broken free of racial and class stereotypes. The following chapters examine and present a fascinating life and lead the reader through the changing cultural world of late nineteenth- and early twentieth-century America. For, in the end, perhaps the most unforgettable character that Amélie Rives ever created was herself.

ONE

"There May Be Something Yet for Me to Do in This Big World"

Beginnings

From her earliest days, Amélie Rives commanded attention. Even amid war, the extended Rives family greeted Amélie's birth, on August 23, 1863, in Richmond as a major event. Her father, Alfred Landon Rives, was an engineer with Lee's army; her mother, born Sarah MacMurdo (known as Sadie), was a Richmond native. Her paternal grandmother, the redoubtable Judith Page Rives, declared, "This happy result is the greatest possible relief to our minds." Asked for help in choosing the baby's name, the elder Mrs. Rives promptly lobbied for one that could not be shortened into a nickname. Judith soon decided that the name of her own daughter Amélie would be particularly apt for this grandchild: "How would it do to call her after Amélie? It would be a loving and tender souvenir for us all."[1] Thus the new baby acquired from her aunt an odd, foreign-sounding name with an unusual spelling.

Amélie's name connected her to an extended paternal family who dominated much of her emotional as well as physical life. Her grandfather, William Cabell Rives, had studied law with Jefferson and was a protégé of Madison. In 1819 Rives married Judith Page Walker, who had inherited the plantation "Castle Hill" with its huge acreage in northeastern Albemarle County. William served two different stints as the minister plenipotentiary to France, from 1829 to 1832 and from 1849 to 1853. During his first term, the Revolution of 1830 brought Louis Philippe to the throne as France's constitutional monarch. Louis Philippe and his wife, Queen Amélie Marie, welcomed the American diplomat and his wife, who then named their newborn daughter Amélie Louise in honor of the queen. In addition to his

Alfred Landon Rives, the father of Amélie Rives, was a French-trained engineer. (Amélie Rives Troubetzkoy Collection, The Valentine)

diplomatic posts, William also served in the U.S. Senate in the 1830s and 1840s, first as a Democrat, later as a Whig.

The family of Amélie's mother, the MacMurdos, seems to have been less prominent in Amélie's life. Among Sadie's progenitors were a Scottish merchant and an Episcopalian minister, Richard Channing Moore, who served as bishop of Virginia. Over the years Amélie said and wrote relatively little about her mother's family. The MacMurdo relatives, however, played an important role in 1864. Although family legend later indicated Robert E. Lee as a godparent to baby Amélie, a modern researcher has found that her MacMurdo grandparents and Aunt Amélie Rives Sigourney were the listed sponsors for the infant at her baptism, which occurred at St. Paul's Episcopal Church in Richmond, right across the square from the state capitol, in February 1864.[2]

As the war was ending in 1865, Sadie Rives, against the advice of relatives, traveled through the unsettled countryside with baby Amélie to join her in-laws at Castle Hill. There, the family cooed over Amélie, and Sadie and the baby stayed until autumn, before returning to Richmond. Castle Hill became so important to Amélie that, even years later, she mentioned in notes for a biographical sketch that she had been "taken as a baby to the estate of Castle Hill, Virginia, which belonged to my Rives grandparents. . . . my first memories are of the lovely countryside which lies at the foot of the Western Mountains, near the Blue Ridge."[3]

After the Civil War, the Rives family began renewing its ties. Amélie's kinship network was particularly far-flung by the standards of the day. Her uncles and aunts—William Jr., Francis, and the older Amélie—had married wealthy northerners and moved to New York and New England. The Civil War broke mail communication between the sections. The separation from the aunts and uncles in the East ended in 1865, but an economic gap had emerged. The Rives cousins in New York and Boston, and the Sigourney cousins in Connecticut, were extremely prosperous and even pampered, whereas Castle Hill was sinking into shabbiness. Although the northern relatives were kind and even generous to their southern kinfolks—for example, sponsoring a visit to Newport, Rhode Island, in summer 1866 for Judith and William Cabell Rives and their unmarried daughter Ella—criticism and condescension frequently accompanied such largesse.[4]

An important part of the family reconstitution was finding a job for Amélie's father, Alfred, who had studied engineering in France. Although he considered positions in the North, he preferred to stay in the South—whether because his Confederate army service had made a southern post necessary, or only because that was more comfortable, is not clear. In the immediate postwar period, building and rebuilding railroads offered a great deal of work for a trained engineer like Alfred. His first jobs in the postwar period took him to his wife's hometown of Richmond.

Sadie and Alfred lived a comfortable life in Richmond, with a succession of nursemaids for toddler Amélie, who was weaned around age two. Their household, with its African American domestic workers, resembled others in an emerging southern urban middle class. Yet links to the family plantation remained strong, and they spent most summers and long vacations at Castle Hill. Before Amélie's third birthday, she acquired a baby sister, Gertrude.[5] In 1870 Sadie, visiting Castle Hill, reported to Alfred that when the

Sarah C. MacMurdo Rives, the mother of Amélie Rives, had in her youth been considered a belle in her native Richmond. (Amélie Rives Troubetzkoy Collection, The Valentine)

nursemaid "Mary got mad at Amélie," the aggrieved employee declared that "she had stood it as long as she could." This servant's comment suggests that six-year-old Amélie was asserting a strong will and definite opinions.[6]

By then, a family routine had emerged of spending long summers at Castle Hill. From an early age, Amélie loved the estate. She called Castle Hill "the old ancestral home, which was a royal grant and [had] been in the

The Princess of Albemarle

family ever since," and later recalled early days there as idyllic: "Her childhood was a most happy one, spent chiefly in her beautiful old country home, with a father and mother so loving and indulgent that she never wanted for a 'fairy godmother' as so many children do!" Indeed, as an adult, Amélie erased the Richmond sojourn from accounts of her early life to concentrate on the delicious summers at Castle Hill, which held "everything to delight a child": "fine horses to ride, wide fields and woods to ramble in; mountains up which we scrambled on ponies or on foot, and one of my happiest memories is the old Water Mill, which belonged to the estate."[7] Amélie as a child and even later apparently thought little about the labor of over sixty enslaved workers, who at the eve of the Civil War had been crucial to this estate's prosperity. Instead she associated the plantation with her relatives and her northern uncles, aunts, and cousins, whose visits created fun and excitement. In 1868, when Amélie was only five, her grandmother wrote to the Boston relatives: "Little Amélie was quite heartbroken at seeing you all depart in masse, and her grief was really touching to me."[8]

Part of the appeal of Castle Hill lay in the erudition and sophistication that Amélie's grandparents, William Cabell Rives and Judith Page Rives, had brought to the house and its grounds. They greatly expanded the house, adding a modern wing to embellish the original eighteenth-century farmhouse; and upon their return from France in the 1840s and 1850s, they redecorated Castle Hill with French furniture, prints, and textiles. A twentieth-century observer thought that the house appeared at first "a modest mid-nineteenth-century planter's mansion." Upon entering, however, he "found still another atmosphere. The simplicity of the exterior was tempered by something more sophisticated, more elegant, within. A wide noble hall stretched to the back of the mansion, past a circular stairwell, to unite what had once been two houses, the nineteenth-century brick front with the simpler clapboard eighteenth-century rear."[9]

The literary turn of the Rives family was apparent in the voluminous library at Castle Hill and the breadth of writings by family members. William published biographies of two of his political mentors, Thomas Jefferson and James Madison, while Judith, whom Amélie called "Bonne maman" (the French term for grandmother) published two memoirs about her time abroad as wife of the minister to France. During the dark days of the Civil War, Judith also penned an autobiography intended for her children and grandchildren, especially those separated from her by war. Amélie's

Castle Hill showed this imposing front in the 1870s when Amélie Rives and her family often visited. (Amélie Rives Troubetzkoy Collection, The Valentine)

namesake, her aunt Amélie Rives Sigourney, was an unpublished writer, celebrated among family and friends for her poetry and stories.

Hours spent in the Rives family library at Castle Hill helped to create Amélie's love of literature, as she later remembered: "When I was a little girl I spent all my spare moments with the quaint old volumes, and oh, how I enjoyed the rich literary treats that some of those old books offered." To readers of her early stories written in Elizabethan dialect, Amélie offered: "I owe all my quaint expressions, all my peculiarities of style and the success I may have attained to the fact of my browsing so continuously among such a wealth of knowledge."[10]

The Castle Hill relatives thoroughly cosseted and spoiled young Amélie. When she was only three, her grandmother and unmarried aunt tried to buy enough chances at the church bazaar to win a china doll for her. Bemoaning a lack of success, Judith Rives declared: "Certainly if there had been anything in the number of chances, dear little Amélie would have won the prize." The following year, Grandmother Judith worked on a special Christmas gift for Amélie, "making a variety of pretty little additions to her baby house. As I could not take the shorter way of making her a handsome Christmas gift, I have given my time to some tiny works of art."[11]

At Castle Hill Amélie acquired her lifelong love of the outdoors and animals, especially horses and dogs. Grandmother Judith purchased a pony,

In this picture of women in the Rives family, Amélie stands between her mother, Sarah Rives, and her grandmother, Judith Page Rives. (Amélie Rives Troubetzkoy Collection, The Valentine)

Fairy, for eleven-year-old Amélie to share with her younger sister Gertrude. Although the children from an early age had ridden horses and ponies, Fairy was a special treasure. Amélie's glee was apparent in her grandmother's description: "It is really a beautiful sight to see Amélie mounted on her 'fairy,' her golden hair flying in the wind, and her blue eyes dancing with glee, and her cheeks glowing with excitement as she gallops off."[12]

In 1870 Amélie's father accepted the job of chief engineer of the Mobile and Ohio Railroad. Working out of Mobile, Alfred decided to move his family there, in what was a traumatic uprooting for seven-year-old Amélie. Her grandmother Judith vividly recorded the leave-taking, in December 1870, as the family boarded the train to Mobile: "I was deeply touched at the simple but great sorrow of dear little Amélie in bidding me good bye. The tears *rained* down her cheeks as she clasped her arms round my neck with 'Oh me! oh me! how *can* I go away from you!' running back again and again to repeat the same words and the same fervent embrace."[13] Amélie herself in a youthful letter described a similar scene: "When I left Castle Hill I cried so[,] Papa could not comfort me, first I looked at the mountains then back at the [railway] car until I was quite tired then I sat still hugging my doll closer and closer until I fairly thought I would mash her to pieces."[14]

Few descriptions of Amélie Rives's life in Mobile have survived, even though she lived there for almost twelve years, from 1871 until 1883, in part in a comfortable house on the corner of Government and Franklin Streets. As in Richmond, the Rives household enjoyed urban amenities. In June 1873 Alfred noted about his wife: "Sadie now has a piano & first class sewing machine, so that she has the elements of constant occupation, the great source of contentment, if not happiness."[15] In 1874 Amélie acquired a second younger sister, Sarah Landon Rives, called Daisy as a child.

To be sure, young Amélie still expected to be the center of attention. At age eleven she recorded in her diary how she wanted a singing lesson from her mother, who then allowed other family responsibilities to crowd it out: "Mama ment [*sic*] to give me one but she wanted to finish a little pincushion that Gertrude had made. . . . so she worked on[.] when she had finished . . . it was entirely too late and to clap the climax Daisy began to cry so mama had to go to her and my singing lesson landed in the mud."[16]

In Mobile, where Amélie had tutors and governesses, her education was heavily weighted toward the arts and languages. She began music at age six and studied French and Latin at a young age.[17] Considerable parts of her learning came in unsystematic fashion, as from an early age Amélie spent much time reading and writing, drawing and painting. Her actual interaction with the world of books came from her family and her own efforts. A precocious lover of language, she was reading by age four and writing soon after. Amélie later recalled that she "began to write both in prose & verse when she was so small that she had to write all her letters in capitals." She declared that she could not "remember when I did not want to 'make up stories' or spin queer rhymes. As soon as I could write, I began to set these on paper." In an oft-told family story, when Amélie was restricted in the amount of paper she was allowed, she began to write an entire story on the broad hem of her starched petticoat. Her father then intervened, declaring that "such ingenuity and persistence deserves encouragement. She shall have all the paper that she wants."[18]

While still a child, Amélie began to assemble publications. She later recalled: "At ten years old I used to issue a small Magazine (all written and illustrated by my own hand) for family consumption! I have still some copies of this quaint weekly which I found among my dear mother's papers!" Yet

The Princess of Albemarle

another family anecdote referred to her habit of reading thoroughly before writing. When Amélie's father suggested she worked too hard before even beginning, she replied to him: "Papa, I am not a very clever writer and I must know all about my subject, so people will not notice that I am a beginner."[19]

With her great fondness for storytelling and description, eleven-year-old Amélie, in her diary, showed precocious skills at character depiction and dialect dialogue. She opened her tale with a request to be allowed to ride her pony to the gates of Castle Hill one summer day: "When I came to breakfast this morning I suggested for Bonne maman to let me go ride by myself down to the duble [sic] gates. 'well I think,' said she that you might try it." Young Amélie then, in her account, "went right straight to Colin he is the coach man and told him in a very authoritative manner that he might bring Fairy to the door as soon as possable. 'Yes marm, sartin marm, jes as soon as I get a finished my breakfast' was the reply. Well said I with dignity be sure." Here the imperious child chronicled her demand for her pony, only to be met by the quiet composure of Collin Byrd, the family's coachman, who insisted on his right to first finish his breakfast.[20]

Other diary entries at this time showed Amélie's fascination with miscellaneous matters pertaining to the workings of the Castle Hill estate: "The key of the wardrobe downstairs will open the door of the wardrobe upstairs in the hall I found it out." Others concerned the natural and social world. "I noticed that if you put hats on a butterflys hed it will kill it," Amélie noted. While chronicling daily activities, she also experimented with cameo sketches. Anticipating a letter, she described her friend Ellen Smith in expressive, misspelled words: "she is my frind my best my dearest frind soft large blue grey eyes a sweet sad mouth and soft shining brown hair streaked with gold at the temples[.] her helth is rather delecate but I love her dearly very dearly[.]"[21]

Part of young Amélie's education was religious. Piety was thriving in late nineteenth-century America, and the Rives family was strongly observant within the Episcopalian tradition, which while inflected by evangelism retained its decorous, ornate nature. Like others in her maternal family, Amélie prided herself on being descended from Bishop Moore. But such religiosity was apparent in her paternal family as well. Indefatigable grandmother Judith and her unmarried daughter Ella were mainstays of the Cobham Episcopal church. In 1875 Judith reported that they had raised $225 to repair the church's roof, "mostly by the sale of fancy work done by Ella and me, and a few donations."[22]

At age twelve, Amélie Rives wanted to be a writer; a year earlier she wrote a diary about visiting Castle Hill. (Amélie Rives Troubetzkoy Collection, The Valentine)

The religious orientation of the Rives family, as well as its cosmopolitanism, can be found in the reading material provided young Amélie in the well-stocked library at Castle Hill. Among the books there was *Conseils de morale* (*Moral Tales*) in the original French, by Elisabeth Pauline Guizot, first wife of the French prime minister—a volume that may have been brought from France by Amélie's grandparents. An 1868 edition of *Rosamond: A Series of Tales for Girls,* by the well-known Anglo-Irish author Maria Edgeworth, bore the inscription to "Amélie L. Rives from her loving Mamma."[23]

In addition to these books from foreign authors, Amélie also received other religious publications, especially from her mother. Such books held a hardy dose of Christian benevolence and correct deportment. Three-year-old Amélie received the book *Songs for the Little Ones at Home,* published by the American Tract Society, a well-known organization specializing in moral uplift. Nine years later, Sadie gave young Amélie a collection of sermons for the young by the Episcopal minister Richard Newton, entitled *Rays from the Sun of Righteousness.* Focusing on the life of Jesus as a guide for moral behavior and benevolent action, Newton averred that Jesus resembled the sun because he had "a great *drawing power,* a great *healing power,* and a great *comforting power.*"[24]

Even some of Amélie's lighter reading held a strongly moral message. In 1875, as a twelve-year-old, she was reading a book by the best-selling author Susan Warner entitled *Opportunities: A Sequel to "What She Could,"* which retailed the story of Matilda, who, after her baptism, sought to care for the poor and needy and convert them to Christianity.[25] Particularly interesting is that the dates of the presentation of these books did not coincide with birthdays or other holidays, such as Christmas. Rather, gifts of books came at various times, showing the Rives family's bookishness, affluence, and generosity.

Anecdotes about the youthful riding activities of Amélie abound and show how important equestrian and outdoor activities were to her family. According to family lore, her first ride on horseback came at age two as she lay on a cushion in front of the family's African American coachman. Rives later recounted her proficiency in terms that other sources echo: "At six years old she rode well, and by the time she was twelve had come off her pony to other horses in every way that it is possible for a human being to descend involuntarily to earth! After that time she was fairly seasoned and her horse had to fall itself to make her fall." At fourteen, Amélie received the mare "Queen" as a birthday gift from her parents.[26]

As Amélie became a young lady in the years between twelve and eighteen, her life may have changed less than those of many of her privileged peers. From the beginning of organized academies in the early nineteenth century, women's education North and South had become more common and more intellectually rigorous. The Civil War had devastated higher education in the South, but in the 1870s and 1880s some families in both the North and the South were sending their daughters to high schools and intellectually challenging academies. Thus, one might wonder why Amélie did not receive a more rigorous education. Her father seems to have considered this question in relation to his family of daughters. In 1876, as Amélie was turning thirteen, Alfred told his brother William: "I am especially anxious that the children should have better advantages for receiving a thorough education than is possible in Mobile, but of all this you are fully advised." Alfred was then attending a convention in Louisville, Kentucky, which he considered the best of the western cities. Nonetheless, he observed that in relation to education "none are equal in this respect to the Seaboard great centres."[27]

The formal schooling that Amélie received appears to have been limited. Late in life, in an autobiographical note, she indicated that she "had governesses, tutors, up to 18 years old, but continued to study ever since." Little suggests that she closely studied mathematics, science, or history; her knowledge of history most likely came mainly from literature. At age twenty-six, Rives exclaimed to her eighteen-year-old sister-in-law, "How you must be studying!! I shall be quite in awe of you—for I couldn't say the Kings of England in order, not if I were going to be guillotined for it!" Rives's education, instead, leaned heavily toward the arts. She was drawing, painting, and sculpting sometime in her teens. In 1880 her father wrote from Mobile: "Amélie has taken to modelling in clay of late, and has really made a very creditable bust of Dido."[28]

As Amélie entered her teen years, her love of Castle Hill remained strong, and the family continued to spend the summer there. Even by the standards of the prosperous, Amélie enjoyed a carefree existence and a far less organized life than most well-to-do young women, North or South. The servants at Castle Hill—in 1875 Judith Page Rives was employing a staff of six—added to the family's comfort and well-being.

Amélie's diary as a sixteen-year-old, which began in October 1879 at the end of her family's summer visit at Castle Hill, chronicled days of leisure—sketching and visiting with her close friend and cousin Leila Page. Rives was living an exaggerated version of the increased freedom from chores that girls from privileged families began to enjoy in the late nineteenth century. Earlier, young American women, even some of the wealthy on southern plantations, had been brought up to housewifery—learning how to provision a house and clothe its inhabitants. Historians have observed that after the Civil War young affluent women "stopped doing substantial housework." Instead they performed light chores connected with tidying their bedrooms and overall helped with the "genteel presentation of the home."[29]

Amélie seems not to have undertaken even the chores connected with keeping her own room neat. At Castle Hill she depended on Martha Jane Bullock, an African American servant. Though Martha Jane was only a decade older, Amélie called her "Mammy." A diary entry described an early morning routine in 1879 that included Amélie trimming her nails and taking a bath. And she continued: "Mammy . . . created clouds of daily dust with a broom, and some other kind of thing which she fancys [sic] especially effective where room cleaning and dust raising is concerned."[30]

Amélie made it clear that her slovenly habits in the bathtub created work only for Martha Jane, not for her: "Mammy says, I slop, or else am 'powerful

The Princess of Albemarle

dirty' as she is pleased refinedly to express it. Well, poor thing, she has to clean up after me. I cannot blame her, and—I rather fancy I *do* slop. I always feel a kind of vague sense of thankfulness that in the course of human events, I am always *before* and not after all the messes I make in this 'mortal life.'"[31] Possibly believing that her own mother expected from her a higher level of neatness and neatening, Rives noted that during one good-night visit: "Mamma kisses me in her own sweet fashion, and after making a sighing tour of my betossed apartment, slips quietly away."[32]

Amélie seems to have displayed fewer skills in housewifery than most nineteenth-century young females. She never indicated any facility with cleaning or in the kitchen. Even though she seldom referred to sewing, she probably learned such skills from her mother. When her parents were experiencing financial difficulties in 1886, Amélie told her uncle that while it was a "little thing," she had "made many of my own clothes since our misfortunes." Later in life, Rives noted that she "loved to build my own wood fire," indicating that "I still make my bedroom fire in the morning, though I am now such an ancient person and though the scandalized servants disapprove strongly."[33]

Amélie's lack of domestic skills contrasted with those of women in her own family, especially her grandmother Judith Rives, the chatelaine of Castle Hill. Back in 1865 at Christmas time, Judith wrote her daughter-in-law Sadie in Richmond: "Not knowing what better to send you and my dear son as a Christmas box, I have packed up a jar of the nicest sausage meat I ever made, (made with my own hands, too) and a bandbox of eggs." Not only did Judith prepare food, she also knitted socks, undertook fancy work, and toiled with the gardener.[34]

Perhaps more troubling than Amélie's limited interest in domestic chores was her restlessness with respect to the piety of the Rives family, especially at Castle Hill. As a sixteen-year-old, Amélie noted the beginning of a day: "Got up this morning[.] Late for prayers as usual." And she added a question and answer: "Query—(was it much of a loss after all?) I have searched the innermost deapths [*sic*] of my soul—and decided myself incapable of answering so momentous a question—however *will* try to be in time tomorrow to please Mamma." The next morning Amélie recorded: "Made better time this morning and arrived in time for the Lord's Prayer. Mamma looked approving."[35]

Pleasing her mother obviously played a part in Rives's religious practice. She included in her teenage diary another account of how her impulses differed from her training in the form of a dramatic dialogue between her mother and herself:

> Mamma and I thus—Scene I.
> Mamma (suddenly)—After all what happiness to compare with the happiness which is connected with religion. Not fanatical religion—I do not mean that, but the peaceful, quiet happiness of Faith. So
>
> I—O Mamma! Do you think so?
>
> Mamma—Why my dear, what do *you* think?
>
> I (with youthful ignorance) I think that there are moments of joy wilder and more intense—moments to which no *peaceful* happiness can compare.
>
> Mamma—But what a flat, everyday feeling follows! That is not true happiness, darling.
>
> "Well," I say with a sigh. "Perhaps so."
>
> Curtain and Crickets.[36]

Amélie's attempt to discuss with her mother secular joy and perhaps even touch on passion had run into Sadie's insistence on the primacy of religious feeling—if not too emotional.

As this encounter with Sadie Rives indicated, Amélie at sixteen considered herself not completely in alignment with religious ideals. Back in Mobile, she recounted her recent attendance at church, most likely Christ Church, where the Reverend Alexander Drysdale was the rector, and noted: "Mr. Drysdale is just a wee too pompous to suit me. I must be very rebellious—I am." Rives further facetiously compared herself to Satan in a discussion of an evening at the theater: "I didn't have any one to speak to but Papa, and I don't like to show my cloven foot to Papa."[37]

As she praised her cousin Leila's purity of thought, Amélie veered close to questioning religious verities as well as Victorian ones: "I like to think of men as pure and great—of women as good and true. Of the world as fair and the heavens as beautiful. To feel with the sun and the rain and the vague grandeur of the winds, which seem to sweep ones soul out of one—and whisper of things better than these. Is it not better to be believing this—to believe too much, than in believing otherwise, to believe too little. Thank God! thank God! I at least believe this!" Yet in this first stab at recording her own religious stance in her diary, Amélie suggested the possibility "not to believe at all." But she may have shocked herself, since she then lined through those words and replaced them with "to believe too little."[38]

To be sure, Amélie's diary also indicated a recognition, though perhaps limited acceptance, of the Victorian projects of self-improvement urged upon young ladies. On November 17, 1879, she sighed: "I ought to be study-ing—unfortunately am not and don't feel at all like beginning. Dear me! How long it does seem to next summer! Today has been abominably warm, sun-shiny and damp. I have been reading a kind of reciept [*sic*] in *St. Nicholas* [the upper-class magazine for youth], for keeping a journal." Most likely, she had encountered an article that had appeared approximately a year earlier, urging young women to keep a journal for self-improvement. The frequent linings-through of Amélie's diary show how she used her journal to improve her self-expression rather than her character as she endeavored to find the perfect phrase to describe or encapsulate her thoughts and actions.

Those who stressed journal writing for young women expected that self-reflection would help build virtue. Rives's journal, however, recorded thoughtless actions with little indication of any need to mend them. Here her relationship with her unmarried aunt Ella Rives, who lived at Castle Hill, shows some of the tensions that Amélie, even at age sixteen, felt to-ward Victorian gentility. Indeed, only a few paragraphs into the journal she had begun, Amélie indicated that at breakfast she "made Auntie angry by chopping off both ends of the loaf [of bread]." Rather than repenting, Amélie criticized Ella: "She certainly has been a faithful and dutiful daugh-ter, however, some people manage to make themselves very nasty in doing their duty."[39]

Amélie dissected her forty-five-year-old aunt in terms of beauty and fashion. In an unsparing depiction, Amélie termed Ella "most ugly": "First She *will* wear her collars low, and her neck looks as if it had been wrung, and then upon wrung. She is as flat as a flounder, and looks as if she had been fashioned precisely the same both 'before and behind.' If I were that 'un-figureless,' I vow I'd stuff a *pincushion* in somewhere. Anything would be preferable to that utter desert of Sahara look which pervades the figure of my aunt."[40]

Amélie then moved to her aunt's choice of dress: "She is one of those people who cling lovingly to a fashion long after it has been consigned to the 'dust-bin of oblivion,' and after wreathing herself in hoops and huge panniers, this many a year, mildly informs me that she is waiting for 'that style' to come around again." Amélie delivered a final crushing blow: "Unless angels affect 'that style' and harp it in big hoops and hideous bunches of overskirt, much, much, do I fear me, my maiden aunt will never again be quite in style."[41]

Despite her dislike of her aunt, Amélie could actually value female friendship and support. Although not mentioning her younger sister Gertrude in her diary, Amélie frequently referred to her friend and second cousin Leila Graham Page, who was almost five years older. "Leilas and my friendship," Amélie mused, "is not a sentimental one—at least not to us. We may call each other 'dear' and 'darling'—but we have been doing so for the past fifteen years, and never—as well as I can remember—excepting one or two little differences—have we even cross words." Predicting the future, Amélie continued: "It is one of those rare friendships which I fancy, come only to some women—and lasts them all their lives. One of the secrets of it is, I think, our respect for each other—and our total lack of any great confiding of secrets and mysteries. We seem to comprehend one another without that—and what we do not comprehend we take for granted."[42]

Rives lauded twenty-year-old Leila's essential nature in terms that showed the Victorian norms then ascendant: "It seems to me that hers is one of the purest, truest, sweetest natures which I have ever known. Like Charity she 'believeth all things, hopeth all things.' I am only afraid that the descent from her ideal world, the world which she has peopled with all that is great and good in human nature will be hard for her."[43] Amélie then tried to include herself among the idealists, though her attempt fell rather flat: "I am glad that I have my share of the romance of youth—glad that I do not know—or cannot tell just how much to believe or not to believe."[44]

Back in Mobile, Rives was heartened by a letter from Leila: "God bless Leila. She is the one true girl in the world to me, and has her faults, for which I am very thankful seeing that to a woman the friendship of a woman is more acceptable than that of an angel." Although the two young women would drift apart in later years, Leila remained special to Amélie. In 1893, a year before Leila's death, Rives included the following in her book *Athelwold:* "To my Dear Friend and Kinswoman Leila Graham Page This Little Book is Most Lovingly Dedicated." Rives may have chosen this historical drama because she had originally written much of it in the 1880s, when she and Leila were closest.[45]

Perhaps inspired by the same *St. Nicholas* magazine article that, along with diary keeping, urged young women to make lists of what they read, sixteen-year-old Amélie declared, "By the by, shall put down all the books I read." Among her reading over the previous month, she listed:

> Have read since I came. Adam Bede (George Eliot)—"My Lady Green-sleeves" (an odious bundle of trash by Helen Mathers—wherein the authoress tries to be "grand-gloomly & peculiar" and fails.) "One Summer" that bright little novel for the sixth time. Wilson's Abode of Snow an extremely interesting book about the Hymalayas but rather stilted in its style. Levers' "Sir Jasper Carew, knight." and went over some old ground in Tennyson, the purest poet undoubtedly in existence. It is a pity that he will degenerate sometimes into mawkishness.[46]

After mentioning *One Summer,* by the popular American writer Blanche Willis Howard, which detailed the romantic adventures of privileged youth in Maine, Amélie moved to European authors: the highly admired Mary Ann Evans, who wrote under the pen name George Eliot; Helen Mathers, a popular writer; and Charles Lever, an Irish storyteller.

Rives then reeled off an enormous list of books and articles covering an array of genres that she had read the past summer. While she admitted to reading current best-selling authors such as Jules Verne, Mary Elizabeth Braddon, and fellow southerner Christian Reid, Amélie also dipped into Henry Hallam's *Introduction to the Literature of Europe in the Fifteenth, Sixteenth and Seventeenth Centuries* as well as classical authors Euripides, Tacitus, Herodotus, Cicero, Demosthenes, and Sophocles. She noted the latter's *Ajax,* "which I remember very well, and some of his other trajegies [*sic*] which I do not remember so well."[47]

A member of a cultured, leisured family, Amélie obviously had access to contemporary authors and literary magazines. Her list included "numerous essays, reviews, criticisms etc." in *Scribner's* & *Harper's* monthlies as well as "Innumerable 'Punches' and Illustrated London News." Like many aspiring female novelists of her day, Amélie greatly admired George Eliot; in addition to *Adam Bede,* she had read parts of *Daniel Deronda.* Indeed, at sixteen, Amélie already held strong opinions and called Eliot's *Middlemarch* "one of the few great novels." Dismissing Mary Elizabeth Braddon's *Pilgrims and Strangers* as "an odious book," Rives was no kinder to Anthony Trollope, whose *Mistletoe Bough* she deemed a "collection of terrible tales," or to Wilkie Collins, whose *Armadale* was "a disagreeable powerful book." Even though Henry James's first novel, *Watch and Ward,* had appeared only eight years earlier, Amélie had read it as well as his more recent novel *The Europeans.* She called James "a cold, pedantic, clever writer and not much to my taste," but she had also perused "parts" of his newest novel, *Confidence,* which had begun to appear in serialized fashion in *Scribner's.*[48] As a voracious reader, Rives knew the current heralded British and American authors but also devoured, even while criticizing, popular writers of the day.

Poetry and drama especially entranced Amélie and formed a significant part of her reading. She listed parts of Milton's *Paradise Lost,* most of Shelley's poems, and "the greater part" of Longfellow's book on European poets, as well as a huge compendium of translations of German, Spanish, Italian, Scandinavian, and Portuguese poems. Long enamored of the bard of Avon, she included "several works on Shakespeare." Earlier she had confided to her diary: "Have decided that I like 'Hamlet' best of all Shakespeares dramas. Next 'Julius Caesar'—'Othello' and 'Macbeth.' Of course there are others quite equal to them in portions, but these are as wholes the most perfect. The dramatic action is more complete, and well, you can see I am a kind of Shakespearian idolator."[49]

Rives read widely and seems to have been relatively encyclopedic in her choices. Later she reminisced that she had been "allowed the range of her grandfather's library, with the exception of the works of Smollett, one of which her Grandmother found her with at the age of nine, and promptly took with the fire-tongs and thrust behind the biggest log in the great fireplace." Judith apparently thought Tobias Smollett's eighteenth-century picaresque novels such as *Roderick Random* much too boisterous and suggestive for a young girl. Amélie also noted in her diary in 1879: "Let me add that I might have read any amount of wicked but interesting old yellow bound English plays, had not mine anxious Papa, met me coming from the Office with my skirt & arms full—and with righteous indignation rifled their contents."[50] Most likely, Alfred Rives had objected to English Restoration comedies by authors such as William Congreve and William Wycherly, whose mockery of sexual propriety appeared immoral to Victorian observers.

Drama was very important to young Amélie and helped construct the persona that she was developing. Part of her interest in plays was merely fun, as on the day that she and her friend Leila reenacted the balcony scene from *Romeo and Juliet*. While Leila wore pantalets as Romeo, Amélie was Juliet. She described herself in her diary: "I was Juliet in a counterpane (which by-the-bye has as good an effect for drapery as satin) with my arms bare to the shoulder, and wrapped near the elbow with pearls. Very little waist to speak of (my unadorned beauty being highly applauded by Romeo in character). And my hair most artistically 'frizzed.'" Rives then adapted John Milton's description of Eve in *Paradise Lost:* "in fact I was almost 'under the flowing gold of my loose tresses hid.'"[51]

As a young woman drawn to the stage, Amélie accompanied her father to at least two productions. At sixteen, she saw the operetta *Giroflé, Girofla* at the theater in Mobile. Rives found the lead actress impressive: "Adah Richmond is a very clever actress, has a sweet mezzo-soprano voice, and is possessed of lots of 'chic' (and *cheek* too). She is quite modest for Opera-Bouffe 'singer'—viz—doesn't affect tights." The implied sexuality of the program simultaneously captivated and repelled Rives, who described the supporting actresses as "a lot of disagreeable women who depended entirely upon the 'garment of *un*righteousness'—for clothing, and who kicked up their heels in a supple and indecent manner, wonderful to behold."[52]

Rives was not alone in her fascination with the stage, as drama trans-fixed many bookish girls of the late nineteenth century. In her memoirs, the New York socialite Margaret Terry Chanler, known as Daisy and later in life Amélie's sister-in-law, described her own family's interest in the theater. The Terry family added a stage to its ballroom, and Daisy, who had been reading Schiller's version of the Joan of Arc drama, "was fired with the ambition to play Joan of Arc." At a Twelfth Night party given by the noted British ac-tress Fanny Kemble, young Daisy was chosen queen and was "thrilled to the core." Daisy later reminisced about how the actress placed "a wide-flowing purple silk scarf about my shoulders as a royal mantle and showed me how I must hold my head high and walk regally."[53]

Some privileged young women took this love of the stage further and wished to become actresses. Growing up in north Mississippi, the novelist Sherwood Bonner, the daughter of a local doctor, daydreamed in the 1860s about becoming an actress. Perhaps because Rives came from a distinguished family that was more ostentatiously proud of its lineage, her fantasies seemed slightly different and more conventional, even though she described herself as "a little 'stage-struck.'" After attending the theater in Mobile, Amélie whimsically envisioned herself as a future patron of the arts: "I thought—other people may give to the Chinese, the Hindoos, the Domestic Missions, but I—I will give as my first charitable donation—a curtain to the Mobile Theatre!!" She imagined the reward: "The idea struck me as dramatic. Already I could see myself in 'robes of spotless white' led forward upon the stage, before the new curtain, as its 'presentress'—welcomed by enthusiastic newspaper boys, and the 'beautiful girls of' Mobile!"[54]

At sixteen Amélie had begun to approach writing more seriously. Books on the British peerage and "any number of guide books old and new" were hardly scintillating fare, but it seems likely that she was gathering material that took her beyond her sheltered worlds of Castle Hill and Mobile and allowed her to imagine other times and places. In October 1879, she noted in her diary: "Am glad that I completed old 'Massinisa' even if he is very blood and thundery. I felt rather proud of him, as being the first of my dramatic children, and hope I may prove a fruitful mother." Here Rives had dramatized the career of Massinissa, who had been a foe of Carthage in the second and third centuries BCE. She was beginning to assume a critical angle on her writing: "We all feel a weakness for our first-born," but "I shall be a severer critic of my future 'offspring.'"[55]

Amélie had been writing for years, but she obviously believed that in her late teens she had entered a different phase. That same October, she detailed her reaction to some of the stories she had created at age twelve, which she called "some of my scribblings of four years ago."

Four years ago I was at that stage—when all beauty was alabaster, lily or rose—all eyes large, deep blue or dilating. All voices, sweet, silvery or enchanting. When all men worshipped all women, and as I poetically put it—the rustling of my heroine's gowns were to my heroes—"as the flutter of angel wings." My heroes all strode or proceeded. My heroines glided or fluttered. They never thought, they meditated—never drank but sipped, never spoke but murmured wailed or muttered. As Leila graphically said, "your girls were all eyes and voice[,] Amélie, one had to take arms, legs, and heads for granted."[56]

Clearly Amélie had begun to question Victorian conventions and beliefs prevalent in her family about the portrayal of women.

Moreover, even at sixteen, Amélie showed the kind of ambition that was usually thought unseemly for women—she dreamed of accomplishment and acclaim. Aware of the strictures that guided young women, she used gendered terms to discuss both her hopes and misgivings: "I shall continue to write as much nonsense as I like so long as it amuses me. I shall not follow Brutus and slay my ambition because it seems so impossible. We women hope so much and accomplish so little—, and yet—who knows? There may be something yet for me to do in this big world. Shall I go bury the talent which God in his infinite wisdom, has chosen to give me, merely because of a sneaking fear of being called presumptious, contenting myself with the 'yea and ay' life which so many women lead?"

Her answer was: "So help me God, no! I will try for the highest and then if I fail—I will still endeavor to say—feeling it—'God knows best.'" Because she knew that her family wished for her to lead a conventional life as a wife, she paused after her bold statement and followed it with the suggestion that that she would try to temper her ambition with Christian resignation.[57]

Given Amélie's talents and ambitions and the relative affluence and prominence of her family, one might question why she did not attend one of the southern women's institutions, such as Greensboro Female College in North Carolina or the newly founded rigorous women's colleges in the North, such as Vassar and Smith. To be sure, although only about 2 percent of American women were college educated in the early 1880s, the Rives family, while not among the wealthiest, could have afforded the tuition. Perhaps neither Alfred and Sadie Rives, nor even Amélie herself, thought a college education particularly needed or appropriate. Her parents seemed to subscribe to the traditional expectation that Amélie would lead the life of a typical woman of good family, one who made an advantageous marriage and "adorned" her household through her cultural and artistic attainments. Such traditionalism was especially strong in the South. Moreover, some educators and other commentators were arguing that a strenuous education for young women overtasked their bodies at a crucial time. Some physicians argued that overstimulating the mind and overloading the emotional circuits would make it harder for women to conceive and nurture children.[58] Such concerns may have had particular resonance with Sadie and Alfred, given that Amélie was high strung and already prone to migraine headaches and other less easily diagnosed ailments.

Then, too, a college education may not have beckoned to Amélie, who seems to have considered only drama, fiction, and art as important to her intellectual life. Comparing her to a privileged northern contemporary, Jane Addams, the founder of Hull House born only three years earlier, can be instructive. Both Rives and Addams were inveterate readers, born to privileged families. Yet Addams not only attended the local college but also began medical school, only to drop out over health-related issues. College attendance in the 1880s seemed most appropriate for those looking for a vocation in teaching or medicine rather than those searching for creative outlets. Early in the twentieth century the *Washington Post* published an article arguing that neither actresses nor female writers were products of the women's colleges. The reporter asserted that, generally, college-educated women could be found among the educators, philanthropists, and suffragists, along with a few younger female authors. While piling up lists of prominent women with or without college educations, the article did not attempt to reach any conclusions about reasons for the differences between them.[59]

By 1879, Alfred and Sadie Rives could see that their young daughter was likely to turn heads and might well become a belle. Males were beginning to figure in Amélie's life. Her diary at sixteen mentions two men. She seems to have had a schoolgirl crush on Captain George Gambier, a British officer who visited the Charlottesville region. Although Gambier was a mature man of thirty-five, the women of Albemarle, and especially unmarried Ella Rives, thought him captivating. After reporting her aunt's comment that "Captain Gambier has magnificent eyes—dark. He is just thirty-five, very charming," Amélie remarked, "In all probability I will never see this Captain Gambier even to speak to him."[60] Yet in fact, within a month she had not only met Gambier but also impressed him enough that he gave her a book about the Himalayas, called *The Abode of Snow* written by Andrew Wilson in 1876. Gambier added a personal note—a short account of how he had replicated

Wilson's trek of over a thousand miles—a feat obviously intended to impress the young woman.[61]

Although Amélie merely recorded in her diary on November 7, 1879, "Have met Captain Gambier," that encounter came just before she returned to Mobile, a trip that she bemoaned: "It is very hard every year, the same parting, the same horrid journey to that *horrider* Mobile." Back in Albemarle, she had written a poem about Gambier, something she called her "Gambiad." Her aunt Ella had, in Amélie's words, "stolen" the poem and shared it with a local matron and apparently even Captain Gambier. In a section of her diary full of crossed out paragraphs, Amélie expressed her embarrassment over the episode: "What must that man think of me? Oh, dear! Oh! dear! Well at all events—I said nothing improper or wicked—and as for thinking him the handsomest man I ever saw, it is a fit [i.e., a fit description]." On November 17, she further mused about whether Gambier would remember her poem: "Absurd! Of course he will not! How credulous is 'sweet sixteen!'"[62]

In addition to her fascination with an older British army officer, sixteen-year-old Amélie mentioned receiving a "most extraordinary epistle" from Joshua Fry Bullitt, a law student, with two enclosed photographs. As Rives flippantly put it, Bullitt "sent me a photo of 'Booth' as 'Hamlet' and one of himself as nothing in particular." In fact, the letter led her to grumble about men in a fashion that mixed the hauteur of the belle with an appreciation of her fellow women: "Young men are assuredly the most verdant productions of Mother Nature. They have such a fine appreciation of themselves too, finer than anyone else could have. Am sure young women are not half such bores." She then jokingly reproached herself, pointing to the postage that Bullitt had used: "This is certainly most uncharitable, and just after 'Jn F Bullitt' has wasted his sweetness and thirty-five cents on me too."[63]

This reference to Bullitt provides clues about the sorts of men who were encouraged to romance young Amélie. Bullitt, who grew up near Louisville, Kentucky, was the son of the former chief justice of the Kentucky Court of Appeals. Educated at Washington and Lee University, he seems by 1879 to have been studying law at the University of Virginia Law School. Bullitt was not only an elite southerner but also a distant relation, probably a fourth cousin of Amélie's. He later embarked on a lucrative career representing the coal industry in southwestern Virginia.

That Bullitt wrote to Amélie shows that she had begun seeing young men in social settings. It also suggests that the world of the debutante, in which young women formally made their entrance into society, probably did not prevail in Albemarle County. The gifts that Gambier and Bullitt gave Rives also indicate a certain level of romantic entanglement. They wooed her with a book about the Himalayas and a portrait of Edwin Booth, a famous Shakespearean actor and the most noted portrayer of Hamlet, rather than with flowers or chocolates. Gambier and Bullitt clearly saw Amélie as a person of elevated interests. Indeed, Bullitt's choice of a portrait of Booth as Hamlet suggests that he had spent enough time with Amélie to know her as a "Shakespeare idolator" who declared "Hamlet" her favorite of his plays.[64] That Bullitt included his own portrait showed his personal interest.

Sixteen-year-old Amélie, returning to Mobile in November 1879, still showed a deep emotional attachment to Castle Hill and to her native state of Virginia. In fact, she pointedly called it her home, contrasting it to Mobile, a city that she detested: "I am most wretchedly homesick, at that stage when to look at or think of anything connected with Castle Hill brings a great 'choke' to my throat and tears to my eyes. When I wonder how I shall ever live through these nine long months ahead, and think of the past summer as a happy glint of sunshine, gone even in the shining. . . . How I love my home, my home, my home!"[65]

In later years, Rives rarely mentioned her years in Mobile, which had then been experiencing stagnation in both its population and economy. One might expect her to have been interested in the French-influenced aspects of Mobile, but she did not mention them. Some of her dislike of the city obviously came from its climate. "How I hate this southern town with its warm enervating winds—its sickly scent of flowers—its lazy drone citizens!"[66]

Also important seems to have been Rives's distaste for her father's friends among the directors of the Mobile and Ohio Railroad. Using a French phrase for high fashion, she declared: "I wish Papa's friends were a little more 'bong-tong-y.'" After mentioning two whom she found particularly objectionable, she summed up his other associates: "The rest are all very good humoured and generally stupid, caught in business affairs. I hate to see a man sit beside a woman with [h]is eyes buttoned to the floor, and gasping under a kind of mental pressure for want of words. So many of them do it."[67]

While Amélie looked to the near future when she returned to Virginia, she also was thinking about a future when writing still mattered to her. "Probably in four years from now," she mused, "what I *now* write will seem as preposterous to me as those doe eyed heroines, and dark eyed herose [*sic*] of four years back seem today." Nonetheless, she rounded out her vision: "Well in burying each year my old self, I laugh at what I was. I may at least be laying up a fund of amusement for the new Amélie of four years hence. It is well to be able to amuse one self."[68] Here, in fact, she showed an awareness of the self-fashioning that was going on in her writing as in her persona building as she anticipated the next steps.

· TWO ·

"A Gifted and Promising Young Authoress"

Becoming a Belle and an Author

Between 1879 and 1886, Amélie transformed herself from a romantic teen-ager who cared deeply about literature into an accomplished flirt, a cele-brated belle, and a published author. Becoming an author, while earning a reputation as a noted beauty, was an unusual combination for any period, but especially Victorian America. Yet in Amélie's case, the two intertwined. As she tried to make a name for herself as an author, she also sought the good marriage that her parents expected and the exciting pleasures of "so-ciety" that she herself desired.

Exploring Rives's world of courtship and her reputation as a belle reveals much about gender ideals and the possibilities available to young women in the late nineteenth century. Her experiences also reveal the changing nature of courtship among late nineteenth-century elite Americans and the response it evoked. In Amélie's case, she fit into the system but also played a part in altering it. As a southern woman she participated in two different so-cial scenes: that of the South, as experienced in Richmond and Charlottes-ville (and to a far lesser extent Mobile), and that of the wealthy Northeast, where her prominent relatives provided entrée.

The world of the belle had long been part of southern culture. At its root the anointing of belles added a competitive fillip to the game of courtship. Gauging the status of a young woman by how much she dazzled and was sought after—in terms of dances and proposals—expanded the social scene to include much of the community, not just young unmarried people. In this system, courtship was a spectator sport, with its own method of notching triumphs and missteps. In the postwar South, focusing on belles seemed to recall the social world before the Civil War, even though the war and its aftermath had greatly changed society. Many among the former elite were coping with the loss of wealth and prestige. Moreover, the postwar world allowed greater social and geographical mobility, which affected the kinds of interactions available. Enlarging the social scene for Amélie were the ties that her family retained to Virginia. Her part-time residence at Castle Hill gave her a potential audience of young elite men, especially those in Richmond and nearby Charlottesville, location of the University of Virginia.

Even as a young girl, Rives seems to have noticed that marriage and courtship might be the most a woman could expect in life. She later described her youthful self as "an observant little thing, sedate and quiet when in doors," who carefully watched "the different behaviour of married couples & pairs of sweethearts who visited 'Castle Hill.'" Then, as Amélie later remembered it, "she wrote a sentence in her *cahier,* at the age of twelve, that shocked and startled her mother and made her father give way to Homeric laughter." Her sentence: "Married love is like champagne with the sparkles out!"[1]

Other evidence suggests that young Amélie viewed marriage with a jaundiced eye. In fact, she liked her childish bon mot about marriage and champagne so much that she used it in one of her early novels, *The Witness of the Sun,* published in 1889, when Rives herself was a newlywed. Ilva, the heroine of the novel, penned this line at age ten, only to have that page ripped up by her disapproving governess. Foreshadowing her later independence, Ilva then retorted: "No matter! It is written in my brain. You cannot tear my brain up and put it in your waste-basket."[2]

As a privileged woman of the southern upper classes, Amélie apparently pursued two ambitions, secretly cultivating the unconventional one of becoming an important author, but in daily life following the traditional path of seeking marriage with a wealthy man. For the most part, her life resembled those of other young unmarried women in privileged American families. She wrote letters; she drew, painted, and sculpted; she rode; she paid social visits and received the attentions of eligible young men. In 1885 she was sculpting a "dryad" (a tree nymph also called a naiad), which by September she pronounced "lovely" and ready for paint.[3]

Amélie's extended family seems to have bolstered her marital prospects by sponsoring visits to Newport, Rhode Island, where her aunt and uncle had a summer "cottage"—which in Newport tended to be a large, elaborate house. Social life there involved the wealthiest, most distinguished families

Davis,

827 Broad St., Richmond, Va.

This photograph of Amélie Rives probably dates from her teens. (Amélie Rives Troubetzkoy Collection, The Valentine)

of the Northeast, and the scene attracted national attention—as did Amélie. In 1882, for example, the Sumter, South Carolina, newspaper reported, "The most beautiful girl at Newport this year, and in the opinion of many connoisseurs of beauty, the loveliest woman in America is Miss Amelia [*sic*] Rives." The article described Amélie, then but nineteen, as "an artist of rare merit" who "to phenomenal beauty adds a brilliant and cultured mind." Moreover, the following year, Amélie seems to have spent a month in Newport during August and September, with her father and her cousin Alice Rives, the daughter of her wealthy uncle William Rives.[4]

In 1883 the Rives family moved from Mobile back to Virginia when Alfred took a job as vice president and general manager of the Richmond and Danville Railroad. The move allowed Amélie to spend far more time at

Castle Hill, but the family at first lived in Richmond. The unusual kind of young lady that she was becoming can perhaps be seen in the contents of the leather handbag she lost in in April 1884: two packs of visiting cards, one her mother's, the other her own (suggesting that she made social calls with her mother), and other items less ladylike—a pocketknife and pencil.[5]

Because little of Amélie's correspondence from this period survives, her circle of male admirers can be only partly reconstituted. She came back from Mobile with at least one committed beau, Edward Spencer Pratt, a young scientist, who was more than a decade older. Pratt was the son of William H. Pratt, a wealthy banker and financier in Mobile. Educated abroad, primarily in France, E. Spencer Pratt was cultured and well-traveled. He trained as a physician and surgeon but seems not to have followed that career. In the mid-1880s he served as a commissioner to oversee Alabama's participation in the World's Cotton and Industrial Centennial Exposition, which opened in New Orleans in December 1884. Described in 1886 as a "devoted student of orientalism," Pratt was named minister (ambassador) to Persia (modern-day Iran) that year. The *New Orleans Picayune* reported in 1887 that Amélie Rives "has long been engaged to marry Persian minister Pratt whose low financial status has delayed the wedding for years." After disclosing that Rives "had the reputation, even in her tender years of being a very lofty personage," the article then related a stinging anecdote. In Mobile, Rives kept a gentleman waiting for several hours while she finished a painting. She finally welcomed him, saying, "Now that I have finished this work, I will devote some time to you." He bowed and departed with the remark, "Now that I have finished waiting for you, I will devote sometime to myself." The story wound to its climax, which involved Pratt: "The minister to Persia figures as the hero in this case, as it was the first occasion she had been matched and she promptly fell in love with the victor."[6]

While the repartee rings true for two such witty young people as Rives and Pratt, the incident may not have had the patriarchy-affirming culmination that the *Picayune* so enjoyed. Nevertheless, a romantic attachment seems to have developed in the mid-1880s. He may have been the "old friend" that, in September 1884, she "expected sooner or later but I do not think will come." After he was posted to Persia, Pratt sent her a piece of "richly wrought" blue silk and cloth of gold, which decorated the mantel in her bedroom.[7] Even if Amélie had earlier been engaged to him, however, it seems unlikely that the engagement had lasted into 1887, as the newspaper suggested. By that time, in Virginia, other serious suitors had presented themselves.

Newspapers in 1888 linked Rives to Archibald Cary Coolidge, a Harvard-educated great-great-grandson of Thomas Jefferson; given that Coolidge had traveled after his graduation in 1887 to Berlin and Paris to study history, any courtship likely occurred much earlier. His brother John, also a possible suitor, had sailed for Japan in January 1887, the beginning of thirty years largely spent in long trips abroad. Both Coolidge brothers fitted the pattern of men who attracted Amélie in this period—well-born and well-educated young men with far-ranging interests. John's globe-trotting propensities and Archibald's love of European history may both have struck a chord of interest in Amélie.[8]

While these young men, like John F. Bullitt before them, certainly admired and romanced Amélie, she may have been considered more of a beauty than a belle. After Rives had become a nationally known author, an article in the *Richmond Times* called her mother a "noted belle" of that city but tellingly described Amélie as "a beautiful girl who contemned the frivolities of society and violated without hesitation the ordinary social convenances."[9]

Why was Rives considered so lovely? Her blond good looks reflected a common emphasis in post–Civil War America on the beauty of fair-haired women. The British Blondes, a music hall troupe that toured the United States in the 1870s, had further popularized light-colored hair; the actress Lillian Russell, a "golden haired goddess," was deemed among the most beautiful at that time. In an era that emphasized facial beauty but provided respectable women few ways to improve their appearance, Rives's eyes, teeth, complexion, and hair seemed remarkably perfect and thus extraordinarily attractive. One newspaper described her: "A complexion clear as health, and peculiar to the Channel Islands and Virginia, nose aquiline, eyes grey, eyelashes black, teeth perfect." The way that Rives herself teased one admirer in 1884 shows her realization that men thought her eyes beautiful: "Why will you have it that I think men must only like me because I've got nice grey eyes with black lashes."[10]

Even as she focused on the social world, Rives also seems to have been acutely alert to the literary and cultural world. As the list of her readings she made at age sixteen indicated, she was a voracious reader with eclectic tastes. The few extant letters by Rives from 1880 to 1885 suggest that she

The Princess of Albemarle

Amélie Rives's flowing hair in this portrait around 1885 made a statement, since at that time a woman's wearing her hair in an updo was seen as indicating adulthood and maturity. (Amélie Rives Troubetzkoy Collection, The Valentine)

continued to follow British authors, as she praised fairy tales by Edward Knatchbull-Hugesson, who had become the first Baron Brabourne, and also avowed herself "a very great lover of Keats." In particular, she seems to have been influenced by the medieval revival that had been prominent in British literature and arts for much of the century. Romantic poets such as William Wordsworth and Percy Bysshe Shelley were particular favorites. A reference by Rives in 1884 to the legend of Copetua and the beggar maid suggests that she had been reading the verses of Alfred, Lord Tennyson. Or she may have learned about the pictures of Prince Copetua and the impoverished woman who captivated him, painted by Edward Burne-Jones, a British artist in sympathy with the Pre-Raphaelite Brotherhood, a group of British artists and intellectuals who beginning in the mid-nineteenth century harkened to an earlier aesthetic ideal. The historian Alice Chandler has pointed out how some nineteenth-century British writers and artists believed the medieval era offered an ordered, paternalistic vision that seemed far better and kinder than their own industrializing society. Rives, however, seems to have paid little attention to such political implications and cared more about the apparent liveliness of the past and its vivid imagery for both art and storytelling.[11]

In addition to her love of the past, especially that of Britain, Rives was attuned to the current world of literature in the United States and Britain. She longed to be a part of intellectual interchange, as shown by an essay that she wrote sometime around 1885 or 1886 entitled "On the Lack of Humor in Great Heroines." Rives pointed to the intensity and seriousness of some of the best-known female protagonists of recent fiction; they were like George Eliot's Dorothea in *Middlemarch,* whose "purity was emphasized by her solemnity." With a lightheartedness that challenged Victorian earnestness, Rives declared, "Humor is to great natures what its foam is to the sea, what clouds are to a starry night; what the grasshopper is to the universe." While concentrating on heroines in George Eliot's novels, Rives also included those delineated by American authors: in particular, Henry James's Isabel Archer (in *The Portrait of a Lady*) and Constance Fenimore Woolson's Margaret Harold (in *East Angels*). Here Rives evinced her familiarity with the newest writers; Woolson, in particular, was among a small group of American female authors who had moved beyond the domestic plot to write stories and novels that sought to win a wide readership and a place in high culture. While these women authors, based in the Northeast, were a generation older than Rives, they, along with British female authors such as George Eliot, may well have suggested to Rives that she might someday participate in the literary world.[12]

Sometime during this period—perhaps even before she became well-known as a beauty—Rives began to dress unconventionally. Both her reading and her love of the art of the Pre-Raphaelites, which valued more natural clothing for women, seem to have inspired her to artistically drape her dresses and eschew the corset.[13] A photograph of her from the late 1870s, when she was sixteen or so, suggests that she was wearing a corset. By the early 1880s she seems to have shed that undergarment, seen by most Victorians as essential to beauty, morality, and fashion.

The literary biographer Welford Dunaway Taylor has raised the possibility that Amélie Rives met Oscar Wilde in 1882, when he made a long American tour. On July 12, 1882, Wilde gave a lecture in Richmond to a crowd of around two hundred that may have included Amélie. At that point

Wilde was less known for his writing than for his celebrity, fueled by his outlandish dress and foppish appearance. A passage that Amélie later wrote in her novel *Shadows of Flames,* published in 1915, seems to echo Wilde's visit. In the novel, Sophy, the Virginia-born heroine, lives in London and sees at a dinner party Oswald Tyne, "one of the most remarkable characters of his day." The heroine then reminisces about an earlier encounter: "Years ago when she was a schoolgirl, Sophy had heard him lecture in her own country. He himself had then been a youth but just graduated from Oxford. She remembered him, a slender, poetic figure." Rives gives this character a name and physical characteristics resembling Wilde's, calling him "a heavy, middle aged man. The long face had become jowled; the light irises of his eyes showed too broad a crescent of white below them. The sensual, heavy-lipped, good-natured mouth seemed to weigh upon the chin, creasing it downward." As Tyne smiled at Sophy, "she thought how much worse it seemed for a poet to have black teeth than for a mere, ordinary mortal." Wilde himself did not show his teeth in photographs because he disliked their discolored appearance.[14]

Modern commentators argue that Wilde blazed new trails in self-promotion, and in 1882 Rives may well have been struck by his ability to draw attention to his ideas and writings.[15] Possibly Wilde's American tour provided Rives with a blueprint for how celebrity and authorship might be combined. His flamboyant clothing and his penchant for bon mots seem likely to have struck a chord with this young lady who very much thought of herself as unusual. Still a lecture tour was out of the question for a young woman of good family. Rives could use unusual garb and even outrageous behavior but would have to make it assume gender-appropriate forms. Yet while she was looking for ways to gain attention, it was the literary world that she wanted to impress.

The year 1884, when Rives was living at Castle Hill, brought important changes in her life as she sought to become a published author. Later she cast her entrance into the public word as accidental. Three years after her first short story appeared, she gave its history to a reporter: "I wrote that story in two evenings, sitting up in bed—wrote it because I liked to write and because I had the story in my mind." Then "one day a very nice Boston boy, of whom we were all very fond, was visiting at the house and found that story in the library." When the visitor was reassured by Rives that she had in fact conceived and written the story, "with that visitor nothing would do but he must take it back to Boston when he went." He then submitted it to the *Atlantic Monthly,* for "a friend who wrote it."[16] While most of these basic facts were correct, they revealed nothing of the deliberate campaign that Rives had waged to place her first publications.

In fact, even before she was "discovered," Rives had already tried to publish a novel. In the autumn of 1884, she submitted a manuscript entitled "Civilization" to the Boston publishers Houghton Mifflin. This was a bold move for a never-published author and an especially audacious one for a young southern lady. One modern authority on the book trade has called Houghton Mifflin's list in this period "surely the most formidable in American publishing." Perhaps not unpredictably for an unsolicited manuscript from an unknown writer, Rives received a rejection letter in January 1885. In ladylike style, she replied, "I thank you very much for having read my story Civilization—and am very sorry to have given you so much trouble for nothing. Of course I am disappointed but feel convinced that you know much better than I could the worth of the story." She further thanked the publishing house for "waiting until Xmas was past to write me the bad news."[17]

Rives's experience with Houghton Mifflin reveals a strange mixture of confidence and tentativeness. Bravely she had submitted her work to one of the most prestigious presses in the country, but at the same time she resorted to a hackneyed reason to explain why she wanted to see her work in print: "I never wrote a novel before—and only tried this one because there is a poor girl I know who hasn't money enough to have anything done for herself and whose face is hideously deformed. Her name is Lutie Pleasants of Richmond Virginia." Here Amélie was excusing her boldness on the grounds of good works: she wanted to publish a book to aid her friend Louisa (nicknamed Lutie) Pleasants, who suffered from a disfiguring cleft palate (then frequently called a harelip). While no doubt wishing to help her friend (she later arranged an operation for Pleasants that aided her speech and eating as well as her appearance), Rives was relying on the code of ladylike conduct and justifying her actions by the sort of reason acceptable to the pious Rives family. Amélie ended her letter: "I tell you this in order that you may not think me very presumptious [*sic*] if I try again."[18]

Despite her excuses, Rives found it hard to remain sweetly stoic about the rejection. When, in a reply, the publisher's representative mentioned grammatical errors in the manuscript, Rives's temper showed, and she retreated to a pose of feminine incapacity as she blamed the mistakes on young

Amélie here poses with her mother and close friend Lutie Pleasants. (Amélie Rives Troubetzkoy Collection, The Valentine)

copyists and even disclaimed authorship of the novel: "I must further tell you that the young Englishman who really wrote Civilization has permitted me to tell you that *I* did not write it. I *do* scribble, but am far too in awe of that mighty clan the Publishers to ever send them anything." And perhaps to differentiate herself from women authors of domestic fiction, she sarcastically ended: "I may some day send you something of mine, but I write only very stupid things on the order of essays."[19]

This first unsuccessful attempt at publishing apparently led Rives to seek another outlet for her work. Historians studying nineteenth-century novelists have found that the most successful, especially among women, relied on sponsorship and mentorship—something that young Amélie Rives seems intuitively to have grasped.[20] She needed a sponsor—difficult to obtain for a southern woman, even one as privileged as she. Yet she had two friends who, if she could interest them in her work, possessed the necessary connections.

Both were young, unmarried men, and she turned to flirtation and flattery to pique their interest.

One of the possible sponsors was already in Rives's sights. For almost nine months she had been exchanging letters with the Virginia author Thomas Nelson Page, a distant cousin ten years her senior. Although a recent biographer of Rives has interpreted these letters as an attempt to woo Page, they seem rather to be part of a carefully crafted campaign that aimed for flirtation, literary companionship, and literary sponsorship rather than engagement and marriage. That Page retained the letters rather than returning them suggests that he did not see them as courtship letters: by the etiquette of the day, a gentleman, as the rather priggish Page certainly considered himself, returned love letters to a lady when the affair was over. The letters between Rives and Page indicate a young woman playing at being fascinating by alternating between sensuality and intellectuality—neither of which was supposed to be part of the southern belle's repertoire. They also show her strong drive to become a published author. Possibly viewing Page as a literary soul mate, Rives hoped for both praise and advice, and even more important, she wanted him to interest an established publisher in her writing.[21]

When Page and Rives began to correspond early in 1884, he was practicing law in Richmond. Born to an aristocratic family that encountered postwar financial challenges, Page had attended Washington College (later Washington and Lee) but did not perform well. A stint at tutoring children helped to finance his law school education at the University of Virginia. Far more conservative personally than Rives, Page also took a more traditional view of woman's place. Yet they shared a common Piedmont Virginia gentry ancestry and an elite status, though one that came with financial insecurity. More important, both had literary leanings with a distinctly historical cast. Both were fascinated by ancient Greece and Rome; Page's professor of Greek in college declared the young man would serve "handsomely as a classical teacher."[22] Both Page and Rives loved Scottish dialect and English heritage stories; both viewed the world through sentimental lenses. All these common intellectual interests made cousin Tom a man of interest to Amélie.

Most important, perhaps, were Page's links to the literary world. To be sure, fame still lay just around the corner for him, but by the spring of 1884 he had already published "Uncle Gabe's White Folks" and "Old Yorktown" in *Scribner's Monthly*, a highly regarded northern periodical. "Marse Chan," the story that vaulted him to national attention, had been accepted by the

Century Illustrated Monthly Magazine (the successor magazine to *Scribner's* after its sale in 1881) and appeared in the April 1884 issue.

When the correspondence began in 1884, Rives gave no indication that she might be engaged, even though she may well have still been involved with Spencer Pratt. Page himself may have been recovering from a failed courtship. A year earlier he had told his aunt that, despite a cold, he was going horseback riding with his sweetheart, and he suggested an upcoming engagement with a woman he had been pursuing for five years: "Barring my anxiety now to get married and so have her for my very own I am as happy as any man can get to be in this world I verily believe."[23] This woman could not have been Amélie, who five years earlier had been living in Mobile; neither could it have been Anne Seddon Bruce, the woman Page married in 1886, since she was only fifteen years old in 1883. The chronic ill health or death of this unknown young woman may have ended the affair.

Rives, in her first letter to Page in 1884, blended mystery, exoticism, and drama with caprice. With seeming frankness, she opened her campaign by telling him how enthralling she had found his letter: "I was feeling so ill when your letter came, and now that I have read it, I find myself following an irresistible desire to answer it." Page apparently had called her a flirt, and she raised the stakes by picturing herself as a dangerous siren: "As for flirting dear Coz—you say that it is in my nature. And what will you think when I tell you frankly 'YES'? It is there, and very strongly, and I am afraid very indelibly. Now what will you say again, when I tell you that I do not flirt? It is true—quite true." She elaborated that she had been "going against her nature" because, even though she had seen no men since the previous autumn, she had recently forgone a conquest: "I could have seen one, who to me as a type, and a strong, and an almost-extinct and an unruly one,—would have been most interesting to talk with, to be with, in a word to flirt with. He was most anxious to know me better. I saw that he was susceptible—and—[I] arranged matters so that he could not see me."[24]

Like a belle who advertised her unavailability but also raised possibilities, Rives assured Page that he held a special place in her regard. "Do you understand that I speak to you as I would to few people men or women,—and that you must not laugh at me?" she chided. "You do not know how anxious I am to see your story," she declared, most likely about "Marse Chan," slated to appear the following month. "I find myself thinking of it sometimes, through the long night. You remember, you told me of it last summer."[25]

As belles were expected to do with men, Rives turned to flattery. After declaring her dislike of modern fiction by Henry James and William Dean Howells (even though "they do some exquisite writing it is true. And James's English is very pure and delightful"), she praised Page's work: "But I will tell you that I had rather read something you had written from your heart, than even that undeniably beautiful book the 'Portrait of a Lady.'" With sensuous imagery, she predicted Page's literary fame: "I am as sure that you will be one of our famous writers, as I am of the moan of the wind down my chimney. That is a most indisputable fact, as you yourself would say, could you see the lilac-flames from the fresh oakwood, spinning about like little salamander coryphés in mauve petticoats." In a later letter, Rives consoled Page for an unfavorable review by comparing him to William Shakespeare.[26]

The remainder of Rives's first letter to Page took the tack that she often repeated, showing off her skill at writing in various genres and alluding to her wide reading. At the letter's end, she returned to the theme of attraction: "I wish with all my heart to see you, to know you better and to love you more—; but how is one to behave when one feels—when I, in fact, feel that you are all the time thinking I am trying to flirt with you, and to fascinate not your true friendship, not your honest love, but that 'Berserk'—(which [Charles] Kingsley says lurks in every Newfoundland dog)—and which I am sure, is part and parcel of every man alive." While assuring Page of her attention, she was also pointing out that she had read Kingsley's novel *Hereward the Wake, the Last of the English* (1866), about the warrior ethic among Anglo-Saxons before the Norman Conquest. Her specific reference suggested a difference between lust and love—a difference that Page, who preferred his white women firmly planted on the pedestal, probably did not think that young ladies could begin to know.[27]

When Page asked Amélie in mid-March 1884 to tell about herself, she seemingly artlessly declared an utter lack of self-knowledge: "I fear I know less of myself than I know of Greek,—and of that, I know only that there is a beginning and an end, which two are 'Alpha' and 'Omega.' The end with me, is not yet." With that "end" as a segue, she then launched into a disquisition on marriage: "They say marriage, is the end with women—I do not know—but I hope not. I do not want to be married myself, and yet—and yet—how lonely are the old-maids!" She proffered a cameo of her despised spinster aunt: "My Aunt Ella Rives is a living warning to me. She is forty eight. She is very yellow. One of her front teeth is lacking. She wears pale brown stockings that wrinkle, and cloth slippers that are out at the toes[.] She is very good, very queer, and unbearably disagreeable. She feeds ducks and plays on a melodion [parlor organ] for recreation." Rives pointedly ended her portrait of Ella: "I do not want a husband, but I think a melodion equally undesirable."[28]

Even if Rives did not want a parlor organ, she most certainly wanted to sustain Page's interest. Thus, she raised contradictions to increase her appeal. She declared in March 1884: "I have as many moods and tenses as a french pronominal verb. I wonder sometimes what your real, profound, never-to-be-admitted opinion of me—is?"[29] Like some southern belles, Amélie professed weakness and softness by emphasizing the illnesses that at times debilitated her and seemingly even threatened her life. Her very first letter to Page had informed him, "I have been very near to death since last you wrote to me." And she continued: "There was a night and a day in which they thought there would never be day or night for me any more forever this side the stars. There! You see?"[30] Her doctors, she added, had warned that her writing was affecting her health—a diagnosis she then dismissed. In her best version of the alluring invalid, she pictured herself as a figure of grace and power. "At present I am maladive—and that is very charming," she indicated. "Everyone comes to see me. My room is a little court, and a big, gilded wicker chair, run-about with blue ribbons, is my throne." [31] Almost a year later, when she had not heard from Page for three months, she again sounded a note of illness: "Is it known to you that I have been nigh unto death? Nay, I am sure that it hath not been told you, else would you surely have writ to me."[32]

While fragility and ill health were quite ladylike, Rives also proclaimed her vibrancy and emphasized her body in a distinctly unladylike way. Celebrating her first carriage ride since her illness with herself as driver, she wrote: "The air was like wine, and had a really vinous effect on me. I laughed and shouted, like a big-boy intoxicated with a sense of his big-boydom. I drove as fast as ever I could. The wind blew all my curls straight up on end,—and so happy was I, that I forgot to be vain, and pull them back into order."[33]

In contrast to the demure fragility expected of young southern white women, Amélie emphasized her physicality. She took what apparently had been a reference in Page's letter to the English literary figures Richard Steele and Mary Wortley Montagu and turned it into a joke that emphasized her own love of bathing: "As for Dick Steele and Lady M.W. M. I hope you will not think of me in the same moment with her, for if deponent sayeth true, she was a most uncleanly body, while I am a very She-Diogenes, and live in my tub. And for this fact my family will sometimes tease me to distraction." Here Rives deftly showed off that not only did she know about the Greek philosopher's reputed lack of belongings and residence in a tub, but she also was aware of the gossip that had circulated about Lady Mary as slatternly. Amélie reemphasized the transgressive image of her own nude body in the bath by closing the paragraph with a whiff of religious heterodoxy: "But cleanliness being next to Godliness, and I, being nearer heaven through that means than any other, do persevere from day to day in spite of their jests." At the same time, she suggested that she wanted her appeal to be based on more than beauty, telling Page in one letter that she believed that he had fetched books for her "because I was kind to Lutie—and not for my eyes."[34]

Amélie showed some impatience with the sexual norms of her society and challenged the notion of privileged women's nature as purer and better. In reply to Page's recitation of the amorous difficulties of one of his friends, she replied: "All these fine lovers who will have it that their mistresses are so many angels up in the clouds above them, are only just many mere Atlases holding up a big piece of earth on their manly shoulders.—and I'll have you know that I speak the truth in this matter."[35]

Even as she paraded her skills at writing and repartee, Rives relied on the belle's tactic of flirtatiousness. "I wish I could see you," she teased, "I am sure you would not fall in love with me. I will let you know me two [*sic*] well. I will not be at all mysterious—if I can help it." She then added: "Like all very healthy and extremely natural women, I like to be considered weird and uncanny. In fact they say that I am—I daresay I am a little mesmeric, but that is all."[36]

Using her letters as performance, Amélie tried to exert a many-faceted appeal, entrancing like a belle but entertaining like a wit. Even when she appeared to woo Page with her sensuality, she did a little sidestep on the nature of their relationship. At what appears to have been the point of their greatest intimacy, late in 1884, she wrote him, "Tom take my face between your two hands and kiss me on my eyes which are full of big tears ready to fall—and they shall be sweeter on your lips than wine, because they will tell you that though comfort has forsaken me, you can comfort me." Yet immediately after that sensual, romantic invocation, she told him: "Dear—I never had a brother, but had I one—I would have him as like you as my two eyes resemble."[37]

This entire letter had been a play on the idea of comfort. Amélie detailed how both her mother and her younger sister Gertrude had come to her in tears, seeking comfort. Exhausted from the effort, Amélie reached for comfort of her own: "And then—and then—When I have in some sort whistled that haggard Comfort, to their cries, lo! she turns wayward & will not perch on mine—and there is to me of all my consolation, not one drop remaining."[38] The invocation of Page's comfort—through kisses on her eyes—then followed, though most likely he realized her construction of an extended metaphor was intended more to show her intellect than any actual passion for him.

As she advertised her fascination, Rives clearly saw her relationship with Page as a chance for literary exchange and growth as well as sponsorship. Her letters to Page slowly pulled him into her world of writing. She did not touch on her writing at all in her first letter, but her second indicated that she had been "writing a great deal this winter." She drew him a picture: "I am sitting before a big, old-fashioned window in my room scribbling, with my portfolio on my knee." Only in her third letter did she mention her poetry: "I send you some jingles I made a year ago. I have made better, but I am a lazy wench, and these being already copied I send them to you."[39]

By the summer of 1884, Rives had begun to confess her literary aspirations. A letter in July 1884 sparkled with literary allusions, devices, and wordplay, and she also begged Page to read his book to her and send her some of his poetry. She then confided, "I too have written a novel this summer, but I fear me that it is not just what one would look for from the pen of a girl,—being meat of so muscular an order that even men would have to chew right manfully to digest it." She then assured him, "Yet do not be thinking that it smacks of immorality. Not so—not so I swear." She revealed little more about the novel, instead pleading for him to visit, anticipating his excuses, and referring to Greek mythology to suggest that she was cold-hearted. "As for you being bound Prometheus like to your office-deck, I will break your bonds with pleading,—as for your Vulture, he is quite welcome to make a meal of my liver. Indeed, if we moderns believed with the ancients that we loved with our livers, the fact of my coldness in matters of love, for one and twenty years, would be quite satisfactorily explained."[40]

Apparently, Page occasionally visited Castle Hill, and when he and Rives spent time together, they indulged in their mutual love of poetry and dialect. Together they read each other's work and played with various literary forms. Old English and Scottish themes particularly bedizened Rives's prose. As she told Page, using archaic English language, "I have read your letter (on my oath) three times, and were it not that there is luck in odd numbers, I would for a fourth time peruse it. Howbeit, it is writ on my heart, and my mind's eye will often con it, whether I will or no."[41]

Rives seems to have seen Page little during the autumn of 1884 and apparently did not hint to him that she was submitting her novel to publishers. She did, however, tell him in September, in veiled terms, that she had "been through the dark valley of trouble since I last wrote to you and the shadows are yet about me." While expressing appreciation for his "sweet letter," she pictured herself as "a little waif whose heart is heavy" and again asked him to visit. Amélie seems to have believed that the friendship had taken more a literary turn; a couple of weeks later she sent Page a ballad that she had written in "less than three hours," telling him: "I consider that it is half your poem, for I don't believe I would ever have finished it had it not been for you." She prodded him to visit again "and bring all that you have written. I have seen your star in the east now let me worship it."[42]

In the winter of 1885 Rives apparently had little interaction with Page or other friends. Early in January, she informed him that she "had not seen but the people of the household since November—no, since the last of October—." And perhaps recalling her recent manuscript rejection (which she did not mention), she obliquely declared: "I think I am a pretty good girl not to fret and go into a green & yellow melancholy. Please write to me. I don't deserve it, but *write* to Amélie."[43]

By the spring of 1885 Page had begun to court wealthy Anne Seddon Bruce of Charlotte County, Virginia, and his friendship with Amélie became only literary. Most likely, she was giving a relatively honest assessment of their relationship when she told Page in July 1885, "O—Cousin—our well-wishing and high-thinking are very dear to me. I would that in truth I could be your Aurora and light up all the days of our life for you." Nonetheless, she again asked him to visit, preferably when there were no other guests: "No I don't want a soul to be here when you are here—and Good Heavens! How I do want to see you." Although they had been sharing poems for almost a year, Page seemed distracted by his other social obligations or simply his own growing literary reputation. That fall, after the *Century* had accepted his story "Meh Lady," Charles Scribner's Sons expressed its interest in publishing both his first book and his stories in book form. This increased renown gave Page the authority to show some of Rives's poems to Richard Watson Gilder, editor at the *Century*.[44]

Amélie sent Page two little songs in late September but told him that she would not send the "Story of Arnon," a story she had recently written, because "I want to watch you while you read it." Asking him to visit, she called herself "so lonely—so desperate." Rather than describing the state of her love life or even the possibility of publishing, this comment may have been occasioned by her father's loss of his position with the railroad. Perhaps indicating the strained relations within the Rives family, Amélie also told Page: "Dear, everyone in this room is quarreling, so you must excuse any incoherence in this letter."[45]

While Rives pursued Page as her mentor, she also secured another male friend, William Sigourney Otis, to help get her work published. Will Otis was "the very nice Boston boy" who brought her to the notice of the *Atlantic Monthly*. A twenty-eight-year-old lawyer in 1885, Otis had graduated from Harvard College and Harvard Law School and was a descendant of the prominent Boston family that had included the Revolutionary-era author Mercy Otis Warren and the Federalist politician Harrison Gray Otis. Marriage and a shared family tragedy connected Will Otis to the Rives family. Will's uncle Henry Sigourney, with his wife, Amélie Rives Sigourney (Amélie's aunt), and three of their children, had died in 1873 when their steamer, the *Ville du Havre*, collided with another ship en route to Europe.[46]

Will was, according to contemporary accounts, "a strikingly handsome man, and noted for his geniality, wit, and readiness of repartee." He precisely fit the profile of young men who were accepted by the Rives family as guests and suitors for Amélie. Athletic and active, Will was a member of several yacht clubs and the Hasty Pudding Club. Showing other mutual interests with Amélie, he belonged to the Harvard Art Club and had been a founding editor of the *Harvard Lampoon*.[47]

No letters between Will Otis and Amélie Rives have survived, but she seems to have had a longer, closer relationship with him than with Page. Otis and Rives may even have been briefly engaged—at least that is the impression she gave in October 1885 when she told Page: "It is all off between Will and myself—and oh! I feel as free as air." That this revelation came immediately after Page announced his engagement to Anne Bruce makes it suspicious. Rives had then teasingly abused Page: "You villain! You rogue!!

William Sigourney Otis, shown in his class picture at Harvard College, helped to secure publication of Rives's first story in the *Atlantic Monthly*. (HUP Otis, William Sigourney, (1A), Harvard University Archives.)

You wretch!! Why ever didn't you tell me you were engaged to be married? 'o these men—these men!' Never mind I am going to heap coals of fire on the tortoise-shell of your conscience." And she further elaborated, "I do love Will. He is good, & dear, & sweet, & noble, but I don't want to be married—and oh! dear—I didn't think you did either."[48] More tellingly, almost a decade later, Amélie's first husband was still jealous of Will Otis.[49]

It was Otis, rather than Page, who scored the first success for Rives. This came in late October 1885 when her first story was accepted for publication. Cautioning Page not to tell "a *soul,*" she revealed her good fortune: "You know Will Otis took on with him to Boston a short story of mine, called a 'Brother to Dragons'—(you read one scene from it). He took [it] to Houghton Mifflin & Co and Mr. Aldrich (reader for the Atlantic Monthly) got hold of it. I can't pretend to tell you all the nice things he said. He sent for Will immediately. He thinks I am a man & insisted on my coming at once to Boston. When Will told him that would be quite impossible, he laughed & asked if I were in Jail."

Amélie was ecstatic, marveling, "just to think of the first short story I ever wrote coming out in the Atlantic."[50] But she was shaky on the facts: Thomas Bailey Aldrich was not just a "reader" for the *Atlantic;* he was its editor—a position that he had held for four years at the magazine, which was especially esteemed for its fiction. A novice author having a story immediately accepted there was an accomplishment indeed.

Among the first editors of the *Atlantic* had been such literary luminaries as James Russell Lowell and William Dean Howells, but Aldrich did not command commensurate respect from contemporaries. Although he had published many of Henry James's stories, James rather contemptuously called him "the great little T. B. Aldrich." Some historians have criticized Aldrich, who himself wrote short stories and poetry, as exemplary of the worst of the "genteel tradition." Others allude to his narrowness and lack of innovation, citing, for example, his dismissal of Walt Whitman's talents as minor and publishing a review of *Leaves of Grass* that maintained "the book cannot attain to any very wide influence." A later historian has been kinder, finding a "degree of competent professionalism in his [Aldrich's] editing."[51]

Aldrich's first reaction to Rives's story was wildly enthusiastic. Not only did he plan to publish it soon, she reported, but he told her that "he can give me every atom of work that I can possibly do." Even more significant, "Mr. Aldrich also says he wants every scrap of Ms. I ever wrote." To Aldrich himself that same day, she gratefully gushed: "I can never thank you enough, and I will do whatever you think best, in regard to it or anything else I ever write."[52]

That Rives had placed her first published article in a major journal was an incredible achievement. That the article itself did not deal with regional themes differentiated her not only from most southern women writers but also from most southern writers. For example, two of the best published southern women of the postwar period, Mary Noailles Murfree and Sherwood Bonner, wrote about southern characters who spoke in dialect. In contrast, "A Brother to Dragons," Rives's story accepted by the *Atlantic,* featured dialect, but that of Elizabethan England. Anthony Butter, gardener to Lord Robert of Amhurst and his twin sister, Lady Margaret, tells the story of humor and adventure. The writing is sprightly, though the plot is slight:

Lady Margaret, despite her many suitors, is most entranced by Lord Denbeigh, who has a reputation as a rake. Absence, swordplay, and disguised identities all culminate in a marriage. The story ends on a sad note after Lady Margaret's estranged brother takes her husband's place in the wars and dies in combat. In an era when readers were entranced by chronicles of the distant past and chivalric heroes, Rives had a good entry—though one pointed more toward the national than a southern audience. While the story features a romance, the heroine Lady Margaret shows resourcefulness and daring, a "distinct foreshadowing," as a literary scholar has pointed out, of the strong heroines Rives later produced.[53]

Wishing this story to be the opening salvo in a volley of publications, Rives pelted Aldrich with manuscripts and letters over the next few months as she sought to make him her newest literary guide. In a November letter to the editor, Amélie declared demurely (even while quoting Lady Macbeth): "I have never sent a romance to anyone before this, and indeed I could never have screwed my courage to the sticking place, had not someone kindly aided me. You shall have the very firstlings of my brain and heart, and I will write for no one else in all the world if you want me to write for you."[54]

The next few stories that Amélie sent Aldrich through Otis did not please the editor. At least two of them, "The Story of Arnon" and "The Romaunt of Yovanne," eventually were published and thus give some notion of her approach. Although she was writing historical fiction with rather stilted diction, she had changed her locales. "Arnon" is set in the biblical world of Noah and the flood, while "The Romaunt" occurs in fifteenth-century France. By December, Amélie had begun to worry whether Aldrich would like her stories. She complained to him: "Now in *every* letter Will tells me you want something like 'A brother to Dragons.' I am going to begin at once on 'A sister to Dragons' to be followed by 'A Brother-in-law to Dragons' and these in turn will be the Progenitor of a race of little nephews, nieces, & grandchildren to Dragons, which shall all be sent in due time!—Please, *please* forgive me if I have been at all impertinent—I would not be that for worlds and I am sure you will not be too severe with a somewhat crazy person."[55]

Despite the undertone of exasperation, Amélie pleaded for Aldrich's approval as well as his editing. "You may cut anything out of my stories that you like, & I know you will blame me less when you remember that I wrote them not thinking of anyone in all the world but my characters & their joys and troubles," she declared. Later in that same letter, she reiterated:

"Please say anything you wish to me—Scold me, criticize me, tell me you were mistaken and that I haven't one atom of talent." In the same month as she begged for editorial advice and counsel, Rives also proffered southern hospitality: "If you think it would not bore you too much, or would in any way amuse you, we (my mother and I) would like so very much to have you come to our old Virginian home for a visit." She advertised her elite Virginia background: "I love the old place myself. It is one of the very few old southern Homesteads which have remained in the same family for two hundred years. We will treat you with all ancient circumstance & pomp and put you in the Haunted Chamber!" Finally, she excused her "unconventional" request: "The truth is I am so full of gratitude, that I want to tell you of it, to look it, and show it. Oh! I think I want to wait on you a little, and fetch things for you,—and know you, and learn to do the things you like, and to earn your approval and the right to your friendship. It isn't too much—is it?"[56]

In truth, it seems to have been far too much for Aldrich, who, as he put aside her letters, labeled them "Miss Rives's singular correspondance."[57] Although he had professed interest in visiting her Virginia home, he grew irritated by this author who was not the young man he had first imagined. Aldrich soon reached the end of his tether over the question of how her story should appear—whether it should be anonymous or signed with her own name, initials, or a nom de plume.

Even as Rives was exulting over the *Atlantic*'s acceptance of a story, she received other good news. Richard Watson Gilder, editor of the *Century*, expressed interest in publishing a sonnet by Rives that Page had shown him. Differing greatly from Rives's story, this poem, "A Sonnet," speaks fervently of love, beginning:

Take all of me, I am thine own, heart—soul—
Brain, body—all, all that I am or dream
Is thine forever; yea, though space should teem
With thy conditions, I'd fulfill the whole—
Were to fulfill them to be loved of thee.

The middle stanzas even more passionately declare that if love were a method of killing, then dying would be a way to live forever. Declaring her lover a king, the poem ends: "Bring / O time! my monarch to possess his throne / Which is my heart and for himself alone."[58]

Suddenly Rives was dealing through proxies with two publishers, both of whom warmly praised her work. For a young woman of twenty-two, who less than a year earlier had received a summary rejection of her novel, this was a heady experience. Clearly, her flirtations with Will Otis and Tom Page had yielded important entrees to the publishing world. Rather than offering her stories directly, Rives in ladylike fashion had used intermediaries to gain acceptance of her writings. Yet how far she should go in publicizing her authorship was a problem. Most southern female authors in 1885 used pen names—Augusta Evans Wilson was a notable exception. However, Amélie's first letter to Aldrich told him, "You may also use my name just as you please. If you would rather have it known at once, I am perfectly willing to submit everything to your judgement."[59]

Rives soon backed away from that straightforward response. In November she responded to Page's news about the acceptance of her sonnet at the *Century* by begging him not to tell the editor her name. She added: "I am beginning to get frightfully shy & alarmed, & feel like tucking my head in the sand of twenty noms de plumes like a silly little Ostrich. Aldrich knows my name now, but I would *so* much rather Gilder did not." Using a quite unconvincing self-characterization, she reiterated: "I *hate* to be known—I don't suppose a more utterly shy little person ever lived."[60]

Over the next four months, the question of whether Amélie would publish under her own name or a pseudonym recurred repeatedly. This problem forced her to confront the conflict between her ambitions and the gender conventions of the day. Although her first letter to Aldrich had assented to publication over her own name, only a month later she was retreating from that possibility. In November 1885 she suggested a pen name: "If you do not mind, I would rather not be known, just yet. And in that case what name would you write over? Fairfax is a Virginia name you know, and William Fairfax sounds simple & unpretentious, does it not?" By December, Rives asked Aldrich "not even to print a nom-de-plume—just print the story without any name." Later that month she was considering using only her initials. She elaborated on this point in January 1886: "Don't put any name if you do not like the initials of my own name. I suggested William Fairfax to you once, but I had rather just be no one at all—if you do not care."[61]

Amélie well understood that the question of a pen name was a gendered issue. In her letters to Aldrich, she used boyish slang to discuss the topic: "I wish I could *talk* to you. If I were a boy I would say—hang this writing!

The Princess of Albemarle

as I am a girl I must satisfy myself with thinking it." Rives's indecisiveness apparently irked the editor, and the entire matter took a bizarre twist late in January 1886. Both Aldrich and Page received letters, allegedly from Rives, that indicated she would use her name on her publications for the *Century*. The one to Aldrich read in part, "I am just writing to tell you that I have told Mr. Gilder of the Century, to publish my name with some poem(s) of mine that he has—& I do not want you to think it strange that I have asked you *not* to publish my name after my short stories and whatever of mine *you* have." The letter then explained: "What you have are very dear to me as the children of beautiful *Now*, what Mr. Gilder had, are the offspring of a childish *Then*. I wrote what he has when I was fifteen and eighteen, and when my father asked me to allow my name to appear with them I said 'Yes.'" After these rather thin reasons, the letter ended: "Please understand—dear Mr Aldrich—In a year you may do with my flimsy little French name whatever you please. Only *now*, I would like to keep under the shadow of your wing for a little while." The note to Page was much simpler and shorter and requested his immediate attention: "My father has asked me to publish my name in the Century. *If it is not too late* please tell Mr Gilder just to publish my name 'Amélie Rives.'"[62]

Aldrich in reply apparently charged that Rives had deceived him by corresponding with Gilder, a rival editor. Rives telegraphed an immediate, though disjointed, disavowal, noting that "the letter you say you received from me was either a forgery or written in my sleep." She followed with a short note, reiterating the claim of imposture: "I am sorry you should have believed me capable of such childishness and double dealing, and I am always Very sincerely yours."[63]

In a longer message, Rives insisted that the letter about Gilder publishing her poem under her name had not come from her and was a forgery: "There are only two people who write a handwriting identical with mine:—one is my sister, and one a person, perhaps the only enemy I have. But that is all over. Once before, this has happened to me." Apparently, Aldrich had conferred with Will Otis, who knowing Amélie's capriciousness, had not defended her. "I am only surprised that Mr. Otis should have thought me capable of such a thing," Rives told the editor. "*You* do not know me and it was natural for you to believe only what you saw." She also added self-righteously that she had contacted Gilder only through a proxy: "I have had no correspondence with Mr. Gilder. The verses were sent to him by Mr. Page, my cousin."[64]

At the same time, Amélie sent Page a distraught note to stop publication of her name in the *Century*. Overlooking her own past inconsistency on the subject, she declared: "I do not wish my name published. I have said so over & over again. Please god for heaven's sake Tom, tell him not to publish it, & explain it to him. I don't care a rap about the wretched verses, but I wouldn't have Aldrich to think me so childish & double dealing for anything in the world."[65] Later that month, after Rives received and scrutinized the letter in which she purportedly directed that the *Century* publish her name, she claimed that it "as a forgery is perfect."[66] In March she told Page that yet another letter to him must have been concocted and asked him to keep the matter quiet, adding, "It is frightful."[67]

Was someone forging letters from Amélie Rives or was she, under pressure about the publicity, simply pretending that she had not given her assent? Obviously, for a forgery to have occurred, the perpetrator needed a detailed knowledge of her literary ventures as well as the ability to duplicate her rounded loopy writing, characteristic of educated genteel women of that era. One allegedly fraudulent letter that survives does appear slightly more rotund in script than Rives's usual handwriting. More important, rather than her common salutation of "My dear Mr. Aldrich," it opens "Dear Mr. Aldrich," and the closing is "Yours most sincere," which she did not use in other letters of that time. Even more dubious is the reference in the letter to "my flimsy little French name," which seems an uncharacteristic way for Amélie to mention a name of which she always appeared quite proud. The purported forgery to Page was a very short note—and it included a closing, "your devoted little cousinkin," that Amélie herself had earlier used.[68]

If these letters to Aldrich and Page were fraudulent, the most likely culprit would have been Amélie's younger sister Gertrude, who, as Amélie pointed out, had a similar handwriting. More significant, Gertrude would also have known the details about the acceptance of her sister's article and poems. Growing up in Amélie's shadow (except for a greater excellence as an equestrian), Gertrude may well have resented her older sister's newfound celebrity. Later in life, they frequently quarreled, but nothing else suggests a rift at this time.

Perhaps Amélie actually wrote the letter and then denied having done so. Her vacillation on the subject lends some weight to this hypothesis. Good reasons also exist to think that numerous family members and friends would disapprove of her name in print. Indeed, Amélie's late grandmother, Judith

Page Rives, who had died four years earlier, may have influenced Amélie's literary aspirations as well as her beliefs about the way a genteel lady should appear in public. Before the Civil War, Judith published a book, combining fiction with a European travel account, under the pseudonym "A Lady of Virginia." Judith's introduction included a ladylike demurral: "Farther apology for these 'souvenirs' is needless as it is not probable that their merits will carry them beyond the limited circle for which they were designed."[69]

In an unpublished autobiography written for her children and grandchildren, Judith Rives recalled how she and her sister carefully scrutinized forms of female self-presentation and rejected the "hoyden or fast" style, which "excited our indignation and disgust." She also criticized "the bluestocking and eccentric," believing the comportment of an intellectual "irreconcilable with graceful manners and an elegant toilette, both of which we decidedly admired." Both fast and bluestocking styles were to Judith "only excuses for vanity, idleness and a convenient pretext for the neglect of the graces and elegancies of social existence, a scrupulous attention to which is so peculiarly attractive and lovely in a young lady, or indeed, in a lady of any age."[70]

Amélie, as a close observer of behavior, must have understood quite well that her provocative letters and expressive conduct fell squarely within her grandmother's definition of a hoyden, or saucy girl. Amélie may also have feared that her publications would brand her a bluestocking. Indeed, her final comment to Aldrich following the alleged forgery fell back on the language of proper southern behavior: "I think Mr. Aldrich if you ever know me, you will believe me when I say that as a lady I am incapable of conduct so false and so unladylike."[71] Despite these brave words, Rives in her self-presentation during her efforts at publication had wandered far from the ladylike conduct expected in the antebellum South.

Rives also showed in these early letters a concern with gender's relation to writing. When she disavowed the novel she had submitted to Houghton Mifflin in 1884, she asserted that a "young Englishman" had written it—a statement that suggests a certain lightness with the truth as well as considerable unease about her gender.[72] As she was using Tom Page to publicize her poetry, she mused to him about sending Gilder a poem: "And *I* want to send him something thro' *you* someday which he thinks a man wrote. You know both the sonnet & the maid & her mother are so *evidently* written by a woman."[73] Both of these comments suggest that she believed that poems and articles would receive different evaluations according the gender of the writer.

Receiving payment for writing seems also to have troubled Rives. Even though gender conventions were in flux, many held that ladies should undertake paid labor only when impelled by penury; over the years many successful southern women writers had cited familial poverty as their reason to write. Given her family's relatively comfortable circumstances, Rives had no reason to seek compensation. She had instead mentioned her friend Lutie Pleasants's need for surgery as justification for writing a novel and later gave away at least one payment for a story to a "poor, pretty, clever French girl." Moreover, Amélie also had little idea what remuneration she should expect for her writings. In April 1886 Rives, after asking an editor to tell her emissary "what you might think proper to give me" for a story, added: "I will be content with any amount you may decide upon."[74]

Even while sometimes flouting convention in her self-presentation, Rives also showed significant worry about propriety, and even purity. Back in 1884, after admitting to Page that she was indeed a flirt, she mentioned a wish: "To be called a good, true woman. 'A maiden, most excellent, shining, white and clear,' this is what I would rather have, even than fame, even than honour." She also suggestively added: "—and when you know me better you will know how dear to me is my ambition." When she first mentioned to Page that she was writing a "muscular" novel, she immediately disavowed any offensiveness in her writings. "Yet do not be thinking that it smacks of immorality," she claimed. "God being my witness, I would not shake such golden apples as he has let grow on the tree of my knowledge into the pig-stye of vulgarity. It is rather that I fear me, I have gathered my apples a little green." She returned to this theme of proper moral tone with Aldrich, after the acceptance of her first story, when she sent him other stories. On December 31, 1885, she had written him: "Thank you beyond all words for offering to read my stories and plays and for saying that they were pure and womanly."[75]

Even as Amélie was setting her stories in the distant past, problems were already emerging with "The Story of Arnon," a tale of Arnon and Asenath, two star-crossed lovers in the time of Noah and the biblical Flood. In December 1885 Rives confided to Aldrich: "It seems that Will Otis thinks I write very dreadful things in my stories, and I am sure if he says so it must be true, for he is a very dear friend of mine and would not say anything but what was for my good. Now I want to implore you to believe me when I tell you, that any such things as he speaks of, are the result of sheer ignorance." Defending herself against any criticism of her character, she continued: "Please, *please* do not think that I am voluntarily vulgar or coarse." And she added:

> Now about "The Story of Arnon"—Will, says that he is *sure* you will not like it—and that some part of it, he must cut out. This is very dreadful! Fancy my sending people improper literature, and not even knowing it! I am afraid you will not like Arnon. Well,—when I wrote about him I thought only of him, and his Asenath, & his troubles, and his hard hearted old father, and it never entered my head as to whether he would some day figure in print—.[76]

Whether the objections to "Arnon," a story that presented an alternative reading of the Flood, arose from moral or religious grounds cannot be determined, but the former seems more likely in the case of Will Otis. In Amélie's attempt to use Old Testament language, the lovers Arnon and Asenath exchange songs that echo the themes of the Song of Solomon. "He hath bound me to him with chains of kisses. He hath set the seal of his love on my mouth. I am his forever," the lovely Asenath chants soon after their meeting. And in return, Arnon declares his love: "Be in mine arms as the sea is in the hollow of the land. Rest upon me as the sunlight on a field of flowers." Moreover, the story presents Noah not as the savior of a righteous people but rather as a stern patriarch who disinherits Arnon because he will not marry the woman chosen for him; instead Arnon hides his beloved in the ark. When at the end of the flood, Noah discovers the couple and denounces them, they go to live in the wild, where Asenath gives birth to a child who dies during a drought.[77]

Some of Will Otis's objections seem to have been stylistic. Amélie had written a dark drama, but as she told her editor: "You know dear Mr. Aldrich, or at least I will tell you that my sense of the humorous is very keen, unfortunately so perhaps, and in writing the story of Arnon, the temptation to indulge in the ludicrous as opened to me by the quaint, and dignified old fashioned style, proved too much for me." She had meant her description of Arnon's proposed bride in an arranged marriage "to be as funny as possible." Finding the depiction ridiculous, Will Otis told her: "The picture was so perfectly absurd, that I nearly collapsed with laughter. *Now as you did not mean it to be funny,* it spoils the effect of the story there." In fact, Rives had intended to be humorous, but the tragic story could poorly carry such broad humor.[78]

Aldrich, apparently tiring of Rives's personal style, rescinded his acceptance of two of her stories and some poems. Possibly he believed her overly emotional and even hysterical. By the time "A Brother to Dragons" appeared in print in March 1886 (listing no author, pseudonym, or initials), Aldrich and his new author were no longer in contact. Two years later, Rives sent him one of her pieces, probably already in print, and in reply he criticized it. With her best ladylike charm, she responded, "I am so sorry that you don't think I have improved." Summing up their relationship, she rather wistfully added, "Never mind, if you ever really think so, I am sure you will be generous enough to tell me of it. . . . I am glad too, that you [already] have the story of mine that you like best."[79]

After the break with Aldrich, Rives quickly began to submit her writings to Richard Watson Gilder at the *Century*. "I hope very much that you will like it," she told him, referring to one of her stories. "I think it the best story I have yet written. . . . Be sure that I will send you the best of which I am capable." All went swimmingly with the *Century* that spring of 1886. By mid-March, she was conferring with Gilder over the romance set in fifteenth-century France that Aldrich had criticized. On April 3, Rives sent Gilder "many thanks for accepting 'Yovanne'" and discussed two changes he suggested. Perhaps remembering her disastrous experience with Aldrich, Rives asked about future submissions: "When the Virginian story is finished, do you want it sent to you? I don't want to inundate you with my Mss, so please let me know about it."[80]

Later that day Rives wrote and requested modifications in the story's language because "I wrote it very quickly as I always write, & on reading it over was struck by the repetition of 'she *did* bend or talk, or weep, etc' instead of 'she bended, wept, talked.'" The following day, Rives returned to Gilder "the pages of 'Yovanne de Savaré,' which you sent me to correct." After mentioning an objection that she thought she had addressed, she closed, "If I have not, send the ms to me again with any suggestion you may choose to make, and I will willingly follow out your instructions."[81]

In May, Rives visited the *Century* editorial offices with her father, who proudly described the scene: "While in New York she was received with the greatest cordiality by the editorial staff of the Century & was made the recipient of quite an ovation at their headquarters." At that point, according to Alfred, his daughter had "sent them another story which is now under advisement. You know that a story of hers has already been accepted but when it is to appear is not yet known." In July, however, Gilder turned down one of Rives's stories, and she told him, "Indeed I do not think it too bad of you to find my scribble unavailable. I will feel all the more pleased if eventually you accept one."[82]

It seems likely that the piece Gilder had rejected was "Virginia of Virginia," a novella later published by *Harper's Monthly*—and one that some critics believe to be the very best of Rives's early writings.[83] That story presented with verve and sympathy an ill-starred relationship between a tenant farmer's daughter and an English horse breeder who had bought a plantation in post–Civil War Virginia. This was not a portrayal that idealized old plantations ravaged by war, though in many ways her realism barely exceeded that of her fellow white "local colorists." Both her plain folk and African Americans speak in dialect. The working-class white men are boorish and uncouth. An African American cook, though warm-hearted and generous, utters malapropisms, and a young black boy primarily provides comic relief. Both common whites and even the Englishman show a casual racism which the story does not directly criticize. Yet the heroine, despite her impoverished origins, exhibits kindness and a heroism that brighten the story. Rives was showing great talent in sketching young women who, like she, were willing to push against social norms.

Gilder's reasons for rejecting "Virginia of Virginia" may have stemmed from his vision of himself not only as an arbiter of taste but also as a guardian of morality, determined to avoid any "salaciousness and gross sensationalism." In the words of one literary historian, Gilder "excluded from his family magazine whatever he thought would offend the mothers of the nation or corrupt their daughters."[84] The headstrong nature of Rives's heroine, who is passionately attracted to the upper-class Englishman and at one point spends a night in a cemetery mourning lost love, probably appeared unseemly to Gilder. That he worked closely with authors and pushed them to excise offending passages suggests that his objections to Rives's story sprang more from the general outlines of the piece rather than a few specific points that could have been corrected. Rives's portrayal of her heroine as a child of nature who experiences a soul-wrenching jealousy that then brings her to atonement and redemption may also have seemed overly sentimental to Gilder. Moreover, many of the whites and blacks in Rives's story appeared poor, uneducated, and disheveled—a far cry from the harmonious communities depicted by plantation romancers like Page.

Here some comparison of Rives's experiences with the *Century* with those of other female writers can be instructive. Gilder did not shut the door to female writers—northern authors such as Rebecca Harding Davis and Constance Fenimore Woolson had been publishing in the *Century* and its predecessor *Scribner's Monthly* for years. Nevertheless, Rives's experience with the *Century* was in line with the shift that the magazine had been making away from female contributors. The southern author Grace King, who penned tighter, more restrained stories than Rives, was rejected by that magazine about the same time. The historian Mark J. Noonan has recently argued that as the *Century* moved increasingly toward realism in the 1880s, it also became less receptive to female authors, whom the editors held to be overly sentimental and lacking in mental toughness. According to the realists, such literature played into women's "addictive consumerism" and, in Noonan's words, "only served to keep women in a state of emotional excitement or dreamy fancifulness" rather than providing the uplift and practical guidance they needed. From such a viewpoint, Gilder perhaps saw "Virginia of Virginia" as not only displaying immoral tendencies but also lacking any socially redeeming message. Yet this distaste accompanied Gilder's growing interest in southern authors and settings; indeed, the *Century* promoted to fame three southern authors, Joel Chandler Harris, James Lane Allen, and Thomas Nelson Page.[85]

Gilder probably found "Virginia of Virginia" coarse and objectionable, but he may also have been influenced by Aldrich's low opinion of Rives's character and stability. In her letter about her manuscript's rejection, Rives mentioned Aldrich when she thanked Gilder "for your kind word to Aldrich in my behalf." While Gilder may have portrayed himself as putting in a kind word, his actions suggest that he came to share Aldrich's assessment. The *Century* never published "Yovanne," the story by Rives it had accepted, even though it was one of the few magazines to pay upon acceptance of an article rather than on its actual appearance in print. Several years later the story came back into Rives's possession when her husband repurchased it from the *Century*. In 1897 it appeared as a novella, *A Damsel Errant*, published by J. B. Lippincott, over a decade after Gilder had first accepted it for publication.[86]

As Rives first submitted her poems and stories to publishers, she continued to depend on Thomas Nelson Page. The nine letters that she wrote him in November and December 1885 all focused on her fictional writings and repeatedly entreated him to visit. In mid-December she asked: "And when are *you* coming? It would be perfectly convenient for us to send for you—and I have three stories to read to you, a handful of verses and some other things of which I will not tell you." She continued to praise him extravagantly. In December 1885 she sought to console him for some criticism he had received: "Never mind what any one says about 'Marse Chan.' In some things I think this last exquisite romance [probably Page's 'Meh Lady'] is even beyond it. There are a hundred touches in it tenderer and quite as beautiful as the tint on the morning clouds." She also pointedly reminded him, "You have never seen one of my short stories—and I want your criticism so, so much."[87]

Nonetheless, as Page's wedding approached, he and Rives corresponded less frequently. She told him in March: "I want to shew you some of my things & to read some of yours, and as *I* am going to be forever an old maid, I want you to promise me that I shall bully your children just as much as ever I like, and be the godmother of one and (if he doesn't claim the right to that foregoing pronoun) have one named after me." Despite this professed intent to continue the friendship, their contact lessened. In July 1886, as Amélie wrestled with illness, her father wrote Page requesting him to return her manuscripts still in his possession.[88]

How much had the friendship with Page affected Amélie's writing style and substance? Despite his attention to Anglo-Saxon and Scottish dialect in poems, Page at this period published almost exclusively in southern, mainly African American, dialect. "Marse Chan," "Meh Lady," and "Unc' Gabriel" present a mythical southern past full of mannered white gentlefolk who live a kinder, more relaxed life. Yet he may well have influenced Amélie, who in some early stories resorts to Page's device of having a servant frame the story. In "A Brother to Dragons," an Elizabethan gardener, who seems roundly attached to the noble family he serves, narrates the tale. Still, he could not serve the purpose that Page sought—that of justifying the old slave regime, apparently through the fond reminiscences of those who had been enslaved. Early in 1886, Rives echoed some of the racist condescension of Page's accounts as she praised his work and declared: "If immortal Will [Shakespeare] himself had tried to make an old darkey (even with the advantages of a Virginian home) he couldn't have done it better."[89]

Rives's literary career thus shows an interesting twist. With literary performance and flirtation, she convinced male friends to show her pieces to publishers. But even as she quickly found her way into print, that same coquettishness, combined with her intensity, unusual vocabulary and unorthodox style, caused enormous problems. Expecting her feminine charm to pave the way, she had no idea of how to move cautiously. Her erratic behavior with Aldrich and unconventional subjects for Gilder convinced these two publishers to abandon her and even forgo publishing pieces that that they earlier had accepted for publication. Her talent for self-promotion seemed to be imploding her writing career, even as it was barely launched. Nevertheless, Rives's letters to Page suggest that she was enjoying her entrance into the literary world and was in no hurry to marry. While she probably did not intend to be the "old maid" that she teasingly mentioned, she also did not seem to be moving closer to a marital choice.

The publication of Amélie's first story, "A Brother to Dragons," in March 1886, and her first poem, "A Sonnet," that June, immediately drew local and national attention. In Virginia, Sarah Seddon Bruce, soon to become Thomas Nelson Page's mother-in-law, wrote her son, "Miss Amalie Rives, daughter of Col Alfred Rives, has a story in the March Number of the Atlantic Monthly which has created a sensation at the North—get it for it will interest & astonish you that such a story should have been written by a young girl." And the *Richmond Dispatch* in April 1886 reported on the New York trip: "Miss Amelie Louise Rives, the gifted and promising young authoress, will leave for New York early in May to spend some time with relations in that city." While this item may have owed more to the prominence of the Rives family than to any fame of Amélie's, two months later the *New York Tribune* noted that Amélie Rives, the author of "Brother to Dragons," was "only twenty-three years old" and "very beautiful."[90] The press and ordinary people, North and South, had begun to take notice of the lovely young author with the unusual name.

THREE

"The Most Noted of the Younger Writers"

Becoming a Southern Writer

In the spring of 1886, Amélie Rives found herself in the enviable public position of being a published author but the difficult private one of having alienated two influential northern editors. The appearance of her short story "A Brother to Dragons" in the eminent *Atlantic Monthly* brought her attention on a national stage. Yet at the same time, her family's growing economic woes also impelled her to merchandise her talents—for writing and for courtship—and to grasp the opportunities that position, talent, and exposure were bringing. In the next two years she would make life-changing decisions. As her foray into print gave her celebrity, her Virginia birth allowed her to take advantage of a rising popularity for southern authors.

In 1885 and 1886 economic affairs took a turn for the worse for Amélie's father. As a railroad executive, Alfred had found the Mobile area promising. Back in 1878, when his regular salary as chief engineer and vice president of the Mobile and Ohio Railroad had increased to ten thousand dollars a year, Alfred told his older brother: "I shall continue to devote my surplus to laying up nest eggs, and trust by hard work a few years longer to lay up a modest competency—more than I ever expected to do until very recently."[1] Five years later, in 1883, Alfred returned to Virginia to take a more prestigious position as vice president and general manager of the Richmond and Danville Railroad. At this auspicious point he undertook a general renovation of Castle Hill, which he owned jointly with his unmarried sister. Unfortunately and unpredictably, his position deteriorated with the Richmond and Danville, which moved from the Pennsylvania system to become part of a newly emerging monopoly in Virginia and North Carolina. In 1885 fifty-five-year-old Alfred was forced out of his position into "retirement." Informing his wife that August that he had been asked for his resignation,

Alfred added: "I am so very tired of the wretched life I have been leading, that I am resigned if Heaven so wills it. We now will be forced to economize but I will be with you to strengthen guide & defend."[2] To make matters worse, he had made some speculative investments that had soured.

By the spring of 1886, the Rives daughters were learning about these financial problems. That summer his wife and eldest daughter listened as Alfred paced day and night from room to room at Castle Hill. Pouring out his worries, he confided to Amélie: "My poor little girl—you never thought it would end like this. I am too old. They have done with me. What shall I do?" His entreaties to his wife were even more pathetic: "Sadie—I don't think this can last much longer. I think my heart is breaking. Be patient with me. Oh! if I could only earn fifty dollars a month."[3]

Scrambling to find a new position, Alfred sought his brother William's aid. In June, Alfred wrote that he had delayed "in the hope of being able to send you some good news in regard to my prospects. In this I am disappointed. I have had more promises & more assurances—voilà tout." William was orchestrating support for a position for Alfred as chief of the U.S. Coast Survey, and Alfred reminded him to "stir up Lamar," probably an attempt to encourage Senator L. Q. C. Lamar of Alabama to support Alfred's candidacy.[4]

Troubled by her father's state of mind, Amélie Rives wrote her uncle William in July 1886 about her father's financial and emotional instability. Estimating that Alfred owed William five hundred dollars and another seven or eight hundred elsewhere, she continued: "He lost a thousand by these terrible storms of the last month." In this search for aid, Amélie did not seem to have a firm plan. Naively depending on fraternal solidarity, she apparently thought that her uncle might supply the emotional bulwark that her father badly needed. She suggested: "If you could only write to say to him, 'Go ahead Alfred & buy something for yourself. I will stand by you & tide you through.'" And she cautioned, "If you could only help him & not let him know I wrote to you. Just of your own free will."[5]

To be sure, Amélie intended to repay any money from her uncle, telling him: "Then, *then* Uncle Will, I would think it a privilege if you would let me spend my youth drop by drop to repay you in money what could never repay your kindness." In part, Rives's new status as author allowed her to ask her uncle for aid, aid that she was quite sure that she could reimburse. "You know dear uncle," she declared, "this is not idle and the high flown sentiment of a school girl. I find—thanks to a good God that I can make money—that such brain as He has given me, means downright, sterling coin." She then rattled off her recent earnings and her unused literary stock: "For my last accepted story I received $175. My latest (unaccepted) they tell me is worth six hundred. I have eight or nine more. I have several hundred verses. Several dramas." And she assured him: "It will be a matter of time I know. Some years. Maybe a good part of my life, but it will make me happy—, happy to feel this debt on my shoulders."[6]

Amélie had approached her uncle with a mixture of self-assurance, charm, and guilelessness. Whatever she expected, she was unprepared for the mix of morality and condescension in his reply. While William assured his niece that he would try, without mentioning her letter, to assist her father, he also unctuously commented: "I have seen with the deepest regret, for a good while past, & yet with powerlessness to change the result, that your Father was unconsciously to himself, laying up a large store of unhappiness in his declining years for himself & perhaps for his family." William then partly blamed Alfred's family: "His love for his wife & children is so ardent that he cannot bear to disappoint their slightest wish & has long been accustomed to look on money as of value chiefly as it might enable him to gratify & anticipate their fancied desires. For many years in the receipt of a larger professional income, its sudden & unexpected withdrawal has been a terrible blow to him."[7]

Asserting that "railroad men" had led Alfred into dangerous speculation, William ventured the hope that Alfred had saved money from his past salary. William further suggested that future expenses could be few: "He has no sons to send to College or to fit out for professional life, no impecunious sons in law to support. He has a beautiful & comfortable home, with a farm around it, yielding abundant & varied provisions."

The opening paragraphs of William's letter had assured Amélie, "You have health and youth and beauty and genius, all admirable & precious gifts." He later proposed that she could best help her father "by showing him your capacity to be happy & rich in the paucity of your wants. As to mortgaging the fruits of your fertile genius to me, or to anyone else, that would be in the highest degree unwise."[8]

Amélie was deeply offended by her uncle's criticisms of her father, family, and herself. Writing in pencil as she seldom did, with the injunction "Forgive the apparent slovenliness of this letter, but I am still confined to my bed," she assumed a lofty, distant tone: "I am sorry that you should have thought it necessary to suggest my 'largely helping' my dear father 'by shewing my capacity to be happy & rich in the paucity of my wants.'" She appeared to agree with William's notion of proper womanly exertions as she self-righteously asserted: "It is a little thing, but I will tell you that I have made many of my own clothes since our misfortunes." Perfunctorily thanking him for his advice, she indicated that she had misrepresented her father's position, since his only debt was the five hundred dollars owed to William. She ended with a chilly statement of her intent to be the family savior: "I thank the dear God that by His help, I have lately been placed in a position which will enable me unassisted to assist those who are most dear to me. I therefore beg that you will forget the contents of my last letter to you."[9]

Later that year a post on a federal commission that was inspecting forty miles of the Northern Pacific railroad gave Alfred a brief respite from his financial problems; and he found a permanent position with the French-owned Panama railroad company in 1887. Amélie, meanwhile, had preoccupations of her own, as family letters suggest that she was unwell much of the spring and summer of 1886. Only a few days before she huffily replied to her uncle, she had described her last few months: "You know I was so ill this spring that I cannot remember all that happened during & after my illness, & ever since my return home, I have been ill off & on with neuralgia of the brain." Earlier that month, she at times had been delirious.[10]

Despite these problems with her health and possibly even her emotional stability, Amélie was finding new publishers who tolerated her eccentricities and even used her unconventionality to their own profit. In early August 1886 she was in contact with Harper Brothers Publishing. Her father at that point told his brother that despite Amélie's illnesses, "We continue to be more and more encouraged in regard to her literary career. I think in a month or two her best effort so far will appear, & very probably in Harper's."[11] Although Alfred's optimism about Harper's was borne out—over the next twenty-five years, that publishing house presented many of her poems, articles, and books—his timing was somewhat amiss. In the summer of 1887, almost a year later, her next story appeared in *Lippincott's* with another in *Harper's* that autumn, as well as an essay in *Harper's Bazaar*. In the meantime, she had published three pieces of poetry by June 1887, one in the *Century,* the others in *Harper's New Monthly*.[12]

As the last chapter has shown, Rives was searching for a way into literary life and seeking more mature guides. As well as benefiting from her family's position and its wide-ranging ties, she also was—at least briefly—in the right place to gain from current developments in literary life, which had come to focus on the South. In the 1870s, "local color" stories, especially those by New England writers such as Sarah Orne Jewett, who described small town Maine, had gained popularity. That growing fascination with regional cultures and stories featuring dialect quickly came to include southerners. While Joel Chandler Harris's "Uncle Remus" stories paved the way, southern women, especially those who focused on Appalachian hill folks, African Americans, or creoles in New Orleans, joined with southern men and New Englanders and midwesterners in presenting particularistic portraits of the United States. Mary Noailles Murfree, who wrote under the pen name Charles Egbert Craddock, had begun publishing in the 1870s. Thomas Nelson Page published his first dialect poem in 1877, but "Marse Chan" and "Meh Lady," published in the *Century* in 1884 and 1886, greatly increased his fame. Some literary scholars have found perplexing this focus on regional peculiarities in a time of national growth, while historians such as Nina Silber have argued that the massive growth of cities and the influx of immigrants in the North made presentations of an allegedly simple life in rural areas and the organic relationships on the plantation particularly alluring to many readers.[13]

In July 1886 Henry M. Alden, editor of *Harper's New Monthly Magazine,* a popular magazine with a middle-class readership, sent Thomas Nelson Page a long list of southern authors who interested him, including Page, George Washington Cable, Mary N. Murfree, M. G. McClelland, Grace King, Frances Hodgson Burnett, and Amélie Rives. The publisher added, "I wish you would as soon as possible send me a good photograph of your-self, of Miss Rives (author of 'A Brother to Dragons') & of Miss McClel-land."[14] (Alden presumably knew that Page had a personal as well as kin relation with the two women.) Alden, in fact, had already begun to publish southern fiction. Earlier that year Page's story "Unc' Edinburg's Drown-din'" appeared in the January issue of *Harper's New Monthly,* and the July issue included a story by the New Orleans writer Grace King.

Some educated southerners were becoming aware of this new appreci-ation for southern writers. In July 1886 John R. Proctor, Kentucky's chief geologist, wrote Thomas Nelson Page: "I am very proud of the reputation gained by southern authors of late. I was in England last winter and the brightest man I met there thought the new literature of the South—the stron-gest, the most imaginative and the most hopeful production of the English speaking world for the past few years. He had read and reread 'Marse Chan' and Craddock's 'Prophet of the Great Smokey Mountains.'" Proctor, who later became a noted civil service reformer and president of the Civil Service Commission, also mentioned Amélie's recent poem: "Miss Reeve's Sonnet in June Century whets my appetite for more."[15]

That same summer, Robert Burns Wilson, one of Page's cousins who was both a painter and a poet, pictured the situation as a cultural upsurge in the South: "The eyes of the world are on us now. There must be no dropping of the line. There must be no going back. By Gad I feel the blood tingle under my fingernails when I think of it. Miss King is 'up.' God bless her. And Miss Rives is more than 'up.'" Wilson's sectional pride became even more overt: "We *must* keep the line from sagging. They are after us—all of them—did you see in the last Critic? Literature in the South. Read it." In closing, Burns sent his love to Page and Anne Bruce Page and added, "Speak me fair to the Goddess of Castle Hill," obviously a reference to Rives.[16]

At this time in the summer of 1886, Rives had published only a poem and a short story, neither of which even mentioned the South; yet as these references indicate, fellow southerners and some critics were beginning to call her a southern writer. Newspapers and magazines agreed. In July of 1886, the *Staunton* [Va.] *Spectator* copied an item from the *Baltimore American,* which began, "The southern woman is coming to the front," and then claimed that Miss Murfree "sprang into lasting fame in almost a single year, and now a Virginia young lady follows in the same path. Her name is Miss Amelie Rives and she is described as very beautiful."[17]

Moreover, some contemporary critics and editors were suggesting that a southern literary renaissance was underway. The May 1887 issue of *Harper's* included a group biography of southern writers, entitled "The Recent Movement in Southern Literature." Likely an outgrowth of Alden's interest, the article argued that a new generation of authors was arising in the South, and that "accuracy of observation, delicacy of portraiture and artistic finish, and, above all, their freshness and earnestness, entitle these new writers to no mean rank and the utmost consideration."[18] While George W. Cable, Joel Chandler Harris, and Mary N. Murfree received the most attention in the issue, Rives was among the dozen authors pictured and discussed. Noting that she had "burst into prominence with a single short story," the article described her "distinguished lineage," "rare personal attractions," and "extended social reputation, not only in her native South, but at the North as well." Also receiving attention was Rives's propensity to "shut herself in her studio, and stand before the easel ten hours at a time; or else, having read everything bearing upon the subject chosen, write as many hours with a rapidity and exactness wellnigh inconceivable."[19]

A follow-up piece in the literary journal the *Critic* discussed this new phenomenon at greater length, calling it "singular" that the South's "wealth and leisure of ante-bellum days . . . actually produced nothing, . . . it is yet more singular that this sudden Southern literature has leaped Minerva-like from the brain, perfect of its kind from the beginning."[20] In June 1887 the *Chicago Daily Inter-Ocean* declared that "Southern names will be conspicuous in *Lippincott's* for July." Rives drew attention in the notice for one of her Elizabethan pieces, which appeared along with a novella by her friend Julia Magruder and poems by Page and Robert Burns Wilson.[21] That an almost

Fellow author Julia Magruder, shown here with Amélie Rives, was a dear friend. (Amélie Rives Troubetzkoy Collection, The Valentine)

identical notice was published in the *Morning Oregonian* in June suggests that *Lippincott's* was the source.[22] Ironically enough, it was only after Rives had been publicly identified as a "southern writer" that she began to publish stories set in the South. The sobriquet of southern writer does not appear to have been one that she ever sought, and it rested uneasily upon her.

In 1887 Rives's writing career again surged. That spring, in addition to a poem in *The Century Illustrated,* she published "Grief and Faith," a thirteen-verse sonnet in which a widower mourns his wife, who has died giving birth. Like Rives's first offering in *Harper's New Monthly,* the poem shows her penchant for choosing topics considered unusual for a twenty-three-year-old unmarried woman. While the poem eventually justifies Christian resignation, it also frames the loss in terms of passion and yearning. The narrator speaks to his deceased wife:

> I thirst for thee
> As thirst the summer meadows for the rain
> As longs the main-land for the tarrying sea
> As stricken souls do yearn for bodily pain
> Oh, God in heaven! Must such anguish be?[23]

Although the grief-stricken narrator questions his faith in God and the order of the universe, the deceased wife reassures her husband, "Love can never die, Though hearts that loved be dust." She then beseeches him: "Dear, have faith; be strong; / Take up this cross of living with a zest; / Help others in their woe; make right of wrong." In the last stanza, the bereaved husband again bids his wife farewell and pledges that "faith shall answer when thy God doth call."

In this rather conventional Victorian sonnet, faith triumphs over grief and promises an eventual reunion of lovers. As the modern scholar Edward Tucker has pointed out, it follows "the strict Italian form of an octave (abbaabba) and a sestet (cdcdcd)."[24] Thomas Nelson Page penned an answer, which he entitled, "To Miss Amélie Rives, on Reading Her 'Grief and Faith.'" Page's sonnet of fourteen lines takes a different tack than Rives's exploration of love and faith. Mustering his classical references, Page in his first octave pictures the ruin of the ancient world where, in its concluding line, "Thou, Amélie, dost lift thy sun-crowned head." The remaining sestet praises Rives as a wise though youthful oracle:

Thou comest filled with Heavenly ecstasy,
Thy virgin lips speak with diviner sooth
Than e'er was heard from Earthly minstrelsy,
Like to Minerva, full grown in thy youth.
Thou dost fulfill the ancient prophecy,
And with thy earliest speech declarest truth.[25]

Page, however, never published his sonnet. Newly married when "Love and Grief" appeared in 1887, he had ceased communicating with Rives almost a year earlier. He may have previously written this sonnet for her, perhaps during or after one of his visits to Castle Hill. It remains unclear whether Rives ever read Page's encomium to her, which

HARPER'S NEW MONTHLY MAGAZINE.

This engraving of Thomas Nelson Page comes from an article entitled "The Recent Movement in Southern Literature," in *Harper's New Monthly Magazine* in May 1887. (Library of Virginia)

rested among his papers until a scholar published it in the twenty-first century.[26]

Also published in spring 1887, "Love Song" was a conventional romantic poem that sent kisses, love, and an appreciation of nature's beauty to a faraway suitor. Although less fervid than Rives's poem in *Harper's,* "Love Song" too drew a response, this time from Francis R. Lassiter, a distant relation with a good education and a similar background to her earlier suitors. Although a recent graduate of the University of Virginia Law School, Lassiter apparently had not been formally introduced to Amélie and so sought Rosalie Rives, a mutual cousin, to send his poetic reply to Amélie's published poem.[27] Rosalie then reluctantly provided the wished-for introduction: "Though she does not know me any more than that 'bunch of turnips' to which with such charming sensibility you liken yourself, I reflected that it was expected of me less to introduce myself than you so your herald sounded a *pretty* flourish of trumpets before the castle of the beautiful princess. I . . . made it easier for her to reply to you than to me, but if she has the bad taste to prefer writing to me, I will forward her letter without delay." Rosalie added a snippy barb: "If however our gifted relation is as capricious and self-absorbed as rumour attests, we must both be philosophically prepared for down-right suffering."[28]

In line with Rosalie's pessimistic assessment of Francis's chances, Amélie replied in a rather distant tone. Addressing him as "My dear Mr. Lassiter," she thanked him for "your answers to my little song" and graciously allowed: "I do not think you should call them bad at all. It gave me much pleasure to read them." She asked if the poem was, as Rosalie had indicated, to be published in the June issue of the *Century*—an event which apparently did not occur.[29]

Francis Lassiter was only one of several young men drawn by Amélie's beauty, talent, and emerging repute, and her social life was enjoying a great uptick in 1887. The beautiful young "authoress" received much attention; perhaps her health had also improved. She spent part of her spring in Richmond and took part in social activities there. In March the Richmond newspaper reported about the musicale in which Miss A.C. Doggett of Fredericksburg sang three alto solos, including "a rendition of the 'Barley Break' by Miss Amelie Rives, music by Mr. Iredell Jenkins, [which] was well done."[30]

That April, Amélie acted in two plays in Richmond, one of which she had written. On its front page, the *Richmond Dispatch* raved that the "social world of Richmond turned out en masse . . . at the theatre." The reviewer also indicated: "The audience was a beautiful one, most of the ladies being in evening dress, and was enthusiastic in its demonstrations of pleasure and satisfaction with the excellent way the two plays were put on the stage." That the article intended to highlight the social elite could be seen in its listing of the worthies who had boxes (including the governor and wife) and its detailed descriptions of the costumes of the actresses in both plays. The reporter, seeking a professional tone, commented that "to criticise amateurs is a harsh and thankless task at best, yet it is a pleasure to say that the acting of last evening, for such an occasion, disarms criticism."[31]

Amélie, like the other participants, received praise for her acting: "'Matilde' was beautifully portrayed by Miss Rives. And many a young man last evening must have envied 'Anatole' his love-making to so captivating a sweetheart." The reporter, while twice calling Rives "charming," was not captivated by *Mad as a March Hare,* the play that she had penned for the second part of the evening's entertainment. "The farce is cleverly written," the reporter allowed, "and while it does great credit to the charming authoress, does not act as well as it reads. It is wanting in dramatic points; and for this reason especially are the cast of last evening to be congratulated on their very pleasing presentation of an entirely new play."[32]

Later assessments of Rives's dramatic experience were more biting. In February 1888 the *Atlanta Constitution* denigrated her skills as playwright and actor: "Last season she produced a play entitled 'Mad as a March Hare,' which was performed by a company of amateurs in Richmond. Miss Rives herself appeared in the leading female role, but the great expectations of her friends were not realized. The play was a failure; the performance execrable." Even harsher was a story from a writer based in Baltimore who asserted: "The play and the acting were seen to be failures ten minutes after the curtain rose before a distinguished gathering of Richmond people. Miss Rives grew impatient and fretted and then angry, and [it] is said she destroyed on that occasion what popularity she had enjoyed in the gay society of that delightful city." The play and Amélie's part in it probably fell somewhere between the immense success and utter failure described in these accounts. In December 1887 many of the original participants reprised their dramatic performance for the benefit of Richmond's Confederate Soldiers' Home, with Governor Fitzhugh Lee serving as the acting company's general manager. The notice of the upcoming performance indicated "the young ladies who are to take part are such beauties as Miss Amelie Rives, the authoress, Mrs. Willie Allen, Mrs. Philip Haxall, Miss Myers. . . ."[33]

During the summer of 1887, Amélie explored the world of wealthy northern suitors. Twenty-four-year-old Amélie was returning to the opulent resort town of Newport as an author as well as an acknowledged beauty. Although a Kansas newspaper reported in August that "Miss Amelie Rives will probably spend two or three weeks at Newport this summer," it is unclear how long a visit she actually paid to her wealthy relatives.[34] One historian records that Amélie attended a ball at the resplendent Casino club that August. Amid the Japanese lanterns, beautiful flowers, and ocean breezes,

> a petite red satin slipper flew off the foot of a dancer and went skimming across the parquet floor. For a moment the room froze, then at once the young men made a mad dash for the shoe. The winner, Donald Swan, gallantly presented the shoe to its owner, the Cinderella-like Amélie. Resplendent in a crimson gown, she dramatically lifted her leg while Swan dropped to his knees and placed the slipper on her foot. He then stood and bowed deeply before her. The dancers on the floor and the gallery of onlookers in the balcony burst into applause.

Among the onlookers was John Armstrong Chanler, known as Archie, the twenty-four-year-old great-great-grandson of John Jacob Astor. According to his biographer, Archie later recalled the incident on the ballroom floor as "the instant that he fell in love with Amélie Rives."[35]

After Amélie was feted and wooed during this golden summer in Newport, more of her stories and poems appeared. That September, her new publisher *Harper's Monthly Magazine* brought out "Nurse Crumpet Tells the Tale," an Elizabethan story, framed by the elderly nurse who related it. *Harper's* also ran in its November 1887 issue "The Story of Arnon," the tale that Aldrich of the *Atlantic Magazine* had so disliked.[36]

Amélie's courtship and authorial experience seemed to be coming together as she explored the world of wealthy suitors. Her newest stories appearing at the end of the year—which may have been written during that summer— moved her focus to the contemporary South, and some of her most riveting productions focused on women in her native Virginia. In particular, "Inja," published in December of 1887, seemed like a script for self-improvement as well as a cautionary tale for herself and other young women mired in the

The Princess of Albemarle

rural South. Told largely from the point of view of Reuben Sterling, a barely literate Virginia farmer, the plot revolves around the courtship and marriage of his daughter India ("Inja" as Reuben pronounces her name).[37] Reuben, a widower, adores his only daughter, whom he apparently has educated and pampered. A worthy man, as indicated by his surname, Reuben nonetheless is also a plain farmer who speaks in dialect and adheres to a masculine code that despises men who smell "sweet" and cannot properly whistle dogs to attention. A man of the earth, Reuben holds simple values.

In contrast, India herself, while lovely, is calculating. She has a handsome head and black braids; her one peculiarity is her eyebrows, which, "though shapely, were singularly thick and broad, looking much like strips of fur above her claret-colored eyes." The opening scene evinces her coldness when she deliberately feeds an annoying katydid to a chicken. Moreover, India's exotic name suggests horizons beyond the Virginia farm; her education has given her a taste for fine things and the larger world. Unlike her father, she rarely speaks in dialect. In bed she surreptitiously devours a current novel, Ouida's *Princess Napraxine* (1884), and is entranced by the world of European society that it portrays.[38] Clearly, Rives expected her audience would know that Ouida (the pseudonym of British writer Maria Louise de la Ramée) wrote racy society novels. Those who had actually read *Princess Napraxine* would also realize that it chronicled the adventures of a hard-hearted, rich, and beautiful woman who deliberately manipulated the world to her advantage.

Rives highlights the gulf between India and her father when Sterling surprises her with a bolt of green silk. The green reminds him of apple blossoms and a beautiful dress worn by his late wife; India, in contrast, compares the color to a "stagnant pond" and insists that, arrayed in such a dress, she would resemble a katydid. A love interest develops when Ruthven Lely, a New York stockbroker who had purchased a nearby farm, courts India, much to the distress of Sterling, who prefers John Nixon, a neighboring farmer. India, however, declares that she would never marry "a man who smells of guano and kills his own pigs."[39]

As the plot progresses toward marriage, the question of love moves to the forefront. After Lely asks to marry India, Sterling queries his daughter about whether she loves Lely. Tellingly, she refuses to answer directly: "I have told you that I am willing to marry him." At the wedding, she with a "half vacant look" rushes to her father, asking him if he thinks she'll be happy: "Say it. Say it anyhow. I'm so afraid that I won't be happy."[40]

After six years in which the young couple lives mainly abroad, with India giving birth to a son in Nice, France, Reuben Sterling decides to visit his daughter and grandchild. At Christmas, he shows up unannounced at their house in New York City while a party is underway. He encounters India dressed in red satin with rubies sewn into her hair. When a guest mistakes Sterling for a family servant or overseer from the imagined aristocratic Virginia plantation past that India has fashioned for herself, she is speechless about his true identity. Running after him, she tells him of her poor health and weak heart and asks him to return the following morning.

As the story wends to its end, Reuben visits his spoiled grandson and stops in a theater where the noted actor John McCullough is portraying King Lear. The king's conflict with his ungrateful daughters inspires Reuben to return in the snow to India's house to force her to acknowledge him. Then, as she falteringly calls him "father," he angrily declares, "Yuh ain' no daughter o' mine! Yuh lie to call me father!" Tragedy ensues, as Reuben flees his daughter's house and she rushes after him. "She stood there in her gorgeous fire-colored dress, and the wind and sleet drove in upon her. She called him wildly, over and over, many times. . . . When they came to her, she had fallen athwart the threshold, and her white hands grasped the ice-coated stones beyond." After storming out of India's house, Reuben takes refuge with a small newsboy in a warm corner by a large building. There, at the story's end, he dreams of his wife and India, as he apparently drifts into unconsciousness and death.[41]

Early in her story Amélie underlines the way in which India's love of material possessions leads to a mercenary marriage. Entranced by the beauty of the handsome designer wedding dress with orange blossoms that Lely has sent her, India returns it only at her father's insistence. At the wedding she then wears a simple white muslin dress. In New York, her jewels, fine house, and scarlet satin evening dress show her defiant grasp of wealth and lead her father to believe her the scarlet woman described in the sermons heard in his youth. Even while the story proclaims the integrity and selfless love shown by Reuben, Rives dwells on how India has been enticed by the high life. In a particularly telling section, the young unmarried India, lying in bed, stares at herself in a mirror: "How red her lips were in the soft light! She smiled, and was in love with the whiteness of her small, sharp teeth. . . . She was thrilled with the beauty of her large, clear eyes, and her white brow shining through the parted tangles above. The contour of her neck and throat seemed so lovely to her that she caressed them with her long, sensitive fingers. She half closed her eyes that she might catch the effect of sleep upon her face, and slightly disarranged her night-gown to show the beauty of her white shoulders and arms."[42] In this autoerotic passage, Rives signals India's self-absorption and the way she considers beauty as a commodity to further her dreams. Some readers may well have wondered whether Rives shared that view.

Those expecting a new South in literature warmly greeted the publication of "Inja." Writing for the *New Orleans Picayune,* Catherine Cole mentioned some of the eccentricities attributed to Rives, but declared it a "beautiful story," of the kind "that make one the better and softer and kinder for the reading."[43]

Only one month after the publication of "Inja," *Harper's New Monthly Magazine* published Amélie's novella "Virginia of Virginia." Like India, the protagonist is a young southern woman from the rural classes, but this tale of tragic attraction takes a very different turn. Both stories, while featuring a young woman, allow a central male character to narrate the story. However, Virginia, as a tenant farmer's daughter, belongs to a poorer class than India's farming family.

The story opens as the English narrator, Jack Roden, who has come to Virginia to run a horse farm called Caryston Hall, meets a rain-swept figure and ponders that person's gender. His uncertainty arises mainly from Virginia's attire: a hat, long tunic, and gaiters over "sturdy leather boots." The daughter of the overseer of Caryston, Virginia Herrick is tall, blond, and muscular. She carries a gun and a game bag and is accompanied by four dogs. As Roden comes to know Virginia better, he finds that, despite her local accent, she plays the piano well and knows the poems of the English poet Robert Herrick. Along with her menagerie of pets—a raccoon and chipmunk in addition to the numerous dogs—she spins yarns and sings African American spirituals and work songs in a throaty contralto. An unconventional heroine, she avows unorthodox religious opinions and declares she will never marry. Roden also finds himself increasingly impressed by her local knowledge and horsemanship. She guides him to the top of a local mountain, and, as her father puts it, "that girl kin ride like an Injun."[44] Able to ride Roden's prize possession, the beautiful and high-strung mare Bonnibel, Virginia also crochets a change purse for him.

In narrating the growing relationship between Jack Roden and Virginia Herrick, Rives pictures each as conscious of the other's body and appearance. As they ascend a mountain, Virginia sees Roden in a new light: "He had taken off his coat, as the increasing sunlight and the exertion of walking had overheated him, and his flannel shirt expressed damply the splendid modelling of his supple body." When they are caught in a storm, the wind pulls loose Virginia's hair: "She looked like some mountain Godiva hidden all as in a banner of cloth of gold." Roden's admiration for Virginia's beauty, however, is always tempered by his class prejudices: "Roden watched her as she stalked away with her splendid swinging stride, thinking vaguely of her beauty and its absolute waste in her position." Indeed, he believes he knows her future: "'She'll marry some "po' white" who talks as much like a nigger as her own father,' he thought, half regretfully; 'have a lot of children, and end by smoking a pipe—ugh!'"[45]

Roden soon meets Mary Errol, daughter of the owner of a neighboring plantation, Windermere. A tall slender woman with dark curling hair, Mary immediately draws Roden's attention as she rides up, mounted sidesaddle. "He watched admiringly the long supple waist as it swayed to the motion of the horse, the bold graceful sweep of the shoulders, and high carriage of the small head." When Roden comments on Mary's fine riding form, Virginia questions his estimate of her own ability. "He answered her, still with his eyes on the vanishing figure of the girl in the Quorn-cloth habit. 'You ride like an Arab,' he said. 'She rides like—like—like an English woman.'" Here Roden shows his adherence to conventions of gender and class. He calls upon Mary Errol, who in turn visits him and stays for lunch. The class divide becomes more apparent as Virginia, who usually delivers his lunch, resentfully tells him that she will serve him, but not Mary. Crying, Virginia storms out, indicating her notion of the servility required: "I don't care! I ain't anybody's nigger!" Roden obliviously responds: "How vulgarity will crop out! . . . That poor little girl has behaved so well until to-day!"[46]

From this first meeting with Mary, Virginia becomes increasingly jealous: "A feeling of utterly unreasonable anger and rebellion was swelling in her heart and straining her throat." The play of love and jealousy in a young woman pushes the story forward. Virginia is a natural woman, given to deep, unmediated emotions. At a steeplechase, she rescues Roden when a jumper throws him. Receiving Mary's thanks for saving Roden's life, Virginia reacts rudely but inwardly rages: "She hated the girl with a mad, barbaric impulse, which was as much beyond her control as its tides are beyond the control of the ocean."[47]

The Princess of Albemarle

After Roden and Mary Errol become engaged, Virginia's emotions begin to devour her. On learning the news, she spends the night crying at the estate's cemetery to mourn the death of her love for Roden. The next day Virginia arises with a sense of vagueness and resignation. In an authorial aside, Rives comments: "She was a savage. She suffered like a savage. Will any say there was no justice in it? It is something, is it not, to be capable of passion such as that? She suffered beyond most people, men and women, it is true; but was she not in that much blessed above them?"[48]

Virginia struggles with her envy of Mary. "She had tried honestly to over-come the all-powerful, unreasoning dislike of Miss Mary Errol, and the result had been worse than if it had not been tried."[49] When Mary arrives at Caryston Hall during a sudden rainstorm, soaking wet, Virginia lends her a plain dress. Mary with her long slender neck, wants a velvet choker to ornament it; Virginia herself has none but knows of a velvet ribbon worn by a baby killed by the fever. Hoping to remove her rival, Virginia gives the ribbon to Mary Errol. Even though Virginia attempts to undo her action—tearing off the ribbon after seeing Jack Roden kiss his fiancée's throat—Mary indeed becomes ill.

Virginia seeks redemption by nursing Mary and spends twelve days by the fever-wracked victim's bedside. Mary recovers, but Virginia herself falls ill with the fever. Tormented by her guilt, she confesses to Roden, who angrily refuses to forgive her. Virginia's jealousy and failure to win love have all but destroyed her: "Virginia lived on, if one can be said to live whose heart is dead within her. She did not dare to pray for death; she did not dare to hope for peace; she feared to die, poor ignorant child, because of the roaring flame which waited to devour her. She feared even more to live, because of the fire with which she was already consumed." A barn fire provides her a last chance at atonement. She bravely rushes in to save Roden's beloved horse, Bonnibel. As they emerge from the barn, it collapses, sparing the horse but severely burning Virginia. Aunt Tishy, the African American cook and Virginia's former nurse, cares for her as Virginia alternates between reason and delirium. With her father and Roden at her bedside, Virginia expresses her joy over saving the horse and sorrow over losing Roden. Just before she dies, she says, "I loved him, father dear—I loved him so! An' I've been mighty wicked; an' God's been mighty good ter me; an' I'm goin' to heaven, mammy says. But I won't have him even there—I won't have him—even there."[50]

Despite its melodramatic ending, "Virginia of Virginia" is far more so-phisticated than Rives's earlier stories. To be sure, the author adhered to Victorian standards and showed her own pious upbringing in creating a natural woman who experiences a soul-wrenching jealousy, then finds atonement and redemption. Rives intended her reader to see an altered her-oine when the fatally injured Virginia asks Aunt Tishy to sing a hymn about sins being washed away and later acknowledges God's blessing.

Even with this conventional religious ending, Rives nonetheless subverts Victorian demands for meekness and self-abnegation in women. This story, like "Inja," features a young woman who is deeply concerned about physical appearance and who self-consciously evaluates her own beauty. India, with her desire to become a lady, pays close attention to her image in the mirror, but so does Virginia: "It was one o'clock on that same night. Virginia Her-rick leaned with round bare arms on the table, above which hung a little oblong, old-fashioned mirror in a warped mahogany frame." Clad only in her chemise, she studies her face and body: "The contrast between the dead white of the stuff, and the living white of her neck and arms, was as perfect as when Southern peach-trees, blossoming before their time, are seen next day against vast fields of snow." Virginia scrutinizes her features and won-ders about her sexual appeal: "Suddenly she spoke. 'I wisht I knew ef I war pretty,' she said. Then, with passionate reiterance, 'I *wisht* I knew ef I war pretty.'" Finally, as she looks at herself in the mirror: "This time she put another question. 'I wisht I knew ef—it—pleased—*him.*'" Here Virginia is imagining herself as the object of attention and even desire.[51]

While such scenes allow Rives, as a novelist, to outline the lineaments of her subject, she depicts her heroines moving toward self-awareness and autonomy. Yet, according to the ideology that had long reigned among reli-giously observant nineteenth-century men and women, such notions seem overly self-involved, and even depraved in their sensuality. India Sterling glories in her attractiveness to a wealthy man, and the same themes of female beauty and power mark "Virginia of Virginia." Moreover, these stories pre-figure Rives's future novel *The Quick or the Dead?* in the modern southern settings and people they depict.

"Virginia of Virginia" also represents Rives's first effort at a southern plantation novel that includes African Americans. Her black characters all speak dialect and often appear closer to minstrel characters than fully drawn people. "Aunt Tishy," the housekeeper and "mammy" for Virginia, is a kindly woman given to malapropisms, superstition, and at times outright incomprehensibility. Still, she shows a basic humanity and a deep loyalty to her charge, protecting Virginia's secret of spending the night in the cemetery. She also seems truly touched by Virginia's death. Broad racist humor is provided by three young African Americans named after volcanoes and an African American couple called Prince Albert and Queen Victoria.[52]

The whites in this story all claim to be authorities on African American life, as when Virginia informs Roden about nomenclature: "'All the darkies took th' name o' th' fam'lies they b'longed to after th' war,' she explained. 'I had a cook here oncet called Faginia Herrick; she used to b'long to father fo' th' war.'" Moreover, all these white characters, even the Englishman Roden, use racial slurs and voice prejudiced views that Rives presents without comment. Indeed, her principal attempt at countering such casual epithets comes in a contrast she draws between Virginia and the Englishman Roden. When the young Black boy Popo checks on Virginia's safety during a storm, she sees that he is shivering and wraps him in the jacket that Roden has lent her. Later, back at Caryston, Roden uncharitably muses about her action: "he really rather liked it on the girl; but d—n the little nigger!—that was my pet coat!"[53]

Even as her African American characters are largely humorous stock figures, Rives shows little empathy toward poorer whites in "Virginia of Virginia." In "Inja," Reuben Sterling, although a plain farmer, has a basic integrity that overshadows his naïveté and lack of knowledge about urban life. The same cannot be said for Mr. Herrick, Virginia's father and an overseer, "a tall, gaunt man, with a beard that seemed flying away with his round head, after the fashion of a comet's tail; little steely blue eyes drawing close to the bridge of his nose as though it magnetized them; long, crooked teeth, not unlike the palings in one of his own fences for tint and irregularity; and a wide-open square smile, like the smile of a Greek comic mask." Other than his love for his daughter, Herrick has few virtues and little intellect. His favorite sayings are ungrammatical and nonsensical: "Consequently were, the beauty of the question air [are] my darter Faginia wont get married twel she gets a mighty good offer."[54]

Even more unappealing than "Old Herrick" is Joe Scott, Virginia's would-be beau, who brings her the latest news and flowers for planting: "He was a person of sinuous, snake-like presence, and seemed capable of shedding his complete attire by means of one deft wriggle. . . . His long locks, of a vague, smoky tint, exuded an unsavory smell of (I am ashamed to say) rancid pomatum." Scott's insipid, banal conversation focuses on illness, especially scarlet fever and typhoid, in neighboring villages.[55] Rives's heroine comes from the common people, but the men in the same rank of life are distasteful.

In spite of shortcomings, both "Inja" and "Virginia of Virginia" show that Rives was beginning to tread new paths. Both stories are set in her native state and feature rural people of various classes. Both include a romantic plot and focus on the decisions of young women. These characters, unlike the valiant maidens of Elizabethan England, are modern young women, dealing with life and love. They represent Rives's attempt at narrating a different South, one not filled with belles and beaux of her own class. And to some extent, they move away from the plantation—certainly the working staple-crop plantation of the nineteenth century did not figure in her stories. Her distaste for many of the common whites and her comic Black characters indicate that Rives had moved little beyond her fellow white southern local colorists and their stereotypes. Nonetheless, to her credit, she was sketching young heroines of various backgrounds who were willing at times to push against the boundaries confining them.

By 1888 Rives's southern ancestry, the southern locales of some of her stories, and her use of African Americans as humorous figures had made her a "southern" writer. That April, when Henry W. Grady, managing editor of the *Atlanta Constitution* and advocate of New South industrialization, was laying plans for the Piedmont Chautauqua, to be held at Salt Springs (roughly twenty miles from Atlanta) in July and August, he turned to Thomas Nelson Page for help. Declaring that he intended to make the Piedmont Chautauqua "a literary center for the South," Grady outlined plans to send an agent to London to engage "distinguished English lecturers, authors, and musicians," and also "to have at the chautauqua yourself, Miss Amelie Rives, Miss N. M. Murfree [*sic*], Mr Robert Burns Wilson, Mr Cable, and Mr Harris, as representing the best we have in southern literature." Grady wanted "each of these to read from his or her writings, or deliver an original lecture, and spend three or four days at the chautauqua." The editor rounded out his vision: "It is probable that I will get all the southern authors named during the week, and make it a southern literary week." Later that year, a Chicago literary paper included Rives in its list of Virginia writers such as Page who "have lifted Virginia much higher up the slopes of 'twin-peaked Parnassus' than it stood three decades ago."[56]

In 1891 Page published an article, "Literature in the Postwar South," describing the conditions that he believed had produced a southern literary renaissance. First, the Civil War had been "a crisis" in which "the fervor of the South burst forth in passionate utterance, assuming generally, as was natural, the lyrical form." Defeat and humiliation created a new southern world view: "The conditions for a literature had sprung into being. A civilization had been overthrown by a convulsion. A heroic past had been created." Page thus saw himself and others in the South describing a civilization that war and emancipation had destroyed. Although he tried to be inclusive and applauded women whose contributions were poems or short stories, he reserved his highest praise for the male writers, especially new writers such as Joel Chandler Harris and Irwin Russell who wrote the same sorts of dialect stories for which Page himself was becoming famous.[57]

To Page, Joel Chandler Harris was the representative genius of the new southern movement, not merely for his "accurate and entertaining" African American dialect: "Reading 'Uncle Remus,' we are not studying animal myths nor learning phonetic arrangements; we are translated bodily to the old man's fireside in his cabin, listening with 'Miss Sally's Little Boy' to Uncle Remus himself as he tells us stories the merit of which as stories springs directly from the fact that Uncle Remus knows them, is relating them, and is vivifying them with his own quaintness and humor and impressing us in every phrase with his delightful and lovable personality." Harris's artistry, Page held, lay in reproducing the "Southern civilization" of the plantation regime that had produced such "delightful and lovable" characters as Uncle Remus. Page believed that elite whites of the plantation "understood the negro," especially those formerly enslaved, and could speak for them, in a kind of ventriloquism, even as they were silencing Blacks in public life and at the ballot box.

In this summary of southern literature, Page depicted an entire movement of southern writers. With a delicate touch he included many writers, some of whom had published little. Yet there was no mention of Sherwood Bonner, a Mississippi author whose *Like unto Like* had depicted a romance between an Alabama woman and a northern abolitionist. Nor did he include Samuel Clemens, who as Mark Twain was in the eyes of many modern critics the greatest of southern writers. Page similarly omitted Charles Chesnutt, the African American writer whose first story, "The Goophered Grapevine," had appeared in the *Atlantic* in 1887. Like Page, Chesnutt used an elderly

African American narrator, Uncle Julius, to frame his story, but Uncle Julius did not have pleasant memories of the prewar days of slavery.[58]

Most indicative of Page's stance was his discussion of the Creole writer George Washington Cable. Agreeing with critics that "cultivated Creoles" in Louisiana did not speak the "patois" that Cable used, Page nonetheless praised him: "The pictures may thus not be true to Creole life, but they rise into the high plane of ideality; they are true to human life." In any case, "much, however, must be forgiven to sincerity. The heart that made possible the characters of Aurore, of Raoul, and of Dr. Sevier must have depths of tenderness as surely as the brain which conceived them has genius." Page, though, assured his readers that he did not share Cable's support for racial equality: "The writer reprobates Mr. Cable's theories of politico-social economy as unsound and unsafe, but he will never cease to be proud that, whatever direction Mr. Cable's philosophy may assume, his literary genius is the offspring of the South."[59]

In this account of southern literature, Page included Amélie Rives as "the most noted of the younger writers not only of the South but of America." Arguing that "her poems possess a finish which her prose has not yet attained," he singled out the "chief qualities" of her prose to be "its vigor and its fearless originality." Alluding to her popularity, he chided: "She is at present among the quicksands of successful authorship, and in danger of being misled into sacrificing through hasty and unconsidered work, for an ephemeral popularity, powers which, properly husbanded, might give her a high and lasting place in our literature."[60] Page's words resonated as a forecast, but Amélie Rives, even as she was writing a new novella, was concentrating on other matters than her long-term reputation in southern literature.

· FOUR ·

"A Hot, Tempestuous Story"

Fame and Marriage

In 1888 Amélie Rives found herself beset by crisscrossing currents: famous, even notorious, as an author, and almost as well known for her beauty. It became a year of decision for Amélie in terms of her literary and courtship prospects. In the flurry of publications she produced in 1888, one in fact intriguingly included a real-life suitor, Archie Chanler, and episodes from their recent courtship, a combination that perhaps spurred him to greater efforts. Her beauty offered Rives the possibility of a marriage that could bring wealth and economic stability to her family as well as cushion herself from the growing torrent of attention, much of it unfavorable, that her writings were drawing. As Rives depicted courtship and contemplated marriage with a northern plutocrat, she might have been drawn to the idea of the North-South romance that, for at least two generations, had caught the American public imagination. But this trope of sectional reunion seems not to have particularly interested Rives.

The Rives family had educated Amélie to preside over a wealthy household in which music and artistic accomplishments counted for far more than housewifery or other practical matters. Her parents certainly expected their lovely daughter to follow the conventional road for young elite women. As Alfred Rives once remarked to Amélie's youngest sister, Landon, when she was in pain from dental work: "This is but another instance of the truth of the Old French adage; il faut souffrir pour être belle [one must suffer to be beautiful]."[1] There can be little doubt that the Rives family prized beauty and expected it to pave the way to a life of luxury for Amélie.

Not only did Amélie's family look to an advantageous match, but much of the world into which she had been born admired the story of Cinderella and her prince, even while expecting most unions to be more prosaic.

The South traditionally gave great respect to the belle. In Richmond and Charlottesville, however, Amélie had lessened her appeal by her bookish inclinations and her unconventional behavior that gave her a reputation for capriciousness. On the national scene, however, she suddenly appeared the quintessential southern belle.

The rich of Boston and New York dominated the Newport social scene where Amélie had made such a splash in the summer of 1887. This social world showed some differences from, as well as underlying similarities with, the world of southern elites. By the mid-1880s an urban elite was emerging in both areas, though it was far larger in the North. Members of the northeastern elite clustered around New York City were far richer than even elite southerners, and their opulence set much of the tone for the nation. In Gilded Age America, a growing mass media increasingly broadcast the social choices made by its wealthiest members. Both money and beauty mattered. Although many remained suspicious of romantic love, they expected personal attraction to play a significant part in marital choice. At the same time, parents and other adults had long smiled on advantageous marriages that promised a solid financial future for a deserving young man or woman, even as they decried matches struck merely for monetary gain.

Earlier in the century, as political relationships between the North and South became increasingly strained, a literary type that modern critics have called the romance of reunion—in which a wedding unites a passionate young southern woman with a masterful northern man—had become part of American fiction. These imaginary stories used marriage to bring together the two sections, but actual North-South romances—many of which connected elite families—had long existed. Marriages such as that of Eliza Chew of Philadelphia to Virginian John Murray Mason, or of New Yorker Sally Baxter into the Hampton clan of South Carolina in the 1850s, had long been occurring. Indeed, there were three such marriages in Amélie's immediate family: her aunt Amélie had wed Henry Sigourney, while her uncles William and Francis both married wealthy northern women.

During the turbulent 1850s, in literary North-South plots written by southern women, the young southern woman in the marriage taught her northern lover to overlook sectional differences, so that domestic and political harmony could reign. In contrast, during the Civil War, similar stories by northern authors tended to picture brave Union soldiers who subjugated southern female spitfires by winning their love and instilling loyalty to the Union.[2]

The Princess of Albemarle

After the Civil War, North-South romances—both in fiction and in real life—seemed to change. The war's destructiveness, along with emancipation, had impoverished many in the southern antebellum elite. Images of the intersectional romance then took a more determinedly mercenary turn as they depicted an impoverished southern woman (preferably of aristocratic lineage) marrying a well-to-do northern man, sometimes a soldier. As the number of millionaires rose in the North, such intersectional romances could be interpreted as fairytale romances bringing a poor but beautiful southern woman to the lap of luxury or, at the very least, a comfortable home.

The author and former soldier John W. De Forest followed this postwar scenario in his novel of reconciliation, *The Bloody Chasm* (1881). Unlike his earlier wartime novel, in which the southern woman independently comes to realize the true worth of a northern soldier, the heroine of the *Bloody Chasm* must be tricked into the marriage that reunites the sections and brings her back to affluence. In De Forest's hands, a Massachusetts man saves a South Carolina woman from both penury and her misguided love of Confederate memorial poetry.

Two close friends of Rives's resorted to the theme of the intersectional marriage in their fiction. In 1886 Thomas Nelson Page used it in his popular story "Meh Lady," which chronicles the romance between a southern woman and a Union officer. As in his earlier story "Marse Chan," Page uses an elderly African American family retainer, formerly enslaved, to tell the story. The narrator calls the lady "Meh Lady" rather than her given name and thus allows her, as one commentator has pointed out, to symbolize all genteel southern white women. "Meh Lady," whose brother was killed in the war, nurses Union officer Captain Wilton back to health. When he proposes, she demurs and sends him away. As poverty and desolation prevail, however, he returns to marry "Meh Lady" and save the Virginia plantation, then falling into disrepair after the death of its male patriarch. Page slyly inserts his own stamp of southern chauvinism in this romance of reunion by making his Yankee officer half Virginian. According to a biographer, Page intended the captain's southern ancestry to be "at least partially responsible for his instinctive knowledge of the code of behavior, the code of Southern heroism." Moreover, "Page writes what he considers to be a story of reconciliation, but it is a story in which the characters are reconciled to the Southern way of life."[3] Page had thus found a way to make the romance of reunion a southern victory as well as a patriarchal one.

Rives, however, had another model of the romance of reunion at hand, one written by her intimate friend Julia Magruder, who, although born in Charlottesville, grew up in Washington, D.C. Almost a decade older than Amélie, Julia never married, but she wrote numerous novels that revolved around the marriage plot. Although the first meeting of Rives and Magruder cannot be determined, they shared a love of literature and numerous friends and relatives among the Albemarle County elite and probably were friendly by the mid-1880s. Julia inscribed a copy of her first novel to Amélie; by 1887–88 they clearly had become companions.

Magruder's first novel, published in 1885, created an alternative to the male version of the romance of reunion. Her book's title, *Across the Chasm,* recalled De Forest's *Bloody Chasm,* published only four years earlier. In Magruder's chronicle of the romantic adventures of Margaret Trevennon during a visit to Washington, D.C., the action centers on the rivalry of four men for Margaret's affection. Both the lackadaisical Virginian lad from Margaret's hometown and the former Confederate officer appear poor choices, especially the Confederate veteran, Major King, who is loud, uncouth, and insensitive. Margaret immediately rejects King; over time she increasingly values the virtue, work ethic, and honesty of Louis Gaston, a northern architect.[4]

Even with these literary examples right in front of her, Rives did not look to the romance of reunion as a meaningful theme for her own work. Although her story "Inja," in which a Virginia farmer's daughter marries a wealthy New Yorker, contains the essential elements, Amélie does not focus on sectional reconciliation but instead emphasizes urban wealth seducing rural virtue. Similarly, when Amélie began to write the story that became "The Quick or the Dead?," she did not frame that courtship story as a romance of reunion, perhaps because she did not want to acknowledge the power disparities involved. Moreover, she chose an ambiguous ending, which while indicating her own undecided stance, worked poorly in indicating either national or sectional allegiances.

While Rives was writing about the South in the autumn of 1887, she also was managing the effects of her summer in Newport. She was a published author with poems and stories in the best magazines, and the season with her wealthy relatives in Newport had yielded well-heeled suitors, many of them northern born and some of whom appeared particularly serious. Rumors in the summer of 1887 suggested that she was engaged to "a widower who was quite devoted to her at Newport . . . [who] married for his first wife

John Armstrong Chanler began to romance Amélie Rives in the summer of 1887. (Virginia Historical Society, Virginia Museum of History and Culture)

a member of the Astor family." This widower was most likely forty-year-old James J. van Alen, who had married Emily Astor over a decade earlier (she died in 1881). An Anglophile and Tudor enthusiast, van Alen probably found Amélie's stories with historical settings particularly interesting. Nonetheless, a wealthy young New Yorker, John Armstrong Chanler, known as Archie, appeared the most determined among the beaux. After calling upon Amélie in Newport, he came south that September for quail hunting. His success at that time as a suitor, though, appears to have been limited; many years later Chanler referred to a breakup with Amélie in the fall of 1887 when he was wearing a French goatee.[5]

The world of courtship offered new artistic as well as social possibilities, and Amélie, basking in the success she had enjoyed in Newport, prepared to explore them. Even before writing "The Quick or the Dead?," she had been choosing and framing her subjects in innovative ways that emphasized emotion. With "The Quick or the Dead?" she moved from her history-themed stories—and her newer southern tales featuring the poorer classes—to a more daring subject: contemporary courtship. She began to write this work late in 1887. Interrupted by a courtship visit from Archie Chanler at Christmas, she turned down his marriage proposal and finished "The Quick or the Dead?" early in 1888.

Framed as a psychological examination, "The Quick or the Dead?" derives its impact from a focus on sexual attraction and personality in courtship and marriage. Moreover, Rives brings passion to the forefront of the story. Even though her story deals with "womanly" themes of devotion, self-abnegation, and mourning, she does not resort to the veiled sentimental language of the day and instead tries to appear particularly modern. Rives intended "The Quick or the Dead?" to frame her writing in a new way; she seems to have little imagined that it would turn her life upside down when it appeared in the April issue of *Lippincott's Monthly Magazine,* with a biographical piece on her to make up most of that issue.[6]

The plot of the story can be easily summarized. Barbara Pomfret, a young Virginia woman widowed two years earlier, meets Jock Dering, her husband's cousin from a northern state, who physically closely resembles the deceased man but has a different personality. Barbara's first marriage, though lasting less than a year, had been extremely happy. Although passionately attracted to Jock, Barbara believes her first marriage a barrier to any new love and doubts whether she should or even can ever marry again. Thus, the book chronicles a tempestuous courtship.

The scene opens as Barbara Pomfret returns on a dark and windy night in early autumn to her Virginia plantation, Rosemary. All through the story, Rives relies on the weather to build emotional scenes. Virginia, even in the Piedmont, has never been as storm-filled as in this story. As the lovely autumn turns to cold and snowy winter, the love affair between Barbara and Jock heats up; despite this paradox, the relationship between these two characters seems to parallel the wild winter landscape.

While an omniscient third party narrates the story, Barbara dominates it; and her thoughts and dreams are most evident. A high-strung young woman, Barbara feels "vast waves of passionate regret, and longing, and rebellion."

This frontispiece of "The Quick or the Dead?" was intended to advertise Amélie Rives's youth and beauty. (Library of Virginia)

Even before meeting Jock, she lies in bed and suggestively whispers to her dead husband: "Touch me, come to me, here in the darkness,—here where you used to love me." Despite this simmering sexuality, Barbara's response to her widowed state is to return to her girlhood, dressing simply and walking for hours in the countryside.[7]

The first meeting with Jock shows Barbara's emotional temperament; not expecting a visitor, she faints at the sight of a man who looks and sounds like her dead husband. While the first meetings are tense, a storm brings Jock and Barbara together, and they discover a mutual fascination. As Rives describes the change: "The hands of friendship and love are drawn apart as by two passing trains, and friendship is left on the siding." As Barbara and Jock act on their sexual attraction, she actively shares in the lovemaking. When a mock battle over a locket ends in a closet: "Dering, rather out of patience, stooped down; she turned her head, a little frightened, and her lips brushed his,—a touch light as flower-leaves, fine as fire. In another instant both mouths had clung into a kiss."⁸ Here it is the woman who initiates contact, and the move to passionate kissing is mutual.

On the other hand, the kiss reminds Barbara that she is being unfaithful to her dead husband. After telling Jock to return to New York, she writes him, first to ask him to stay away. When she reads a newspaper story that mistakenly suggests that he had been injured, she then writes to ask him to return. As he arrives on a snowy day, their fiery interchange contrasts with the frigid weather. Declaring his love, Jock asks her why she called him back. Barbara interrupts his soliloquy, not once but seven times, with the plea "kiss me." This rising chorus reaches a climax with her affirmation: "I love you more than anything I have ever dreamed of,—more than anything in earth or heaven,—more than anything alive or dead,—or *dead!* You understand? Now kiss me!"⁹

To this female willingness to share in lovemaking, Rives adds yet another unconventional element. Barbara is positively unladylike in her demonstration of passion. On one occasion, when Jock tells her that he adores her and "stopped and pressed his lips, now on one foot, now on the other; then kneeling up, he kissed her dress, her knees, her waist, her arms," Barbara responds by bending over him "panting, intoxicated, half reassured." This is no isolated incident: "It was in some such way that nearly all their misunderstandings ended."¹⁰

Barbara visits a widowed minister to discuss whether fidelity to a dead spouse stands in the way of remarriage and whether married couples will be united in heaven. He gives no helpful guidance. She sends Jock away again then summons him back. She burns her wedding gown, to break her ties with the past. Yet in the end, after an emotional upheaval in a deserted church, she quarrels with Jock over her wedding ring, which she has retained, thus showing its continued hold over her.

While the descriptions of passion no doubt engaged readers, the story had other appealing features. The staging of the story shows Amélie's fascination with drama and a sensibility that prefigures the modern film. Barbara changes her mind about the new love affair several times in the course in the narrative, and readers probably wanted to know whether she would choose the living suitor over loyalty to the past. No doubt some Victorian young men and women read it for what they believed to be the "dirty parts"—for the sexuality expressed in passionate kisses and embraces—but others read it because Barbara and Jock talk of love and play outdoors, whether in the forest, barn, or a haystack. In fact, while Barbara calls swimming the only outdoor activity that she really cares about, she also declares that a "man should swim, and ride, and wrestle, and fence, as he breathes." Barbara and Jock clearly are privileged people who seem never to have to think of work; instead they romp in the woods and play hide-and-seek and other children's games in the house.[11]

Even the more sedate activities of this couple sometime involve games. Jock has what he calls "an odd trick" of randomly picking a book and putting a finger on a specific passage on a page—to see what it will tell him. Barbara, while expressing an abhorrence of anything supernatural, admits that she sometimes does the same with the Bible. Jock convinces her to play the game; her finger lands on "I would love infinitely and be loved"—well-known lines from Robert Browning's "Paracelsus."[12] Even those readers unaware of the literary reference might well be caught up in the growing attraction of the two.

Combining witty dialogue with a detailed description of the countryside, actors, and action, Rives grabs her readers' attention. Her major characters enjoy talking. As Barbara tells Jock, "Every time we talk together I feel I know you ten years better."[13] In contrast to much of the moralizing writing of the time, Rives tries to make her characters indicative of a new day. For example, she inserts the brand names of various products, a kind of "product placement" then unknown to Victorian literature.

One historian of advertising, Ellen Gruber Garvey, has focused on a scene when Jock and Barbara, playing in a haystack, discuss the smell of her hair. To Jock's question about its origin, she replies, "Soap and water." He immediately counters: "Oh, Barbara! Do you want me to believe all this is only due to Pears [soap] and your cistern?" Barbara protests that perfuming her hair would be "vulgar" and hopes that it doesn't smell as "though it were all horrid and Lubin's Extracty." Jock answers, "That is as original a compound verb as the one the Punch's little girl made use of a year ago."

"The scene is a commercial interlude between kisses," Garvey writes; "it demonstrates that Barbara and Dering read the same magazines, that they inhabit the same world—in fact, a specifically material world." She maintains, "The use of the brand-named product similarly plays at a boundary: the conversation maintains an intimate and presumably individual focus on Barbara's body and Dering's response to it, while commenting on it in a way that lets

the reader participate too, through familiarity with the products discussed."
At the same time, Barbara's response authenticates her, "because her smell is
seen as not deliberately or artfully applied as perfume would be: like all good
romantic heroines, she must be unconscious of her own attractions."[14]

Rives here is describing a particular kind of material world, one of global
cosmopolitanism. Pears is an elite English soap, while Lubin's is an expensive French perfume. Jock and Barbara are global consumers who both have
read an issue of the English magazine that featured a child making a joke
about "Liebig's-Extract-of Beef," a beef concentrate manufactured from a
German formula. All these products show Rives's characters to be acutely
aware of the European world outside their door. A recent historian has
argued that late nineteenth-century American women manifested "international sensibilities" in their use of fashion and imported household objects.[15]
To such readers, Rives would appear modern and particularly au courant.

"The Quick or the Dead?" is not, however, a fully integrated story. In
addition to its allusions to emotion and sexuality, the story also has gothic
overtones. Worrying about her dead husband, Barbara often ventures into
macabre musings. At one point, as she is falling asleep, she is beset by fantastic images: "God's imagined face took on a horrible grinning. The min-
istering angels seemed deformed creatures who writhed, and twisted, and
uttered wanton gigglings as they circled about the Throne after the fashion
of the witches in 'Macbeth' about the caldron." In such a frame of mind,
Barbara's thoughts drift to her deceased husband: "He was mere mass of
repulsive formlessness in a slimy wedge of earth; perhaps he was not even
that. She imagined his ghastly skeleton tricked out in all the mockery of
fashionable attire. What delightful, smart, of-the-world-worldly coats he had
worn! Why if he were a skeleton now, one could see his tailor's name in gilt
letters through his spinal column!"[16]

The gothic theme recurs when Barbara thinks about the past and her
husband. In one of the last scenes, she and Jock are caught in a rainstorm,
and he returns to Rosemary for a carriage while she takes refuge in "the
pretty, Gothic church of the neighborhood." While exploring inside the
church, she discovers that the doors have been locked from the outside. The
storm worsens: "The rain was now falling more heavily than ever, and sheets
of bluish lightning threw into pale relief the tall windows, with their lead-
framed panes of glass, . . . but failed to penetrate the arches of the vaulted
roof, from which the gloom seemed to hang like dust-clogged cobwebs."

Although Barbara tries to remain calm and count to one hundred, she becomes increasingly nervous. Being marooned in the church prompts the memory of her wedding service and her husband's words: "Death will not part us, Barbara. We will laugh in his face, my Barbara." As she waits, increasingly overwrought, she comes to expect the dead Valentine to arrive. The plot unspools much as in the movie thrillers that this scene anticipates. When Jock arrives in the church to find Barbara lying face down, "he thought that she was dead."[17] At the cost of the unity of message, the gothic themes may have added to the suspense that kept readers turning the pages.

Another part of the story's appeal lay in its wit, as Rives often inserts sardonic asides about both Barbara and Jock. For example, the appearance of Barbara's bedroom indicates her character: "The number of mirrors suggested a certain vanity on the part of its occupant: there were eight in all, none of them small, and all framed heavily in old gilt." In another section, while Jock is deciding whether Barbara is a beauty, she is wondering whether she has overdone her mourning attire. Rives then comments: "If acknowledged beauties could know the thoughts of most men when first introduced to them, there would not be so much vanity in the world." The striking remark and the indelible image are parts of the book. When Jock tells Barbara that her dead husband, like any true honest man, would want her future happiness, she lashes out: "You don't know. Men never know. They never really suffer. They get over things so. Their memories are like—like photographs,—they fade out so. Women's memories are like statues: you may break them in pieces, you may leave them out in storms until they are discolored, you can always put them together again. No matter how stained they are, they always retain their shape."[18]

Despite all the play and action, Rives lets Barbara at times be a stereotypical Victorian heroine. For example, she swoons at least three or four times, at one point for several hours. Moreover, she also cares deeply about religion, as her long talk with the widowed pastor and a night of prayer on the cold floor beside her wedding dress are meant to suggest. Both aspects seem tailored to attract a popular audience.

Also obviously playing to popular tastes are the humorous sections that jibe strangely with all the passion, gothic lugubriousness, and emphasis on the physical landscape. Rives adds a local-color cast of African American characters, including the maids, Martha Ellen and Sarah, and the coachman, Unc' Joshua, all of whom speak in dialect. They differ in appearance and character, but all focus on helping Barbara through her grief, while sometimes being amazed by her overly emotional reactions. At one point, when Barbara is overcome by hysterical laughter, her personal maid Martha Ellen fearfully sits up in bed and between "clacking teeth, mutters 'Miss Barb'ra done gone mad! She done gone mad! I dunno what tuh do! God knows I dunno what tu do!'"[19]

Rives seems to have added other Black characters primarily for comic relief. A small African American boy, Beauregard Walsingham, has a pretentious name (part of which ironically is that of a Confederate general) and a bedraggled appearance. He is a one-dimensional cartoon. While Barbara calls him Robin Goodfellow to compare him to the puckish figure of English folklore, the young African American is sullen, avaricious, and terse; only his stubborn individualism distinguishes him from a stock minstrel show character.

Poor whites are figures of derision. Rives pokes fun at local common white men, particularly a member of the Buzzy family. When the coachman Unc' Joshua is driving Barbara and Jock to the railroad station, they encounter Mr. Buzzy, whose wagon has broken down in the road. They end up giving him and his cargo of apples and potatoes a ride. When Jock exclaims to Barbara, "What a name! *Buzzy!*" she gloomily replies, "It isn't near as bad as the man." Buzzy is peculiarly dressed in a striped brown and black suit and red satin tie with green bars; his appearance is uncouth. He has eyes and cheeks of "mottled plum" color and has "lost a tooth directly in front, and could not keep his tongue from incessantly playing in and out of this unpleasing hollow." Buzzy, "inclined to be talkative," tells long involved anecdotes, and his insensitivity and wordiness act as a counterpoint to the romantic conversation between Jock and Barbara. They speak in French to mask their meaning and furtively grasp one another. "Please put your hand on my knee again," Jock implores Barbara, "and was presently rewarded by a soft clasp upon his knee, which sent such a delightful thrill through him that he actually smiled in response to Mr. Buzzy's toothy grin."[20]

Readers found "The Quick or the Dead?" fascinating, while the critics fumed, and the parodists had a field day. The romance, modernity, and sexual tension of Rives's writing in part explains the readers' reactions. Critics were divided between those who saw great potential and those who were morally offended by the plot and its workings. Some reviewers were irritated by Rives's strange word choices and her mixture of styles. Her prose frequently built to a fever pitch, and the humorous episodes with elements of minstrelsy comported oddly with the modern love story and gothic effects.

The lovemaking and repartee central to "The Quick or the Dead?" offered one additional selling point: Was it really fiction? Did it involve actual people? Readers had already been introduced to Amélie Rives as a young southern beauty, and many assumed that she was writing a book about her own life, an assumption further fueled by newspaper reports that suggested as much. In February 1888, shortly before the story's appearance, the *Atlanta Constitution* had speculated about Rives's novella "Virginia of Virginia": "A friend of the writer tells me that there is a growing suspicion that the heroine of the story, Virginia, is a somewhat exaggerated pen-picture of the novelist herself. Bits of color here and there through the narrative are local, and traces of personal character are frequently recognizable."[21] Rives, keenly aware of her aristocratic heritage, most likely would have been surprised to see herself likened to a tenant farmer's daughter. Yet "The Quick or the Dead?" only added to earlier speculation by including many people and places that were, in fact, drawn from the author's own life experience.

Twenty-four-year-old, never-married Amélie created a heroine, Barbara Pomfret, a twenty-six-year-old widow who lives on a Virginia plantation with an elderly aunt and servants. Barbara's plantation house Rosemary resembles Castle Hill and is not far from the Blue Ridge Mountains. Rives describes Rosemary as "one of those old Virginia houses which have not been desecrated with modern furniture, as gray hair with hair-dye." Like Castle Hill, it is an old red-brick house with "many old portraits in the large hall, as darkly ruddy in color as the outer walls of the mansion which they adorned." One reaches Rosemary by crossing Machunk Creek, the name of an actual stream near Castle Hill.[22]

Moreover, many of the characters had real-life equivalents. Barbara's elderly aunt, called Fridiswig, resembles Amélie's own despised Aunt Ella Rives. Fridiswig, like Ella, plays the piano poorly and, also like Ella, dresses strangely and is "amiable and unobtrusive." Rives even makes Aunt Fridiswig speak in dialect, as she worries that Barbara's supper of two partridges, biscuits, and three cups of tea would "ruin her stummick." Barbara's "childhood maid" is named Martha Ellen; in fact, African American Martha Jane Bullock (called "mammy" by Rives) was for many years a valued employee in the Rives family.[23]

Rives played a slightly different game with the two major characters, Jock and Barbara. Her hero has the same first name, John, as Archie Chanler and, like him, is known by a nickname. Jock's appearance also strongly resembles

Chandler's: "his curling brown hair above a square, strongly-modelled forehead; eyes the color of autumn pools in sunlight; the determined yet delicate jut of the nose; the pleasing unevenness in the crowded white teeth, and the fine jaw which had that curve from ear to tip like the prow of a cutter." Like Archie, Jock is a hunter and athlete. Also like Archie, he is a clubman who lunches at the Manhattan Club with Mr. Everstone Beanpoddy of Boston (whose character allows Rives to lampoon the New England wealthy).[24]

Physically, Barbara does not resemble Amélie; while she is tall and Junoesque, Amélie was petite and slender. Barbara has copper brown hair, sometimes worn in braids, while Amélie was an ashen blonde. Still, both women are seen as gorgeous with particularly striking profiles. In fact, Jock does not realize Barbara's beauty until he sees her profile: "Barbara, who was an acknowledged beauty, did not strike any responsive chord in Dering until she turned him her profile in settling the folds of her dress. It was vigorous, classic, enthralling, and he admitted as much to himself while regarding it. 'Good brow,' he meditated; 'good nose; good line of lips—well balanced, upper and lower equal; good chin, splendid chin, massive, but not heavy. Lots of will-power,—no end to it."[25]

Both Rives and her fictional character spend a great deal of thought on clothing and dress rather unconventionally. Although Barbara does not ride horseback, her love of nature is apparent as she frequently hikes around the plantation. One might argue that the differences in Barbara's appearance and interests gave Rives a plausible deniability about any overlap between her and her heroine.

Some of that difference was undercut by a biographical sketch of Rives in the April issue of *Lippincott's* that, in both focus and wording, drew parallels between her life and the story of "The Quick or the Dead?" The sketch's author, J. D. Hurrell, a pen name for a "friend of the Rives family," visited Castle Hill and extravagantly praised Amélie. According to Hurrell, "Someone, in writing of Miss Rives, says, 'She has dipped her pen in herself,' and so she has, but always in Virginia." Hurrell describes a walk with Amélie and her father, accompanied by a collie, two greyhounds, and a fourth large Bordelais dog. At one point, when the greyhounds chased the sheep, "Miss Rives took an abrupt leave of me, and dashed over the fields in her mud-stained corduroy skirt, tan gaiters, and sturdy porpoise hide boots, hallooing for the greyhounds and keeping the other dogs at heel." The writer then depicted Amélie chastising the greyhound for killing a sheep: "What a picture she made, with the crouching, yelping hound, her face swept with color from brow to chin, the dark blue of her Tam o' Shanter crushing the short brown-gold curls against her forehead!" This description almost completely matches the story's description of Barbara's "boyish costume": "a dark-blue flannel shirt, a short, clay-stained corduroy skirt, a leather belt, a pair of chamois-skin shooting-gaiters, and a pair of stout laced boots" topped with a "dark-blue Tam O'Shanter."[26]

One might question whether Rives wrote the story as a kind of flirtation device. The seasons in the book follow those of Rives and Chanler's relationship. Archie visited her in the fall, met rejection, and returned in the winter, Christmas to be exact. He then was probably rejected again, much as in the story. Rives may well have meant "The Quick or the Dead?" to tell the story of Chanler's courtship and make him wonder whether she ever would choose him. The story certainly showed how much physical appeal he held for her. In numerous scenes, Barbara exhibits a keen sense of Jock's body: "He reached up and swung her to the ground. It was a light, easy gesture, full of the restrained power that women like. To feel a strong man minister to their fragile wants has all the fascination of watching a steam-hammer employed in the frivolous occupation of cracking almonds."[27] Such feminine interest in male strength and sexuality clearly challenged Victorian norms for innocent young women.

And what of the plot? Aside from the implausibility of the two almost identical cousins, why would Amélie present courtship as a battle in which one of the suitors is dead and thus could not really compete? Walter Wellman, a newspaperman based in Washington, D.C., presented the version that Amélie and Archie gave the newspapers after their marriage: "Jock was Chanler. Val was—Amélie's girlish ideal. . . . There was nothing shadowy or ill-defined about the ideal of a girl like Amélie Rives. She knew him because she had created him, as only a woman of genius can create in her imagination."[28]

One of Rives's biographers has suggested that Amélie wrote the story "while wrestling with her decision about Archie. She was faced with a choice between the 'quick' persistent Astor descendant or the 'dead'—the idealized version of what her lover should be—a man perhaps in the mold of her aristocratic Virginia cousin, Thomas Nelson Page."[29] Even though it seems doubtful that Page was ever more than a possible literary mentor, examining Amélie's earlier suitors does suggest one way to interpret her story, as the "dead" Val Pomfret shares similarities with some of the men linked to Rives. Will Otis, the Coolidge brothers, E. Spencer Pratt, or even Thomas Nelson Page—all were men of wide-ranging culture. Interested in the arts or science, they were better educated and intellectually broader in their pursuits than Archie Chanler. Will Otis's attraction to art and humor seems to have paralleled that of Amélie. Both Pratt and the Coolidges had spent time abroad and were fascinated by foreign cultures. Page was by far the most parochial of this group, but even he cared about classical Greece and Rome. Any of these men was likely to be a more intellectually stimulating companion than Archie Chanler.

Yet another possibility is that the dead husband Val was a kinder and more thoughtful version of Archie himself—a self that he only occasionally showed. Lending credence to this interpretation is the passage in which Jock claims that he is "not in the least like my cousin; that is, except as far as looks go." He then "with a grim humor" reveals: "I'm a brute. If he was Valentine I'm certainly Orson."[30] Here Amélie is referring to the medieval French folk tale about twin brothers, Valentine and Orson, abandoned in the forest as infants. Valentine is rescued and grows up to be a knight in the Carolingian court of Pepin, while Orson, reared by animals in the forest, becomes a wild man who in time is civilized by his brother. Thus, Jock's identification with Orson suggests a certain untamed quality.

Elsewhere the story foreshadows the eccentricity and emotional turmoil that Archie Chanler showed in later life. In particular, toward the story's end, as Barbara is arguing that it would be wicked for her to marry again, Rives renders Jock's side of the interchange: he speaks "savagely," "fiercely," "harshly," and "acridly." As Barbara tells him that she cannot marry again, "he had a horrible revulsion of feeling, and felt his mouth beginning to twist into that strangely distorted grin which characterized him in moments of violent emotion." He declares to her that if she is not mad, "you are the most unutterably cruel creature I ever imagined." When they have made their final speeches, he leaves, "only to re-enter stumblingly, to catch her to him, to bruise her face and throat with short, hard kisses." Averring again that he loves her despite everything, he asks her to think "of the way you have clung to me, of the way you have kissed my hair, my eyes, my throat—as I kiss yours now!" But Barbara is emotionally exhausted: "He almost hurt her in his desperate eagerness, but he might as well have tried to rouse response in a corpse."[31] Here in the conclusion of her novel,

Rives portrays a harsh, almost violent aspect to her male protagonist's passion for the heroine.

Even before its publication in April 1888, "The Quick or the Dead?" was drawing attention; once in print, it was reviewed and discussed in journals and newspapers across the nation. By March 1888, news-sheets advertising the story called it "full of passion and interest" and "strong in the working and very holding."[32] The issue of *Lippincott's* included a portrait of Amélie as its frontispiece, and the publishing house was soon offering "The Quick or the Dead?" as a stand-alone novella; sales reached 300,000, an enormous number then.

Upon publication, a volley of attention, much of it negative, focused on the story. Some critics compared it unfavorably to Rives's earlier work. For example, when a book reprinting her Elizabethan stories appeared that spring, one critic opened his review: "It is pleasant to be able to remove the disagreeable impression of Miss Rives's much assailed novel by returning to the 'old-time tale' which introduced her to the public." Others found "The Quick or the Dead?" symptomatic of the worst in American culture and intellectual life. In April 1888 the magazine *Life* deemed it "hysterical and entirely morbid." Calling the novella an "unhealthy book," the reviewer averred, "Everything about it is false to the best instincts of a sensible woman" and further declared, "One might call the love-making gross, were it not so ludicrous."[33]

The *Atlanta Constitution* reprinted part of a review from the *Criterion* that described "The Quick or the Dead?" as "not delicate, it is scarcely pure, and it is irreverent to a shocking degree. . . . It is a hot tempestuous story, full of unmoral suggestions, and, in some parts, bubbling over with lustful intimations." While partly excusing "the gentle Virginia girl" as "handling matters that she does not understand," the author concluded, "It is a pity to be compelled to say it, but any person who puts this story in the hands of a young girl is not her friend." Yet another column, allegedly written by a young woman, asserted that "The Quick or the Dead?" was "most uninteresting , . . . the three elements which struggled for preeminence in its composition were vulgarity, blasphemy, and gush."[34] (The reviewer, while pronouncing the characterization of Aunt Fridiswig vulgar, never actually indicated what was either blasphemous or gushy about the piece.)

Closer to home, Rives's story created unease, as some members of her extended family worried about the morality of the tale. Her uncle Francis

Rives complained to his brother Will: "I cannot help hearing at second hand a good deal about the 'Quick or the Dead.' I have not read it." Francis even reverted to the French term for "dirty" in his report that "the idea of the clubs seems to be that it is cleaver [*sic*], *sale* & salacious." And he asserted that some ladies questioned whether Amélie had a living father or mother (suggesting that any parent would have censored such a story).[35]

At least one writer questioned the originality of Rives's novella. A critic at the *New York World* apparently asserted that the story too closely resembled Lucas Malet's *Mrs. Lorimer,* published in the early 1880s, whose plot concerned a beautiful young English widow who was besieged with suitors. Although Rives told one journalist that she had decided not to reply to "any charges whatever," she said: "This one appears to me even more absurd than usual." Comparing the two publications suggests Rives was correct. Defending herself, she stated: "All love stories must be as old as love itself. It is only the different garb in which they are dressed that makes them interesting to us."[36]

In the long run, the ridicule that "The Quick or the Dead?" received may have injured Amélie's literary reputation more than the charges of immorality. In addition to a book-length lampoon, some papers printed shorter parodies. One version published in May featured "Miss Barbarity Pompadour," who "returned to her old Virginia home on a tempestuous night, which had been specially selected for her by the author, so that she could drive through the soughing [moaning] rain and allow the ragged trees to brush her face as she dashed onward in the gloom." This parody supplied Barbarity with a suitor, Dock Jeering, who shared many of her deceased husband's "artless Virginia ways, such as expectorating on the floor and eating pie with a knife."[37]

Some newspapers treated the author herself as a joke. The New Orleans paper reported that Rives would visit relatives in Cincinnati, where she "will have the chance there to write 'The Fresh and the Cured,' without being slaughtered herself with the critic's meat-axe." A squib in a Kansas paper joked that Rives "reads French readily and has begun to take an interest in German. She expects to study English when she has leisure." Other critics took a sectional bent. Quoting R. H. Stoddard, literary editor of the *New York Daily Mail,* who had asserted that that no New England woman would have received a positive reception for a similar story, a Milwaukee writer added: "It is sorry trash that Miss Rives writes, and the magazines that accept and parade it before their readers are doing literature a disservice."[38]

The most thoughtful reviews indicated that Rives's prose was uneven and her scenes sometimes strikingly overdrawn. She showed "all the faults and good qualities of youthful genius," one columnist wrote, continuing: "There is entirely too much power in her sketches to be overlooked, yet the scenes are often grotesque, the development awkward and the plot wildly unnatural." Another opined: "It is a book that certainly has faults, yet these faults are of over opulence rather than aridity and betray an undisciplined temperament rather than a commonplace intellect." This critic described himself as "diverted" by "the portrait of an impetuous, foolish, lovable woman whom fate had treated with a really woeful amount of severity."[39]

This latter critic also compared Rives to Rhoda Broughton, an English writer whose work was viewed as sensational and rather racy. "Miss Rives forcefully reminds us," he wrote, "of the wayward novelist who won ephemeral notoriety. . . . Miss Broughton frittered away on trifles talent that might have given her a lasting place in Victorian letters. Let Miss Rives beware of the possible parallel!" Criticism also came directly from irate readers. One newspaper described the "avalanche of mail" to Amélie—over "five hundred missives of all kinds from men and women, and particularly from young girls have reached her." Rives herself privately wrote in late April that she had received "nearly two hundred letters" about the story, although she indicated only "three that were unkind, and they were anonymous!"[40]

Some heated discussions may have developed over the story's critical reception. A Maine paper reported that the editor of the *Critic* (which it wrongly placed in Richmond rather than New York) "has created a sensation by his bitter criticisms" of "The Quick or the Dead?" The *Critic*'s editor, it claimed, "was in receipt of many anonymous letters threatening him with terrible vengeance if he does not stop his attacks on the handsome and gifted Virginian. Undismayed, however, he continues to free his mind on the subject of her latest effort with the warmth of an obstinate man defied."[41]

Whatever the critical response, the story continued to sell. In early June the *New York Tribune* reported that *Lippincott's* found it impossible to keep up with the demand for its April issue, adding snidely that "such is literary appreciation in the United States!"[42]

How did Amélie react to the uproar her work caused? At first, the enormous attention she received seemed to please her. Apparently, many admirers asked for a picture as well as an autograph. In April 1888 she told a Miss Dickinson, "The tears came into my eyes as I read your sweet letter and learned that my picture pleased you and that you kept it near you." Acknowledging another "most kind letter," she told its writer, "you can get the original photograph for the Lippincott engraving of me, by writing and sending this note to Mr. George C. Cox, Photographer Broadway, New York, N.Y."[43]

She also put up a brave front as the vituperation began to pour in. A reporter pictured her that spring as "not at all upset or disconcerted by the crisis in her life brought about by what she is pleased to tell me 'was my somewhat crude and hastily written study.'"[44] Before the novella had been out a scant month, Amélie had found a way to defend herself against charges of immorality. She hit on a tack that earlier authors, especially scandalous ones such as E. D. E. N. Southworth, who wrote melodramatic novels, used: relying on their own reputation to protect their writings from any notion of wickedness. Rives, falling back on traditional notions of womanhood, affected a complete innocence about the sensual nature of her story. On April 22, she replied to a letter from Alice V. Broadus, a friend of Julia Magruder and the daughter of John A. Broadus, a Baptist minister and faculty member of the Southern Theological Seminary in Louisville. Alice, who belonged to a devout household, had apparently written that both she and her mother regretted the criticism that Rives and her story had received. Amélie thanked Alice "with all my heart and soul, with all the true womanhood that is in me, for this your belief and staunchness." Indicating that her own "modesty" had been shocked by "the Critics and evil-minded ones," Rives averred: "I have been so bewildered and amazed ever since this dreadful attack, that I have only just begun to comprehend the horrible motives and thoughts which are imputed me."[45]

In this private letter, Rives then launched the defenses that she would use publicly. She insisted that her work did have a moral: Barbara was a "study of a morbid, introspective, selfish woman—as a warning for other Barbaras." Amélie also pooh-poohed critics who suggested that her depiction of Barbara was autobiographical, declaring that they were "ascribing to me an honesty such as has surely never characterized any other human being! Fancy any woman, deliberately setting to work to draw such a minute, hideous picture of herself!" She closed with a paragraph, the first two sentences of which she later used in the preface to an edition of the novella: "Books strongly written and from a clean-heart, resemble mirrors, in which all who read behold their own images. The pure will see purity—the foul-minded foulness. Until people understand that it is sensuality, and *not* Passion which is impure, I fear my poor friends will have to submit to hearing my books classified as immoral, and my own nature as 'too opulent.'"[46] During the summer of 1888 Rives took a similar tack as she described her book's object as "to show that a woman loves her husband's soul, his ego, rather than his body. If this were not so[,] Barbara would have given herself unquestionably to Dering, who was physically the exact reproduction of her dead husband."[47]

Even as Rives faced mounting negative evaluations of her writing, her courtship prospects soared. Archie Chanler, perhaps after seeing himself in the novel and thinking that boded well for his chances, renewed his attentions. He was accompanied by a party of eight or so young men and women, including his brother Winthrop and wife Margaret Terry Chanler, known as Daisy, on a visit to Charlottesville and Castle Hill in early May. A New England counterpart of Amélie, Daisy was literary, interested in the theater, bright and lively. She quickly formed an opinion of the woman whom her brother-in-law was romancing, calling her "very extraordinary— really beautiful with wonderful hair & eyes and teeth & complexion." In fact, Amélie was so extraordinary that Daisy used that adjective twice in the same paragraph. Although she thought that Amélie was "certainly one of the cleverest women I have ever met," Daisy, from the beginning, had doubts. Rives seemed far too self-regarding: "she is in love with her own person & intoxicated with her own success." Amélie was one of those successful people who "get to have an idea that the whole outside world is merely occupied with themselves."[48]

Meanwhile, Archie Chanler was pushing his suit by visiting Amélie three times in less than a year. The last time she was swayed. By the end of May they were announcing their engagement. Daisy Chanler gleefully broke the news to her mother: "Prepare yourself to be utterly astounded and guess a hundred times what has happened. I may as well out with it at once as you can never imagine. Archie is engaged, and of all people to the beautiful and gifted young authoress Amélie Rives, whom we went to see in Virginia."[49]

How did Archie Chanler come to win the hand of the "beautiful and gifted young authoress," reputed to have made so many conquests? The love scenes of breathless kisses and stolen embraces in "The Quick or the Dead?" suggest that a certain sexual magnetism existed between the two.

One biographer theorizes that, in writing "The Quick or the Dead?," "Amélie may have written herself into a passionate frenzy even she could no longer resist. She had written herself into love."[50]

This seems highly unlikely. At age twenty-four, Amélie had for many years shown herself quite willing to calculate the value of love and marriage, and Archie did in fact hold many attractions for her. His wealth, for example, promised a way out of the Riveses' straitened circumstances. Even though her father Alfred had found work with the French-based Panamanian railroad, Amélie was well aware that her family members were the poor relations in the Rives clan. In contrast, Archie, as an Astor heir, controlled a large fortune that he with his seven siblings had inherited upon the deaths of his father and mother in the 1870s. Still, he was only one among other wealthy men who had romanced Amélie—for example, James J. van Alen could call on both his own family money from railroads and the fortune of his deceased wife.

Making a difference was not only Archie's wealth but also the attractive possibilities that he could dangle before Amélie. He seems to have suggested that she could study art abroad, especially in France and England, two countries that had long interested her. Lending credence to the importance that Rives placed on foreign study is a letter she wrote the popular author Frank Stockton in July of 1888. She reminded Stockton that she had promised to "sketch some outlines on the book you left with me," apparently some illustrations for a future edition. Apologizing for her failure to do so, she brought up a past conversation about studying art abroad: "Don't you remember at the time that I told you how much I wished to study a winter or so in Paris, before attempting anything of the kind?" The newly married Rives added: "My opportunity has at last come, and if you do not despair you shall yet have your desired drawings." In the possible future life that Archie depicted for Amélie as an artist, he may also have promised her an atelier at Castle Hill. In 1889 when the young couple was still in Europe, Alfred Rives speculated that "if she [Amélie] carries out her idea of a studio at Castle Hill," the Rives daughters could all become "swell artists."[51]

Yet another, particularly promising, lure from Archie may have been the possibility that Rives might become not only a literary lady and artist but also a noted reformer and philanthropist. All these roles played on her ambition for fame and fortune. Even as a sixteen-year-old, Amélie had laughingly forecast herself as a "patroness" of the Mobile theater, bestowing a new curtain upon their stage. In keeping with the intensity of her Episcopalian upbringing, she also felt the need for good works. In early attempts at publishing a novel, she justified the possible earnings as a way to help her friend Lutie Pleasants. Similarly, Rives, early in her publishing career, had given away one hundred dollars received for her writings.[52]

Rives's actions soon after her marriage also suggest that Archie had encouraged her interest in philanthropy. During the Yuletide season of 1888, Amélie handed out gifts from an oxcart to poor neighbors, including "$200 worth of blankets and warm clothing, which she presented in person at this festive season." In January 1889 she offered a prize of a hundred dollars for the best American essay on child labor. The money "received by Mrs. Chanler for some sonnets on the subject" would be "placed in the hands of Prof. Richard T. Ely . . . Secretary of the American Economic Association."[53]

The decision to marry Archie also came as Amélie was experiencing the uncomfortable aspects of celebrity. Despite her optimistic assertion in April that she had received only a few critical letters, some newspapers indicated that many among the hundreds of letters sent to her were insulting. In May 1888 one literary journal noted, "All of Amélie Rives's correspondence, sent in care of her publishers, is opened by them before forwarding, at the author's request, to protect her from abusive letters, which are at once destroyed."[54] The deluge of fan mail and hate mail, combined with scathing reviews, denunciations from moralists, and joking asides from newspapermen, may have led Rives to consider Archie and his fortune a bulwark against such hostile forces.

Upon Amélie's acceptance of his proposal, Archie himself was so overjoyed that he sent a short, cryptic telegram, more like an exclamation, to his sister Elizabeth (known in the family as Bessie): "Just engaged Miss Rives." Indignant that he should not have described his romance in detail, Bessie complained: "If I had been in London with no one to explain it I should never have made out what it meant." As Archie's siblings tried to adjust to the sudden betrothal, Bessie expressed their surprise: "I long too to get a letter from you & to hear your plans, & to hear a little about how it all happened." She continued, "What exclamations on all sides! Cousin Stuyve, for one, will be delighted, I know. He told me last winter that she was charming."[55]

Archie also cabled his sister Margaret in New York, and Amélie herself wrote friends and acquaintances, such as Alice Broadus of Louisville: "I write to tell you of my engagement to Mr. John Armstrong Chanler of New

York. He is most splendid and noble in every way and I am very happy." She ended the note with the injunction, "please pray for me and write me some loving word dear Alice."[56] By the third of June the newspapers were running accounts of the engagement.

Archie returned in May to New York to spread the news. According to a biographer, he visited numerous friends and family among the city's elite to share the startling news about his engagement. Clearly, Archie believed that he had won a prize. When Coleman Drayton, a lawyer on Wall Street and Archie's cousin by marriage, wondered how another beau of Amélie's, "a prominent swell approaching middle age" (probably James J. van Alen), would react to the news, Archie exulted, "Make the best of it I imagine."[57] The newspapers formally announced Archie and Amélie's engagement on June 3 and suggested the wedding would take place in the fall.

The combination of Amélie's new notoriety as an author and her engagement to a very wealthy man led newspapers into unusually aggressive reporting. The normally staid *New York Times* society reporter asserted that simultaneous rumors of Rives's engagement to Archie Coolidge and to Archie Chanler were "rather confusing." The befuddled reporter also noted: "It has always been supposed that Miss Rives was engaged to Mr. Spencer Pratt, now Minister to Persia, and the story runs that she would not become his bride until he had won a diplomatic position." The article reached its summation: "But those persons who know Miss Rives would not have been surprised at the announcement of her *engagement* to six men, for it has been hard to decide which of the small army with whose individual members the fair authoress, it is understood, has carried on a more or less desperate flirtation for some years she would choose."[58]

The combination of a racy novel and a rich suitor brought to Castle Hill hordes of newspapermen, who filled their papers with information, gossip, and rumors about Amélie Rives. A Chicago paper in its announcement of the engagement mistakenly speculated that the couple had a longstanding secret understanding: "The courtship was quite romantic in some respects, the couple falling in love with each other at sight. It is whispered she enjoined secrecy, and for two years the engagement has been kept from the friends of both, though not the immediate relatives, who, it is said, sanction the match."[59]

When Archie returned to Castle Hill with his younger sister Margaret, he confronted a media circus. In this situation, Archie's money and position could ensure some protection. Both Archie and Amélie had reasons to consider an immediate wedding, although she may have verged on panic at the sudden intensity and ferocity of the national scrutiny she was receiving. With her relatives and friends nearby, Amélie and her mother could arrange a wedding very quickly. On June 12 the news went out from Charlottesville that a marriage license had been issued to Archie and Amélie. While regional newspapers such as the *Raleigh News and Observer* picked up the feed, the New York press—not surprisingly, given the Astor family's prominence and New York's importance in the publishing industry—also paid great attention to the wedding.

To be sure, the Rives family tried to restrict news of the upcoming marriage from the press. Even on June 14, the actual day of the wedding, the Richmond paper was stating: "Though every effort was made to keep the matter as silent as possible, report was rife that the wedding would immediately take place." The reporter then indicated that he had learned that "her two most intimate friends among her own set had been sent for."[60]

The wedding itself was a small but elaborate ceremony, at two o'clock in the afternoon, in the drawing room at Castle Hill. Because Alfred Rives was away in Panama, the bride was escorted by her uncle, William C. Rives Jr. Amélie wore a high-necked, long-sleeved dress gown of white silk; her mother, Sarah MacMurdo Rives, wore black silk; and sisters Landon and Gertrude also wore white. The rector of the local Episcopal church performed the ceremony. Later the guests enjoyed "a bounteous dinner, many of the dishes of which were prepared in the old ante-bellum Southern style now almost unknown."[61]

While Amélie's immediate family and friends attended the ceremony, only Archie's sister Margaret was there to represent the Chanlers. This happened in part because of Archie's rivalry with his married brother Winthrop. While Wintie's wife, Daisy, had privately expressed joy over the engagement, she had also criticized "The Quick or the Dead?," calling it: "One of the earthiest, most disagreeable pieces of literature it has ever been my misfortune to read." When the engagement was announced, Daisy had found a more conciliatory context for Amélie's literary endeavors: "Her stories are many of them very charming—all in fact, except the last one ["The Quick or the Dead?"] which was a mistake." Wintie, however, apparently had a more imperiously critical response; years later Archie recalled that Wintie had sent him a copy of "The Quick or the Dead?" with "objectionable parts" pointed out in blue pencil. Archie then suggested that this action had resulted in Wintie and his wife not being invited to the wedding. More likely, the hurried and secretive aspects of the wedding were largely responsible for the absence of almost all the Chanler family.[62]

In any event, the wedding started Archie and Amélie off on the wrong foot with his siblings. Daisy Chanler tried to put the best face on it when she wrote to her mother: "They decided to hasten matters & have the affair over as quickly and quietly as possible in order to get rid of the endless curiosity & impertinence of the newspapers. The articles about Miss R. in connection with her last book have been something too atrocious." In her letter to Archie, Daisy was more straightforward. After congratulating him "on your winning such a fair and noble prize in the life race," she upbraided him: "I don't think you realize in the least how very keenly we all felt your treating us as if we were outsiders to be classed with reporters and other noxious and inquisitive bipeds. The news of your marriage was known to hundreds of people before it reached us." She made it clear that she was expressing the dismay of all the Chanler siblings: "Naturally we felt very much hurt at such neglect, poor Alida has cried her eyes out several times feeling that you do not care for her, the boys are all vexed and affronted." Daisy tried to explain that it was the secret wedding and lack of notification rather than any objection to Amélie herself that had created these problems: "The world which you seem to care about a good deal—as who does not?—has got hold of the idea that your family is not overpleased with your marriage, nothing as you know could be falser than this, but it is you who have given it this impression, it rests with you to efface it."[63]

Daisy's attempts to smooth over the family relationships did not placate Archie. Wintie had further infuriated his brother, both with an angry note and by two messages written to their siblings that referred to Amélie as "Armida," a sorceress featured in several well-known operas. On June 27, Archie curtly informed Wintie: "I shall want an apology from you in writing, before anything further can pass between us."[64] Relations between the two brothers were never again friendly.

While the omission of the Chanlers from the wedding ceremony pained and insulted them, Amélie's family seems to have approved the union as advantageous. Her father wrote his brother from Panama: "I received with the greatest pleasure your sympathetic letter referring to Amélie's engagement—by telegraph I have since learnt of the marriage. It gives me great comfort to know your high estimate of Mr. Chanler & I fully agree with you

Amélie Rives signed this photograph with the pet name that Archie Chanler had given her. (Amélie Rives Troubetzkoy Collection, The Valentine)

Archie from Amy.

Paris - 28th Feb. 1890.

that of all Amélie's admirers he combines the most recommendations. I cannot but believe the happiness of our Home circle will be greatly enhanced, although there are always inevitable wrenches—change & separation—due to the happiest marriages." The northern branches of the Rives family were relieved that Amélie had apparently made a good match. Acknowledging a note from Sara Pryor, a fellow Virginian expatriate, William Rives thanked her "for so much kind interest" in Amélie. He further prophesied: "Her marriage promises to be a happy one & I trust will save her from censure to which the imprudence of her passionate and artistic nature would be apt to expose her—if relying for guidance on herself alone."[65]

In marrying an immensely wealthy northern man, Rives had made what might appear a "reunion" marriage, but she never portrayed it in that light.

Her family had not felt ideologically divided between its northern and southern wings. Moreover, the conservative Democratic politics of the Chanler family as well as Archie's admiration of the South might have made the Chanlers appear little different from her northern relatives.

Even though Rives seems not to have dwelt on her own marriage as a North-South one, fellow Virginians and other southerners did see her as a southern belle who was advertising her fascinating ways nationwide. By the last decades of the nineteenth century some intersectional unions, as before the Civil War, were coming to involve well-to-do southern families and thus had no rags-to-riches story attached. Nonetheless, newspapers still liked to chronicle the triumphs of southern beauties. For example, in 1891 the *National Intelligencer* (Washington, D.C.) recorded that May Handy, a belle from Richmond, had left Narragansett Pier for the South, and "her recently announced engagement to Mr. Arthur Rotch of Boston is denied." (Only in 1904 did May Handy wed the wealthy northern banker James Brown Potter.) Other, more publicized, marriages that involved a southern "belle" and a wealthy northerner were undertaken by the beautiful daughters of the wealthy Langhorne family in Virginia: Irene, who married illustrator Charles Dana Gibson, and her younger sister Nancy, who first wed a wealthy Boston man, Charles Gould Shaw II, before divorcing him to marry William Waldorf Astor, Archie's titled cousin. Among those attending the large Richmond wedding of Irene Langhorne and Charles Dana Gibson in November 1895 was Amélie's sister Gertrude with her beau Allan Potts.[66]

Back in 1888, Amélie's own marriage had seemed to offer many possibilities; then she immediately had to cope with its outcome.

· FIVE ·

"My Life Is Ruined for Me"

Transitions at Home and Abroad

The first few months of marriage were difficult for Amélie and Archie. Her family—mother, aunt, and sisters—left Castle Hill for a week after the June wedding to allow the young couple some privacy. Yet time alone did not build happiness. The Chanler siblings expected Archie and Amélie to visit Rokeby, the family home on the Hudson River, but Amélie delayed, claiming that it was too hot to travel in late June.[1]

If Rives had expected her marriage to be a refuge and a protection, she was deeply disappointed. At first, she felt the need to conciliate Archie's siblings, who remained upset at having been left out of the wedding. In late June, she wrote his sister Elizabeth: "Perhaps someday when we know each other, and are really as sisters, I can tell you what your dear letter was to me. I am always afraid of giving way to my heart, which is very impulsive, especially on paper, for fear that those to whom I write, will think me 'gushing.'"[2] Nonetheless, Amélie adopted a highly emotional style in her letters to the Chanler sisters and, perhaps in deference to their religiosity, referred more frequently to prayer and religion.

When Archie escorted his sister Margaret back to Rokeby, Rives stayed back at Castle Hill. In late June she thanked Margaret for "the comfort your little note brought me. It was like a kiss on a bare and aching heart, and the tears came into my eyes and stayed there as I read it." In this overwrought epistle, Amélie struck an ominous note: "No matter what happens, no matter how life may widen or contract for us both, we have each other, and so much sweetest and best of all—love each other with all our hearts." In keeping with the letter's dreary yet emotional tone, Amélie also confided: "God has let you save me from the very pit of gloom, and grief, and terror."

In July Amélie assured Margaret: "Every day I miss you more . . . and I am hungry and thirsty for a letter from you."[3]

Later that month, as Margaret sailed for Europe, Amélie told her: "I have been fighting battles of such mortal anguish in my soul." Apparently, the upcoming meeting with Daisy Chanler and the rest of the family at Rokeby was raising fears that threatened to overwhelm Amélie. "Oh! Margaret," she declared, "how I wish you or someone who loves me could be there when I first go. If only your mother were living—I would feel no fear of her—but Margaret—I *dread* Daisy—I am not afraid of anyone, but I am afraid of treachery, oh! so tremblingly afraid." Later in the same letter, Amélie returned to that subject: "You know how I dread the Rokeby visit. I never had anything quite so distasteful to do in my life, but duties aren't to be shirked, are they dear?"[4] Rives's emphasis on her terror of dealing with the Chanler siblings suggests that she feared the judgments of his family and knew that Rokeby was their turf, not hers.

Obviously Rives was distraught in the month following her wedding. Donna Lucey in her biography of Rives has suggested that sexual relations lay at the root of her unrest: "Could it be that the love goddess herself . . .— the woman who made men quiver with lust—was actually afraid of sex?" Lucey then quotes from a letter written by Elizabeth, the oldest of Archie's sisters, who in 1924 described Amélie as one of a "type of a cold blonde" who "have an almost hypnotic charm for the fiery men who fall in love with them." Elizabeth concluded that marriages with such sirens could come to no good end: "In all their marital relations, that type of woman looks upon a hot-blooded husband as an *aggressor*. And after a nightmare on both their parts, she throws him out." Rives, according to Elizabeth, had a "strange mixture of coldness & warmth, advancing & retreating like a white cat . . . who rubs against your hand & seems to want a caress, but who walks off in a huff if you give it to her."[5] This scathing assessment came years after the marriage had dissolved and after Archie's emotional stability had disintegrated.

Nonetheless, moving from flirtation and sexual suggestiveness to an actual physical relationship may well have posed problems for Amélie, as it did for numerous women in the Victorian era, when some doctors and ministers were still arguing that passionlessness was the state of the ideal woman. To be sure, even as a young woman Amélie did not believe that women were or should be immune to sexual desire. At age twenty-one, she had poked fun at one of Thomas Nelson Page's male friends for expecting excessive prudery among young white women: "I am so sorry for poor Bruce—but if a man will go and put a woman on a pedestal, he deserves to have both her and the pedestal come toppling down and mash his silly toes for him."[6]

Still, Amélie's defense of the purity of her motives in writing "The Quick or the Dead?" suggests that she too had been influenced by Victorian notions of sexuality. There she had contended that people should "understand that it is sensuality, and not Passion which is impure."[7] Some might assert that it would be difficult to discover exactly where passion degenerated into sensuality and lasciviousness; nonetheless, Amélie's distinction between the two hints that she may have worried about unbridled passion. Religion and other beliefs about marriage may also have complicated her views of sexuality and the distinction that she tried to draw. She wanted to be passionate yet pure, spiritual without being overly preachy—extremely difficult combinations to imagine working in tandem and still more difficult to carry out.

Moreover, Amélie, a spoiled and pampered young woman with a strong sense of her own rights, had long felt some incompatibility with the institution of marriage. Back in 1885 she had told Page that she did not want to be married. In a similar vein, a friend from Amélie's youth remembered her saying: "Yes, I've sometimes thought it would be very nice to be married for a week or so, say, but when I think of sharing my life, myself, my environments, with any one, I have the most stifling and rebellious sensation." In this anecdote, Amélie most resented the intrusion into her personal autonomy: "Just to think of giving a man the cited right to come in one's boudoir, put on his dressing gown and slipper and ensconce himself quietly with cigar and paper by one's fireside for the whole evening—why, it's perfectly exasperating!" The youthful Amélie had then pictured herself as a runaway bride: "As the evenings lengthened into weeks I'd grow wilder and wilder, and when they began to settle themselves into the monotony of years I'd run away from them into the darkness of some stormy night."[8]

Amélie may also have had medical problems that made sexual activity painful. Despite her active life, she had been ill a great deal, possibly since the onset of menarche. Although diagnosing the ailments of people in the past gives even trained practitioners enormous problems, speculation can point to tentative conclusions. The kinds of pains that Rives chronicled, as well as her failure in two marriages to ever become pregnant, suggests she may have suffered from endometriosis, the growth of uterine tissue outside the uterus. While the tissue growths are benign, they can be painful, lead to internal swelling and bleeding, and cause infertility.[9]

Endometriosis manifests itself in several different forms of pain including uncomfortable menstrual periods, lower back and pelvic aches, and, most relevant for Rives's case, pain during intercourse. Women afflicted with this condition sometimes experience particularly deep uterine spasms during sexual encounters which continue even after intercourse has ended. If Rives suffered from endometriosis, her initiation into sexual relations may have seemed a nightmare.[10]

Certainly, Rives early in her marriage often referred to pain and suffering. In early July, she informed Margaret: "I am trying to be brave, but *you* know how hard some things are—that terrible feeling of foreboding has not left me yet." Amélie added that her prayers were always "to ask Gods love and, blessing on those I love, and sometimes to plead for mercy and comfort." Later that month, she elaborated: "I am not happy, but the dear God for Christ's sake, has wonderfully mitigated my pain, and I am now able to bear it calmly—(I trust—with—Christ's help)."[11]

In addition to her worries about sex and possibly her health, Amélie had to cope with the man she had married. Almost immediately she learned that her husband had a difficult personality and strong obsessive traits. He also exhibited a jealous possessiveness that sometimes became menacing. During the summer of 1888, Amélie very plaintively queried: "Margaret, tell me as though you were my own sister as well as Archies, have you ever thought in the bottom of your soul, that Archie's mind was not quite right?" She continued, "He laughs at me in such a dreadful way sometimes until I am crying & trembling with terror. And the more I cry & beg him to stop or to tell me what is the matter, the more he laughs." Rives sought comfort against menacing portents: "Oh! Margaret, Margaret write to me darling. Pray for me. Oh! pray for me for Christ's sake, that I may be guided & do what is right. Pray for poor Archie too."[12]

The relationship had quickly hit the rocks, and a struggle between two strong wills may have played a part. After the wedding, Amélie was dealing with a new status as well as her continuing celebrity. When she wrote to "Mrs Holloway" (apparently a friend or relation of the noted Virginia-born author Mary Virginia Terhune) in July 1888, Amélie signed her note "Amélie Rives (Mrs. Chanler)."[13] The culture of the day expected and applauded a husband's rule, and Archie apparently wished to exercise it. Indeed, exercising dominance over Amélie, a woman well known for her willfulness, may have held a special appeal. Through charm and persistence, Amélie had often gained her way in the past, and she probably still expected to prevail in disagreements. Archie, though, as the oldest in a family of immense wealth, was accustomed to doing whatever he wished; and the early death of both his parents had likely increased his independence. Although Amélie successfully resisted accompanying Archie to Rokeby in July, other possibilities for marital tugs of war soon occurred, especially around the subject of travel. Describing Archie and his siblings as in continual motion, Daisy Chanler had at one point commented: "The Chanlers are like turkeys and must not be enclosed. They cannot thrive unless they be allowed to range."[14] While the possibility of visiting Europe most likely had increased Archie's appeal to Amélie, she actually felt most comfortable at Castle Hill.

Two months after the wedding, Archie and Amélie were on the move. In early September they spent a night in Washington, D.C., on their way to Newport, Rhode Island. There they stayed almost two weeks at Wakehurst, the imposing summer residence of James J. van Alen, who, as a noted Anglophile, was showing off his British antiques. In turn, Archie was flaunting his new bride. He was well aware that van Alen had unsuccessfully courted Amélie.[15]

On September 3 Amélie, on van Alen's arm (and accompanied by Archie), turned up at the Casino's theater in Newport, where, according to a Chicago newspaper, "instantly" she became "the centre of attraction to the entire assembly." The reporter called her "a remarkable woman . . . who could not fail to rivet attention wherever she appeared" and further noted: "Certainly no one has created such a stir this season, though there have been belles, and beauties, and Princesses upon the scene." A week later at the last dance of the season at the Casino, Amélie again was "a centre of attraction, this time dressed more conspicuously and becomingly than before in a white tulle, with a scarlet sash and gold embroidery, which accented strongly her peculiar beauty." While she danced and conversed with admirers, spectators in the gallery "nearly fell over the railing, while some of the more enterprising, not to be caught napping, produced opera-glasses and proceeded to inspect her with all the due pomp and circumstance as if she had been the leading lady at the play." Archie reveled in the attention that his bride received. Writing about the Newport visit, he boasted to his sister: "We went everywhere, to Casino dances, dinners & luncheons. The papers were full of Amélie & all complimentary. They couldn't be anything else about her looks."[16]

From there the young couple visited one of Archie's favorite cousins in New Hampshire, but Amélie found it dark and cold. In late September they arrived in New York City, where she received celebrity treatment. Calling her a "famous little woman," a Boston newspaper described how her "cream colored silk tea gown half disguised and half revealed the lithe figure that still hesitates between that of maid and very young matron." The reporter asked many questions about where the young couple planned to honeymoon and settle. Archie appeared in the account as "the big, broad shouldered young fellow" who protectively remarked about his wife: "that poor little girl in there has been at high tension for a year and a half now and I am determined that she shall rest."[17]

As Archie and Amélie visited New York, "The Quick or the Dead?" was being dramatized, if that word can properly indicate its staging. Drawing upon minstrel traditions, the show emphasized the role of Cupid, the young African American servant whom in the book Rives had called Beauregard Walsingham. An article in the *New York Times* about the lad chosen to play this role ridiculed both the actor and the character: "Ulysses Simpson Grant Wilson is the equally ponderous name borne by the funny little black boy who was selected yesterday to play Cupid in the dramatized version of the story as it is to be given by the Estelle Clayton Company at the Fifth-Avenue Theatre." After lampooning his dress and behavior, the item noted: "There were ludicrous antics and absurd songs, but Ulysses was incomparable. He remembered perfectly Cupid's song, 'I'm Nuttin' but a Pickaninny, Mammy's but a Coon,' though he had heard it but once, a week before, and gave a topical song of his own that brought down the house." In keeping with the emphasis on minstrelsy, the story closed by pointing out that "Cupid develops into a very important character in the play, as also does Buzzy." The poor white character, Mr. Buzzy, despised in the story by the heroine, "will have to fall in love with Miss Clayton's Barbara, and to make complications for her T.D. Frawley's Jock Dering." Whatever Rives's part in selling the rights to the production, she later regretted it. In 1905 she told an interviewer that although she had been in New York City while the play was on and had attended it, "There was really nothing in it I could recognize as mine." She then rebuffed the intimation that she had had input into the production.[18]

After the couple returned from these peregrinations, Archie wanted to leave for Paris or New York, but Amélie again turned stubborn. Newspapers reported in September that Archie and Amélie would depart for Europe in a couple of months. It seems likely that she had undertaken the northern swing through Rhode Island, New Hampshire, and New York City with the expectation that she would be able to squeeze in some writing, but amid the travel and hectic social and publicity schedule, she found that she could accomplish little. A few months later she complained: "I cannot write amid strange surroundings. . . . If I cannot have my own room my mind refuses to work. I tried it in Newport last summer and in New York, but I could not write a page of manuscript."[19]

That autumn at Castle Hill, problems with Amélie and Archie's marriage intensified. Confiding again in her sister-in-law, Amélie wrote that she and Archie agreed that he would go abroad without her, but despair framed her decision: "You know of course that my life is ruined for me. My chains cut and gall me at every turn. I am to be a prisoner (God knows a willing one!) in my old home." Archie and Amélie also decided that he would remain outside the United States for two years while she would stay at Castle Hill. He had also convinced her that she should not discuss any of their marital woes with his sisters. As she put it to Margaret, "I am not going to write of him any more after this letter, because I want to be perfectly loyal to him." Nonetheless, Amélie did intimate that Archie had been mercurial and cruel: "Think of how he has made Bessie cry, & then know how I have been tortured."[20]

Even as the marriage became a battlefield, Amélie returned to her writing. In the fall and winter, when Archie was away, she seems to have written steadily. During the past two years she had published a wide array of poems and short stories. Some of these may have been written five to eight years earlier, but she continued to tackle new subjects. Only two months after the wedding, extracts from her new drama, "Herod and Mariamne," based on the exploits of the biblical king, were published in the *New York Herald*. According to a piece that first appeared in the *New York Graphic,* work on a novel, *The Witness of the Sun,* had hindered "the young authoress from accompanying her husband to Europe."[21]

Rives was now seriously thinking about future writing and publication projects. In November, J. M. Stoddart and William Walsh of Lippincott's, the editor and publisher of "The Quick or the Dead?," accepted an invitation to visit her at Castle Hill to discuss financial arrangements. Walsh assured Rives that he was willing to accept her terms and he also had "a proposition that will be at least as good as the one you suggest, viz, that you share equally in the profits of all sales, if not more satisfactory."[22]

The months at Castle Hill apparently calmed Amélie, and early in February 1889 a reconciliation of sorts with Archie occurred. She shared it with her sister-in-law: "I look at Archie and think that he must be part of a dream not the real Archie, not the man who has given me such unspeakable anguish during the last seven months. He is so gentle, so quiet, so considerate, so tender, so loving." Rives finished: "All and more than my old trust in Archie has come back." Archie on his part was enchanted by their new rapport, telling another sister: "I had not been with Amélie half an hour after my arrival from Europe before she blossomed in love for me like a flower before the sun. I just thawed & convinced her of my tenderness & love at the same moment." In his view, "Everything I ever wished for in my Ideal—before I met it—I get in Amélie."[23]

Even as love seemed to return, Amélie continued to receive scathing criticism, mainly of "The Quick or the Dead?" Along with all the parodies came reviews that skewered her ability, her character, or both. A piece in the *Critic*, in November 1888, asserted that Rives's stories "lack original quality," and argued that her gender made the stories all the worse: "It *is* [emphasis in original] worse for a woman to write in her fashion than it is for a man." The author drove home the point: "To say with truth that a young author like Miss Rives is unmaidenly, is condemnation severe enough. . . . The line that separates strength from coarseness, the clean from the unclean, the sensual from the spiritual, is not an imaginary line." The following month, *Current Literature* placed Rives in the "school" of young women who had published novels of "physical passion" and asserted: "The success of The Quick or the Dead has stirred up the morbid brains of women who have been theorizing on forbidden things for years, and the result is calculated to simply paralyze old ideas." Although "purity and innocence" were believed to emanate from young women, "it would seem as though the fountainhead were strangely soiled." When Andrew Lang, a well-known British journalist and writer, summed up "The Quick or the Dead?," he maintained that too much attention had been paid to the question: "Was this a nice book for a young lady to write?" Still, he concluded: "The truth about the novel probably is that, amidst a perfect tempest of deranged epithets and deplorable style, a gleam of real and rare talent may be seen like a star through a witch's storm."[24]

The Princess of Albemarle

Rives's new novel, *The Witness of the Sun,* appeared in the spring of 1889 and soon drew unfavorable reviews. This novel, set in Italy (which Rives had never visited), depicts an ill-fated romance between Vladimir Nadrovine, a Russian author, and Ilva Demarini, a seventeen-year-old Italian woman who hopes to become a famous writer. The novel alternates between believable dialogue about a developing relationship and melodramatic scenes, including a duel and refuge in a monastery. Rives may have penned at least part of it sometime earlier—it recycled clever sayings from her own childhood, and the story begins with Ilva a precocious girl.[25]

To be sure, the novel exhibited some new strengths. Nadrovine had chosen as his motto "Let the sun be a witness" to indicate a commitment to living an irreproachably upright life; and Rives reinforces her symbolism by her depiction of the natural world. Literary biographer Welford Dunaway Taylor has asserted that this story "showed the author's most controlled use of symbolism thus far." The sun is a symbol for the search for truth; insects and other winged creatures suggest the quest for beauty and fame. In contrast to the butterflies that greet Ilva in her garden, Madame Nadrovine, after inciting her son to a duel in which he kills her lover, finds instead moths "fluttering and singing about the glittering candles on her toilet-table and writing-desk. Some of them were half burned to death and buzzed in anguish among the silver and ivory brushes and toilet-articles; others, half plunged in the melted wax, strove to free themselves with desperate contortions of their long legs."[26]

Rives devises an interesting subplot involving Nadrovine's beautiful, cruel mother. Although the tall, striking, green-eyed Madame Nadrovine appears similar in appearance to many of the dark women of sensational literature, Rives creates tension by describing a mother who obsessively loves her son. So unwilling is this mother to acknowledge that Vladimir might marry, she tells him: "I think I shall go very quietly to your bride's house to take her a wedding-present; and when she is asleep, with her white throat bent backward for your dreamed-of kisses, I shall give it one snip, deep to the left, with my little, crooked toilet-scissors, and then strike her across the lips, very lightly, once with my glove."[27]

Madame Nadrovine's love has incestuous aspects, as when she kisses her son on the mouth. At the novel's end, in a feverish delirium, she recalls his babyhood: "And he pinches my breast with his little fingers when he is nursing, until it hurts; I tell you, it really hurts. Oh, it is divine to feel the little mouth drawing my life into his! . . . All the love that I ought to have given my husband I give to his child." A literary historian has posited that "Amélie almost certainly failed to realize the full psychological ramifications of Madame Nadrovine's love for her son, and this assumption is confirmed by the fact that none of the critics realized it either." Archie certainly missed it, as he told his sister that "the only passion in the Witness is the maternal or Mother's love for her son."[28]

The Witness of the Sun received few favorable reviews. One newspaper commented: "There is just plot enough in the one hundred large pages to make a respectable one-column story." Another writer adopted a folksy tone, pretending to address Rives: "I hear jealous critics saying that your clever little skit is inexcusably horrible and fantastically improbable, and that your characters are unnatural beyond the stretch of imagination." He added, sarcastically: "Why down where I live, one can find 'em [such characters] in almost every house in one's block."[29]

In the following months, other criticisms appeared. Some tended to view *The Witness of the Sun* in light of "The Quick or the Dead?" Susy Clemens, Mark Twain's seventeen-year-old daughter, lamented that she was not allowed to read the book: "I want to read 'The Witness of the Sun' so much, but the story is forbidden [*sic*] fruit to me." A newspaper review ventured that Rives lacked originality and had merely appropriated the work of the sensationalist novelist Ouida (Marie de la Ramée): "The yarn is composed of scraps from various novels of Ouida, which are readily recognized by the confirmed novel reader." What praise there was tended to be qualified. Even a critic who discovered fewer "of the objectionable features found in her former works" emphasized potential rather than actual achievement: "This young writer possesses undeniable force and originality, and should she successfully pass the gush, swush, and swirl, swish and blissfully kissful stage of her career, she will doubtless earn some substantial literary fame for herself."[30]

Even as these barbs landed, Amélie was trying to balance work and social duties. In March 1889 she and Archie visited Washington, D.C., where one of her Cabell cousins (probably William D. Cabell, who with his wife, Virginia Ellet Cabell, had opened the Norwood Institute for Girls and Young Ladies) threw a reception in their honor featuring prominent southern members of Congress. Although First Lady Caroline Scott Harrison was ill, Amélie, Archie, and her mother were received at a private reception in the White House: "Mrs. Chanler enjoyed a pleasant informal chat with the ladies of the White House, the only drawback to the pleasure of the visit being the enforced absence of the hostess." The next day, Rives met guests during a three-hour public reception at the Hotel Arno.[31]

In April 1889 Archie and Amélie were on their way to Europe. Over two years would pass before Amélie again made her home primarily in the United States. In those years she learned much about the world and herself. Mired in a difficult marriage, she found that the drugs prescribed for her illnesses, especially the paralyzing migraine headaches, provided a welcome release—not only from the marriage but more generally from life. The trip was a chance for Archie to introduce Amélie to Europe, but only sporadically did the thrill of exploring new countries seem to mend relations between them. In fact, the time abroad, especially in England, may have suggested to Amélie other ways of living and other, less confining, forms of marriage.

After a brief visit in Paris, the Chanlers landed in England and made their way into London's social scene. A London paper wrote of Amélie: "Those who have met her socially speak enthusiastically of her charm of manner, her absence of all affectation and conceit; and her ears would tingle at the glowing accounts of her beauty." Archie and Amélie had an entrée into London high society through his older cousin Margaret (Daisy) Rutherfurd White and her husband, Harry, the first secretary of the American legation there. Harry White, although born in Maryland, had spent much of his life abroad and was well accepted in English social circles. After marrying Daisy in 1879, he pursued a diplomatic career, serving as secretary of the American legation in Vienna in 1883 and becoming the second secretary of the American legation in London in 1884.[32]

Daisy White introduced the Chanlers to London society and also initiated them into the Souls, a social set of aristocratic young people who saw themselves as arbiters of artistic and literary taste. Arguing that "there has seldom been a more delightful group," the historian Allan Nevins pointed out "their brilliant social gifts . . . and the breadth of their interests. . . . Sports, games, literature, art, philosophy, politics, religion were all open for discussion at their gatherings."[33] Noted for their high spirits and literary badinage, the Souls were socially exclusive but cared about intellectual life.

Members of the Souls had wide-ranging and varied interests. Many of the men in the group looked to political careers—Arthur J. Balfour and H. H. Asquith later became prime ministers, while George Wyndham, George Curzon, and Harry Cust were all, at various times, members of

Parliament. Among the more prominent women were the Tennant sisters, Charlotte, Lucy, Laura, and Margot, daughters of a wealthy Scottish Liberal politician and businessman and close friends of Chanler's cousins Harry and Daisy. Margot Tennant, who later married Asquith, a future prime minister, was noted for her wit and wide reading. Other leading women in the Souls, such as Ettie Grenfell and Mary Elcho, were noted hostesses; and Violet Manners (then the Marchioness of Granby) was a talented artist. While the titled aristocrats set the tone of the Souls, the group also interacted with poets, writers, painters, and architects.[34]

Archie and Amélie were immediately accepted into these elite circles. They spent the week of the Royal Ascot races in June 1889 at Taplow Hall, the home of William and Ethel Fane Grenfell (known to friends as Willy and Ettie), who afterward became Lord and Lady Desborough. Ettie welcomed a wide group of friends to Taplow Hall on the Thames in Buckinghamshire; she "kept a full house during Ascot week: her invitations were much prized." One participant in the Ascot festivities that year noted: "It was rather a nice Ascot. . . . They had splendid times at Taplow, bathing, boating, and wild fun of all sorts."[35]

Fun among the Souls included both social and intellectual activities. A defender later called them "lighthearted but not frivolous; unconventional, but neither fast nor loose." The group enjoyed impromptu games such as creating poems or other pieces that mimicked the style of a particular writer. One favorite pastime was guessing games: for example, what had a member of the group left behind from a previous weekend's visit? Another was identifying a participant by comparing him or her to colors, animals, vegetables, and the like. These entertainments could at times be rather cruel—as when the player had to choose among three friends marooned in a high tower: whom to save, push, or simply leave abandoned there.[36]

A strong flavor of sexual tension and flirtation also marked these gatherings. In this period sexual affairs among men and married women of the British upper classes might have few repercussions. Some members of the Souls, such as Ettie Grenfell, merely had ongoing flirtations with devoted admirers, while others, including Violet Manners, Lady Granby (later the Duchess of Rutland), were involved in serious long-term sexual relationships. Beautiful, raven-haired Mary Elcho seemed almost unconscious that her husband, Hugo (later Earl Wymiss), pursued many affairs. Such liaisons sometimes resulted in children, but rarely, among this group, in

The Princess of Albemarle

Violet Manners, Lady Granby, made this sketch of Amélie Rives, probably when they became friends during social gatherings of the Souls. (Amélie Rives Troubetzkoy Collection, The Valentine)

divorce. One might wonder about Amélie's first reaction to this behavior, accustomed as she was to the rigid sexual mores impressed upon elite southern ladies. Rives later commented on these sexual mores in her 1915 novel, *Shadows of Flames,* set in London. There the Virginia-born heroine muses about one of her close friends: "Three years in England had taught her that a woman may be an excellent mother, a good friend, an attentive wife, and yet have 'lovers.' How strange it seemed to her!"[37] Aristocratic English sexual conduct certainly made real to Rives some of her past reading about the European aristocracy and perhaps suggested that extramarital affairs could enliven, even gladden one's existence.

The Souls were a fashionable and lively group, but their challenges to society lay in aesthetics and personal conduct; they were not political or social reformers. "The Souls' independence from the prevailing orthodoxy," writer Angela Lambert has noted, "was purely aesthetic or social. Not one single member of the intelligent, independent, strong-minded women who made up the inner circle of the Souls ever spoke out in favour of any reforms that might have eased the lives of their less well endowed contemporaries."[38] Whatever Rives's reform and philanthropic tendencies, interaction with the Souls did not increase them.

Archie's money, family connections, and position paved the way for his and Amélie's entrance to the Souls, but it was her personality and literary flair that charmed the group. Although Amélie left few letters describing her time with the Souls, she later reminisced about her relationships with some of them and corrected the impression that she had corresponded with Arthur, Lord Balfour, later prime minister: "I merely mentioned that I saw a great deal of him as a fellow member of 'The Souls.' He was never an intimate friend of mine though I liked and admired him, and he was always very nice to me."[39]

One of Amélie's closest relationships was with thirty-year-old George Curzon, son of the fourth Baron Scarsdale, later viceroy of India, foreign secretary under King George V, and Marquess of Kedleston. In 1889 he was a bachelor, recovering from a long affair with Lady Sybil Grosvenor, who, after the death of her husband, Lord Grosvenor, had married another man. A member of Parliament, Curzon took great interest in international diplomacy. He was just beginning to undertake the travels that he would write about at length, and that would make him such a knowledgeable foreign secretary.[40]

Curzon and Amélie met sometime in 1889, before July. Margot Tennant wrote an account of a memorable dinner held when Curzon was "threatened with lung trouble and was ordered to Switzerland by his doctors. We were very unhappy and assembled at a farewell banquet, to which he entertained us in the Bachelors' Club, on the 10th of July, 1889."[41] There Curzon presented a poem, toasting each person by name. It began by calling Arthur Balfour, leading light of the Souls, "the heart that to all hearts is nearest." Curzon then moved to Archie's cousins Daisy and Henry White:

America lends,
Nay, she gives when she sends
Such treasures as Harry and Daisy;
Tho' many may yearn,
None but Harry can turn
That sweet little head of hers crazy.

The Princess of Albemarle

Curzon ended the series with an encomium to Amélie, calling her

A gift of true grace,
Virginia's marvellous daughter.
Having conquered the States,
She's been blown by the Fates
To conquer us over the water.[42]

Clearly, the Souls had fitted Amélie into their coterie. Archie, however, was in a different position. Curzon's poem generally saluted both husband and wife, but Archie was totally omitted and at this dinner remained invisible. Given his wealth and position, he may well have felt insulted at the slight. To be sure, Curzon made amends in a poem presented at a second dinner of the Souls, in 1890, by referring to "bold Chanler," who by some star's "augury" had won "the enchanting little Amélie." But Archie was not present to celebrate his inclusion because he and Amélie were then in Paris.[43]

Archie may have suspected that Curzon, an inveterate womanizer, found Amélie alluring and that she reciprocated that feeling. Curzon seems to have considered female authors quite enticing; at least two of his serious relationships were with women who became well-known novelists: Pearl Craigie, who wrote under the pseudonym John Oliver Hobbes, and the American author Elinor Glyn both had affairs with Curzon, though in 1889 these lay in his future. Curzon also evinced some similarity to the suitors who had earlier romanced Rives. Like Edward Spencer Pratt and the Coolidge brothers, Curzon had traveled widely, was knowledgeable about foreign countries, and was fascinated by history and foreign affairs.[44]

Even as Curzon expressed his appreciation of Amélie, he may have played a darker role in her literary career, regarding their shared interest in poetry. In 1889 a collection of her poetry was under consideration at Houghton Mifflin. Shortly before she left the United States, Amélie had submitted the poems "with the hope that you may decide to publish them for me." She told the publisher: "I have not offered them elsewhere, and many of them have never been printed in any form." Indicating her willingness to correct the poems, she said she might also add others "should you consider their publication in a favorable light."[45]

Houghton Mifflin apparently replied affirmatively, and a month later Rives wrote the publisher again: "I cannot express to you my appreciation of your generosity in regard to offering to select the best poems for me, and I thank you again for your interest as so fully expressed in your letter." Not then ready to settle on terms, Rives alluded to her husband's absence: "Mr. Chanler is New York at present and I do not like to conclude business arrangements without consulting him. As soon as he returns he will write or call on you."[46]

Even in this correspondence with the publisher, Rives showed a lack of confidence in her poetry: "The friend who copied them, copied indiscriminately all that she could collect. I am in no hurry for them to appear, and wish you to feel that you have ample time at your disposal, especially as I wish to correct carefully the proofs. I have suffered so much from incorrect printing of my verses particularly." Much like her early pleas for editorial guidance at the *Atlantic,* she told the press: "Please criticize severely regardless of my feelings, & if you leave out one or two poems that I have a particular weakness for I am sure you wont mind my asking you to retain them." She also intended to send new poems, "two or three of the best things that I have written," and a still incomplete sonnet.[47]

Just before sailing to Europe in March, Rives had informed the publishing house that her trip might "interfere somewhat with the publishing of the poems," but "if you will send the proofs to Mrs. Chanler, c/o Rothschild et Cie, Paris, France, they will be forwarded to me promptly and I will attend to them at once." That June, *Current Literature* announced that "Amélie Rives is to have a volume of her published and unpublished verses brought out in September." This collection never appeared, and some evidence suggests that George Curzon encouraged Rives not to publish it. One Curzon biographer alluded to his intimacy with Rives and argued: "What she lacked and what she required was a stern literary censor; and on one occasion at least, George Curzon assumed the rôle, for in 1890 she placed all her poetry in his hands and agreed to abide by his decision as to whole or partial publication or suppression. He decided on the latter."[48]

Although Curzon may have found Rives's poetry less compelling than that of his idol Alfred, Lord Tennyson, at least two other considerations may have influenced his advice not to publish. Although he was no fan of fiction, Curzon had earlier read "The Quick or the Dead?" and had, according to a biographer, "before he met her [Rives] . . . speculated on the character of the writer." Believing that her book was "disfigured . . . by sensuous phrases and morbid turns of thought," Curzon took quite an opposite view of Amélie

Amélie was photographed with flowers in her hair during her visit to England in 1889. (Amélie Rives Troubetzkoy Collection, The Valentine)

after he had interacted with her; he came to believe her "innocently unconscious of the interpretation placed on them by her readers." Curzon saw Amélie "as sensitive and highly strung . . . and, above all, the purest minded and least suspicious woman he had ever met; one who was shocked by the slightest breath of impropriety."[49]

Given Curzon's estimation of Rives as a writer prone to verbal excesses that needed to be reined in, he was unlikely to encourage her emotional and passionate poetry. Moreover, Curzon "viewed with real apprehension a growing tendency to break down the natural barriers between the two sexes." No feminist, he successfully opposed a proposal in 1893 to allow women to become members of the Royal Geographical Society. Claiming that women's "sex and training rendered them equally unfitted for exploration," he saw his stand as part of a larger battle against the equality of the sexes. In one letter, he proudly proclaimed that he had "pulled off my combat against the ladies at the Royal Geographical Society successfully," despite criticism from the newspapers "because 'woman's emancipation' is the fashionable tomfoolery of the day."[50] Such ideas would surely have pushed him toward discouraging Amélie from publishing her poetry.

Although Rives long admired Curzon, she later seems to have regretted taking his advice about her poetry. In 1892 she used an extended metaphor to complain to her sister-in-law that Curzon had "tried to drag out my wings with forceps." Admitting that he had succeeded "in maiming me for a time," she insisted that "the matrix of my brave pinions was not destroyed and behold me in full feather again & soaring away as obstinately as ever toward the sun."[51]

While in England, Amélie deepened her acquaintances in literary circles that included people not part of the Souls. Considering Oscar Wilde's origins far too middle class, Curzon and the Whites were displeased when Ettie Grenfell and Violet Manners invited the Wildes to social occasions. During Amélie's stay in England, Wilde sent her a note with two of his recent works including *The Happy Prince,* a collection of fairy stories. He described them as "slight and fanciful and written not for children, but for childlike people from eighteen to eighty!" He inscribed the book: "For Amélie Rives, from her sincere admirer, Oscar Wilde. London." He then cryptically added: "A rose-red July, '89." Wilde also included his recent article "The Decay of Lying," which had appeared in the magazine *Nineteenth Century.* Describing it as "written only for artistic temperaments," he added, "The public are not allowed a chance of comprehension, so you will know what I mean by it." At the end of his note, Wilde asked when he might call to see her, suggesting that they two had met earlier or corresponded.[52]

While these encounters show Rives experiencing an unprecedented level of fame, she still had to cope with denunciations of her writing. Curzon's dismissal of her poetry came while she was experiencing a particularly difficult stretch of criticism, to the point that she seems to have vacillated about even continuing to write. Earlier in the spring, as she was preparing to depart for England, one newspaper disclosed that "she contemplates doing considerable literary work while abroad, but it is understood her productions will all be published in America." Reports from the summer of 1889, however, suggested trepidations on her part. One magazine item stated that

Rives had recently written a friend that she "had decided to abandon literature for art, because the prizes of literature were not worth striving for: a book, she said was certain to create discussion among a large number of people unfitted by education to comprehend the fine points of an author's work, while a picture attracted attention only from those competent to pass upon its merits."[53]

Some of the stories that Rives seems to have been trying to write did not pan out. According to an item in the *Washington Post* of June 12, Rives "is at work on a new story on the employment of children in factories." In an interview several months earlier, she described her novel-in-progress as concerning "child slavery." She declared that she was "pouring out my heart" in it because "I only hope to do some good." Her interest in child labor had led her to contact Richard Ely, an economics professor at Johns Hopkins University. After he mailed novels to her, she demanded, "Send me facts and figures." Rives's proposed novel, which has not survived and was probably never completed, chronicled the family life of an industrial worker who fell ill and sent his young daughter out to factory work. In the author's outline, the young daughter "becomes a white slave, an industrial slave, and it is her career and its strange vicissitudes, through childhood and early womanhood, I shall ask my readers to follow."[54] Rives apparently abandoned this topic, perhaps in the summer of 1889, and did not mention it again.

The first year of marriage had revealed that Amélie and Archie had serious incompatibilities of temperament and interests. Yet, given nineteenth-century expectations, both wanted to make their marriage work. Rives's commitment to her writing career seems to have been a point of contention. Chanler was proud of his wife's beauty and acclaim but wished her to retreat to the private sphere. He apparently wanted her to accompany him on his frequent travels, where he could listen to praise for her beauty and charm. While the summer in England had shown that she could receive admiration and acclaim from a wide circle, Archie may have chafed at the way in which she overshadowed him among the Souls. He seemed to hope that in Paris their attention to art—he exercising sponsorship and she improving her artistic technique—would provide greater contentment and even happiness for both of them.

SIX

"I Would Teach Her That Passion ... Is a Great, Pure Fire"

Marriage, Drugs, and Despair

After the summer in England mingling with aristocratic society, Amélie and Archie headed in August 1889 for the European continent, where they would spend much of the next two years. Their relationship became rockier. While Rives seemed to enjoy her increased focus on art, she was unwilling to give up her writing. Over time, morphine and cocaine offered her forgetfulness of illness and marital torments, taking her into a downward spiral of dependence.

Archie and Amélie first visited Bad Kissingen, a resort in Bavaria, ostensibly for their health. Quarrels repeatedly erupted, and there were signs that these were more than passing spats. A scrap of ledger paper in Amélie's handwriting, dated "Kissingen 26th of August" and saved among Archie's papers, hints at the discord. Cast as a dialogue, one of Amélie's favorite forms, the memo apparently records a quarrel. Archie opens with an accusation: "I firmly believe that when you said that time that you had no disagreeable feeling in your heart that you were untruthful." Amélie replies: "(After a considerable pause) Well—you say I haven't written the whole sentence. What comes after?" After parrying several phrases, Archie contends, "You *were* untruthful to me once in Newport[.] you confessed it." Amélie then admits, "Yes, I remember now, and it's always been my grief that instead of a pride[,] it has always been a regret to me."[1]

The dialogue indicates that Archie was bringing up past quarrels, and that Amélie's past actions—whether in Newport when they first met in 1887, or simply during the previous fall—greatly perturbed him. Even if only an imaginative reconstruction of the young couple's arguments, the memo—and its retention—suggest an impasse developing between them.

In Germany, Amélie and Archie consulted a doctor. At much the same time as the quarrel, Rives wrote her sister-in-law: "I know you will be rejoiced that the doctor thinks that he can benefit Archie's nerves also to a great degree. O what a blessing for us all!—we have had some sad & dreadful scenes since I last saw you, but things are much, much better, & poor Archie does honestly try with all his might." While Amélie seemed to be putting an optimistic spin on their difficulties, she confided far greater worries about Archie's mental state: "The doctor here also says that he is not always responsible for what he says & does." Rives also depicted her own behavior in a far more positive light than had the memo: "That helps me so to be patient & gentle, & what with praying and thinking of the great blessings that God has showered on me in other ways, I manage to struggle on after a fashion."[2]

In their travels, accompanied by their servants, Archie and Amélie continued to experience ups and downs. That fall he fell ill, and Amélie again apparently put the best face on it, at least to her friends and family. Her dear friend Louisa "Lutie" Pleasants reassured Archie: "How dreadful it must have been—as bad for Amy [a nickname for Amélie] as for you—for terror is worse than pain—and mental pain far, far before that of the body—but, my dear boy, I am *not* belittling your trials. Amélie writes me how heavenly sweet you were in your illness."[3]

From Germany, Archie and Amélie went to Venice; by November they headed to Algiers, where she sketched under an art master as part of the studies that Archie was determined she should follow. Their new surroundings fascinated Amélie, who vividly limned the street life: "The fluttering draperies of the Arabs and the bare brown legs of scampering children. Crowds of meek little furry donkeys go pattering through the streets loaded with dates and straw and very often with great solemn Arabs draped and cowled elaborately & beating a tattoo on their sturdy beasts' sides to encourage them to trot!" Yet the change brought by travel was not a happy one. By Christmas, Amélie was sick and miserable: "I never never never *NEVER* spent such a Christmas in my whole life," she wailed to her sister-in-law. "The only cheerful thing in it was the really *lovely* service in the little English church."[4]

As 1890 dawned, Amélie and Archie settled in Paris, where she was thrilled to study painting with Charles Lasar, an American painter living in Paris. "In my opinion," she gushed, Lasar "grows every day, more and more the most wonderful teacher I have ever imagined." But other tensions bubbled. Amélie had made a marriage that vaulted her into a life of luxury, but problems loomed in both her writing career and personal life. In the spring of 1890, Jules Renaud, a young art student who had become obsessed with her, committed suicide in Algiers. The news stories posited that "he worshipped her as a goddess. Long before he saw her she seemed to him the very embodiment of genius. Her pictures, gleaned from the American magazines, he had framed and hung in profusion around his room." It remains unclear whether Renaud actually ever met or conversed with Rives, but "he was constantly telling his companions of the smiles which she had given him and the opportunities she made to allow him to show her his devotion."[5] In a society not yet accustomed to people having an obsessive interest in a celebrity, this episode further injured Rives's reputation.

After traveling with only Archie and servants in 1889, Amélie tried to ensure that she would always be surrounded by a circle of companions to amuse and, more important, support her. Before her marriage, friends had frequently visited her at Castle Hill; but in the early years after marriage, an entourage, which would accompany her for years, more fully took shape. Sojourns by her intimates, supplemented by those from her mother, sisters, and Archie's siblings, formed an important part of the Parisian interlude. Lutie Pleasants arrived as they were settling in; Julia Magruder later that year. Although Amélie seems to have supplied most of the friends—Pleasants, Magruder, and cousin Leila Page—Archie also appreciated these women and bankrolled opulent accommodations for them all. Indeed, the entire expedition had an air of youthful, almost juvenile, fun as Archie and Lutie called each other Archems and Luttems, and Magruder often signed her notes "Doola."[6]

At this point Archie, in seeking to find his own special causes, had seized upon the idea of supporting artists. Securing the funding for what was then being called the Paris prize, a five-year stipend for young American artists, took him back and forth across the Atlantic. As the award took shape in 1891, it guaranteed nine hundred dollars per year for five years in support of an aspiring artist, male or female, over twenty-five years of age. Archie also envisaged a fund from American cities to support local art students.[7] In keeping with this philanthropic agenda, Amélie had bestowed a prize for the best essay on child labor, shared by two economists. Yet, after the announcement of the prize, she seemed to lose interest. On his part, Archie was encountering difficulties in convincing others among the wealthy to supplement his generous gift.

This depiction of Amélie Rives at her desk, possibly at the house of Madame de Pompadour, was taken by a French photographer. (Amélie Rives Troubetzkoy Collection, The Valentine)

In the spring of 1890 outside Paris, Amélie, Archie, and her friend Julia Magruder were visiting Fontainebleau and stumbled upon the Ermitage de Pompadour. The white stone gateway bearing the gilded name of the estate caught their attention, and they vainly attempted to convince an implacable concierge to give them a tour. "Everything was in a state of the most perfect preservation, and it seemed a thousand pities that so fascinating a house should have no occupants." As Amélie wistfully stared at the forbidden mansion, she summoned up magical beliefs from her childhood: "If a fairy gave me a wish at this moment I should ask that someone would offer me that house for the summer."[8] With an wealthy husband to play fairy godfather and grant wishes, the Ermitage de Pompadour became the summer residence of the Chanler group, with its visiting relatives and friends.

Julia Magruder published an account of their summer visit that reads much like a travelogue. Describing the "really charming" house of about thirty rooms ("besides the ample accommodation for servants above the stable"), she noted, "It is furnished in pure Louis XV style, and a good many of the original pieces of furniture owned by Madame de Pompadour are pointed out." Since this piece appeared in a family-oriented publication, Magruder added a note of propriety: "If one could only think of that old palace as the setting for an idyllic romance, without any of the hideousness of Madame de Pompadour's career of extravagance and vice, how perfect it would be!" Julia's enthusiasm seemed unbounded: "Never were there lovelier walks than under those great old trees, with their screening vines; never sweeter trysting places than the old stone seat in the lilac hedge and the ruins of the summer house, hung with ivy that stands at the entrance to the beautiful French kitchen garden."[9]

Writing for an audience that knew Rives had gone to Paris to pursue art, Magruder coyly indicated that the party included a "painter, working indefatigably at her art." She drew an idyllic picture, without mentioning Amélie's name: "In a secluded corner of the grounds she posed her model and worked for many hours a day. Here we had a rustic table, with books and writing materials and canvases and paints heaped upon it promiscuously; and sometimes one of us would read aloud while the model posed and the picture went forward; or, when the model rested, we had our afternoon tea brought out, and the gentlemen joined us with their cigars and newspapers, and so many pleasant hours were passed." That summer Amélie told her sister-in-law Margaret about days spent painting, writing, and reading French authors such as Stendhal, Flaubert, and Théophile Gautier. Rives exulted: "O I do find the days about forty hours too short for all that I want to do."[10]

Other parts of the time in Paris were also enjoyable for Amélie. Years later she recalled her art studies at Lasar's studio in the rue de Vaugirard, where "I used to go at 9 o'clock in the winter mornings dressing by candle light, and gazing out at the carvings on the lovely pediment of La Madeleine (My apartment was in the Place de la Madeleine) as they slowly emerged out of the purplish grey dusk of early morning." Her routine was to spend the day at the studio and walk home at sunset "for the exercise": "I wore a simple little black frock & hat, and walked fast, carrying a dry canvas (or a wet one sometimes!) in my hand and looking straight ahead. Though I was rather a pretty person in those days, *no one ever spoke to me! Vive* Paris!"[11]

Reports from Paris pictured Amélie as intent on her art studies. According to a fellow student: "Her studio was just above mine and I saw her pass nearly every day. I never saw her with her husband. She was always with a tall, handsome woman, her husband's sister, I think." The artist noted: "Everybody thought she'd try to have a picture hung, but she has not. Of course, she could on account of her reputation in other ways, even if she was not a great artist. She makes many friends. All her fellow students like her. They find her simple, modest, and unaffected, 'just as if she'd never done anything,' they say."[12]

Despite the wonderful summer at Fontainebleau and the joys of exploring Paris, this time also marked a new, darker period in Rives's life. Like her grandmother Judith Page Rives, Amélie suffered from migraine headaches that incapacitated her, sometimes for days. During this European stay she began to use opiates, most likely prescribed by a physician to deal with her excruciating headaches.[13] Although she later talked about her addiction to close friends, she never wrote about her ordeal nor did it become public during her lifetime. Her fictional writings, however, hold numerous clues about her addiction and her state of mind in 1890–91.

Long fascinated with sacrifice and death, especially in religious contexts, Rives came to obsess over forms of sacrifice, perhaps as part of her depression about her marriage. A poem of six parts, composed as a Keatsian sonnet and published late in 1888, expressed her despair. Entitled "To All Women," it expressed solidarity with other women dealing with pain and sorrow:

O sorrowing women, yet who weep in vain
Who uncaressed sob on through the dark night,
With broken wings that ache to feel the light,
Strained out above joy's corpse untimely slain,

The poem's six fourteen-line stanzas focus on redemptive suffering as well as death. In the first stanza the poem addresses

All ye who pine to cease rather than die,
Who dread a second consciousness, and long
Only for peace as peace is known to graves,
Not to the buried—unto you I cry, . . .

Longing to strip roses of their thorns and give the blossoms to female victims, the narrator also voices the wish: "Oh, I would live and die a thousand times / Could but my death at last buy women rest."

Calling for tolerance, love, and an end to hatred, Rives in her last stanza reaches out to "hearts forsaken, hearts forlorn, oppressed" and promises "dear unquestioning sympathy" and "rest." The last six lines of the poem again sound the theme of her own self-sacrifice.

> Come to me, come, queen, beggar, vile or pure,
> So yet but love and long for higher ken,
> With tremulous eyes fast on eternity,
> And faltering feet that faith will yet make sure
> O sad ones, come! Christ Thou didst die for men,
> Let me but die for women,—live for Thee![14]

While Rives's sonnet connected self-sacrifice with Christian rebirth, a novella that she wrote in 1890–91 took a more morbid, death-centered view. *According to St. John* was first issued in serial form, beginning August 1891, in *Cosmopolitan Magazine,* one of the best-selling magazines of the day, especially popular with middle-class women. The novella was published in book form later that year. Its descriptions of Parisian life echo the realism that Amélie had been encountering in nineteenth-century novels; the story's original title had been "A Girl of the Pavement."[15] The later title, *According to St. John,* indicates a shift in focus, as the plot came to pivot around the biblical verse John 14:13, "Greater love hath no man than this, that a man lay down his life for his friends," featured on the book's title page.

According to St. John follows a few months in the life of Jean Page, a young Virginia woman studying in Paris. After the death of her neighbor and dear friend, Lilian Farrance, Jean marries the widower, Adrian Farrance, a painter, but soon discovers his diary in which he pines for his dead wife. Jean decides that Adrian would be better off without her—the best thing that she can do is to kill herself. An encounter with a Paris street gamine, who is thinking of drowning herself in the Seine, brings Jean to save the girl even as she herself drifts closer to suicide.

Rives also lays out in *According to St. John* a parallel story of unrequited love: that of the Parisian concierge Madame Vamousin, known as Maman Cici, who is deserted by her coachman husband. Maman Cici's descent into alcoholism and morphine addiction provides a means of suicide for Jean. Borrowing a syringe from Maman Cici, Jean "with a quick movement, ran the sharp needle into the smooth flesh of her slender fore-arm, and pressed the piston slowly until its head rested on the frame." After "a sharp burning sensation," she became "quite light hearted." Rives closely details Jean's reaction to the morphine: "Next came a delicious languor—it was as though warm-rosy wine were streaming through her veins. Her mouth became slightly dry, and it was an effort for her to moisten her lips or move in the least, but this strange, thrilling heaviness of her body was in some way delicious. . . . Oh, how lovely this is—like floating on a magic carpet."[16] Rives did not deal with the question of how a naive young woman obtained the morphine and knew just how to inject it. Instead the focus is on how lovely Jean was as the drug allowed her to slip easily from life. Upon encountering Jean's body, but not realizing that she is dead, Adrian Farrance thinks: "I've never seen her so beautiful."[17]

This passage shows how alluring the use of morphine had become to Amélie; its beautification of death suggests her own depression. In her novel *Shadows of Flames,* published in 1915 after years of battling drug dependency, Rives chooses another interpretation, describing the "wild sense of triumph" that morphine could give: "The sting of the spot where the needle had thrust into his flesh was sweet as the sting left by a kiss to the normal lover." The addicted character is aware of the peril: "He knew that he risked the danger of an abscess every time that he thrust the needle into his arms or legs, already so thickly punctured. He did not care. Morphia gives this carelessness—this calm recklessness of all that may follow." Later, Rives sympathetically reveals the agony of this addicted man: "Yes, at times, so great was his suffering over his own abasement that he had frequently thought of self-destruction as a means of escape from the dark coil. These were during the luridly lucid moments which come to fine natures in such thrall—the moments when they see themselves as they are."[18] In the early 1890s, as Rives was beginning to use opiates, she pictured suicide as akin to "strange, thrilling heaviness." Later she wrote about the "calm recklessness" of opiate use, but in 1890–91 she showed little realization that opiates were the "dark coil" that she later called them.

Even before Rives's story appeared in July 1891, an item in the *Southern Cultivator* that month announced that "in the estimation of critics who are most competent to judge, this last story will be the most finished as well as interesting product of this versatile Southern pen." The *Cultivator* assured its more conventional readers that "its publication in the Cosmopolitan is a guarantee that it will contain nothing of the kind that excited criticism in Amelie Rives' earlier productions."[19]

In fact, *According to St. John* offended many readers. In August, the *New York Tribune* commented: "There's a good deal of tinsel in Mrs. Amelie

Rives's story in 'The Cosmopolitan': it is much to be feared that the young lady has not greatly improved her literary theories and performances." A caustic review in *Current Literature* that September maintained: "If the newspaper comment on the first chapters of Mrs. Amelie Rives Chanler's new Cosmopolitan novel . . . be a criterion, the fair author will never again be taken seriously." The critic further asserted: "The modern instances of this writer's work have been judged even by sensational newspapers as—hysterical nonsense." While the review allowed that "Mrs. Rives-Chanler is not—like some of her fellow-sufferers with the literary measles—a naturally vulgar woman," it condemned Rives's description of lingerie and an uncorseted female as "certainly not lady-like literature."[20]

Rives's depiction of the *déshabillé* French concierge nauseated more than one reader, including an anonymous reviewer in the *Critic,* who pointed to the same passage. Calling it "unflinching realism," the reviewer argued that Rives's "warmest friends must acknowledge her decadence." That reviewer found the book's tone "morbid and hysterical at times, especially toward the end, and there are several unpleasant episodes which have no bearing on the story, and are plainly only brought in to show that the writer can deal with them." Despite all these "defects," the reviewer also perceived "power and earnestness, and criticism must recognize aim as well as achievement." As in this example, much of the censure focused on the moral tone of the work. One review noted: "It is certainly original, and there is nothing weak in the manner of the telling, but to any thoroughly healthy-minded person there is something revolting about such a morbid study, such a perversion of all that is sweet and high and noble in life." Rives, in the reviewer's opinion, should not have published the story.[21]

Others judged the premise of the novella's ending to be unconvincing. In deeming it an error in judgment, Rives's literary biographer described the suicide that ended the book as Amélie's most "egregious . . . literary offense." Even the praise the novella received in other quarters was qualified. The *New Orleans Picayune* declared: "The story, of course, is well written, but it is none the less absurd." More positively, the *Boston Globe* argued that "the story is worked with skill, and in parts is strong in dramatic power."[22]

At some point in Paris, Rives's drug usage had begun to compromise her health and well-being. Years later, Archie's sister Margaret referred to her growing disillusionment with Amélie. Archie, in Margaret's opinion, was married to a woman "who did not love him in the least." Moreover, Amélie's

The Princess of Albemarle

opium habit had made her "no use as a housekeeper or hostess. I saw my brother living in extreme discomfort, adoring his wife, and allowing her to reduce his life to complimentary interviews over her." In the autumn of 1890 Rives became ill for several months, and newspapers speculated that she was suffering from consumption (tuberculosis). In January 1891 the *Chicago Tribune* reported that she "has just recovered from a dangerous attack of bronchitis which threatened her life."[23]

During this period Amélie and Archie spent a great deal of time apart, and the relationship was often chilly. So indifferent in correspondence did Archie become that Lutie Pleasants wrote him in January 1891, almost begging him to write to Amélie, then convalescing in San Remo. Amélie had asked Lutie not to send a cable to Archie because, in Lutie's words, "she seemed so afraid of worrying you with womans fears." After secretly telegraphing but receiving no answer, Lutie again contacted Archie, telling him: "Amélie simply *suffers* under your silence—you know how proud she is—and she always loyally says, 'I understand him *perfectly* I know just how he feels—but oh! I do *wish* he would write—It seems so long.'" Lutie also admonished Archie: "Amélie longs for the words of love which I *know* you are saying in your heart—day and night, day and night for your Amy. I really think constant letters from you would help her in her getting well."[24]

By the summer of 1891, when Rives returned to the United States to help publicize the forthcoming novella of *According to St. John,* difficulties with the Chanler family had worsened. Archie's nineteen-year-old brother Robert, who was in rebellion from the family and his tutor, had an emotional breakdown in Paris that June. Part of his problem was an obsession with Amélie, who had become especially close to him and had painted his portrait. The extended Chanler family, especially cousin Daisy White, blamed Amélie, believing that she had encouraged the infatuation. After Robert was packed off to convalesce in rural Wales, Daisy decreed that if Amélie corresponded with him at all, she should be cautioned to write only letters that were "short, natural (what other people call natural[,] not what is natural to her)."[25]

In this ongoing tiff, Archie defended his wife and alleged that Robert's "hallucination" sprang from Amélie being "the first person he met who understood & fully sympathized with him." Years later, after Robert became a well-known artist, with numerous works exhibited at the famous International Exposition of Modern Art in 1913 (housed in the 69th Regiment Armory in New York City and often called the Armory Show), he credited Amélie with being "the one who helped me to my freedom."[26] But in the summer of 1891, the Chanler family found much to criticize in Rives's behavior.

Archie planned for a grand return to the United States after which he and Amélie would spend much of the summer in Newport chaperoning his three sisters. Amélie, however, was in no hurry to leave Paris, where an operation that spring had corrected Lutie Pleasants's cleft palate. Amélie had long wanted this outcome for her close friend—in fact she had justified her first stab at publication as a way to raise money to help her. As Amélie made her plans to return to the United States, her uncle Francis Rives died in July. Observing mourning conventions gave her a pretext to cancel participation in the Newport season. Upon landing in New York on August 23, 1891, she proceeded directly to Castle Hill.[27]

How much Rives would devote herself to art rather than writing remained up in the air. That August she informed the *Boston Globe* that *According to St. John* was the "last thing I shall write for some time." She added: "I intend for the present to devote myself entirely to art. I find that painting does not undermine my health so much as writing does." At about the same time, Archie told a Chicago paper: "Mrs. Chanler will not exhibit any of her work for a long time. . . . We shall be in New York for a month next winter, and will look at the work of some of the best American painters." Denying that she was currently writing fiction, Archie stated: "Her time will be divided between writing and painting, six months in the year being devoted to each pursuit." When they returned to Castle Hill that summer, Amélie's art teacher Charles Lasar accompanied them. Thus, the experiment in art went on—although Archie's comments intimated that he wanted her art (and perhaps even her writing) to stay out of the public eye. The intensity of Archie's belief that Rives should focus on art can be seen in a statement he gave two decades later that "her artistic gift was as far stronger than her literary gift as the sun is than the moon." He concluded that with the exception of some stories and two novellas (including "The Quick or the Dead?"), "none of her literary work has satisfied said Art Patron [Archie], when measured by the side of her splendid artistic power."[28]

Late in 1891 a newspaper speculated that the Chanlers would spend the winter in New York, where Amélie would be a "society belle," but still she stayed at Castle Hill. She and Archie remained in the United States the next year, but their marriage was reaching a new low. Amélie's health—worsened by drug dependency—constantly caused concern, and Archie's jealousy and emotional instability were increasing. Over the previous years, they had tried separation, with limited success. A remarkable letter of over sixty pages that Archie wrote Julia Magruder, in June 1892 reveals his fears and some of the most severe problems in the marriage. Although the letter was addressed to Julia, he expected her to share its contents with Amélie: "I leave it *entirely* to your discretion as to what of its contents you show, read, or it may be only *translate* into calmer language to her." So intimate and revealing was Archie's letter that he did not use full names but throughout the letter called himself "Ulysses" (the Roman version of Odysseus, the hero away on adventure), and Amélie "Penelope" (Ulysses's wife, who patiently awaited his return, though surrounded by suitors who begged her to remarry). Pronouncing himself in "the Valley of the Shadow of Soul death," Archie claimed nonetheless that his health was normal. Earlier problems with sleep had abated and "my nerves are quieter than they have been for four years." What had plunged him into despair was a letter from Amélie, which he pronounced "lovely" but which included one phrase that "sets my ever over-ruly imagination at work and the scorpions which lie coiled within its domain and with which it lashes its enemies, finding the house divided against itself, turned on and gnawed me."[29]

What was the one phrase? "I like Mr. F very much," Amélie had written. It turned out that Archie was deeply jealous of Mr. F, identified as Moreton Frewen, brother-in-law of Lady Randolph Churchill, the former Jennie Jerome. Frewen, then forty years old and sometimes called "Mortal Ruin" because of his financial recklessness, was the younger son in an English gentry family and had made and lost a fortune ranching in Wyoming. Archie associated Frewen with a cesspool of "corruption and marital infidelity—the Prince of Wales' set." Believing Frewen morally tainted from his relatives by marriage, Randolph and Jennie Churchill, Archie also wrote: "Lord R.C.'s wife has been one of the most openly unfaithful women in London, and Lord R. carries horns on his head as long as an antedeluvian monster's."[30]

Four hours after reading Amélie's letter, Archie began to feel "an absolutely unaccountable and mysterious depression creeping up on me. . . . I had a feeling as of some approaching sinister blow. I tried to rally—found it impossible. As the sun sank my spirits kept him company." Archie's depression stemmed in part from his belief that Amélie, because of her gendered, womanly nature, could not understand men, even though she was "invariably right about women." She had an "un-secretive sunlight loving nature."[31]

Amazingly enough for a man who had been married almost four years, Archie envisioned himself involved in a competition, and as he put it: "My life has been one long battle with rivals." In his view, he was shielding Amélie: "This letter will serve as a charge against the first married or unmarried man that tries to ingratiate himself with her." Even as he imagined himself fending off romantic rivals, he was also celebrating her as irresistible. Convinced of the continued "shadowy" antagonism of Will Otis (who had himself since married), Archie thought that Will still preferred Amélie. In fact, Archie believed that Will, in a conversation with Amélie, had admitted "his failure & mistake in his marriage."[32]

Amélie held an incomparable appeal to Archie. Holding her to be "invincible, Matchless, all Love conquering," he rhapsodized: "Her record is now unparalled [*sic*]. *No* man who has known her has failed to fall desperately in love with her." Archie was convinced that every man would try to steal her and that Mr. F. would undoubtedly try to seduce her. Archie's fevered imagination conjured a wild scenario: "From being the same, cool, friendly, flattering, but sad, indifferent friend he will transform himself, at one bound into the unbridled, the impassioned lover. Throwing himself at her feet,—or perhaps he would compromise on a one-knee posture—he will pour out a flood of the most passionate endearments using words which he has *never* used before. Under cover of her surprise he will cover her feet and hands with kisses—will he stop there! He will appear overwhelmed, crushed by the vehemence of his confession. It was plus fort que lui! [He couldn't help himself.] It would out!" Archie then envisioned Frewen entreating Amélie: "Come into my dreary, weary life—come sweet golden flower of Purity & Peace. Leave the world—fly with me!" At the climax of this delusional seduction, Archie asserted that Amélie would not succumb: "God, loyalty, and *herself* would keep her from that." Nonetheless, he worried that Frewen would try to "picque" Amélie's interest by appearing "invulnerable" and thus "in her character of Woman Invincible," she "would be decoyed into the pleasures & excitement of the chase after the subjection of this vauntingly invincible man."[33]

Perhaps most revealing was Archie's intimation that he and Amélie had a mutual understanding about a certain element of contingency to their relationship. He sought to explain: "When I agreed with Penelope [Amélie] that if either found their Heart's Desire in a man or woman, the finder was so, at once to tell the other, I did *not* mean, or even mean to suggest that either of us was to try to set out *now* to find a Heart's Desire. I suggested this as a mere pis aller [last resort] at the end of a long long period in which we had given our poor hearts a chance to recover from the fearful strain passed through and we could look with full justice and more untroubled love on each other."

Archie tried to make clear to Julia, who after all was Amélie's intimate friend, that he expected the current separation to be more a respite than a parting. "It would be unfair to the sacred memory of our past love and tenderness—spasmodic but intense, either to jeopardize its resurrection by allowing our hearts during this period of rest & self-examination to be assaulted or even approached by man or woman." He also explicitly wrote of letting their love die, only to be resurrected. If that did not happen, he and Amélie then could look elsewhere for love. This separation was different, from his departure to Europe alone in 1888, he insisted, "because then the agreement was that there was to be *no* competition." He thought that Amélie back in 1888 "would bar the door to suitors—now she's opened it, unconsciously, but open it is, and the garden of my love is unguarded, . . . and the suitor can prowl in and out, at will. This makes me feel lonely, desolate, unprotected."[34]

Archie's long letter reveals a man at the end of his emotional tether. His emphasis on competition and feeling "unprotected" particularly indicates how such a man, intent on self-defense, may also have been threatening to Amélie. Years later she told her friend Louis Auchincloss that "Chanler used to sleep with a revolver under his pillow, threatening that one night he would do what Archduke Rudolf had done at Mayerling," a notorious double murder-suicide that occurred in 1889 when Austrian Crown Prince Rudolf killed himself and his mistress, Baroness Mary Vetsera, at a hunting lodge.[35] The Chanler marriage in 1892, after years of tumult, was running off the rails.

Other evidence from that June suggests that Archie was encountering greater emotional difficulties. At the end of that month, Amélie wrote a Dr. Bleyer (possibly Dr. J. Mount Bleyer of New York), thanking him "a thousand times" for his interest in Archie's well-being. "I have seen him since your first note," she informed the doctor, "and he does indeed seem much calmer and more natural."[36]

While no relationship between Amélie and Moreton Frewen has come to light, her friendship with George Curzon did take at least a brief romantic turn in the summer of 1892. Apparently, Rives was only one among several interests for Curzon. He had been romancing Mary Leiter, an attractive young American heiress, during the previous two years, while also carrying on a flirtation with Ettie Desborough, a fellow member of the Souls. Still, in August 1892 when Curzon visited Castle Hill, he recorded Amélie's dazzling effect on him: "Upon me Amy shone with the undivided insistence of her starlike eyes. Oh God! . . . the nights on the still lawn under the soft sky with my sweetheart." It is unlikely that either Curzon or Rives, whatever their mutual attraction, looked toward a permanent relationship, which could promise little in the way of financial security to either. Such a commitment also might damage Curzon's political aspirations. In spring 1893 he became engaged to Mary Leiter and married her in April 1895 in Washington, D.C. He and Amélie remained friendly; many years later, in 1914, she and her second husband, Pierre Troubetzkoy, spent several weeks with the widowed Curzon in London. In 1932 Rives, in a discussion with a potential biographer, declared: "My friendship with Lord Curzon was of long-standing, but I have destroyed most of his letters to me as they were concerned with his personal life and affairs and I felt that he would have preferred me to destroy them."[37]

At about the same time that Curzon visited Amélie at Castle Hill, she drew in charcoals a nude self-portrait. Although the picture itself has not been found, a photograph of it has survived.[38] Like the fling with Curzon, the portrait seems to signal a search for greater self-awareness, which had a sexual component. Rives also explored sexuality in a more public venue, when she penned an editorial, "Innocence versus Ignorance," published in the prestigious *North American Review* in September 1892, that called for young women to be taught more about sexuality.

This essay pointed out that children's curiosity "on religion or physical subjects" was too often "hushed and reproved." Rives carefully couched her argument in negative language. Rather than straightforwardly advocating teaching the facts of life, she more cautiously declared that girls should not be sheltered from them. "That which, according to my views, should be avoided," she admonished, "is a system of training from which all instruction, or at least all clear instruction, as to the rules of health and life, has been rigorously eliminated." She stated more clearly: "Boys are educated, girls are not; yet girls should be educated first and taught the most impressively." She further asserted an "intelligent and thoroughly instructed young girl" will

Only a photograph survives of the nude self-portrait that Amélie Rives drew in 1892. She carefully signed and dated it either August 21 or August 31. (Albert and Shirley Small Special Collections Library, University of Virginia)

have a "purity which shines, not through the opaque medium of ignorance, but through the clear texture of that lofty innocence which is the choice of what is worthy, made by one having the knowledge of good and evil."[39] Despite Rives's circumspection, her essay earned a rebuke from Bertha Monroe Rickoff, a female poet who argued that a mother should guard "the maiden's natural faith in human nature" and know that the young woman's "defence from evil lies, not in a knowledge of the world, but in a loftiness of ideals." While Rives had contended that young men would be more likely to confide in and be inspired by a knowledgeable sister, Rickoff insisted: "Does not the fact remain that a sister's innocent horror of evil is a more effective restraint on her brother than a knowledge which would place her on a level with his boyish comrades."[40]

In addition to her essay, Rives showed her growing awareness of issues impinging on women's autonomy in a novel that she published in 1892. Advertising itself in the subtitle as a sequel to "The Quick or the Dead?," *Barbara Dering* also reflected Rives's interest in how marriage affected women's role and autonomy. While "The Quick or the Dead?" had focused on the suspense of courtship, Rives meant her new book to explore modern marriage and its challenges. The title, *Barbara Dering,* informed her readers that Barbara Pomfret would choose Jock Dering; by the seventh of the book's thirty-three chapters, the protagonists have married. Much of the book pivots around the need for Barbara and Jock to accommodate themselves to each other's different pastimes and style of life.

Rives was sharing with the reading public her concerns about the constraints that marriage placed on women as well as some of the problems of her own marriage. This was unusual in the Victorian era, and a biographer has characterized the book, much like the nude self-portrait, as an attempt to "bare herself literally."[41] Yet Rives apparently hoped she could inspire herself to continue the marriage. In this sense the novel was an attempt to save the Chanlers' rocky union by showing how the Derings had mended theirs and how another marriage in the book—the Bransbys'—appeared past retrieval. Moreover, Rives in tackling the institution of wedlock was participating in the movement of the "New Woman"—new in the sense that this ideal challenged Victorian strictures on female activity and independence.

As the story unfolds, Barbara Dering and her friend from school days, Eunice Bransby, renew their acquaintance and become close, confiding in each other about problems caused by their insensitive husbands. Rives portrays Eunice's husband, Godfrey, as a prudish, old-fashioned patriarch, who dislikes the modern world and arbitrarily rules his sweet-natured wife—forbidding her to sing or wear dresses with décolletage. The novel also includes commentary on a third marriage, that of Barbara's African American maid, Martha Ellen, and her kind but disappointing husband, Tobit.

Amélie evidently drew on her experiences with Archie as a source for her picture of marital friction. Barbara confides in her friend Eunice, in words that recall Amélie's letters to her sisters-in-law: "He can be so horribly cruel. My soul cowers sometimes under his words like a dog that has been often beaten. Sometimes he seems to hate me, to be possessed of some evil spirit." The specificity of detail that Rives employs for one confrontation over a poem suggests that she was dredging up a past quarrel with Archie. Barbara lauds the sonnet "Her Love," written by the well-known poet Dante Gabriel Rossetti, to celebrate love as a unity of mind that surpasses physical passion. When Jock dismisses it as "rather a molly-coddle," Barbara heatedly upholds the theme: "Any one knows what you mean when you try to express passionate love, but even when poems attempt to put into words that spiritual essence of love . . . it is like trying to describe a subtle harmony to some one who has never heard it." The quarrel escalates as Jock peremptorily orders her to sit by him, and she objects to the command and its tone, "I am certainly not going to run at your bidding like a good little girl."[42]

In arguing for companionate marriage, *Barbara Dering* points out that selfishness, lack of communication, and jealousy must be overcome to achieve a good relationship. Even as Barbara wishes to patch up a spat with Jock, he leaves for a hunting trip with friends. Rives depicts both Barbara and Jock as self-absorbed and thoughtless, especially during quarrels. The novel, however, introduces an element completely absent from the Chanler marriage—a baby. Baby Fair becomes yet another point of contention when concerned mother Barbara refuses to leave the recently ill infant to travel to the West with Jock and his friends. Even though Amélie and Archie never had children, she from her youth had considered her writings a kind of offspring. Thus, his attempts to move her away from a public career can be interpreted as a struggle that paralleled the competition for a mother's attention.

As a literary historian has pointed out, Rives uses the example of the Bransbys to show Barbara and Jock how much they share, since both find Godfrey insufferable, narrow, and priggish. Indeed, Rives seems to have fashioned Godfrey along the lines of many of her detractors. Criticizing authors such as Dante Gabriel Rossetti as "unwholesome and unnatural," Godfrey tells his wife, "These overstrained sensations are not what men and women feel nowadays."[43] While Barbara helps Eunice to resist Godfrey's domination and prods him to be more sensitive to his wife's demands, at the story's end Eunice remains married to a cold, rigid man. To be sure, *Barbara Dering* focuses primarily on marriage among the wealthier classes and is silent about women's economic or legal disabilities. Even Amélie's own struggle to maintain her writing career finds no parallel in the novel. Insofar as *Barbara Dering* is social commentary, it tackles personal attitudes and power relationships rather than social and economic structures and inequalities.

Ironically enough, the most compelling relationship in this book about marriage is that of Eunice and Barbara, who candidly discuss their lives and marriages as they support each another. The closeness of the relationship recalls nineteenth-century female friendships recounted by the historian Carroll Smith-Rosenberg. Moreover, this fictional rapport may have drawn some of its inspiration from Rives's own attachment to her female circle. Barbara describes her affinity with Eunice: "We have grown so close during the last weeks that I seem to feel your dear heart beating next to mine." Criticizing her own marriage, Eunice expresses her repugnance at feeling to be "the property of another" and claims that her husband does not even have the excuse of jealousy: "If I could feel that he loved me,—was jealous even; but no, no! It is not that. He merely wishes to domineer, to compel, to master." Eunice then compares herself to "a silly bird that streaks the ceiling with its blood in trying to get out of the room where it is captive. I don't seem to care for anything to-day but my freedom, my freedom, my freedom! I want to be a girl—free—myself!" The intimacy grows as each woman tries to bolster the other. Eunice tells Barbara: "I have never lost my faith in friendship, and now I have you."[44]

Rives also shows some self-knowledge. In a section echoing her essay about girls' need for education about sexuality, Barbara denounces the false modesty encouraged among young women: "We are trained to be hypocrites. We are trained to regard all healthy, natural, vivid impulses as unrefined, unfeminine, immodest." She proceeds to lay out her creed: "Oh, if I had a daughter, I would teach her that passion in love, in religion, in friendship, in patriotism, is a great, pure fire created by God, and not to be scorned by man!" Perhaps best illustrating Rives's self-criticism is her condemnation of mercenary marriages (an adjective that many might have applied to her own): "A woman who errs through love is a nobler creature than her sister who marries for convenience."[45]

Barbara Dering, despite its happy ending in an apparent reconciliation between Jock and Barbara, paints two marriages filled with misery. In fact, the tortures of an unhappy union form the novel's most vivid images. At one point, Eunice tells Barbara: "Sometimes when—when I was first married, . . . I used to stretch out my arms, when I lay awake at night with Godfrey asleep beside me, and I used to think, 'It is like being crucified. This is my cross I am lying on.'"[46]

Particularly self-revelatory is Rives's decision to make both her major female characters her own age and to emphasize that age. Eunice cries: "Look at me as I stand here! I am thirty years old and I have never been loved in my life!" Later, while estranged from Jock, Barbara also muses: "It cannot be that I am only thirty and that life is over for me. . . . I cannot think that it is all over."[47] At that point Jock returns, and a happy reunion—brought about by his determination to be more thoughtful—ensues. Amélie, herself just about to turn thirty, could not foresee such marital bliss.

Barbara Dering was a far more disciplined piece of writing than Rives's earlier works. While the beauty of her two female protagonists lessened their believability, she created two characters in search of better marriages. Some critics believed Rives to be growing as an author. One critic said that "a good deal of the old slushiness has disappeared from the style, which is pleasant news." The review concluded: "There is so much that is clever and original and daring and dramatic about Amélie Rives that her books will always be read." Others were more dismissive. A reviewer who disliked the passionate aspects of *Barbara Dering* remarked that "the courting scenes between her and Dering remind one of two young tiger cats." Even though Rives was developing fuller, less stereotyped characterizations, this sequel held little of the staccato tempo that had vaulted "The Quick or the Dead?" to enormous popularity. *Godey's Lady's Book* found "none of the audacity of 'The Quick or the Dead?'" and predicted "it will be forgotten sooner than that was."[48] Perhaps because Rives stuck to an ending with marital reunion and did not portray heroines who, like Emma Bovary or Anna Karenina, had tragic adulterous affairs, the passion of her heroines would have far less lasting influence in the literary world.

Rives used *Barbara Dering* to testify to the importance of female friend-ship, and her intimate companions continued to be central in her own life. In September, Rives assured Joseph M. Stoddart, her publisher, that "I am correcting the proofs for *Barbara Dering* with the utmost care." Telling him that her next instruction was "*very important,*" Rives asked him to forward a set of "*revised proofs*" to Julia Magruder, then in North Carolina, "as she is going to help me with them, and this is very necessary as a writer overlooks so many things in her own work."[49]

The other novella that Rives published in 1893, *Tanis: The Sang Digger,* like *Virginia of Virginia,* chronicles the choices made by a young white woman from the poorer classes when confronted with the power of sexual attraction. *Tanis* focuses on a young Appalachian woman caught in an abu-sive relationship but offered a chance at a different life. A ginseng gatherer by profession, Tanis has a strong sense of personal honor and is not beautiful. Intrigued by a young idealistic couple who offer her a better life in the valley, Tanis must also cope with the sexual explosiveness of Sam, a handsome, alcoholic backswoodman known for his exploitation of women. When Sam and other mountain men kidnap the middle-class woman Alice Gilman, Tanis secures Alice's release by promising to return to the mountains with Sam and thus forfeit her own future autonomy. One male bystander watching Tanis leave the valley describes her as "a statue of Eve gazing back at the garden of Eden." Although Sam had earlier inspired a passionate response in Tanis, at the book's end she appears emotionally drained.[50] After writing *Tanis,* Rives abandoned the theme of female self-sacrifice that was nobly or religiously motivated; she possibly had come to doubt it.

While Rives in her fictional works was creating happy endings or redemptive sacrifices, her own life was careening out of control. Late in 1892 her dependence on drugs apparently hit the point at which intervention was necessary. Her struggle with opiates, which likely lasted a decade, can best be understood from her 1915 novel, *Shadows of Flames,* which features Cecil Chesney, an addict who is the younger son in an English aristocratic family. Chesney is married to the novel's heroine, Sophy Taliaferro, a young Virginian, whose marriage has become a burden. Ill for the last two years, Cecil puzzles his wife with a condition that interposes "violent interruptions of alternate rage and high spirits" with "long stretches of indifferent apathy."[51] He experiences mood swings and eats little but drinks much.

Even when her friend Olive warns Sophy that her mother-in-law has slandered her by claiming she introduced Cecil to drugs, naive Sophy does not suspect drug usage. In her estimation: "Opium gave wonderful dreams—deep sleep. Morphine was used to quiet delirium." Thus, she reasoned, Cecil's overly excited mania "could not be the effect of either of those drugs." After Cecil falls unconscious from an overdose, Sophy consults with Dr. Carfew, a "nerve specialist" who diagnoses Cecil as a "morphinomaniac." The doctor spells out that Cecil "is so addicted to the drug that he varies the effect with cocaine—takes them alternately—both drugs hypodermically."[52]

Rives's explanation for the onset of Cecil's addiction likely resembled her own introduction to opiates. When Cecil on a voyage was suffering from a daylong violent headache, a doctor injected him with morphine, warning that it should be taken only under a physician's supervision. Reasoning that doctors "prescribe a bit of heaven—then order you to stay snug in hell," Chesney, upon returning to London, "bought a fitted hypodermic-syringe— that is, a little case containing a syringe, needles, and tiny bottles of morphia, apo-morphia, strychnine, and cocaine." Chesney then turns to cocaine and alcohol, particularly brandy, "in the time of great weakness . . . after the morphine."[53]

The moods of the "morphomaniac are very inconsistent," Rives writes. Sometimes the addicted person "agonised over this degrading vice which was slowly sapping his manhood and self-respect." At other times he was entirely callous about others and cared only about procuring drugs. Especially vivid is her depiction of the boundless determination of the addict to obtain the drugs. Cecil calmly manipulates and tricks his wife and valet to feed his drug habit. Cecil's nurse tells Sophy, "If the angel Gabriel was given me for a morphia patient, *I'd pluck his wings*—for fear he'd hide the nasty stuff among the feathers!"[54]

Rives convincingly depicts Chesney's physical and mental tortures during withdrawal and his relapses. When he first is slowly weaned from the drug at his country home, his vigilant nurse, who estimates it will take six weeks to clear his system, has to leave after two weeks to care for her ill parent. By the nurse's return, Cecil has begun to self-dose with morphine and cocaine from a hidden cache. A two-month stay in a sanatorium then cleanses his system. Even after Cecil joins his wife at Lake Maggiore in Italy, a vigorous day of sailing leaves him chilled with intense pains in his legs and back, which provide an excuse to return to morphine, though he is at first cautious.[55] All through his short life, Cecil's ability to resist the lure of morphine seems weak, a shakiness that paralleled Rives's own experience with drug addiction. Her solution to this character is to kill him—in an accidental drowning rather than a drug overdose.

Rives's health and emotional well-being were deteriorating in 1892. She visited Hot Springs, Arkansas, in the winter of 1892–93, accompanied by her mother, Lutie Pleasants, and longtime servant Martha Jane Bullock. Lutie described the doctor's diagnosis: "He says Amélie is full of Malaria, and has taken cold, but above all the condition of her nerves is the chief trouble." That the problem with her "nerves" correlated with renewed drug usage was revealed by the next intervention: hospitalization in a sanitarium. In March 1893 Archie described Amélie as too unwell to answer her correspondence; by May she was at the Philadelphia sanitarium of Dr. S. Weir Mitchell, a prominent neurologist of the day—an experience Rives may have later used to depict Cecil's stay in a similar institution. Mitchell became best known for what he popularized as the "rest cure." Generally prescribed for the nervous disorder neurasthenia, defined as a physical and emotional breakdown, the rest cure involved nonstressful tasks such as painting and a great deal of sleep, reclining, and eating, all intended to make the patient gain weight and thus strengthen the nerves. Charlotte Perkins Gilman's fictional treatment of her own experience with Mitchell and the rest cure in "The Yellow Wallpaper" (first published in the *New England Magazine* in January 1892) has introduced it to modern readers. Gilman's story follows the narrator as the confinement and idleness of the sanitarium slowly pull her into hallucinations and insanity.[56]

Although Dr. Mitchell was among the physicians who asserted that women had a special nervous system that could be damaged by too much exertion, mental or physical, he apparently made exceptions for his more intellectually inclined female patients. A novelist himself, he admired creative patients, such as Edith Wharton, who complained that during her rest cure with him, he pressured her to add additional characters to her novels. It seems likely that Mitchell discussed literature with Amélie; perhaps he even gave her a copy of his own novel, *Characteristics,* published in 1892. Although some historians point to the way that the rest cure defined female ambition and activity as abnormal, at least one scholar has stated that Mitchell resorted to a variety of strategies for dealing with women's nervous disorders, and in some cases, he did not dampen their intellectual drive and activities.[57]

Rives never directly commented, in letters or stories, on her own time at Mitchell's sanitarium. Her brother-in-law Wintie Chanler speculated about the regime: "Amélie is with Weir Mitchell in Philadelphia, . . . They say he makes her get up at 7 a.m. & scrub the floor." No one ever described Amélie so much as lifting a finger to clean or cook, and Wintie himself gave little credence to the rumor. "I don't believe it, for they also say that he goes about attesting to her matchless charm. Rats! Doctors are all old women." Insofar as Rives's stay made it into the news, one item reported that after six weeks in Dr. Mitchell's sanitarium, "Mrs. Chanler returns home this week completely cured from a nervous depression." From her stay, Amélie forged an ongoing relationship with Mitchell's colleague, Dr. J. Madison Taylor. Over the next few years he frequently visited her at Castle Hill, most likely when her dependence on opiates peaked.[58]

Rives, with her health improving, rented a home for the summer of 1893 at Little Boar's Head, a seaside resort near North Hampton, New Hampshire.

Her veiled remark to Archie hints at her opinion of the rest cure. "You can't think how delightful it is to be free as I am here," she wrote. "No one trying to guide or advise me in any particular path except that of health. I feel more myself in some ways than for ages—but still *very* weak & lots of rheumatism." Perhaps in reaction to weeks of enforced inactivity in the sanitarium, she spent much of her day outdoors, whether riding in a carriage or sailing on a little catboat with a skipper and her friends. According to a Boston paper, she had resumed writing: "It is said that when the whim seizes her she spends a whole day at her desk dashing off a story, poem or play."[59]

In 1893 Amélie and Archie were often apart—partly because of his growing interest in creating a model industrial village at Roanoke Rapids in North Carolina and in developing a self-threading device for sewing machines. Even when Archie tried to please Amélie, as when he gave her a beautiful mare for Christmas, things went awry. Amélie apologized: "Somehow darling boy, I feel that I couldn't or didn't make you understand how dear and generous it was of you, to give me the lovely, lovely mare." She then assured him: "I shall love her all the more because you first rode her & had her & then gave her to your Amy." Yet she undercut this conciliatory note when, in asking whether they could soon ride together, she made togetherness seem more obligation than affection: "I am trying to do my duty, or rather I am deliciously *glad* to do my duty. I love you darling & you are good to me & make me happy. God bless you & your Amy in this His year *1894*."[60]

That year of 1894 would be a turning point in Rives's life. As she tried to break her dependence on drugs, Dr. Taylor came to Castle Hill four times between January and April. At some point, Archie decided to buy Edgefield, a house and land near Castle Hill, which he came to call Merrie Mills. By summer he was transferring much of the furniture purchased for himself and Amélie at Castle Hill to his new lodgings. Reporting that the bedroom furniture had been moved, Rives encouraged this step: "Our only difference of opinion in this matter, as far as I can see, is, that I do not even wish a '*fairish* division of the chattels.' I really have no use for them, and, in fact, I'd rather think of Castle-Hill as looking like its quaint, bare old self."[61]

Amélie's decisions about where to spend the summer of 1894 caused greater friction with Archie, whose business and reform interests were taking him to London. When Amélie, from Paris, informed Archie, then ill in London, of her plans to visit London but not stay with him, he apparently remonstrated that people would talk if they did not share the same hotel.

Amélie Rives, simply dressed, autographed this photograph, taken by the English firm James Russell and Sons, in 1894. (Amélie Rives Troubetzkoy Collection, The Valentine)

She rather huffily replied: "Now about people 'talking'—They would talk much more, I assure you, if I broke engagements which I have up to the 10th of July, & *left you ill in London, remaining myself in Paris* [Paris double underlined]!!!"[62] She proposed that she and her party (her maid and a female friend) stay in the hotel where Archie was located but in a different suite for an evening; the three of them would then move to the lodgings she had secured.

In this period during 1893 and 1894, female friendship seemed to remain as important for Rives as for her character Barbara Dering. At Little Boar's Head in New England, she was surrounded not only by her sisters and sisters-in-law but also by her dear friends Julia Magruder and Lutie

Pleasants. Amélie had also been making new friends, one of whom was the poet and Boston socialite Louise Chandler Moulton, who spent summers in Europe, primarily in England. By July that attachment was already deepening as Rives wrote Moulton from Paris and described the pomp and emotion of the funeral of the assassinated French president Marie François Sadi Carnot. At the end of "a terribly fatiguing day spent in watching the phenomenal funeral procession of poor Carnot," Rives told Moulton, "it gives me a feeling of deep peace and rest when I think of your love for me, and of how soon I shall see you." On July 6, the day that they had chosen to meet, Rives was the guest of honor at Moulton's weekly reception in London, attended by the English social and literary elite. A wealthy young American woman who attended these soirées in 1894 called the guests "[Mrs. Moulton's] usual menagerie," probably because of the mixture of affluent Americans and Britons, writers and poets.[63] The friendship with Moulton helped to extend Rives's ties to the Anglo-American literary elite.

An even more momentous event occurred that summer in London when Amélie first encountered Pierre Troubetzkoy, a portrait painter and son of an exiled Russian prince. As a young Virginia friend of Rives later re-created the scene: Oscar Wilde "made a special point of interrupting the two in their conversations with other people because, he said, they must meet. He did not explain why, but it was undoubtedly because that aesthete of aesthetes had decided that they were the two most beautiful persons at the party. They met again shortly in Wilde's house."[64]

Troubetzkoy, whose mother, Ada Winans, had been an American opera singer, combined many of the qualities that Rives found most exciting. Tall— well over six feet—and athletic, he had grown up in northern Italy. As the oldest of Ada's three sons with Prince Pyotr Troubetzkoy, Pierre had been born out of wedlock. Pyotr, after a divorce from his first wife, married Ada and apparently legitimated their children. Interested in botany, he created beautiful gardens at their home Villa Ada in Ghiffa on Lake Maggiore. Pierre combined dark good looks, aristocratic ancestors, and European manners with wide-ranging interests in culture and art. He and his brother Paul were both quite artistic—the latter became a well-known sculptor. Contemporary observers called Pierre kind, gentle, thoughtful—attributes that must have appealed to Amélie after the volatility and unpredictability of Archie.[65]

Rives's meeting with Troubetzkoy seems indeed to have been electric. Soon he was painting her portrait. Amélie, on her part, was writing her dear

Pierre Troubetzkoy's good looks and dashing manner are apparent in this portrait from 1894 when Rives first met him. (Library of Congress)

friend Louise Moulton: "Don't you want to go with me to Troubetzkoy's studio some morning or afternoon? If you could look in tomorrow at any time after three, just for a few moments—say for twenty minutes or half an hour, I'm sure he'd love to have you, & somehow I *do* [double underline] so want you to know him."[66]

After the portrait was finished, the relationship with Troubetzkoy deepened. Evidence for this courtship survives only from shreds of commentary from the outside, because late in life Amélie burned every piece of their correspondence. That summer, Oscar Wilde informed his friend and lover Lord Alfred Douglas: "I lunched with Prince Troubetzkoy and Mrs Chanler this afternoon. He has done a lovely picture of her, and would do a beautiful one of you."[67] Wilde added that Troubetzkoy was "going down to the Batterseas to finish his portrait of Cyril but will be back in the autumn."[68] This visit may have been the occasion when Troubetzkoy introduced Rives to Cyril Flower, Lord Battersea, a Liberal member of Parliament, and his wife, Constance de Rothschild Flower. Lady Battersea, who was very active in reform causes such as temperance, women's rights, and prison reform, later remembered Pierre Troubetzkoy as "a great friend of ours": "he had a handsome face, with a good, kind expression, and his manner and manners were perfect." During a visit at the country home of Lord and Lady Battersea near Norfolk, Rives also met the British novelist and poet George Meredith, known for his realist novels such as *The Egoist* and *The Ordeal of Richard Feverel.* According to Lady Battersea, Meredith "gave as his opinion that hardly any woman had produced a first-rate novel, not even Jane Austen, Charlotte Bronte, or George Eliot, whose names we brandished triumphantly before him." Rives, in Lady Battersea's account, "heaved a sigh, less in conscious acquiescence to her own shortcomings than in sorrow that so great a genius should commit such an error in judgment."[69]

By September 1894 Rives was visiting Ada Troubetzkoy, the prince's widowed mother, in Ghiffa. Rives had reached the point where decisions were necessary, and the very fact of her visit suggests that she and Pierre were considering the next step. Archie had been very generous to her, her friends, and family. Had the time arrived when she needed to tell Archie that she had found her "Hearts-Desire" and needed a divorce?

Sometime during her time abroad, Rives's ambitions to become a great writer and philanthropist encountered major barriers. Her husband had encouraged her career in art and had become very active himself, not only in sponsoring young artists, but in planning for his ideal mill village in North Carolina. Yet even as Rives was learning to navigate the intellectual swim, she may have been remaking some of her ambitions. Though George Curzon discouraged her from publishing her poems, she continued to write and to publish, even some of her older works. In keeping with her desire to be a public intellectual, she contributed both fiction and nonfiction that supported the rising tide of women's personal rights. She was publicizing some aspects of the autonomy that the "New Woman" wanted, even though she not had publicly identified with or supported the organized forms of women's rights. Instead Rives wrote in favor of companionate marriage and female education, self-expression, and empowerment.

Even as Rives was becoming a more polished writer, her earlier decision to make a financially advantageous marriage had turned into a gigantic problem. Critiquing marriage in *Barbara Dering* allowed her to confront the wreck of her own personal life. She wanted to follow her muse, but a dependence on drugs was making that increasingly difficult. At age thirty, much like her female protagonists in *Barbara Dering*, Rives had come to question what lay before her. Her addiction to morphine and cocaine meant that breaking free would be a long, difficult process. As she looked toward her career and a new love, she also examined her public image and worked to create a new one that better fit her own view of herself and her goals.

· SEVEN ·

"The Most Beautiful Woman in Literature"

Images of Beauty, Celebrity, and Genius

As Rives looked back on the first decade of her career as an author, she could see a flood of reports covering her writings, appearance, and activities. She had entered publishing at a time when magazines had become an important part of social and intellectual life; the popularity and notoriety of her first book as well as her own unorthodox actions had made her a frequent topic in newspapers and periodicals. As daily journals became an important part of American life, coast to coast, they reached for information, often human-interest stories, to involve male and female readers. Rives and her editors at times sought that attention and worked to create a profile, yet both stereotypes and sensationalism would play a part in the changing image that emerged.

In 1886 no one could have predicted that Amélie Rives would take the literary world by storm. An assiduous reader at that time would have seen a few references to stories by this young female writer and some items about her youth and beauty.[1] Yet in 1887 her name began to show up in literary magazines, and a year later, these mentions turned into a torrent. In fact, the publication of "The Quick or the Dead?" in the spring of 1888 and its reception by both readers and irate critics forever changed Amélie Rives's life. It advertised her as an author, even though her fame lay partly in her celebrity and notoriety rather than the quality of her publications. In 1888 and 1889 she became the subject of gossip, jokes, and other trivia in newspapers, big and small. A *Boston Globe* columnist in 1888, for example, facetiously wrote that an (imaginary) interview with her revealed "that her doctor forbids her to drink anything alcoholic and that everything she has written was the emanation of her own brain, without the slightest assistance from stimulants." He added his punch line: "I wonder what the dear girl would write if she was well braced with brandy and soda."[2]

161

Amélie Rives was creating both a literary persona and a life as a celebrity. Although she very much liked to appear artless, she was not. Moreover, her personal goals, social life, and literary career often collided, and many of her choices had negative repercussions both on the quality of her work and on the tenor of its reception. Even as the great popularity of "The Quick or the Dead?," first as a magazine article, then as a novella, flashed Rives's name across America, she had been building her life in the public eye. But the image that emerged over the two years before her marriage would soon change. Her earlier interactions with Thomas Nelson Page and with various editors had shown her trying to construct her persona as a modern literary woman. Her best-selling novella and her marriage made her a celebrity— and thus known for being herself rather than for any specific achievement. Even though the nineteenth century had seen celebrities appearing in the literary, theater, and even social world, Rives had little guidance to help her handle her notoriety.[3] Later, with the help of Archie Chanler, she apparently attempted to influence the newspapers by granting interviews and planting notices, but at first she had limited control over her publicity.

The character of Amélie Rives that first appeared in papers and magazines was a composite of what she wished to be, how she wished to appear, and what those organs thought would sell their issues. In addition to critiquing her writing, newspapers at first focused on her youth, beauty, southern ancestry, and "genius." They wrote about her love of animals, nature, and the outdoors, and in varying ways chronicled her flouting of social conventions. Over time, the papers moved to different stereotypes: Amélie as eccentric genius or hysterical, overwrought lady authoress. At the same time as the fashioning of Rives's image slipped even more out of her control, she was also trying to balance her various ambitions with her duties and obligations as the wife of a very wealthy man. This chapter explores her changing image and the interactions between her celebrity, her literary career, and her marriage during the first decade of her writing career.

Rives might appear in a newspaper for several reasons. While journals reported actual events such as marriages, speeches, and deaths that involved public figures, they also published notices and reviews of novels and other published work. In addition, the papers of that day contained many items of random information. Literary figures were often grouped together, with facts about their education, relatives, place of residence, or even monies earned. Female writers, while sometimes included among the males, were more frequently bunched together, with an emphasis on their appearance, marital status, and social activities. Female authors were often covered in the woman's pages, on the assumption that their activities, like their writings, mainly interested other women.[4] As newspapers stressed fashion in their woman's sections, they sometimes used the more fashionable female authors as examples. Reputation, personal behavior, appearance, and other issues often inflected or obscured an author's publications.

At the beginning of Rives's writing career, the newspapers emphasized her youth. One item described her at the time of the publication of "A Brother to Dragons" as "a young girl living in a Virginia country house." A newspaper in Maine called her story in *Lippincott's* "the long-expected novel by this brilliant young genius, who has sprung so suddenly into fame through her poems and short stories." Sometimes the squibs lowered Amélie's age to make her appear even younger. An article in the *Richmond Dispatch* in 1895 noted, "She early showed a taste for literature, and at the age of 15 published a sonnet in the Century Magazine" (while Rives claimed to have written some of her early poems at that age, she was actually twenty-two when the sonnet was published).[5]

Perhaps buttressing that image of innocent youthfulness, newspapers in the 1880s also described her as the young woman from the countryside—a persona that Amélie desired or at least thought helpful. Replying to Alice W. Rollins, a critic for various journals who was apparently preparing a notice, Rives misrepresented her upbringing and conveniently suppressed the decade spent in Mobile: "You see I am a genuine country-lass, having lived for the most part of my life among these rubescent banks and meadows of my native state. Indeed for three years past, winter and summer I have been here. And oh! how long the winters seem. And how lonely." She then added a literary touch to her isolation: "I feel as though my home were then part of a little landslip, after the fashion of the one in [Jules] Verne's 'Journey to the Sun.' That we were revolving (so to speak) on an axis of our own, & the big world with its voices and stirring, were way apart somewhere in space."[6]

A story in February 1888 indicated that Rives lived "in practical seclusion on her father's large farm near Cobham, Albermarle [*sic*] county, Virginia" and that "Miss Rives is said to be indifferent to the allurements of society." During that spring, other reports described her as friendly yet aloof from society. A New York reporter declared in May that "she has a charmingly frank way of making strangers feel comfortable. To those who know her well she is a delightful companion and sincere friend. She is not at all spoiled by her success." The following month a Chicago paper maintained: "She is very sensitive and retiring, dislikes notoriety, and cares nothing for society. She is devoted to writing and painting, and has a most enthusiastic circle of friends."[7] Similarly, a June 1888 article in the *Richmond Times,* while noting Amélie's links to that city, described her as practically a recluse: "That she incurred some adverse criticism at that time was natural, for she scarcely ever appeared on the street, declined to receive visitors, except in the evening, and even then it was said, was not particularly careful to conceal her indifference."[8]

Side by side with such vignettes were those touting Rives as "a woman of remarkable and conspicuous genius," as an Atlanta newspaper put it. In keeping with this notion of untutored ability, a Richmond paper reported that "Amelie Rives never went to school, but had governesses who guided rather than taught her." The papers put forward as a mark of her genius her ability to write quickly and well. Stories were represented as flying off her pen rather than being reworked many times. The *New Orleans Picayune,* in a long 1887 piece, asserted: "It is said in the most delightfully gossipy way, that she has trunks full of manuscripts that have never seen the light of an editor's study, and that when she wants a new story, a poem or drama to send off to a magazine, all she has to do is to go to the attic and fish one out of her trunk; that she butters her bread with poems, and instead of 'golden syrup' spreads stories on the white lids of her Virginia beaten biscuits."[9]

This genius apparently coexisted with a strong work ethic. A February 1888 story described her as "an indefatigable worker" who "is capable of producing acceptable manuscript at a remarkable rate of speed. When she begins a story she throws her whole existence into the work." Another item noted her alleged ability to "write as many hours with a rapidity and exactness well nigh inconceivable." Amélie herself helped to spread the notion of her writing as flying off the page when she informed a reporter that writing "A Brother to Dragons" had required only two evenings "because I liked to write and because I had the story in my mind." Accounts of her artistic ability similarly pointed to her work ethic. A Denver paper marveled: "Art divides her time with literature, she sometimes spending ten hours in her studio or else engaged the same number of hours with her pen."[10]

Love of animals, the outdoors, athleticism, and sport were often grouped together in the coverage of Rives in the spring of 1888. A San Francisco paper described her as "very fond of horses and dogs" and declared that she "spends much time in the open air, either riding or walking." According to a Kansas paper, "She knows all the woodland haunts about her home, and is in close acquaintance with horses, dogs, and dumb bells." The *Atlanta Journal* reprinted a story from the *New York Mail* that described Rives as "a graceful equestrian" who "delights in long rambles."[11]

Amélie loved not only the outdoors but also outdoor exercise. One newspaper article noted that she was "passionately fond of horses and dogs, whose pedigree she notes with the accuracy of a fancier. For recreation she drives a tandem team about the picturesque roads in the neighborhood of her home." After speculating about whether "Amelie Rives is somewhat responsible for" the growing popularity of horseback riding, an article in the *Chicago Tribune* added: "Her heroines spend most of their time riding thoroughbreds through rain-storms, beating refractory dogs over the head, or rescuing their lover's favorite coursers from burning barns." As for Amélie herself: "she has always loved horses, can ride like an Apache Indian, and is a lover of races and other sports of the South." Another newspaper piece allowed that "her usual exercise is taken on horseback, dashing at breakneck speed along the roads."[12]

Such reports portrayed Amélie as a paragon of health. While private letters by and about Amélie described a young woman who was often ill, sometimes severely, no hint of such ailments can be found in the early accounts. One newspaper described her as "in the most radient [*sic*] health, and in spirits as brimful of life as any girl in all Virginia." Moreover, "She is an excellent tennis player and handles an oar with ease and grace. She loves outdoor life, and knows how to take care of her health as well as she knows how to write stories." Rives herself, in her novel *Barbara Dering*, depicted its eponymous heroine as a woman who could "ride half-broken colts, train a dog thoroughly, keep a shuttlecock up to a thousand, swim, run, and jump like a boy."[13]

The most frequent comments in the press about Rives for well over a decade concerned her appearance. Back in 1886, when she had only published a story and two poems, the *Staunton* [Va.] *Spectator* reprinted a brief item where she "is described as very beautiful, and having a face 'like a Madonna before she knew her seven sorrows.'" "There is but one opinion about her beauty," opined a writer in April 1888. In 1889 the *New York Times* agreed that "whatever the varying opinions may be in regard to Amélie Rives as a writer, there can be but one verdict in regard to her beauty." As a corollary to her attractiveness, the press depicted Rives as particularly marriageable, as indeed "overwhelmed with offers of marriage since her portrait was published recently."[14]

Early in Rives's career, before her face became well known, the newspapers mingled fact and misinformation about her appearance. One paper, after incorrectly noting her as "tall," called her "slender and graceful; a perfect blonde and very pretty." An 1888 story was wildly wrong in most of its description: "Her features are as regular as if cut in cameo; her complexion is a delightfully rich olive, and heavy masses of blue black hair crown her shapely head. Her eyes are dark and brilliant, and are shaded by long curling lashes."[15]

This emphasis on beauty played out in various ways. Much of this reporting formed part of a more general interest among newspapers in the physical appearance of literary ladies; they often treated Amélie as a member of the growing group of female writers or "authoresses." Long a visible though reviled group—after all, Hawthorne's famous disparaging remark about the "damn'd mob of scribbling women" had been made in the 1850s—female authors in post–Civil War America were both slighted and patronized. Much of the attention they received dealt with their appearance, behavior, or private life. The *Washington Post,* in an article subtitled "Female Writers Improving in Personal Appearance," decided: "Time was when all literary women were supposed to be homely. To-day beauty is becoming fashionable in the clan." The writer listed Rives second among six female writers who were "all handsome women." The journalist Kate Field in 1892 compared Rives to a goddess, calling her a "Psyche in appearance and as charming in manner as in face." She ventured that Rives was among the modern women writers who were "upsetting the old picture of fright and slatternly dressing which a past generation religiously believed went hand in hand with alleged female intellect."[16]

Newspapers also tended to class beauties and other female celebrities with actresses, whose profession and behavior still held unsavory connotations of licentiousness. A gossip columnist in the fall of 1888 described Amélie at Newport: "Her manner was confident, her talk was emphatic, and I cannot better describe her general demeanor than to say that it was exactly like that of most actresses in the drawing room." A few months later, a newspaper commented on the efforts of Rives's publisher to place portraits of her in stores along Broadway. Although the item admitted that the "portraits are admirably executed and framed in good taste," it also compared Rives to two well-known actresses, Cora Potter and Lillie Langtry, who had either married or bedded the elite: "Amelie Rives is being starred in a fashion that ought to cause the keenest pangs of jealousy to enter the souls of Mrs. Potter and Mrs. Langtry."[17]

Quite early, some hints of eccentricity appeared regarding Rives as a "lady authoress." A story about female authors, for example, called Rives "as whimsical about the pens she uses and the small notions about her writing table as she is about her attire and the circumstances under which she receives her guests." At their lightest, such reports suggested tardiness or artificiality. "Amelie Rives has never been known to keep an engagement at the hour named," according to a Kansas paper in April 1888, yet she "is nevertheless a great favorite among her friends." A more fanciful and even mildly racy story concerned a Washington gentleman who presented his letter of introduction to her, only to be told that she would see him at 10 p.m. "He was conducted to a tent on the lawn, lighted by Japanese lanterns, where, in full evening costume, Miss Rives bade him welcome. . . . he swears that the conversation that ensued and the impression he received more than repaid him for the long journey and the weary wait."[18]

Soon, wilder stories began to circulate. The *New Orleans Picayune,* even before the notoriety of "The Quick or the Dead?," gossiped that "stories are told of her libations of cold tea, when writing; of the lovely nude portrait of herself, painted by herself; of her wit, grace, raillery, millinery, of her pathos, Paris gowns, and Pingat bonnets, enough to convince the most skeptical that Amelie Rives is a most remarkable young woman, gifted, beautiful and a genius." The columnist concluded: "As for me, the woman who wrote the beautiful story of 'Inja' may ride bare-backed horses from Cape May to Cape Mendocino, drink cold tea by the gallon, smoke cigarettes like a furnace, if only she will keep on writing stories like 'Inja' that make one the better and the softer and the kinder for the reading."[19] This piece was remarkable not only for its early account of Rives's unconventional and socially unacceptable behavior, such as posing nude, riding bareback, and smoking cigarettes, but also for its suggestion that she wore expensive clothes by exclusive French designers. Given that Rives was an unmarried young woman of good family, the story was explosive.

At least one journal suggested that she had purposefully engineered her fame. A review in *Current Literature,* noting that "The Quick or the Dead?"

had increased interest in her other stories, asked: "Can it be that she wrote her inflammatory novel to that end? If so, she has more cleverness than we have given her credit for." It is unlikely that Rives expected "The Quick or the Dead?" to receive the sort of attention it did, but she and her publishers did try to generate publicity that would sell books and magazines. In 1893 one paper indicated that J. M. Stoddart, editor of *Lippincott's*, had invented the technique of presenting a novel complete in one magazine. "To him belongs a large share of the glory of inventing Amelie Rives," the notice concluded.[20]

The publishers of Rives's books and stories promoted their list of authors in several ways; announcements of new and forthcoming books formed regular parts of many newspapers and leading magazines. Rives apparently received a special level of promotion, as the publishers sought to use her appearance to sell her stories by including a picture of her as the frontispiece of many of her books and magazine issues. As early as May 1887, *Harper's New Monthly Magazine* printed a portrait of Amélie to accompany one of her stories. *Cosmopolitan* did the same in 1891 when it published the serialized version of "According to St. John" with a frontispiece that "is an excellent portrait of the young author, who has gained so much notoriety." In addition to the head shots that adorned her publications, Rives also posed for other photographs to emblazon her image on the mind of America. An item from Richmond in April 1889, shortly before Rives left for Europe, described a photographic session: "Mrs. Chanler had her pictures taken at a gallery here the other day in a number of unique positions. In most of the photos she is dressed in long flowing garments and sits or lies in graceful style. . . . Another style represents her in street costume with a long cape, and in half a dozen others one of her collies which she brought with her from Castle Hill, is seen."[21] Contemporaries may have justifiably believed that Rives loved both the camera and the resulting photographs in which she appeared before the public.

Archie Chanler seems to have helped manage Rives's publicity and promoted her celebrity interviews. In the fall of 1888, as she traveled with Archie to New York, Amélie received the public and press both in Washington, D.C., and New York. In February 1889 she granted an audience to Walter Wellman, a well-known journalist at the *Chicago Tribune*. In the puff piece that followed, Wellman gave a "key" to "The Quick or the Dead?," explaining that Rives was choosing between the real-life Archie and her girlhood

From the latest photograph

Carrying the caption "From the latest photograph," this portrait of Amélie Rives formed the frontispiece of *According to St. John,* published in 1891. (Library of Virginia)

dreams of the ideal husband and lover. The article also testified to her charm and beauty.[22]

Knowing that Chanler and Rives would scrutinize his published interview, Wellman sent a copy to Archie soon afterward. The newspaperman asserted that he was "almost afraid to mail you this paper, but when Mrs. Chanler and yourself consider the friendly spirit in which I wrote I am sure you will forgive some of the liberties I took, and some of the errors I made." In any case, "already I have reason to believe the article has done good, for I have seen it approvingly copied or mentioned in a number of newspapers and journals." Wellman put forward his own view of Amélie's celebrity: "You must consider she is in a certain sense a public character, as is every woman or man of genius and achievement. Notoriety and discussion, unpleasant of course to all of you, are nevertheless unavoidable, and not always disadvantageous." After avowing his intention to become one of Amélie's "knights," Wellman closed his letter with yet another tribute: "Ever since my return from Castle Hill I have talked of little but the genius, beauty and sweetness of Mrs. Chanler."[23]

At the beginning of her fame, publications frequently referred to Amélie Rives as a southerner and representative of southern literature. Southern newspapers often claimed her as a daughter of the region. For example, in April 1888 the *Atlanta Constitution* subtitled a piece about Rives, "The Young Southern Authoress as Viewed on Her Native Heath." Other magazines and newspapers alluded to her southern or Virginian origins. The *Morning Oregonian* carried a story about Rives as a belle: "Miss Amelie Rives had a host of admirers when she lived in maiden meditation at the home of her ancestors, Castle Hill, Virginia." In 1891 the same paper speculated that Augusta Evans Wilson, a popular southern novelist of the Civil War era, "is said to be loathe to welcome Amelie Rives as a rival in Southern literature."[24]

Amélie seems to have used African American characters to present herself as a southern aristocrat who had retainers from antebellum days. Although not a crusader for racial justice, she avoided the racist diatribes that were all too common in that day. In her daily life, she expected to enjoy the privileges of her class and race and relied on both to make herself appear more refined. The *Washington Post* noted about one of her photographs from a Richmond session: "The most striking one is that in which the authoress is lying on a couch, with closed eyes, while a colored maid stands behind and bends over her."[25]

Whether Amélie and her publicists consciously used relationships with African Americans to make her appear more aristocratic and unusual, or the newspapers themselves manufactured such incidents, the effect was the same: Rives was pictured as a benevolent southerner of the old school. An item in the *Washington Post* in 1891 recounted a visit to Castle Hill by "Aunt Polly," an elderly Black woman described as a neighbor's "mammy." Amélie was "indisposed" but had been receiving callers in her "sleeping apartment," and Aunt Polly was the last of the day. Not only did Amélie give Aunt Polly some "pin money," but also insisted on driving her home in the carriage. To be sure, in keeping with Virginia racial etiquette, Aunt Polly sat with Colin, the carriage driver, while "de ladies sot on de back seat

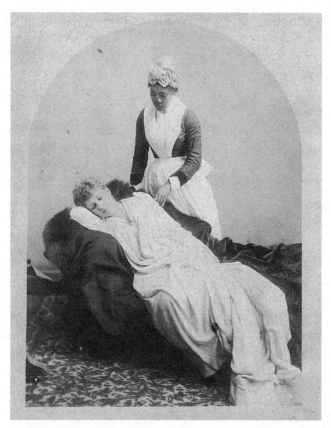

The photograph taken in Richmond early in 1889 shows how
Amélie Rives portrayed herself as a Virginia aristocrat who en-
joyed special care from an African American servant. (Amélie
Rives Troubetzkoy Collection, The Valentine)

and dey driv me clean home." The article omitted surnames for the African
Americans, making them appear to harken back to the days of slavery. While
the narrative resembled one of Thomas Nelson Page's stories in its use of
an aged Black storyteller to wax eloquent about the virtues of an aristocratic
white person, it included some touches that suggest that an actual incident
had inspired it, including a mention of Martha Jane Bullock, Amélie's long-
term servant, as well as Collin Byrd, the carriage driver at Castle Hill.[26]

Other newspaper items also utilized Rives's African American servants
to indicate her aristocratic southern origins. A report on her studies in Paris
in 1890 cited various comments from her fellow students, including "they

say that she brought her old black negro mammy across the waters with her and that this old woman looks after her as if she were a baby." Similarly, a mention of Rives's return from Europe in 1891 described the party that disembarked and hurried to the Castle Hill as including "the old colored woman Martha, who is an ex-slave and the favorite domestic of the brilliant young writer."[27]

Even though a New Orleans organ had alluded in 1887 to possible nude self-portraits, newspapers generally became bolder after Rives became both a best-selling scandalous writer and a married woman. In part, this fits with Michael Trotti's conclusion that southern journals—the Virginia newspapers in his study—were careful in their reporting about young, unmarried white women to present them as spotless "ladies." Rives's fame and notoriety, however, seemed to allow reporters greater latitude to focus on activities that they presented as deviant. Some of this new attention related, or even invented, eccentric or odd behavior, such as the accounts of her wearing "digitated" boots that featured separate toes. Similarly, in November 1888 a Washington paper announced: "Amelie Rives Chanler . . . recently appeared in public with her hair let down behind and parted into two equal strands, which were drawn over her shoulders and fastened in front by a ribbon. Strange to say, this peculiar and original way of wearing the hair was eminently becoming to Mrs. Chanler. It formed a kind of hirsute frame for her beautiful face and caused favorable comment from even very conservative women who were present."[28] These bizarre accounts displeased Rives. In late November 1888, she sent her publisher a request, republished in the newspapers, that he deny as "absolutely false" the reports that "[I wear] 'digitated boots,' tie my hair under my chin, and appear at theatres in large hats ornamented with lilac plumes." "Really, if it were not all so idiotic," she fumed, "one might be tempted to get indignant."[29]

Earlier that August a newspaper offered a vignette that during the preceding summer, the then-unmarried Rives, on vacation in Massachusetts, had hired a dory piloted by a "half-grown, somewhat stupid fisher lad" and remained away until dusk. When searchers pulled alongside the boat, they found that "Miss Rives . . . lay at full length extended on the cushions in the boat, her long hair unbound, eyes closed and wild roses strewn over her in profusion." Rather than having encountered foul play, she was reenacting the legendary voyage of Elaine, the lily maid of Astolat, who perished from unrequited love for Sir Lancelot. While it is unclear whether Rives had even

The Princess of Albemarle

traveled to coastal Massachusetts during her Newport visit in 1887, such a tale held a certain plausibility because of her love of British legend and her theatrical self-presentation.[30]

In the summer and fall of 1888, papers carried stories that Rives's confirmation into the Episcopal Church had been unorthodox. Pleading illness, she missed the group ceremony and asked the bishop to confirm her at her home. In the version in the *Chicago Tribune,* the bishop, on being ushered into the parlor, "found an altar draped in virgin white and decorated with flowers." Then entered "the sensational Amélie attired in long flowing white garments with angel sleeves which fell to the hem of her gown, and all her hair let down and combed out to float picturesquely about her. She glided forward and fell upon her knees at the good Bishop's feet." Despite his discomfiture, the bishop proceeded with the confirmation, and according to the *Tribune,* "Amélie had the gratification of having a special function all to herself and being as different from other people as circumstances would permit."[31] Thus the account of a religious ceremony became a way to comment on her histrionic and self-dramatizing actions.

Rives clearly read newspaper clippings about herself and was aware of the coverage. In 1888, for example, she declared, "I wish you would do one thing—contradict the absurd story of my confirmation." She claimed that being ill the day of the ceremony and being advised by her doctor not to undergo it, she asked to have the rite at her home. "I was so weak my father and mother had to support me as I stood at the table with the Bishop. . . . There were no candles or anything of that sort, and all the foundation there is for the story of the robe is the fact that I happened to wear a white tea-gown."[32]

If eccentricity or love of the limelight came to the fore in some accounts, others highlighted different character deficiencies. An article in 1889 alleged that "Amelie Rives, who has suddenly become one of the highest priced of writers, spends almost all her earnings in dressmaker's and jeweler's bills." Other items conflated her character with her writings. The *St. Paul Daily Globe* in August 1888 declared, "The evident difficulty with Miss Rives is that she is morbid or immature, and that if it is morbidness, it arises from a diseased stomach or an unbalanced mind." The writer argued, "If she were a man, the reading public might seize upon her (or him) and administer physical reproof that would be efficacious," adding rather bitterly that "gallantry forbids aught but courteous criticism of works whose general treatment of what we cherish dearest in life is demoralizing and bad."[33]

Some newspaper coverage took a more scandalous turn. A *New York Sun* journalist, Nellie Bly, then famous as an investigative reporter, retailed a story, supposedly heard from one of Rives's "life-long friends," of an alleged relationship between Amélie and the Irish-born actor John McCullough, deceased since 1885. Bly indicated that Rives in her travels had seen McCullough "and became possessed of a passionate admiration for him," attending his plays in several cities and convincing him to spend his vacation at her homestead, where a courtship transpired. According to Bly, "He admired her and she more than admired him," and he was the model for the deceased husband in "The Quick and the Dead?" McCullough's insanity and death caused a great shock to Rives's "peculiar temperament," making her "more eccentric than ever." Bly cited Rives's 1887 play *Mad as a March Hare* as evidence of the aftershocks from that romance.[34]

Interestingly enough, a letter from "A Son of the Old Dominion" to the *Boston Globe,* apparently intended to refute various calumnies about Rives, actually gave some fuel to Bly's story by stating that "it seems that McCullough did visit Castle Hill some time about the advent of Miss Rives's stage ambition, but that is all that is known."[35] In fact, both Bly's story and that of "Old Dominion" had a very thin basis; McCullough, suffering from acute alcoholism, had retired from the stage in 1884, when Amélie was but twenty-one, and died the following year. Nor is there any evidence that Amélie appeared on the stage before 1887.

In 1890, when Amélie had been abroad for almost a year, an actual scandal occurred, one in which Rives herself may have played little part. A young Parisian artist, Jules Renaud, had killed himself in Algiers, "For Amélie Rives's Sake" as one headline put it. In some accounts, the young artist had become obsessed with Rives even before her arrival in Europe and had committed suicide in despair. Although no evidence indicates that Rives actually met him, at least one newspaper item averred that he killed himself because "Amélie Rives-Chanler jilted him while they were studying together in Paris."[36] Such a reputed relationship appeared particularly dishonorable because those who had followed Amélie's career would know that she had never visited Europe before her marriage.

While reporting such shocking occurrences, the newspapers felt free to speculate about her marriage. Less than six months after the wedding, the *Raleigh News and Courier* reported that "an idle rumor put afloat in New York that Mrs. John Armstrong Chanler (Amelie Rives) had departed from her husband has been promptly and emphatically denied by both Mr. and Mrs. Chanler." In August 1891 Maud Andrews in the *Atlanta Constitution* suggested that the Chanler-Rives marriage was not a happy one, adding her "firm conviction" that Amélie "will some day do something unusual and startling in regard to this domestic relation." Andrews then proclaimed that Rives seemed to be an exception to the rule that all women should be wives and mothers.[37]

At least one newspaper report on the state of the Chanler marriage used it as an opportunity to argue in favor of husbandly dominance over wayward wives. The article pretended to explore the reason that both Rives and Ella Wheeler Wilcox, a popular poet who often focused on passion, had "announced their intention of abandoning the peculiar literary methods by which they have made both money and notoriety." After suggesting that the female writers had perhaps become ashamed of their productions, the paper turned to another possibility: "Or can it be that Mr. Wilcox and Mr. Chanler are something more than Mr. Ella and Mr. Amelie? Can it be that these two gentlemen have asserted their authority for the protection of their wives, and have insisted that the realisms of tumultuous imaginations should be preserved to brighten the sacred precincts of home?"[38]

The mere subject of female writers sometimes provided the pretext for a commentary on proper gender roles. A purportedly humorous essay on the wives of literary men ended with a brief glance at literary women: "one continually reads paragraphs setting forth the helpfulness of authors' wives. . . . But do we ever hear that Mr. Chanler typewrites Amélie Rives Chanler's impassioned romances, or that Mr. Van Rensselaer Cruger interviews editors and critics in the interests of his wife's novel? Alas, no! The millennium has not yet arrived." Obviously, no self-respecting man would, implied this article, be involved in the work of a wifely author. More insulting was the "humorous" item in the *San Francisco Bulletin* in 1891 announcing that Rives's work had unmanned her husband, afflicting him with an ailment frequently associated with intellectual women: "J. Armstrong Chanler, the husband of the sensational novelist, Amelie Rives, is suffering from nervous prostration. He must have been reading one of his wife's novels."[39]

Amid all the reporting on odd behavior and scandal, the emphasis on Amélie's beauty remained. The *New York Sun* noted in 1889 that "the personal friends of Miss Rives . . . are stanch [*sic*] in believing her to be the most beautiful woman in America," and the newspaper went on to agree that a sober estimate "places her at the very head of the beautiful women of the United States." Another paper reported on her visit in Richmond that year: "The authoress is said to be much prettier than she was in the days of her maidenhood, and the local papers go into raptures in describing her beauty. One paper speaks of her eyes as 'great double violets, so indescribable in their hue between purple and blue.'"[40]

Much of this commentary on Rives's appearance focused on her face. The *Washington Post* in July 1888 reported "Amelie Rives Chanler has blue eyes, golden brown hair and a pretty complexion." A September 1888 story described her as "a beautiful 'bluestocking' as rare as a day in June," while a less rapturous piece called her "a beautiful girl, with an expression of good breeding and refinement in her face."[41]

At least one newspaper, soon after Rives's marriage, speculated about whether she enhanced her beauty, while others expressed some dissent from the general admiration. A column describing how the smart set at Newport thronged to see Rives in the autumn of 1888 suggested that she had lightened her hair color. "Her skin is white and fair as a lily," the reporter raved, before noting that "the contrast between the infantine blondeness of her hair with those dark brows and lashes is absolutely startling." Asserting that the question had been "much discussed . . . by the grand jury of society," the article concluded: "Popular opinion, inclined to a malicious view, declared that her hair had been bleached and faded to its auriferous [golden] hue by some of those preparations known to the apothecary." According to a Milwaukee paper, Washingtonians who met Rives in 1889 "assert that she was so 'made up' as to look positively dreadful. Mrs. Chanler, it seems, has bleached her hair, and she has likewise looked upon the rouge pot when it was red, to say nothing of blac de perle and black pencils."[42]

At times, discussion of Amélie's beauty moved into an objectification that treated her almost as a courtesan. One writer, for example, described Rives's lips as very full and very red and then ventured: "She does not smile easily; when she does it comes in a slow fashion. She has some tricks of the lip when speaking that to gentlemen are very fetching. She curves the under lip outward in a way that is very suggestive of 'Quick or the Dead' kisses." And the writer ended: "Her mouth is sadly at variance with the rest of her face, which, in repose, is rather classic."[43]

Beauties in the late nineteenth century popularized the full-figured look rather than the more delicate, frail beauty that had been prized during the antebellum era. By the 1880s, however, this emphasis on voluptuousness and the hourglass figure was beginning to wane. Insofar as early reports mentioned Rives's figure, they tended to be discreet, perhaps because of her youthfulness and upper-class family. One paper in the autumn of 1888 described her as "one of those young ladies . . . who inclose [*sic*] a spirit of adventurous daring in a delicate and demure physique" while another at much the same time alluded to her "well rounded figure."[44]

When the *Washington Post* reported in July 1888 that Rives "disdains gowns upon ordinary occasions and winds herself up in yards of nun's veiling and camel's hair," the newspaper was alluding to Amélie's most outrageous fashion choice: not to wear a corset. A picture dating to the late 1870s, when Rives was in her mid-teens, seems to indicate she then wore a corset, but those from the 1880s suggest that she had made a daring decision, especially for one of her social class, to forgo this nineteenth-century garment. In fact, she came of age during a time when the corset still ruled. A corset molded one's bust, waist, and hips into an hourglass to match the fashion of the tightly fitted dress with bustles, so stylish from 1876 to 1882, as Amélie was maturing. Going without a corset also carried other connotations to contemporaries. Control was a major point in Victorian society, and the uncorseted body was a one lacking control, or more scandalously, out of control. A corsetless form evoked not only the lower-class woman engaged in physical labor but also the prostitute who did not wear such underclothes.[45]

Thus, in addition to the daring of writing trangressively, publicly and privately, about bodies, Amélie also presented her own physical form in a provocative, uncontrolled manner. One newspaper described her participation in a dance: "She was graceful in her poses and movements, and one couldn't help recalling descriptive passages from her wicked story and applying them to her own sinuous and somewhat alluring appearance in the minuet." Rives's turn to art in 1889 brought up the body in yet other controversial ways. A squib reprinted from the *Philadelphia Inquirer* suggested that Rives was not just a sculptor but also—far more improperly—a model: "Amelie Rives Chanler, since she abandoned literature for art, is said to have used her own figure as the model for her sculptured productions, posing in front of a mirror." A Kansas paper asserted that a painting entitled "The Wood Nymph," in the drawing room of Castle Hill, showed a "young woman clad in the airiest of draperies," and more interestingly, was "unmistakably and undeniably a portrait of the artist herself. . . . The features, the hair, the color, expression and carriage of the figure are identical with the personal traits and characteristics of the author-artist herself."[46]

Rives did not, however, have the body type that late nineteenth-century Americans considered ideal. While the emphasis on statuesque women was waning by the 1890s, the new emerging ideal silhouette—which came to be known as the Gibson Girl, after the sketches of Charles Dana Gibson— was of a tall young woman with an hourglass figure and hair in a glamorous updo. In contrast, Rives was petite, and when she appeared uncorseted in flowing gowns, her curvaceous shape was not immediately apparent. Years later, her sister-in-law Daisy Chanler recalled her first meeting with Rives: "A romantic white tea gown draped and flowed from her shoulders in most becoming fashion." Daisy then delivered her brickbat: "all but concealing her want of stature."[47]

Even as early as 1889, one newspaper account of Rives referred to her as "short and plump." Another noted about her "very pleasing" appear- ance: "In height she is about five feet two, and figure, slender, willowy and graceful." Later that year an Oregon paper stated that she "has an ungraceful figure, crowned by a beautiful face. Indeed, if the truth be told, she is short, somewhat dumpy, and although she is very fond of horseback riding, she does not look at all well in the saddle."[48]

In the 1890s, however, interest in Rives's body increased. A New Orleans newspaper in 1893, after commenting on an attack of sciatica that Rives had suffered, commented: "Mrs. Chanler is now about thirty years old and her maturity is said to have heightened the physical beauty for which she was noted as a girl." A Kansas newspaper the next year delineated her: "Her fig- ure has lost its girlish lines . . . and there is a plump and matronly look about the authoress." In 1895 a New York paper cattily commented that Rives "does not resemble the slip of a Virginia girl who made her brilliant literary debut over a decade ago." She was not, though, "of the extreme dowager type who has launched a family of girls into matrimony and grown obese over it. . . . Her outlines are not broad and generous, but she possesses a symmetrical plumpness quite in contrast with her willowy form of girlhood days."[49]

Without the shaping of a corset, Rives often wore looser and more unusual dresses than most women of her day. One description of her at Castle Hill mentioned her "wearing a fleecy gown of white material, a wide-brimmed hat, and swinging a parasol in her hand" while accompanied by at least three dogs. An account of a reception at a Washington, D.C., hotel included a

The Princess of Albemarle

description of Rives's clothing: "This afternoon she wore a highly artistic gown of white China crêpe which fell in the soft folds of Greek draperies."[50]

Along with her unconventional dresses, Amélie may have been wearing unusual footwear. Her penchant for boots in the out of doors had been noted, but she may have helped bring sandals to indoor wear. In 1896 a Chicago paper indicated that Rives "took her aristocratic little instep to a fashionable reception in sandals, after a day's shooting experience." A Richmond paper around the turn of the century recalled "what a thrill of horror arose, a decade ago, when the yellow journal press reporters pictured Amelie Rives in sandals, with a pair of pink and rosy feet adjusted on a silk cushion at a morning reception."[51]

After the notoriety of "The Quick or the Dead?," Amélie became more inured to publicity, even though she began more generally to decry it. In 1890, as she studied art in Paris, a fellow student remarked, "She says she is greatly annoyed by people; that nobody seems to respect her rights to privacy as an individual." A reporter from a Richmond paper consulted with "a lady friend of Mrs. Chanler" (probably Lutie Pleasants, possibly Julia Magruder), who said, "Mrs. Chanler disliked publicity very much and always avoided it when possible." Nonetheless, the reporter learned about Rives's stay in Europe: "she moved in the most refined circles of society and was cordially received by all the celebrated literary personages who were in the same cities with her."[52]

Despite her avowed dislike of publicity, Rives sought press coverage for her books or serialized articles, offering both invitations and interviews to newspapers. In 1891, when she was living in Paris and her book *According to St. John* was forthcoming, Florence Robinson, a fellow art student, was invited to visit Rives and afterward published an account of it. Robinson described Rives as "a perfect beauty, with a mass of golden hair, all natural waves and curls; great soulful luminous gray eyes, and teeth that are exquisite." Robinson continued: "She is a real lily—petite, graceful, and looks about twenty years old. I know of no one nearly as lovely to compare her with. I never saw hair like hers, except in paintings."[53]

When Robinson arrived, Rives was wearing a "white tea-gown, partly open in front, exposing a mass of soft, white beaded lace, a gold girdle about her waist, a tiny red silk turban on her beautiful head, and red hose and slippers." After convincing Robinson to join her for dinner, Rives changed into a dinner dress, "a soft, clinging gown of a light-blue shade, with a heavy blue rope girdle, and a plaited cape, made of the same material as her gown, carelessly thrown about her shoulders." A newspaper interviewer later that year similarly focused on her dress and hairstyle: "She wore a graceful tea-gown of turquois blue china silk, with long, flowing sleeves, the garment being edged all around with a design of swallows in point lace, and the name 'Amélie' on the right side of the drapery. Her blonde hair was beautifully arranged in the Greek fashion, with a knot at the back of her head, and a narrow band of turquois blue velvet."[54]

While Rives was in Europe, a new kind of story began to appear about her health. Although Amélie's bouts of poor health had long figured in family and private correspondence, her illnesses did not surface in the newspapers until her European stay. In January 1891 she was reputedly "seriously ill in Paris." One item indicated that she "has not left her room for six months and has not quitted her bed since early in December." Follow-up stories pronounced her much better and suffering only from "severe bronchitis and not from consumption as was first feared." While Rives's problems in this period probably were related to her abuse of morphine, no hint of her drug usage appeared in the press. A Sacramento paper in February commented on her convalescence in San Remo. Stating that her doctor had vetoed a visit to Florence, the paper then more inventively added: "She says she is sick of authorship, too, and will probably not continue in the field of sensational literature." An item in a Galveston newspaper on her convalescence sarcastically revealed that "her health is sufficiently improved to allow her to disport in picturesque get-ups," along with the detail that "her favorite costume is a tan-colored gown, low shoes to match and brilliant cardinal hose."[55]

When Rives returned from Paris, in 1891, the newspaper article on her ship's landing declared that she looked much stronger than when she had left two years earlier. "A healthy flush relieves her transparent skin, making her look the picture of health. Her face is fuller, and her liquid eyes have lost none of their former lustre." She told the reporter that her serial story in *Cosmopolitan* was the last thing she would write for some time: "I intend for the present to devote myself entirely to art" because "I find that painting does not undermine my health so much as writing does." At this time, one paper announced that Rives played tennis for half an hour, although not well, "for in France one gets out of practice, tennis being too active a game for the Parisians." The writer added: "She is even more beautiful than when she went abroad, for her face has more sensitiveness and expression." The article also included a description of her "picturesque" tennis costume: "a white flannel skirt with a pink silk blouse and the most bewitching of rustic hats garlanded with pink roses." An 1892 item more imaginatively indicated: "Amelie Rives-Chanler rides into Richmond frequently on Horseback from her home, which is a few miles out of the city."[56]

Reports of Rives's ill health continued to dot the papers, even though some still reported her love of activity and the out of doors. In 1893, when she summered at Little Boar's Head, the *Boston Globe* declared: "Mrs Chanler has been living a gloriously independent life here all summer. She is very fond of out-of-door sport, and her passion for being in the open air has been thoroughly gratified." That summer Amélie spent hours on a "little catboat" and either riding or driving through the woods.[57]

The papers also continued to dwell on Amélie's beauty. In 1891 a newspaper item speculated about whether Rives, a "society belle," would spend the winter in New York: "She is," the piece noted, "called exceedingly fascinating in her blonde loveliness. She is slight and graceful and quite dressy." In a *New York Times* piece in July 1894, she was "a striking figure" at a reception given by the poet and society matron Louise Moulton. That same month, another paper announced that "Amelie Rives Chanler is pronounced by the London 'Literary World' 'the most beautiful woman in literature.'" An 1896 list of the most attractive women in the Western world mixed dancers and actresses such as Cléo de Mérode and Lillie Langtry with English aristocrats such as Lady Randolph Churchill and Daisy Greville, Countess of Warwick. Amid this jumble, the evaluation stated, "The most lovely of American beauties is Amelie Rives-Chanler."[58]

More significantly, Amélie herself in 1893 professed to value her beauty over all her other gifts, including her literary talents. The newspaperwoman Augusta Prescott, in a long story based on the premise that loveliness might be a curse, discussed twelve women, ranging from First Lady Frances Cleveland to actress Lillian Russell, but primarily focused on "society women." About Amélie, Prescott claimed: "Like Marie Bashkirseff, Mrs. Chanler enjoys admiring her own features and figure in the looking glass and she goes even further than other beautiful women, by declaring that she thanks her God daily, for his gift of loveliness of face and figure." The comparison here was to the Russian artist Marie Bashkirseff, who had died young from tuberculosis after writing a movingly self-aware journal. Prescott also asserted that "Mrs Chanler is a living refutation of the idea that beautiful women rest upon the beauty that God has given them without adding to it mental charms. She writes, she paints, and though few people know it, she is an authority upon horses and dogs, and rivals Olive Thorne Miller in her knowledge of song birds." Prescott then quoted Amélie: "If I could keep only one gift from those of wealth, position, success, riches, and beauty, which providence has given me, I would choose beauty and let the rest go." Rives then decorously tried to add some perspective, saying, "Next to love of friends and health, I value beauty." Yet any reader would come away with a strong impression that Rives cherished her lovely appearance above all.[59]

Over time, newspapers tended to emphasize Amélie's clothing more than her actual appearance. On her return from Europe, she was wearing a "very becoming costume" of a "trim blue cloth yachting suit, a pilot jacket, open in front, displaying a blue and white loose jersey." In 1891 she is described as "always prettily gowned, perhaps because the artist chooses for the authoress. She delights in cascades of lace, huge puffs, gathers, frills and fluffy effects generally, and in combination with her delicate beauty they produce charming results." A newspaper columnist in 1895 had the same emphasis but a slightly different interpretation: "Her appearance is that of a New York woman who has a rich husband and who knows how to dress in the very best possible taste. Her walking dress looks almost as if she had been melted into it, and is generally of a dark shade." Even in 1896, after her divorce and remarriage, a Milwaukee newspaper carried a squib detailing the "study in lilac" that she wore in Paris, with a bodice "swathed with tissue upon tissue of the two ethereal shades, and so delicately manipulated that it seemed too dainty to be the work of human hands."[60]

To be sure, the newspapers continued to carry general items about Rives's writing. In 1891 an article lauded Walt Whitman, John Greenleaf Whittier, and Oliver Wendell Holmes but then decried "the melancholy fact that there are no younger men upon whom the mantle of the elders has fallen." Looking then to the women, the writer commented about Rives: "Once or twice she has blown a blast that has stirred our blood and made our heart leap within us. But could she be depended on for a sustained effort?" The article concluded sadly that no younger writers were to be preferred to Lowell or Whitman.[61]

By the early nineties, newspapers grouped Rives with writer Gertrude Atherton and poet Ella Wheeler Wilcox as creators of "impassioned" literature. It then became fashionable to deride Rives as out of date. A squib in the

Bookman in 1895, dealing with a group of new British "semi-erotic" novels added: "The English think that it is a new thing, but over here we had it all ten years ago in Amélie Rives's *Quick and the Dead* and the novels of Edgar Saltus." A *Washington Post* reviewer in 1896 contended: "The erotic novel left a bad taste in the public mouth, and it has gone, it is to be hoped, never to return. I know of but a few readers now of Gertrude Atherton, Amelie Rives, Edgar Saltus, or authors of that class." That critic sneered that while the "shelves of cigar shops and miscellaneous fiction sellers" stocked such novels, "they are still demanded only by those whose tastes never rise."[62]

A decade into her career as a writer, Amélie had become a literary celebrity, but the press emphasized the celebrity more than her literary ability. Some scoffed at her writings or even found them dangerously enticing to young women. Most likely, for many readers she remained an intriguing figure as well as a stimulating writer. In 1896 in Fayetteville, North Carolina, the Sweet Bells in Tune, a women's literary club, discussed Rives at its March meeting. Miss Calvert read an entertaining sketch which "first pictured the childhood of Amelie Rives and the attitude taken by Albemarle county toward each new development of this strange girl as it shook its good old Virginia head and styled her 'a caution.'" They then discussed Rives's publications, with Mrs. Lilly reading aloud Rives's story "Nurse Crumpet Tells the Story."[63] Groups as well as individuals had been reading Rives since 1888, when the Southern Club at Harvard discussed "Amelie Rives and her Writings" as well as "Manners and Customs in North Carolina."[64]

By the mid-nineties, though, it was sheer celebrity that commanded the most public attention. In 1893 the *Boston Globe* described the enormous interest she provoked at a New England resort: "Curiosity at that time to see the brilliant authoress ran high, and heroine worshippers resorted to almost every known means to get a glimpse of her face. People sat and waited on the rocks, along the road, or on the verandas, marine glasses in hand, waiting for her to pass. They would rush to the windows to see her, attracted by what they had heard of her beauty and genius."

In reaction, Rives had become increasingly wary of the press. Upon her arrival back in the United States in January 1895, the *New York Times* reporter called but was rebuffed: "Mrs. Chanler said the fatigue of her voyage made it impossible for her to tell anything about her experiences abroad or her plans." The breakup of her marriage later that year called forth a new spate of attention. Archie's valet Charles Hartnett detailed one encounter that Amélie had with the press: "Mrs Chanler went out riding the other evening and met a reporter driving in hot haste to 'Castle Hill' with a letter of introduction from Mr Graham Page and only for this letter Mrs Chanler would not have spoken to him at all, but as it was he found out nothing, although he asked some very clever questions."[65]

The first decade of press notice for Rives had seen reams of coverage. Newspapers celebrated her as a beautiful young genius, but pointed to eccentric, self-centered behavior; they also criticized her work as overly emotional, salacious, or simply not very accomplished. Yet as she now dealt with remaking her life and revamping her image, she soon encountered far more dismissive and disapproving attention.

EIGHT

"All That I Ever Dreamed of Love Is Mine, Mine, Mine"

Building a New Life as a Princess

Looking back late in life, Amélie Rives mused: "I have the most delightful memories of the much-abused nineties. . . . It was the climax of a gracious civilization and the best time to live in England. One could meet an archbishop, an actor, an explorer, a writer, and a débutante all at dinner together then."[1] While she had earlier spent time with the Souls and members of London's literary elite, it was Rives's return to England in 1894 that built her friendship with Louise Chandler Moulton, the wealthy poet from Boston, and gave her contacts with authors such as George Meredith, Thomas Hardy, and the American expatriate Henry James.

In seeking refuge from her unhappy marriage with Archie, Amélie found in London not only new friends and an exciting literary scene but also what she called "the most beautiful love-story in all the realm of romance" with handsome, talented Pierre Troubetzkoy. Having recently finished a portrait of former prime minister William Gladstone, Troubetzkoy was gaining notice for his paintings of aristocrats and high society. Rives and Troubetzkoy, given their mutual interest in art, music, and literature, had much in common. Nonetheless, this budding romance could not obscure the difficult parts of Rives's life. Given her prominent and religiously conservative background, any relationship with Troubetzkoy was fraught. A long-term affair would destroy her reputation in American society and alienate her family. Divorce, while becoming more frequent among Americans, especially wealthy ones, also carried a stigma. Moreover, although Archie was a generous man, a divorce would likely remove his largesse and the financial mainstay he had provided her family.[2] It might also be the more dangerous option; his mood swings had always been a part of the marriage but had become more frequent and more dramatic. Given his difficult and possibly dangerous personality, how could Rives obtain a divorce and feel safe in remarrying?

Amélie drew upon notions that she and Archie had been sharing for years to cast their relationship in a different light. In the summer of 1894, Archie apparently gave her George Meredith's new book, *Lord Ormond and His Aminta,* in which a mismatched couple dissolve their marriage. "Perhaps God meant you to give me 'Lord Ormond & his Aminta' as a sort of prophecy," Amélie wrote Archie: "It seems to have come to me like an inspiration,—the idea, the *sure feeling,* of how much the whole world would 'gain in grandeur & in moral height,' were men & women to face such mistakes simply, generously, nobly & to say to each other, 'I love you—I am your best friend as you are mine—, but in this *one* way we make each other wretched.'" She then struck a high note: "Let us begin life over. Let us give each other our freedom."[3] Amélie seems to have found the right argument to convince Archie that he and she should part.

As Amélie contemplated divorce, other parts of her personal life presented problems as well. She fired her longtime maid and companion Martha Jane Bullock, an African American woman who had been working for the Rives family for over twenty years and who had accompanied Archie and Amélie to Europe for the almost two years they had spent there. Martha Jane had also, with only the slightest name change, served as the prototype for Martha Ellen, the heroine's maid in "The Quick or the Dead?" and *Barbara Dering.* These writings did not present Martha Ellen as the stereotypical mammy, a large-hearted, cheery woman who alternately pets and disciplines. Instead, she is "a dark brown creature with a profile like that of Ramses II." This portrayal is contradictory: Martha Ellen is a "creature," which suggests inferiority, yet she also resembles royalty.[4] Moreover, Martha Ellen speaks in dialect (among the elite white characters in "The Quick or the Dead?," only the despised Aunt Fridiswig does so).

Rives's stories often portray Martha Ellen as a foil to her employer. When out on a walk that turns into a run, Barbara "flew over the frozen ground" while "poor Martha Ellen, whose hand she grasped, panted along as best she might, also laughing hysterically." Still, the scene indicates an important shared camaraderie. Later, in *Barbara Dering,* Rives juxtaposes the maid's experiences with marriage to the heroine's. After Martha Ellen confides that her husband was "mighty aggravatin' sometimes," Barbara asks whether, if he

The Princess of Albemarle

disappeared, Martha Ellen would marry again. Martha Ellen says no, using the third person to answer for herself: "Martha Ellen don' think nothin' 'bout that. She know, ef God wuz tuh lif' her outer trouble onct, she cert'n'y w'an't goin' tuh put her paws in no other trap menfolks could set for her."[5] From a superior pose, Rives has the maid compare herself to an animal with paws. Aside from racist stereotypes, Rives also lets class divisions stand—Martha Ellen is a treasured companion, but not an equal one. In the 1890s the United States was at a nadir of race relations, with numerous white writers such as Thomas Nelson Page moving toward depicting African Americans as savage or incorrigible, and Rives seems to have been influenced by these currents.

Why did Amélie fire someone who had been a part of her life for many years and on whose care she had long depended? Perhaps Bullock herself was distressed by parts of Amélie's personal life, such as the drug dependency, the breakup of the marriage with Archie, and the new relationship with Pierre Troubetzkoy. And Martha Jane may have tired of the European visits and the absences from her own family and friends. Whatever the causes for the break up, it was acrimonious, at least on Amélie's part.

Archie's longtime valet, Charles Hartnett, discussed the firing with Amélie's doctor and then related their discussion to Archie: "He told me among other things that he was surprised that Mrs Chanler should discharge Martha, and he said I'll tell you, Mrs Chanler will never get another Martha Jane. She was truthful and discreet, but she's going to talk now that she has left Mrs Chanler, and it's a pity Mrs Chanler sent her away."[6] (Martha Jane Bullock apparently gave no interviews to the press.)

Whether from sympathy with Martha Jane or to keep her from airing the Chanlers' dirty linen, Archie hired her. Cautioning him against "the little negress Martha Jane," Rives let loose a tirade: "I will tell you frankly, dear Archie, that it shocked me very much, when you wrote that you had taken 'Martha Jane' into your service." Archie apparently had professed that his sister Elizabeth had assured him Amélie would approve. Not at all mollified, Amélie scolded: "It amazed me doubly because I had so often heard you express your opinion very forceably concerning those who took the discarded servants of friends or relatives, into *their* household, their service—especially servants dismissed in the manner & for the outrageous behavior. . . ." The rest of this letter has been lost, thus veiling Amélie's conclusions.[7]

Even as Amélie tried to convince Archie that he and she would be happier living apart, he was pushing forward with his notions of reform and invention. In 1892 he had begun a law firm, Chanler, Maxwell, and Philip, to oversee his private investments. The following year construction started on his model textile mill village in Roanoke Rapids, North Carolina. Archie recruited noted architect Stanford White to design the red brick mill and the workers' cottages. Archie even improved the design for the cottages by enlarging the rooms and adding front porches. He invested large parts of his own fortune and that of his younger brothers and sisters in this enterprise. The Chanler siblings apparently became worried about whether their money would in fact be safe with Archie's elaborate plans.[8] Archie, moreover, had an increasingly grandiose vision of himself as industrial tycoon. He expected great things in his promotion of a self-threading device for sewing machines. Exhibited at the World's Columbian Exposition in the summer of 1893, this device won a prize, as did a patented roadway in which Archie also invested. Despite the self-threader's promise, it was not yet compatible with the major brands of sewing machines.[9]

By the beginning of 1895, wheels had been set in motion to dissolve the Chanler marriage, as Amélie traveled west to St. Louis and on to South Dakota, where she set up residency and filed for divorce. Most likely, Archie and Amélie knew about South Dakota's relatively lax laws on divorce because his cousin the Baroness Margaret de Stuers, sister of his close friend Arthur Astor Carey, had severed her union with Baron Alphonse de Stuers there in 1892. Since that time, South Dakota had lengthened its residency period from sixty days to six months, but the state, along with North Dakota, remained among the most permissive in requiring a relatively short residency. In fact, a coterie of divorce seekers had formed in Sioux Falls, South Dakota's largest city.[10]

Because of Archie's wealth, he and Amélie were able to pull off their split quite discreetly. In September 1895 they received a divorce, likely on grounds of cruelty. Although many states had included some form of mental cruelty among the grounds for divorce, South Dakota, while lenient about residency, accepted only the traditional cause of physical cruelty. Thus, the Chanlers quite deliberately concealed which state had granted the decree. Suppressing this fact allowed them to claim to the press that the grounds had been incompatibility of temperament—obviously, a less embarrassing reason for Archie. In letters to Amélie, Archie agreed that he would pay her at least three thousand dollars annually, although he meant to adjust the amount upward to four thousand in 1897–98. Archie later claimed this payment was not alimony, but rather was intended to support Rives's art career.[11]

In October 1895 Archie's valet, Charles Hartnett, was positively crowing about the success in keeping the entire divorce process secret until its announcement. He also assured Archie of Albemarle County's support for him: "Well, everyone is on your side in this affair, and everyone I saw or heard speak of it say that they feel sorry for Mr. Chanler, that it's too bad it should have happened, but of course no man wants a wife that is all the time in bed sick. Why, anybody could see with half an eye that that sort of living would never go, and lots more to this effect."[12]

The Chanler siblings at Rokeby did not react calmly to news of the divorce. Hartnett reported to Archie, then in North Carolina: "I had a letter from Barrytown [Rokeby], and that place is worked up to the highest pitch over it, it is worse than if a cyclone had struck it and carried off all the buildings." While attempting to conciliate her former sister-in-law Elizabeth Chanler, Amélie indicated in a long letter in December that she would soon be remarrying and "the *monstrous* press was going to have a field day." The attempt to mollify Elizabeth was futile; Archie's family completely removed Rives from its consciousness. Since Margaret Chanler considered remarriage after divorce to conflict with religious doctrine, she had long refused to interact socially with those who had divorced and remarried.[13]

As news of the divorce decree became public, the newspapers again looked to Rives for copy. Although much of society saw divorce as a growing social evil that threatened to reach epidemic proportion, the news outlets sometimes were not as censorious as Rives had predicted. The *Raleigh News and Courier,* while admitting it knew little about the couple's unhappiness, surmised that she had sought the divorce and Archie's only fault "if he had one, was a failure to make wedded life fantastic enough to suit the strained and heated romanticism of his novel-writing wife." The Chicago newspaperman Walter Wellman, who had been acquainted with Rives for over eight years, opened a column of reminiscences by describing her as "always a woman of caprice, wayward, fickle." He mused that the marriage's breakup was probably "no one's fault, but simply a natural though unfortunate result of yoking together a manly and practical young man and a romantic, capricious, genius-blessed and genius-cursed young woman." The *Chicago Daily Inter-Ocean* quoted friends of the couple who asserted: "Both are perfection—but how they did quarrel. Like the married wretches of the comic opera they might say: 'We'd have been perfectly happy if we hadn't been so perfectly miserable.'"[14]

Other papers, as in the past, alluded to Rives's genius and eccentricities. One suggested "that she had always been an impossible sort of character," giving as an example a story about Amélie painting herself nude: "'Are you an admirer of nude figures, Aunt Jane,' she [Rives] asked one day of a starchy visitor, at the same time revealing to that individual's scandalized gaze a half finished canvas with her own undraped loveliness imposed upon it with the assistance of a mirror." A Kansas paper drew a more idealized domestic scene: "She is now at her old home, Castle Hill, as happy with thoroughbreds, her dogs and her faithful negro servants as a young woman of genius can well be to whom marriage has proven a failure." A long item about Rives's peculiar work habits concluded: "The world owes a countless debt to the people who can charm by story or verse; and the people themselves owe it to the world to keep single, as double harness seldom sits well upon the neck of genius."[15]

Some newspapers did malign Rives's character and lifestyle. A Portland, Oregon, news-sheet sneered: "Why should any one feel surprise? Women of this type, whether on the stage or in literature, are constantly changing husbands."[16] The moral was, the same journal later put forward, that "young girls who exalt passion to a seat of love and who are so indelicate as to write for the public eye" are unlikely to find happiness in marriage, "a contract requiring for its successful fulfillment calm good sense, mutual forbearance, and mutual respect." A Memphis newspaper blamed Rives's unwomanly ambition for the divorce: "The wife lived unostentatiously in Paris, and forgot matrimony in art, . . . It was merely another exemplification of the modern woman—of the degeneracy which thinks man secondary to ambition." Some stories linked the divorce to her degenerate novels. Another Tennessee item fulminated: "The world was not yet ready for these unhealthy outpourings of diseased sentiment." Thus, Rives was left with "the ashes of a fame that rested on a monstrosity."[17]

Yet other papers mused, as before, on Rives's beauty. One quoted an acquaintance in Paris who remembered: "She used to say the most daring things—but in that artless manner that would deceive the hardened cynic. She is undersized, you know, but with a complexion indescrible [sic] in its pure rose-leaf and creamy tints. Her eyes, so large and beautiful, are fascinating because of their childlike sweetness of expression."[18]

The Princess of Albemarle

In 1895 Amélie tried to return to writing. Her pace had slowed radically since 1892–93 when she published three book-length works, *Barbara Dering, Tanis: The Sang Digger*, and *Athelwold* (even though *Athelwold*, a play about love, jealousy, and rivalry set in tenth-century Anglo-Saxon England, probably dated from years earlier when she wrote historically themed fiction). During her sojourn in South Dakota, Rives spent part of the spring in Monterey, California, where she again suffered from ill health, perhaps because of a continued dependence on opiates. Nonetheless, in April 1895 she noted progress on an unidentified project: "I wrote a chapter on my novel last night," she told Archie, confiding that a friend had pronounced it "splendid." Back at Castle Hill in poor health in October, Rives was still struggling with writing. Julia Magruder had been invited for a visit then because Rives told her: "If I would come she was sure that she could finish her book and of course I am glad to go, both for that reason & for the pleasure of being with her." In her decade of publishing, Rives had never written so little.

At the end of 1895, Rives was anticipating a happier life. In a letter to her former sister-in-law Elizabeth, Amélie spoke with relish of earning her living in the future: "I believe to contribute mutually by one's separate endeavor to the maintenance of a home, be it only a cheery apartment in Kensington, is one of the solidest foundations for pure, wholesome married-happiness!" Perhaps with more hope than conviction, Amélie further prophesied: "How it will make me write! With what zest, what ardour, what exultation!!"[19] While she eventually regained much of her old zest for writing, it required breaking her drug habit and regaining her health—both of which then lay considerably in the future.

Rives's female friends comforted her as she tried to restore her life, health, and career. Lutie Pleasants spent over a month around the Christmas holidays; Julia Magruder, at Sadie Rives's urging, hurried to Castle Hill in January 1896. According to Julia, Amélie then "was trying to finish her book but said she could do nothing until I came. Once before I went to try to help her, but she made very slight progress with it."[20]

Amélie, despite her ill health, moved ahead with preparations to marry Pierre Troubetzkoy. How they settled on a date and to what extent she consulted with her parents cannot be determined. Whatever the latter's views, they opened Castle Hill for the wedding and made the best of the situation. In a letter to his widowed sister-in-law, Alfred Rives described Pierre as "exceptionally fine looking . . . [with the] most attractive manner & ways."

Alfred added: "He seems moreover good tempered & modest & we hope the couple will be happy." Amélie gave her own reading of the situation, when she confided in her friend Louise Moulton in early February about the upcoming "still secret from the world" wedding: "All that I ever dreamed of love is mine, mine, mine, and I want you to be the first to share this golden delight with me."[21]

After Pierre arrived from Europe, he and Amélie married at three o'clock in the afternoon on February 18, 1896. It was a small but impressive private ceremony with her family in attendance. Gertrude was maid of honor while the four bridesmaids were her younger sister Landon, two cousins Bessie Martin and Eleanor Page, and close friend Julia Magruder. The Reverend Paul L. Menzel of the German Evangelical Church in Richmond performed the ceremony, most likely because the Episcopal Church disapproved of remarriage by the divorced. That Amélie wore a white gown (trimmed with Russian sable) seemed almost to deny her first marriage. A Chicago journal commented that the "simplicity and secrecy" of the wedding was "in striking contrast" to her first marriage. Ignoring the elements of concealment in that first event, the reporter continued: "Then there was gathered a distinguished company and a select lot of newspaper men were invited and were present."[22]

Newspapers of the day were often severe about the remarriage of a divorcée, and Rives's choice of a foreign-born second husband seemed to enrage, or at least irritate, some reporters. The *Raleigh News and Observer* censoriously observed: "It turns out that she virtually became engaged to the Prince while she was the wife of Mr. Chandler [*sic*]." In its speculations about women's various motives for marrying, the *Atchison Daily Globe* commented: "It is said that Amelie Rives admits that she married her Russian nobleman to get material for a new novel. The prince is a Cossack, a nihilist, an exile, and probably a tough and galoot." To be sure, some papers clothed their antiforeign prejudice in seeming jocosity. Asserting that Amélie had received a foreign title by marrying a count, the *Denver Evening Post* opined: "It is not known how it happened. She is not a widow of wealth, nor an heiress. This makes us fear that there is something wrong with the count. . . . Men with names having similar terminations [i.e., Eastern European surnames] have been seen on the American stage for some years past as villains of the deepest dye, and there must be some reason for this." Others called Pierre a "Russian Prince without an inheritance"; one suggested that on the Continent "a prince may be a restaurant waiter, or a fiddler, like Amelie

The Princess of Albemarle

Rives's new husband." Other comments on Pierre Troubetzkoy focused on his physique or career as a portrait painter as well as his name. Often his surname was misspelled—as Triboutski, Troubutskoi, or Troubetzkoi.[23]

Some of the newspapers also presented Rives's interpretation of her two relationships. Thus, one account of the failed marriage with Archie ran: "her friends declare that within three months after her marriage . . . she knew she had made a mistake, but she lived with him for four years. Mr. Chanler, becoming aware of his wife's feeling toward him, took the steps necessary for a divorce." An item about Rives's marriage to Troubetzkoy was also intended to satisfy moral critics: "Although there was never a breath of scandal about the matter she met Prince Trowbetzkoy a year before she was divorced. They were not in any way associated with each other up to that time, but were married shortly afterward."[24]

At least one budding writer with Virginia roots took the remarriage as a chance to lambaste Rives's character and writings. "So Amélie Rives is married again and to a Russian prince," began Willa Cather's essay. Calling up Rives's aristocratic background and a family history of women who "have been models of propriety and social grace for generations," Cather continued, "Life is easy for Virginia women. Virginia chivalry has made it so." With this heritage, "Amélie Rives has not kept the faith; she has made herself ridiculous and has made her name common property among trashy and ignorant people the world over. That, in Virginia, is the unpardonable sin."[25]

Cather moved from an assault on character to an insult to the author. "As to Miss Rives' literary prospects, they are considerably worse than nothing, and it is doubtful if she will ever rise above writing tales for *Town Topics*," she sneered. Cather disparaged "The Quick or the Dead?" as containing "the greatest of all literary faults, it was thoroughly and entirely unnatural." There was "no remedy": "if one does not see at least a few things as they are by the time one is twenty, then one never sees them at all and goes through life with distorted vision." Although Cather conceded the difficulty of writing "the literature of passion," her verdict was that "Amélie Rives tried to write the most difficult sort of fiction in the world and she did it passing poorly. . . . In short the princess of the unpronounceable name is utterly without the blessed quality of common sense, and it is impossible to either live or write decently without it."[26]

Meanwhile, the recently married pair were trying to decide where to live decently and seemed inclined to stay in Europe, most likely England. That

Amélie Rives, on a ship gazing out to sea, subtly advertises her ties to Europe. (Amélie Rives Troubetzkoy Collection, The Valentine)

Amélie used the example of "a cheery apartment in Kensington" for her notion of home in a letter written two months before the marriage suggests that London was on her mind. Her father lamented that, despite Pierre's lovely manners and good disposition, "it is a great strain having Amélie's future cast in all probability in Europe, so that in the natural course of events we cannot hope to often see her."[27]

Late in February 1896, Pierre and Amélie sailed to Italy, where they visited his mother in Milan. Amélie's health woes continued, and a succession of illnesses dominated much of the spring, but as Amélie later recounted, her new mother-in-law "nursed me like a professional sick-nurse." Rives graphically described her illness: "You see, the grip went for my lungs &

both lungs this time, & I spit blood all the time, for some days, & was threatened with hemorrages." Moreover, she had experienced other problems in Milan: "Then I had a really frightful abscess on my thigh, and had to have it cut without anything to deaden the pain, not even cocaine. I'm telling you all this that you may understand how weak & easily made ill, I *still* am, though, really, as far as *general, constitutional* health goes, I am, I believe & fervently pray, much, much better than since long years."

Despite Rives's insistence that her "constitutional health" was much better, the abscess had been quite serious: "That abscess however wasn't just a simple matter of lancing but it had to be cut (a cut of about an inch & a half) *twice*, & then stuffed with something like liquid fire, & dressed & *kept* stuffed for several days." Such serious infections can be a side effect of injecting drugs; probably Amélie had relapsed again into addiction. She jauntily described her reaction to the operation: "I smoked a cigarette at the time, & looked on. It was pride, even a little vanity I fear, that kept me so cool about it."[28]

After the visit in Milan, Pierre and Amélie proceeded to Paris, where she spent three weeks in bed with a bad knee. By July in London, they apparently were encountering financial difficulties. When Archie sent Rives a sheaf of unpaid bills as part of the separation of their financial matters, she professed herself surprised and entreated him, "Only be patient & believe in me, & I will send you this money, bit by bit, as I can afford it. Now, just at this present time, I am too feeble with these low fevers & chills, to count on writing anything, but when I am better, & can write, little by little I hope to retrieve my character as that of a grateful being, in your estimation."[29]

England soon palled on Amélie. In September she and Pierre spent at least three weeks in the north at Sir William Eden's Windlestone in County Durham, most likely for Pierre to execute a portrait commission. In a letter to Archie, Amélie unloaded her frustration about being "for the last three weeks, shut up in the country house" with "English people in England." "In all that time," she protested, "I have met well,—*two* clever people. The most of them however are what you & I loathe so!—Oh, how they suffocate, depress, repress, *shrivel* me, these people!" She compared the country house to a place inhabited by the chief evil genie of Islamic mythology: "I never hear *one* word of encouragement, or of just criticism. In a word no one in these Halls of Eblis, where I have been wandering & must wander, seem even to remember that there are such things as books, even *novels!*"[30]

Amélie then recounted a dialogue that she had heard between two of her fellow guests, an Englishman and a Frenchman. After grumbling about the upkeep of bicycles, the Englishman asserted: "As it is, I can *just* manage to go in for huntin' a bit, & keep two hunters & a lad to look after 'em. Now that lad wouldn't clean my 'bike,' would he now? Not much! *Why,* I'd have to clean the bloomin' thing myself every time I went out!" The Frenchman retorted, "Well! Good Lord! Man! But aint that better than takin' up a book when you're bored! Why, just thinking of cleaning a jolly new machine, a perfect beauty of a 'bike' for one whole hour, instead of poring over a beastly stupid book that *you've got to make an effort to keep your mind on!!*" "And will you please tell me," Amélie queried, "whether it's most comic or most tragic?"[31]

Amélie and Pierre intended to return to the United States by the autumn of 1896, but they prolonged their stay. Possibly they planned to avoid the marriage of her sister Gertrude to Richmond lawyer Allan Potts which occurred that October. It was a lovely wedding at Grace Church, near Cobham, which had recently been rebuilt after a fire. Gertrude wore white satin with a traditional veil and had twenty attendants. Landon Rives, as maid of honor, was attired in violet with a large picture hat. Amélie and Pierre sent a congratulatory telegram but did not attend. As Amélie was a divorcée who had remarried, her attendance at a church wedding would have scandalized some of her more religiously conservative relatives and friends. No doubt her celebrity status would also have diverted attention from the bride. Over the years, Gertrude and Amélie had often been—and would continue to be—at odds, and the wedding was Gertrude's day to shine. Even with Amélie's absence, a long article on the wedding in the *Richmond Times* noted that many of the portraits at Castle Hill were copies that she had painted and further remarked: "Reminders of her talent as an artist are all over the house."[32]

Late in November 1896 Amélie and Pierre arrived stateside and took an apartment in New York City. A few months later, while they were still in New York, a remarkable event occurred. In March 1897 Archie's relatives secretly gained his commitment to Bloomingdale Asylum by alleging that he was violent and mentally ill. While Amélie and Pierre had been abroad, Archie had been pushing his great schemes for the Roanoke Rapids industrial community and the sewing machine self-threader. At the same time, rifts with his family had deepened when he chose not to attend his youngest sister Alida's wedding in October 1896. Possibly Archie's brother Winthrop instigated the commitment, but all the Chanler siblings had come to doubt Archie's financial acumen and even his sanity. Only in October 1897, six months after his commitment, was Archie's residence at the asylum revealed in the daily papers.

Rives soon learned the difficulty that Archie's confinement posed. In 1897 and 1898 she received on Chanler's behalf a total of $5,500 from Stanford White, Archie's friend and then guardian (who would shortly be exposed as an exploiter of young women). The payments then appear to have ceased. In November 1900 Archie successfully escaped from Bloomingdale Asylum and made his way to Virginia. Over time he would attempt to regain control of his fortune; the unusual outcome was that the Virginia courts declared him sane, while the New York courts (where much of his fortune lay) continued to consider him incompetent. During this period, Rives could not count on the monies from Archie. Only in 1911, after successfully suing Archie's guardians, did Rives regain the annual payment of $3,600.[33]

At the fin de siècle, Rives began to assume a new guise in the press—that of a European princess, though aspects of the flighty southern belle and eccentric author still surfaced there. Some of her self-fashioning as a princess built on her reputation for self-regard. Only a month after her marriage, a newspaper that had called her "Princess Troubetskoi" referred to the French derivation of her given name, adding: "It is said there is no more certain way of winning ill will from the new Princess than to slur or miscall her name—making it either 'Emily,' 'Amelia'—when it is properly very near to 'Omily'—with the accent on the first syllable."[34]

Still, that year, as Amélie sought to revitalize her writing career, she encountered a problem that she had not experienced for over a decade—one of her novellas was rejected. The manuscript does not seem to have survived, so only its outlines can be ascertained. Reportedly, she began it in the winter of 1896 and had been working steadily on it. That summer, she granted an interview (picked up by several newspapers) in which she asserted: "My new book is to be my greatest effort. It will be more startling than 'The Quick or the Dead,' and infinitely more interesting." The protagonist was Marc Zeuska, a young man with a Polish father and Virginian mother. Upon coming to Virginia to claim his ancestral estate, Zeuska meets Petronel, a Virginia woman who is the stepdaughter of his maternal uncle. Although Zeuska intended to "better the condition of the negroes and poor whites," the plot apparently centered on the concept expounded in Leo Tolstoy's story "The Kreutzer Sonata" that chastity in marriage produced a higher form of life than sexual activity. Tolstoy's short story had gained intense notoriety because much of it consists of a long diatribe in which the murderer Posdnicheff justifies having killed his wife. According to Rives, Zeuska, after his marriage to Petronel, "models his married life upon his master's creed. He makes the 'Kreutzer Sonata' the family Bible. What happens after all that is still my secret and theirs." In addition to this teaser about the characters and plot, Rives stated, "The work is now almost complete."[35]

In the absence of records, one can only speculate about what happened to Rives's almost complete book. Perhaps the story was too hastily and badly written for a publisher to accept, but in the previous decade, most of what Rives had produced—even stories she had written back in her teens—had been accepted by a variety of leading publishing houses, whether *Lippincott's*, *Harper's*, or *Cosmopolitan Magazine*. More likely, the travails of Tolstoy's "Kreutzer Sonata," both in Russia, where it had been banned, and in the United States, where newspapers serializing it were forbidden the federal mails, had intimidated American publishers.[36] The combination of Rives writing on unfamiliar territory—using a foreign-born male protagonist rather than an alluring heroine—with a subject so controversial may have doomed this proposed book.

The failed project does, however, illustrate Rives's self-presentation after her remarriage. An interview in the *New York Journal and Advertiser* included a picture of Rives "from her Latest Photograph" as well as a reproduction of her signed portrait of Pierre Troubetzkoy and a handwritten page of her book manuscript. The interview also included details that nineteenth-century readers would have found extraordinarily personal, even intimate. When the reporter met Rives at Castle Hill, in the moonlight, "The Princess. . . . was gowned in a graceful, flowing silken negligee, which releaved [revealed] the perfection of her velvety white arms and soft full throat. Clematis vines and Japanese ivy threw fantastic shadows athwart her recumbent form."[37] Rives was presenting herself as a figure of royal privilege and exoticism.

Moreover, she willingly divulged details about her approach to writing. She told the interviewer she had designated the balcony at Castle Hill a favorite place: "I have all my life spent many [an] hour upon it. My reveries, my day dreams, my best work and the happiest moments of my life are associated with the dear old 'Hanging Garden.'" In addition, she declared that she often wrote "tirelessly from noon till dusk" on a rug in a field of oats. Rives's quest to be perceived as serious shone through, as she assured the reporter: "I have made a study of Tolstoi's works for years. After reading the 'Kreutzer Sonata,' I conceived the story about Marc Zeuska and Petronel." She intended Pierre to illustrate the novella, even though she herself was continuing to draw and paint. The interview, in abbreviated form, was picked up by newspapers in towns as diverse as Chicago, Charlotte, Charlottesville, and New Orleans. Because Rives did not mention a publisher and possibly did not have one, it seems highly likely that she herself had set up the interview, or at least had agreed to it, to publicize the novel.[38]

Rives's frequent physical breakdowns in this period, most of which probably stemmed from a continuing addiction to morphine and cocaine, posed a continuing problem, but newspapers, if they learned of her drug problem, never mentioned it. To explain her collapses, Rives increasingly relied on the cover of "nervous prostration." By 1897 she dishonestly claimed that "her ill health was indirectly traceable to a nervous affliction which had its origins in the violent discussion and personal abuse that followed the publication of 'The Quick or the Dead.'" Other reports of her illness posited that it "directly" sprang from "the great tension and mental strain incumbent upon the completion of a new novel," like "a similar illness that began five years ago caused by the bitter attacks made upon her for the views and sentiments she expressed in 'The Quick or the Dead.'"[39] Apparently, Rives had begun to attribute all her problems to the publicity circus that a decade earlier had surrounded her best seller.

Rives's recovery assumed a roller coaster aspect. In June 1897 she was again in "delicate health" and had consulted in Philadelphia with "an eminent specialist." Her father and husband had accompanied her to Philadelphia, where she was a patient in the "private sanitarium" of Dr. Wharton Sinkler, a prominent neurologist with strong ties to South Carolina. In Sinkler's estimation, Rives was "suffering from nervous prostration" and was "completely broken down."[40]

Given her need for money and the rejection of her novel exploring marital chastity, Amélie turned to fiction in more traditional veins. First, she dusted off the medieval romance that Richard Watson Gilder had accepted for the *Century* back in 1886 but never published; she sent it off to J. B. Lippincott, which published it in 1898 as *A Damsel Errant*. She also finished "Meriel," a story for *Lippincott's Magazine* about a romantic adventure set in Italy that she had been writing back in 1892. The heroine, a youthful widow, whose name was almost an anagram of Amélie, shared other characteristics. Although twenty-nine, Meriel looks much younger. She paints and sings, the latter even as she is tossed about the sea on a small boat near San Remo, where she and the hero are summering. The slight plot revolves about whether the narrator, Gordon Dalryn, a forty-year-old Englishman who believes himself unworthy of any relationship because of his cruelty to his first wife (who committed suicide), can move beyond that guilt to find love with Meriel. Here Rives was allowing a male (rather than her usual female protagonists) to expiate past misdeeds through heroic action. Unlike her earlier explorations of modern romance, though, Meriel and Gordon talk much more than they act.[41]

Even as Amélie returned to publishing, she and Pierre needed to decide on their plans for their future. They first looked to Washington. Amélie told one of her friends in 1897: "My prince leaves me in a few days to go to work in Washington where he is to have an atelier this winter. I am not strong enough to go with him. Is that not a little tragedy?"[42] Obviously meant as an amusing aside, this comment intimated problems. The destruction of Rives's correspondence makes it impossible to chart any changes in her relationship with Pierre. His desire to continue his career played a part in their separations during the 1890s, but Amélie's continued battle with opiates was likely a factor. Amélie's preference for Castle Hill over any other residence may also have played a part.

Like Rives, Pierre used publicity to improve his prospects. A *New York Journal* reporter, perhaps even the reporter who had earlier interviewed Amélie, published an interview with the prince in March 1898 about his portrait painting in Washington, D.C., where he had opened a studio in the Corcoran building. The article proclaimed Pierre to be "beyond the threshold of a career both brilliant and swift" and discussed some of the portraits in Washington that he was undertaking. The reporter also provided a brief synopsis of how Pierre's career in England had prospered after he painted a portrait of William Gladstone, the former prime minister. Describing Pierre as "a tall, clean limbed athletic looking fellow, brown haired, brown eyes, standing six feet two and a half inches in his stocking feet," the journalist marveled that Troubetzkoy, "to keep up his wonderful physical strength, practises each afternoon in his studio following the day's work upon a massive iron bar . . . six feet in length, with a weight of one hundred and twenty pounds."[43]

The Princess of Albemarle

Twice in the interview Pierre mentioned his wife joining him in Washington; he also declared that the "greatest pleasure" for them both would be "when she is able, for them to work together in the studio." Even though Rives had been ill with nervous prostration, "there are signs of improvement which indicate that before long she will be able to carry into effect her wish to join her husband in Washington." Pressed about future plans, Troubetzkoy indicated that "so much depends upon the state of my wife's health—all, in fact, everything, depends upon that."[44]

Despite separations, Amélie and Pierre appear to have been forging a partnership, based on mutual interests, admiration, and love. Moreover, Amélie seems to have thoroughly appreciated his gentleness and kindness. In an undated letter written during the first decade of their marriage, she praised his solicitude when she suddenly became ill with sciatica: "Pierre was *so* good to me—Mother, lover, sick-nurse all in one!" While less can be discovered about Pierre's view of Amélie, he left a telling testimony in the dedication to her of his novel, published in 1908: "it is due to you as the light is due to the flame." Troubetzkoy and Rives shared a love of animals, which brought them closer over the years—at one point he adopted a squirrel in New York and took it with them on a transatlantic voyage. He had lured the squirrel into his coat with nuts, which he always carried in his pocket because, as he told a reporter, they "are part of my diet. I not only have stopped eating meat, but I am done with hunting big game."[45]

Even though Rives was publishing little, she still occasionally gained press notice for fashion and beauty. The San Francisco paper in 1898 classed Rives with Sarah Bernhardt because they were "standing in their countries for the esthetic in dress, adapting the style of draping the figure in a loose, light material which was very becoming. Instead of cutting out a morning robe from the regulation pattern and sewing it in seams, they took the goods and gathered it around the neck and provided arm holes for it. They draped them long and loose and caught them here and there with fancy ornaments." Beauty culture was becoming more accepted at this time, and one newspaper featured Rives's personal tips, such as how to obtain "beauty sleep" by a bath "in cool cologne water" before bedtime and the use of a pillow. In the morning, "another cold bath in perfumed water, and the beauty sleep is over, and with most beneficial results, for none is more beautiful than the newly married princess."[46]

Other newspaper items, in keeping with Rives's new status as a "princess," related her to European culture. A Honolulu paper announced that

Amélie Rives and Pierre Troubetzkoy, shown here around 1900, forged a life together. (Amélie Rives Troubetzkoy Collection, The Valentine)

"Amelie Rives, the American author, will establish a literary salon in Paris." That same month a column about Americans in France indicated that "it is rumoured among Americans that Princess Troubetskoi, former wife of John Armstrong Candler [*sic*] and better known as Amelie Rives, will settle here with her present husband's wealthy relatives, about Christmas, to remain permanently, making an occasional visit to the old Virginia homestead. . . . She comes here specifically to use her influence to win literary recognition and will probably maintain a literary salon."[47] None of Rives's surviving letters suggests any substance to these rumors.

By 1900 Rives's physical problems apparently came to a head. In July, her husband closed his Washington studio three weeks early to remain "by her bedside." *Harper's Bazaar* gave a gloomy assessment: "For several years past she has lived an invalid and a recluse in her fine old home in Virginia. Now the end of her life is said to be near at hand, and she is dying, separated from the world and attended only by a faithful old colored

The Princess of Albemarle

servant." Another paper in July divulged that she would leave for Bar Harbor to be treated by a "distinguished Boston specialist for sciatica" and concluded: "The Princess has for some time been a great sufferer from this disease and is now unable to walk."[48]

Later that summer, on a Tuesday afternoon, August 14, perhaps under the influence of drugs, Rives left home (presumably walking). The next afternoon she was discovered sitting beside an old mill pond at the foot of Walnut Mountain. One article pronounced that "her eccentricities, which have always been great and varied, seem to have been emphasized by her invalidism. There have recently been all sorts of reports about her health and her mental condition." The upshot of this incident was a short article later that month with the unhelpful headline "Princess Not Insane." Pierre Troubetzkoy, the story reported, "states in his most positive manner that his wife has not been out of her mind although publication of such stories and the mailing of them to her by maliciously-inclined persons has been of serious injury to her in her admittedly poor nervous condition."[49]

Newspaper coverage during this period treated Rives as an invalid "authoress." An October 1900 story was typical. It called Rives a "beautiful wreck of her former self" who was living as a "voluntary prisoner" at Castle Hill with "her health ruined and her nervous system unstrung," and predicted that the "life of the young princess [is] now evidently near its end." Scattering reams of misinformation, the article then recounted Rives's unhappy marriage to Chanler, "a man considerably her senior," and subsequent remarriage in Paris to Troubetzkoy, "a Corsican" who had painted a portrait of the queen of England. The following month the *New York Times* disclosed that Rives along with her mother and sister were spending the winter in Richmond: "The Princess, it will be remembered, has been in bad health for several months, and was for some time under treatment at Boston by a distinguished specialist for nervous diseases." In 1903 the newspaper indicated that Rives "writes very little and is more or less of an invalid."[50]

It was only a small leap from treating Rives as prone to nervous prostration to criticizing her writing as hysterical. In the mid-1890s, many critics had a consistent critique of Amélie: she was the chronicler of passion and a progenitor of other overly emotional novelists. In 1896 while reviewing a book by Julian Hawthorne (son of Nathaniel Hawthorne), the *Literary World* propounded, "We had not supposed that any one could beat Amélie Rives in her own peculiar province," but Hawthorne's book has "achieved that difficult feat": "a more unpleasant description of love has never been written." In 1902 J. P. Mowbray, in a piece called "The Higher Hysterics," focused on "Lady Literature," which he defined as the chronicle of an irrational wife who places her own emotional state at the center of the universe. Mowbray doubly damned Rives as he argued that the new Lady Literature had "outgrown the tumultuous ravening of Amelie Rives" until it reached "an achievement at once magical and momentous, as if some one had preserved in the pressed herbarium all the fleeting odors and unpredictable [*sic*] wantonings of the summer flowers."[51]

Despite the new rash of unfavorable reviews, Rives, sometime after her illness in 1900, managed to break her dependence on opiates. She never gave any indication of how this came about, possibly because this long battle with addiction was the part of her life she most regretted. Louis Auchincloss remembered that, as an elderly lady, she had assured him "that she soon broke the habit and never went back to it." Amélie also seemed to intimate that many in New York society knew about her victory over drug dependence. She once recounted to Auchincloss how, when she was at the opera in New York with her arm on the partition separating two loges, a mysterious woman clutched her hand and whispered: "Don't look around, but tell me oh please tell me, how you did it." Then "Amélie whispered of her struggles while staring down at the fingers on which, in the dim light, she could make out immense jewels. The lights went up for the entr'acte, and the neighboring box was empty. But she knew it belonged to one of the richest families in New York."[52] Even though Rives admitted her problem to Auchincloss, she apparently found it difficult to be completely honest and purposely glided over the many years—perhaps even a decade—that she battled the craving for opiates.

In the new century, Rives began to regain better health. She was in a sanitarium, possibly for sciatica, when her father died in February 1903, but she soon was recuperating and told her former nurse that April: "I find I can't walk yet. It makes me giddy, but with the first mild weather I am sure that this will be quite right."[53] By the summer she was riding again and also painting. She confided that she found "pastels fascinating."[54] Reaching again for the creative realm, Rives returned to writing and publishing—not only short stories but poetry and novels as well. From 1902 until 1918, she turned out poems, short stories, and novels, not at the fevered pace of her youth, but in a steady stream, publishing six short stories and nine book-length works (including two extended blank verse poems and two novels that were serialized in magazines).

Rives's enduring interest in poetry and classical civilizations rejuvenated her pen. In 1902 the *North American Review* published her poem "A Hymn to the Sea," which combined her long-standing fascination with Greek mythology with a quest for religious meaning. In part, she compares herself to the sea in its lack of control and love of freedom, calling herself "one of those who at the most / Desire no memories, only sleep and night." She also brings up her stormy past romantic history:

> My heart, O Sea! My heart too hath its tides,
> Its moods of rage, its calms, its storms again;
> Its ice-bound regions where no life abides,
> Its snow-fields where a rose would seem a stain;

That heart, in her depiction, held caverns:

> Its wrecks majestic, and its towers tall of moon-white castles built for
>   ecstasy,
> But turned by time to echoing tombs forlorn
> Where many a drowned hope doth lie in state.

Much of the poem lauds the various Greek gods connected with the sea and moon. Rives invokes the power of the sea to lift her higher, but this time toward a secular redemption: "O toss me starward as I were thy spray!" The final two lines read: "O may my soul's tides ever ruled be, / By the pure golden sphere of Love's high mystery!"[55]

Poetry dominated Rives's return to writing. She took up again a blank verse poem on a moon goddess that she had been contemplating back in the summer of 1893, when she told her sister-in-law: "I am going to begin work again on *Sélené* today."[56] In 1905 she published the book-length poem.

Sélené represents the mature version of Rives's interest in Greek myths and ancient history and also builds on her love of Keats, who had related the story of the moon goddess and her lover in his poem *Endymion.* The voluptuousness of *Sélené*'s poetic imagery draws from the aesthete tradition of Algernon Swinburne and Dante Gabriel Rossetti, which Rives had long admired. She interprets Sélené to be not only the moon goddess but also several of her avatars, Artemis, Diana, and Phoebe: "For many maidens in one goddess dwell."[57]

Rives depicts Sélené as being from infancy cursed with unhappiness, whether she made a friend or foe of love. As the goddess of the hunt, Sélené delights in her coldness and virginity, but she is entranced when she happens upon the sleeping shepherd Endymion, whose beauty is as great as her own. Half mortal, half god, Sélené proudly summons Eros for a confrontation. Trying to plunge one of the arrows from her own quiver into her breast, the goddess instead uses one belonging to Eros, which Fate has substituted. Sélené must then drink from the cup of Fate and learn how to choose between good and evil. In the end the impassioned goddess rushes forth in search of Endymion and love.

Rives's poem illustrates her love of word imagery as her vivid scenes pulse and exalt the senses. The reader must see, hear, and feel the onrush of events. Sélené as Artemis appears as the superb athlete: "Her tresses by her vehement speed unloosed, / Melted in golden mist upon the wind." Her arrogance is immense as she tells Eros, "I fear thee not, O Love—I fear thee not." The description of Eros is even more luxuriant:

> A crown of jonquils intertwined with stars
> Rested above his dark and tender brows,
> Wherein was gathered all the mystic gloom
> That haunts the far, faint level of the sea.

The god appears in a boat of ivory:

> Nor robe nor mantle wore he, being clad
> In his own splendor as in golden gauze,
> Where through his languid limbs gleamed silverly
> Veilèd yet hidden not.[58]

Amid this confrontation, Artemis/Sélené proudly declares of herself: "What hath the Goddess of White Chastity to do with gorgeous Love?" Eros then responds: "Chastity is not abstinence but temperance. / True Chastity is truer for true love." He disparages her as being, "chaste [not] because of conquered fire, but merely chill bearing a heart unkindled." When Sélené, after learning the difference between good and evil, chooses love,

The Princess of Albemarle

she declares, "All is changed." She salutes love, even though she knows its passion will bring pain as well as joy:

O pain delicious! O mysterious longing!
O hunger fierce, divine, as of a god
Fireborn for fire! Endymion I come![59]

Although the poem broke new ground for Rives and marked a high point in her explorations of love, passion, and the virtue of chastity, which she redefined, readers no doubt compared its heroine to Rives herself. When Sélené sings, "How from my birth I loved the free wide life / Of wood and meadow," she clearly echoes Rives's own love of the rural Piedmont. Moreover, Sélené says "I loved mine own bright freedom more than love—such love as Maidens dream of ere they sleep!" And she amplifies her power:

No! mine it was to feel the larger zest,
The nobler ache, the frenzy all divine
Of maidenhood that knows itself a power,
A force supreme through very loneliness!—
Mine, mine the ecstasy of fellowship
With winds and waves and frost, and fire itself;
Possessing all things, yet by none possessed;[60]

In addition to the figure of Sélené/Artemis, readers would have found other parts of the poem redolent of Rives's life story. Endymion's pain at his earlier loveless union suggests Rives's broken marriage to Archie Chanler:

For he had known
The sapping, slow, brain-sucking misery
That falls upon the passionate whom error
Unto the passionless hath bound. Full well,
Ah bitter well, he knew the dregs that lie
Within the cup of tepid tenderness.

After chronicling the toll that this dreariness exacts from the body, Rives indicates another pain to the spirit in terms that also evoke her experiences with Archie:

The endless striving to unmake ourselves
Because one loves us for the thing we are not
Nor ever shall be—effort barren, senseless,
Resulting in the death, not of our faults,
But the life within us, till we grow
Into a dull, meek, apathetic being,
Incapable of love or hate or joy,
Incapable of mourning overmuch
Our own incapability. . . .[61]

Readers who knew about the courtship with Pierre Troubetzkoy might also have considered *Sélené* to resonate with Rives's history of seeking love and beauty. After all, both she and Pierre were "beautiful" people.

Sélené focuses on a woman and her growth and emotional empowerment. In contrast to Keats's *Endymion,* presented from the viewpoint of the shepherd lad, *Sélené* features the moon goddess addressing the perplexities of love and sexuality. Indeed, the charge given Sélené—to be neither a friend nor foe of love—seems to have echoed the difficulties that Rives saw in the Victorian era's double standard that deemed sexual urges and activity as natural for men but foreign to and even degrading for women. Since the early nineties, Rives had been arguing that women needed to know more about sexuality and even passion in order to make the right choices.[62]

Sélené, an opulent blank-verse exploration of Greek myth, gained respect from critics. Dubbing Rives "a writer of surprises," the *Reader* magazine held that "the story is told with the real poet's rapture in rhythm and in delicately tinted phrase. Its cadences are true and songful, its imagery fresh in conception and vista opening." Considering the poem "a prism of brightness," Louise Collier Willcox in the *North American Review* characterized it as "a highly modern, romantic, temperamental study of passion." She was especially impressed by Rives's use of color: "The visual sense is predominant, the sense for color almost obliterating line." Willcox concluded with a single word of disapproval: "We trace the same personality in this poet which produced those striking and romantic tales of the time of Shakespeare, a personality exuberant, intense, highly endowed, imaginative, undisciplined."[63]

In *Harper's Weekly,* C. H. Gaines asserted that Rives had treated her theme with "perfect originality": "Her style is not merely splendid in description but it possesses that peculiar aptness of characterization which makes the words of a poet the final expression of an idea." In addition to the poem's beauty of language, he praised its conception: "The author harks back to the older notion of Hesiod, which makes Love a sort of sublime and mystical power, that existed before Jove was, and who, like the Fates, cannot be safely defied, even by Jove himself." Gaines concluded: "The triumph of Love over the goddess of chastity is the conquest of a higher ideal over one less perfect, so that the poem has a grandeur greater than the pomp of pagan divinities contending."[64]

The following year Rives published another work based on the distant past, a blank verse study of the personal relationships of St. Augustine, titled *Augustine the Man*. According to her literary biographer, Rives always considered this her finest work. In it she pens a vivacious portrait of Melcara, Augustine's mistress, who fears his growing interest in Christianity. She deems it a crueler religion than her own worship of the Carthaginian god, Melcarth. Augustine's attraction to Christian sainthood, however, appears from the early pages, when he contradicts a friend who says that in finding oneself, one finds God. Instead, Augustine poses: "Say rather, That he who finds God finds himself."[65]

These two carefully wrought long poems show Rives writing luminously and revitalizing her career. Although she had not gained the high literary reputation she had desired at age twenty-two, when she published her first story and first poem, she was constructing a new persona—that of the enlightened princess who was a patron of literature and the arts. This seems to have brought her peace and even fulfillment. And her happiness with Pierre Troubetzkoy (to whom she dedicated *Augustine the Man*) was an indispensable part of that new persona.

Years of dealing with an avalanche of publicity had, by 1900, given Amélie comfort with public life. During her illness, Pierre had laid out their philosophy: "I know that my wife is a public personage so far as her works go . . . and that her doings are of legitimate interest to the public, but her private affairs are only her own business."[66] No longer the overwhelmed young woman of the late 1880s, Amélie by the first decade of the twentieth century was more consistently able to cope with the press. Usually, just as one of her new books was being published, she gave long interviews—exclusives of a sort—to reporters willing to write favorable stories.

Early in the new century, the tide was turning in favor of her image in the literary world. When the author and critic William Dean Howells, in his "Editor's Study" column in *Harper's Magazine* in March 1901, described genius in art and letters, he mentioned Rives as having "a distinctive quality of genius nowhere else manifest in a so wholly native fashion" and compared her to Emily Dickinson. Howells thought it significant that Rives's education had been at home and through browsing her grandfather's library. "She neither copied nor imitated; she caught dominant notes and passed into harmonies that were variant and distinctly individual." Not only did Howells praise Rives's early stories, his summation of her career looked to future achievements: "It is proper to speak of her in the present tense rather than the past, for she is yet to be heard from in the literary world, and through work as striking and original as any she has ever done."[67]

As she recovered from her past turmoil, Rives came thoroughly to inhabit the role of princess. The visits that she and Pierre made to his family home in Lake Maggiore are illustrative. In the new century Amélie and Pierre at first divided their lives between America and Europe. In 1901 they spent late winter in New York, where he painted portraits, then sailed to Europe in May, at which point the *New York Times* called her health "improved." When they returned from Italy that November, the *Times* reported the prince's intention to "open a studio" in New York. This combination of summers in Europe, winters in New York City or Virginia, lasted for several years, and newspaper coverage of her departures and arrivals cemented her celebrity status. In a November 1904 *Times* item about the Princess Troubetzkoy's arrival on a North German liner with the German consul and the Italian soprana Maria de Macchi, it was Rives who received the headline: "Amelie Rives on the Prinzess [*sic*] Irene."[68]

Once more, Rives was celebrated as a great beauty. In August 1901 the *Critic* emphasized her loveliness in a sketch of "The Princess Troubetzkoy (Amélie Rives)." In 1903 a San Francisco newspaper pronounced Amélie "most charming" and presented her as the cynosure of fashion, "one of the first to discover the beauties of the draped gown, and in her fondness for it, she was closely seconded by Mrs. William C. Whitney and Mrs. Cleveland." Here the newspaper was grouping Rives with the wife of a financier and a former First Lady. A year earlier the same newspaper had included her in a summary of new fashions: "A silk gown which might be described as stunning was worn by the Princess Troubetskoy, who was Miss Amelie Rives. It was designed by the Prince, her artist husband, and its material was changeable black taffeta. It looked all colors in different lights." The article included a detailed exposition of the construction of the dress, including

The Princess Troubetzkoy (Amelie Rives)

FROM THE LATEST PHOTOGRAPH OF THE GREAT AMERICAN AUTHOR

This illustration in *Harper's Weekly* of July 11, 1908, shows how Amélie Rives portrayed herself as Princess Troubetzkoy, wearing a tiara. (Library of Virginia)

the pleats in the skirt, "which seemed to fall straight to the floor from her slender figure."[69]

Rives could rely on that celebrity in dealing with other authors. In 1905, when Mark Twain turned seventy, a large dinner of 170 authors, illustrators, and editors celebrated the event at Delmonico's, then the best-known restaurant in New York City. George Harvey, editor of the *North American Review* and a wealthy streetcar magnate, hosted the party, which featured letters of congratulation from President Roosevelt and numerous British authors. The dinner began with an orchestra of forty playing a processional for the guests. After Twain himself entered with Mary Wilkins Freeman, a New England writer of local color stories, "Col. Harvey led Princess Troubetzkoy who once was Amelie Rives and still writes under that name. Andrew Carnegie and Agnes Repplier, the essayist, followed side by side."

The friends and acquaintances that Rives had made during her sojourns in Great Britain and on the Continent added to her prestige and visibility as well as her intellectual well-being and happiness. Louise Moulton, who had celebrated Rives during her literary teas in London in the 1890s, so valued their friendship that she wrote a poem, "Her Magic," dedicated to Rives. Composed of rhyming couplets celebrating Rives's beauty, the poem proclaimed: "You look at me with those deep, haunting eyes, / and all my life replies."[70] Rives and Moulton remained close for many years.

Rives also became friendly with fellow Virginia writer Ellen Glasgow, who was a decade younger. It is not clear whether they met in Richmond or while Glasgow was taking expensive foreign vacations financed by the generosity of her wealthy brother. By March 1905 Glasgow was planning a visit to Castle Hill, and Rives soon introduced her to other writers abroad. That summer, Rives gave Glasgow a letter of introduction to Louise Moulton, describing her Richmond friend as "one of the most intellectual & spiritual beings I have ever known." Rives also cautioned Moulton that Glasgow was "very deaf & rather shy but I feel that she will not be shy with you for I have told her how I love you."[71]

With her return to publishing, Rives used the press to gain readers. The publicity that rolled forth, though designed to sell her stories and novels, reinforced the image that she was building of herself as a gracious princess, aloof from the bustle of modern life. In a 1905 interview in the *New York Times*, Rives claimed that seventeen years had elapsed since she had been the subject of "a personal sketch . . . that is a true one, taken from life." That assertion was accurate only if one considered the biographical piece published with the "The Quick or the Dead?" to have been the only "personal sketch" and somehow differentiated from the many interviews she had given since that time.

The *Times* interview echoed common depictions of Rives, stressing her beauty and youthfulness. A reporter using the pen name Pendennis described her as "a slender figure in a soft, flowing robe of white, a little woman, perhaps a trifle above the average height." The writer emphasized facial features that had long been remarked upon: "large gray eyes . . . a mouth that was perfect in a woman, feminine in its tenderness, yet clear bold in its outline, . . . her soft brown hair worn low on the neck in girlish fashion . . . a nose that was Grecian in its shape and proportions, a low wide brow, and a smile that was all happiness and health." "She looked like a girl scarce out of her 'teens,'"

Pendennis averred, "and yet the stern statistics of dated time showed she must be nearly forty."[72] In fact, Rives was almost forty-two.

Rives was not a "New York Princess" associated with "bridal suites and a staff of flunkeys" declared the interviewer, who instead dubbed her a "Princess o' Dreams," ensconced in a "quiet apartment" in the heart of the hotel district. Amélie herself emphasized her simple life—rising at seven in the morning, retiring at ten in the evening. During the day, "[I] ride or walk in the country roads, live close to my books, see few people. . . . What fashionable woman could endure my life!" Calling Castle Hill a "dear, old-fashioned, rambling country house," Rives also highlighted her European connections: "then we take trips to the Prince's home on Lake Maggiore, and there we find ourselves amid all the reminiscences of his childhood."[73]

The interview aimed to enhance Rives's reputation as a writer as well as a beauty and aristocrat, and this perhaps had been her intent in granting it. While denying that the story was about her latest poem *Seléné*, Pendennis compared Rives to Keats and claimed that the poem "establishes Amélie Rives among the great poets, contemporary by an accident of time only," and

Amélie Rives poses here with a dog, probably on Lake Maggiore in Italy. (Amélie Rives Troubetzkoy Collection, The Valentine)

further proposed: "It is important that we should acknowledge her, drape her shoulders with the mantle of honor and rank that she deserves and that she has been denied in the contemporary falsities that have been told about her personality." Rives described herself as intellectually independent, saying that "I read very little of modern work," which she then compared to items stored in a chest with rose leaves that then all shared that "same perfume."[74]

While painting a positive portrait and creating interest in Rives and her writings, the article contained some candid moments. She was willing to acknowledge that she had moved away from her religious upbringing. "I am not a believer in any sectarian influences, although I suppose by family instinct and association, I am Episcopalian." Asked whether she attended the Episcopal Church, Rives responded that she accompanied her mother but added: "I scarcely feel that any religion is greater than another; they are all part of the broad way to human sympathy and human sentiment." She admitted her preference for poetry over prose: "I don't like prose and I don't write very much of it now," she confided. And with a touch of imperiousness, and perhaps even overconfidence, she added: "The editors tell me they want prose, but they will have to take my poetry or nothing."[75]

The following year another profile of Rives from the pen of Pendennis, titled "A Week's End Visit with Amelie Rives," appeared in the *New York Times* magazine. Asserting that "so much is said [about Rives] and yet so little told that is true," Pendennis described an intellectual hermit who, "because of her chosen exile from the clamor of a selfish, pleasure-loving world, [is] a woman who has retained great beauty and amazing youth." Rives appears an aristocrat of the world, who spends winters on the Rives estate comprising nearly three thousand acres and summers "at her husband's villa on Lake Maggiore, in Italy." The interviewer gushed: "It is all reminiscent of the English grandeur of country life where so far as the eye can see is private field and woodland and hillside." Despite these aristocratic surroundings, Rives herself has no airs; wearing "a modest little blue serge suit," she is a "trim, out-of-doors person," walking on the estate even on the coldest winter days. When questioned whether she wore furs, Rives replied, "No I just put on a covert coat [a British topcoat often used for hunting], and the world is mine." Rives again was depicting herself as a cosmopolitan country aristocrat.[76]

Pendennis used a quotation from *Augustine the Man* as an epigraph: "But every woman hath some whispering god / Who tells her secrets." As recipient of those divine insights, Rives had a wisdom that exceeded even her literary skill: "She is a woman who has discovered in the secrets that her 'whispering god' has told her the spiritual essences of life: the renunciations, the braveries, the intellectual contentments, the broad mission of tenderness and affection toward those who are still blinded by the glare of prejudices— the pleasures of giving and forgiving."[77]

Even more than the first article, this second interview emphasized Rives's seclusion, intellectual independence, and genius. Castle Hill had no neighbors within four or five miles, according to Pendennis, and "the household itself is small, for so large a place, although usually the poet has with her some intimate friend of the family." Dinner was by candlelight. Never reading a newspaper, Amélie "has no interest in the transient vagaries of the world beyond that Virginia valley, and yet she has a keen sense of humor, and has the courage and initiative of a man when she desires to exert it." Such autonomy extended to her writing: "She writes when the spirit moves, and only a small fraction of all she writes ever leaves her safe." The story contrasted Rives's artistic temperament to the "executive" ability of her sister, Gertrude Rives Potts, who managed the estate as a stock farm. Amélie, in the article's summation, "lives on the remote horizon of a jealous world, and listens to the secrets of her 'whispering god' in the solitude of that dream-valley of Virginia."[78]

In yet a third interview by Pendennis, Rives appeared as a cultural authority, a "poet who has preferred a life of consistent obscurity, an idyllic absence from the world of innumerable celebrities." Commenting on the state of intellectual America, Rives declared that "few dared to live out our primitive instincts, to test the true ideals of life." Religious conservatism was the culprit: "I think Americans are all keenly alive to spiritual meaning, but they seem to me still bound by fixed conventions and creeds and a certain false pretense of morals that cripple the poets." Although Rives asserted that "Americans are the most intelligent people in the world," she also believed that "in poetic sensibility they mistake sentimentality for actual principles of life." Here Rives stood aloof from her American heritage to insist her own vision was wider, ripened by her experiences in Europe. Thus, she decried the "bloodless watchfulness against the intrusion of actual passions, as though the human heart was at its best only when in a state of conventional propriety."[79]

Not only did Rives receive favorable notice in national publications, she was hailed as a dignitary closer to home. When in January 1906 she spent several weeks in Richmond visiting with Lutie Pleasants and enjoying "a round of social functions given in her honor," the Richmond paper effused that the "princess is no less a favorite than when as the beautiful Amelie Rives, she spent much of her time here." The correspondent remarked, "It has been twenty years since the princess has visited Richmond for more than a couple of days at a time."[80]

Even as Rives remade her life, her social circle was contracting in some ways. Her father, Alfred L. Rives, died in 1903; her dear friend Julia Magruder in 1907; Louise Moulton in 1908. Although Archie was living on his Merrie Mills estate near Castle Hill, Amélie apparently spent no time with him. In 1906 Rives asserted that she had not seen Archie since the divorce and added: "I have seen him at a distance twice. I have not spoken to him."[81]

By the end of the first decade of the twentieth century, Rives had radically altered her life. She had left an unsatisfying marriage and found a lover she considered a soul mate. As she and Pierre tried to make a living from their art, she broke free of her dependence on opiates and cocaine. She once again found her literary creativity and produced her finest poetic works to date in *Sélené* and *Augustine the Man,* poems that brought her a higher status among editors and other authors. In the process, she assumed the persona of the European cosmopolitan aristocrat who could instruct Americans in spirituality and human nature. As a cosmopolite, she also smoked cigarettes and wore cosmetics—activities that in fin-de-siècle America were still not respectable. As she attempted to exert intellectual heft and the past allure of her youth, she insisted that she was both an artist and a princess.

· NINE ·

"A Legend with the Men of Father's Age"

The Princess as Author, Playwright, and Muse

As Amélie Rives re-created her image as that of a gracious princess, she also sought to rehabilitate her literary reputation and her writing career. The loss of payments from Archie Chanler for over a decade meant that she and Pierre needed to finance on their own a luxurious lifestyle suitable for an aristocratic position: a studio for Pierre, first in Washington, later in New York City, and estate living at beautiful Castle Hill, which required a staff to care for the family and its animals. Only in 1911 did Rives successfully sue the administrators of Archie's monies to resume this annuity of around three thousand dollars; she also sought repayment of twenty thousand dollars that he had allegedly borrowed from her.[1] A practical streak thus drove her authorial career after 1905, as she returned to both novels and short stories.

Rives also looked to a wider role as a writer. She experimented with playwriting and even took a brief foray into the newer medium of motion pictures—making appearances and selling screenplays. Never an activist, she nonetheless lent her name and support to reform and charitable efforts and causes, such as the author's freedom from censorship, women's rights, support for immigrants, and antilynching. She seems particularly to have enjoyed the support and companionship that she lent to and, in return, found among younger authors.

Although Alfred and Sadie Rives had worried that Amélie's marriage to Pierre Troubetzkoy might move her permanent residence to Europe, Castle Hill remained her base, supplemented by summers in Europe (before 1915) and winter visits to New York City that continued for almost a decade after 1914. Though personally tied to Castle Hill, Rives showed a wide choice of locales and genres in her writing. That, along with her resort to short stories, seems to have been driven in part by the need to sell her work, with

Pioneering photojournalist Jessie Tarbox Beals created this regal
image of Amélie Rives, sometime in the early twentieth century.
(Schlesinger Library, Radcliffe Institute, Harvard University)

the help of agents and other representatives. Taking advantage of the surge
of magazines in the twentieth century, she also continued to serialize many
of her novels.

In the decade after 1905 Rives accomplished some of her most polished
fictional writing and turned to a wider number of themes and styles. Many of
her stories and novels in the 1880s had used dialect or ancient settings. She
retained the dialect in some stories, but after 1905 most of her fiction focused
on modern themes. Welford Dunaway Taylor has denominated this her "second period," in which she became "additionally experienced in the realities
of her art as well as human experience in general."[2] Much of this work, even

The Princess of Albemarle

when obviously aimed at a popular audience, showed a finish that her earlier writings had seldom attained. She had become a working writer.

In the twentieth century Rives seldom wrote about poorer white and African American southerners, but she did not completely abandon the dialect novel. Because she reveled in word choice and subtle meanings, she enjoyed dialect and saw it as her strength. One of her lighter novels of the time—*Trix and Over-the-Moon,* serialized in *Harper's* and published by that house in 1909—features a heroine resembling her sister Gertrude who runs a Virginia horse breeding farm. Rives even dedicated the book to Gertrude. The story also includes a Scottish character who speaks in a broad Scots dialect.

Rives's *Hidden House* (1912) presents a family of Scottish origin in the Virginia mountains. Although the heavy use of Scots dialect among the characters in *Hidden House* was implausible, the plot itself marked an advance in Rives's storytelling. Framed by a northern narrator, *Hidden House* spotlights a Scottish farmer's two winsome granddaughters, Moina and Robina, who care for him. The narrator quickly falls in love with Moina, who is quiet, demure, beautiful, yet very repressed and mysterious. When her sister Robina appears, the narrator finds her electric personality irresistible. Early in the novel, Rives hints at what the narrator will discover when she has him muse: "And life holds no starker fact than this, that a man's heart may bear two loves at once, just as a woman may bear twin children."[3] By the end of the story, when Robina falls into one of her frequent swoons, the narrator realizes that he is not dealing with two people but only one who exhibits what today would be considered multiple personalities (described by Rives as "two souls"). The characters, including a maimed, mute, formerly enslaved Jamaican servant and the grandfather who favors the spark of the Robina personality and encourages her excesses, are drawn as extreme types, but the story moves quickly and easily.

Rives also drew on her residence in England and on the Continent to add a European fillip to her work. In *Pan's Mountain* (1910), she bases her story on the myths that had so often interested her. She sets this love story between a young woman and a visiting Englishman in the mountains of the Italian lake region. While Rives resorts to a melodramatic ending, *Pan's Mountain* shows that she could map out believable and complex modern male characters who were more than mere foils to her female protagonists.

Rives's confidence that she had found a new footing in literature grew. In October 1913 she confided to Ellen Glasgow, "I seem to have come into a new place with my writing and it is very pleasant."[4] In the next two years Rives published two of her best constructed novels, *World's-End* and *Shadows of Flames,* both of which chronicle Virginia-born heroines in American and European locales.

Rives, however, encountered some problems with publishing *World's-End.* She sent it to J. B. Lippincott at the end of 1912; in January 1913 the firm assured her that it had given the novel "more than usual consideration" but "with very great regret" determined that "it would not be prudent business to undertake its publication" on her suggested terms. Although the publisher deemed the novel "exceptionally well done" as a literary piece, he expressed concerns about the "business aspect of the proposition." At 200,000 words, *World's-End* was double the length of the usual novel and thus would entail "double cost of composition, proof reading, plates, paper and press work and considerable increase in the cost of gathering sheets for binding." Yet the real sticking problem was Rives's expectations, as she had apparently insisted on double the ordinary royalty, or even 50 percent more than that paid to "favored authors." Despite this rejection, the press's representative tried to keep alive the relationship by regretting "our inability to meet your views." In fact, *World's-End,* when it was published by Frederick A. Stokes, seems to have done quite well in the marketplace. Rives wrote, "It went into 3 editions in nine days, which I think is very good. The first edition was 7,000 volumes, and the second 3,000, so that ten thousand copies were sold in nine days! Wasn't that encouraging?"[5]

World's-End explores a challenging topic—the problem of premarital pregnancy and the plight of the seduced and abandoned young woman. Phoebe Nelson, an innocent Virginia girl, becomes entranced by Richard Bryce, a pretentious young painter visiting his wealthy forty-seven-year-old socialist uncle, Owen Randolph. After Phoebe becomes pregnant from a passionate encounter, she realizes that Richard has no intention of marrying her and legitimating their unborn child. Attempting suicide, she is rescued by Owen, who proposes marriage. Yet, even though Owen marries Phoebe and gives his name to her child, they have a sexless union and never discuss the relationship that led to her pregnancy. As this marriage, intended to rescue a vulnerable young woman, becomes increasingly companionate, the novel strains credulity. Owen's high-mindedness and Phoebe's reticence about her sexual past probably seemed dated and overly Victorian to many early twentieth-century readers. Although Rives shows the principled hero giving way to rage and assailing his caddish nephew, she provides the story with a conventional happy ending as Owen and Phoebe come to appreciate and love one another, turning their marriage into one filled with passion as well as respect. The ending, much like the couple's earlier failure to discuss sexual behavior, undermined Rives's attempt at realism in tackling illegitimate pregnancy. Moreover, the novel's focus on Owen probably impaired her intended critique of male privilege. On the other hand, her heroine evolves from being a naive, suicidal provincial in Virginia to an accepted, and even celebrated, member of an intellectual upper-class social set when she visits England.

As in earlier works, Rives drew upon parts of her own history for *World's-End*. Phoebe's success in English society recalls Amélie's own acceptance by the Souls in the 1890s. Moreover, Owen Randolph, in his wish to better the poor in Virginia, echoes Archie Chanler's idealism. Dubbed a socialist by his relatives, Randolph admits to such tendencies and calls himself a "question asker."[6]

But Rives's depiction of African Americans in Virginia had become more hackneyed and racist. To be sure, she describes the housekeeper, Hannah, as "a character with all the best traits of the white race yet of full negro blood." She and her husband, Old Jonathan, are kind and reliable; their daughter through the generosity of Owen Randolph has been educated as a nurse in Boston. Despite these stabs at respecting African Americans and their achievements, Rives uses most other Black characters as either unthinkingly loyal or humorous in their idiosyncrasies. Rives goes much further than her earlier works in promoting the notion of the antebellum plantation as an organic community. An elderly African American man, Gared Douglas, who had belonged to Randolph's grandfather, arrives at World's-End from Culpeper and asks Randolph to buy him, because he wants to belong to someone. Randolph, as a kindly patriarch, assures "Uncle Gared" that he can live at World's-End for the rest of his life.[7] Here Rives is suggesting a long line of benevolent plantation owners and devoted enslaved people—a vision congruent with the white supremacist notions of the day and one also emphasizing her own aristocratic background. Segregation and white supremacist claims had gained increasing acceptance in the early twentieth century, and many white southerners voiced or were swayed by them. Moreover, Rives's high esteem for her father and grandfather may have influenced her to prettify the white men of the plantation community. As an author, she had moved closer to the notions that Thomas Nelson Page had been purveying back in the 1880s.

Welford Taylor argues that *World's-End* is Rives's finest work, and critics at the time were generally positive in their reviews. The *New York Times* found the book distinctive because of its assertion that "a woman who has been wronged has not been irreparably stained thereby, that she may still deserve the respect of the world and keep her pride in herself, and that marriage itself may itself be freed from sex jealousy and sex ownership." Although suggesting that some would see the hero Owen Randolph as "too good to be true," the critic also approved of "a new idea given us of generosity in marriage." Perhaps the most insightful reviewer termed *World's-End* "a realistic novel written in a sentimental manner."[8]

That judgment suggests that Ellen Glasgow and Rives, despite their friendship, had been moving in different directions in their fiction. In 1913, a year before the appearance of *World's-End,* Glasgow published *Virginia,* set in Dinwiddie (a town that looked and sounded much like Petersburg, Virginia). *Virginia* chronicles the eponymous heroine's courtship and marriage and the marriage's disintegration, all as she tries to be a southern lady who is a perfect wife and mother. Glasgow also portrays a far grittier and poorer community and dwells on its numerous disappointments and inequities. When in the 1920s, Glasgow visited the topic of illegitimate pregnancy, she again offered a different perspective from Rives's treatment of that subject. Featuring an unmarried Piedmont Virginia woman who becomes pregnant, Glasgow's *Barren Ground* (1925) contains much turmoil and pain as her heroine, though later marrying and becoming a successful farmer, is emotionally hardened by her experience and emerges tough and unyielding. Resonating with readers and critics alike, *Barren Ground* became a classic.

Rives, in fact, had poured her own outlook into *World's-End.* Just before its publication, she gave a long interview to the *New York Times,* laying out her views on marriage and divorce. To her, ideal marriages combined passion with companionship and friendship and stressed mutual respect. As the interviewer summarized it, Rives "conceives the social relation to be ideal when the status of the woman in the case is not that of wife-chattel, wife-vassal, wife-drudge or perhaps, least of all wife-dictator, but that of wife-friend."[9]

When the interviewer probed whether marriage between two artists posed special problems, Rives declared, "Like temperaments understand

The Princess of Albemarle

each other the more readily. Certainly the artistic impulse is a bond in itself." The reporter interpreted this comment to touch upon Rives's own marriage to Pierre: "she considers her marriage with the big painter-Prince as an embodiment of that theory." Amélie herself offered an anecdote about how shared interests kept her marriage fresh: "For instance, one evening not long ago, Prince Troubetzkoy and I were both rather tired, and we had decided to get a long night's rest. Then we began to talk art. We talked on and on, and before we knew it was 2 o'clock in the morning."[10]

Rives was conveying her sense of herself as an artist as well as a wife. When she considered what married women without specific talents or intellectual interests ought to do, she concluded that "it would be best for them to search their natures closely before deciding that they were really without the impulse to do something positive: to sing, to play, to dance, to do any of the thousand and one deeply interesting things." Her focus was not on self-support; instead she wanted a married woman to have "an occupation for the mind, in addition to her home or household occupations, whatever she may choose." To Amélie, such intellectual independence was crucial to the "permanency of marriage, both by doing away with monotony and by keeping husband and wife somewhat apart." In her view, constant companionship risked the relationship "becoming commonplace and losing its charm."[11]

In this highly productive period Rives also created one of her most self-revelatory novels, *Shadows of Flames,* published in 1915. Loosely organized, the book chronicles eight years of the life and loves of a Virginia-born heroine, Sophy Chesney. Although Rives skillfully develops her major characters, she follows the increasingly old-fashioned conventions of the Victorian domestic novel. Her major male and female characters are beautiful; they encounter a range of mishaps and accidental encounters to propel the plot forward. Although Rives does not give the conventional happy ending, she nonetheless bathes the heroine's relationship with her son in the sentimentality and devotion that many associate with nineteenth-century notions of motherhood.

Shadows of Flames showed that Rives still expected her readers to connect her stories with her life; indeed, at times she seems to be positively enjoying the associations she was forging for her audience. Sophy Chesney, like Rives, had published a passionate book (of verse rather than fiction) before being romanced by wealthy men in Europe and the United States, although the author, as she had done before, gives her heroine a different body type than her own.

Rives drew on other figures in her romantic past for her book's cast of characters. Sophy's second husband, the immensely rich Morris Loring of New York, resembles in crucial ways Rives's first husband, Archie Chanler. First came wealth and education. Loring "had an excellent, but lazy mind" and read law at Harvard, only to drop it after inheriting fifteen million dollars. Loring shares Chanler's interest in travel, sport, and membership in elite clubs. Rives also describes Loring's pastimes in terms applicable to Chanler: "His life since college days, had been made up of sport, occasional spurts of travel in wild places, girls—to a moderate degree—the usual convivial, surface intercourse with other young bloods—some ennui, generally dispelled by drink." Apparently reliving some of her own courtship history, Rives depicts Loring's pursuit of Sophy: "he had never in all his exceedingly willful life desired anything with the frantic vehemence that he desired Sophy."[12] While Loring is more classically handsome than Chanler, the character shares Archie's lack of interest in intellectual life and a bitter jealousy of any of his wife's male friends—much like that Archie had exhibited toward Will Otis over two decades earlier.

One male character, Marco, the Marchese Amaldi, seems to have been modeled on Pierre Troubetzkoy. Amaldi is a constant presence in *Shadows of Flames,* entering that 580-page book on page 15. Like Troubetzkoy, Amaldi is a foreign aristocrat, of noble Italian lineage, but with an American mother. As a talented musician, he has an artistic temperament and is handsome—his face is "dark and irregular" and his eyes a "clear olive." Rives uses height to differentiate her hero from real life: Troubetzkoy towered over others; Amaldi was "not very tall" but "appeared strong" and his figure had a "lithe symmetry."[13]

Other parts of Rives's own history were apparent in the description of high society in London and visits to Italy. Sophy condemns New York society in terms that echo Rives's experiences and beliefs: "Its mad speed and ostentation resulted in a sort of golden glare of monotony." Sophy opines that the city held many "charming people caught protesting in the maelstrom."[14]

Perhaps the most important experience that informed *Shadows of Flames* was not evident to Rives's readers: her struggles with an addiction to morphine and cocaine. The novel details the compulsions driving the addict;

The Princess of Albemarle

against such a drive, only the most determined nurse could make any headway, given the patient's willingness to lie and steal. Lauding the manner in which Rives had portrayed the "morphiniac," the critic at the *New-York Tribune* asserted: "The study of the habit, of its degrading hold upon character and body, which the author gives here, is even more realistic than that Robert Hichens gave us years ago in 'Felix.'"[15]

The comparison here with *Felix,* a 1902 novel by an English writer, is telling. Hichens's protagonist Felix comes to know extremely well two English women who are part of "this morphia craze," which according to the author "spread secretly all through modern society." Society women in the novel "begin to inject either because they're bored or miserable, or because they feel over-tired, or out of sheer curiosity." He describes the experience of Lady Caroline under the influence of morphine as an "exquisite languor . . . as if she lay in a world all flooded with gold into which sorrow had never entered." In keeping with this interpretation of addiction as the purview of privileged women, Hichens centers the morphia craze in Paris, where seven or eight "morphinomanes" with "hollow expressionless eyes" gather in a house to await injections of morphine from the female proprietor.[16] Although Hichens writes about the physical compulsions of the addict, his emphasis on drug taking as a voluntary choice of wealthy women makes addiction appear a frivolous vice, freely taken up, in contrast to the dependency stemming from a doctor's prescription experienced by Rives's character.

In *Shadows of Flames* the addict is a male: Cecil Chesney, the younger son of an English aristocrat and Sophy's first husband. Cecil becomes addicted through a doctor's injection to fight his illnesses of "jungle fever" and migraine headaches. Rives vividly chronicles Cecil's mood swings, his determination to quit drugs, and the physical cravings that overwhelm his good intentions. She evidently drew on her own experiences but dropped no hint about how she had become so knowledgeable. Her addiction to morphine and cocaine had never reached the newspapers. By making the addicted character a large English man and by portraying his wife's surprise and horror at his addiction, Rives drew the reader away from any notion that her own past drug usage had educated her.

The *New-York Tribune* adjudged *Shadows of Flames* a story of "matrimonial misadventure" with "all that it implies of disillusion, repulsion, and revolt, in the case of a sensitive, exceptionally high-principled woman made for love at its truest and best." The critic pointed out a contrast "throughout" the novel between the "coarseness" of Sophy's two husbands and her "fastidiousness of body as of soul." The review summed up: "in short, this is an interesting book, ably written."[17]

While the book was generally respectfully reviewed, some critics brought up Rives's past sensational works. Referring to "The Quick or the Dead?," the Washington *Evening Star* dubbed Rives a "writer of perfervid fiction." The critic praised parts of *Shadows of Flames:* "There are pleasing backgrounds to these various adventures—English, Italian, American backgrounds all of which are handled with feeling and skill. The people, too, are believable human beings of appeal and some distinction." Nonetheless, the reviewer could not resist a final barb about the novel's premise of Sophy's unsatisfied love for the Marchese Amaldi: "And, so far as one is able to judge, the only hindrance to her [the heroine's] third marriage is the writer's sure instinct that another venture of the kind would turn what is obviously intended for a serious story into a fantastic and ridiculous farce."[18]

Heartened by her productivity during this period, Rives also found happiness in the trip that she and Pierre made to England in the spring of 1914 for him to paint portraits of the privileged. Rives then revisited her British friends from twenty-five years earlier, when she had been a literary sensation and acclaimed beauty. Hosting the Troubetzkoys in London was George Curzon, who had once written poetic tributes to Rives's beauty and talents. Much had occurred in Curzon's professional and personal life since he had last romanced Amélie at Castle Hill in 1892. He married an American heiress, Mary Leiter, who died in 1906, leaving him with three daughters. Building upon his long interest in foreign affairs, he served as viceroy of India, and in 1911 he had become Earl Curzon of Kedleston. A man with many female friends, he resolutely opposed woman suffrage. Only weeks before Rives arrived, he spoke in the House of Lords against allowing women to vote in parliamentary elections. Although Rives disagreed with Curzon, she deemed the right to vote less important than other aspects of women's autonomy.

When Rives arrived in England in mid-May, her spirits soared. "It is the loveliest May weather here you can imagine, just like our Virginia May," Amélie informed her sister Landon. "As we came up in the train, all the hedges were white with Hawthorn and the skylarks, sweet ecstatic voices hidden in the blue, were singing their hearts out." Lord Curzon welcomed them to the elegant town house at 1 Carlton House Terrace that he was

George Curzon, pictured here as viceroy of India, hosted Amélie Rives and Pierre Troubetzkoy in London in 1914. (Library of Congress)

renting. Rives was entranced by the surroundings, which combined beauty with an imposing view of British power. "From this window where I am writing I look out over Carlton Terrace, one mass of great English elms & grass with blackbirds piping as in the Country," she marveled. "'Big Ben's' round face stares kindly at me above the trees, & I can see the spires of Westminster Abbey & the tower of the Houses of Parliament." Rives was positively joyful. Even London's urban vastness, she wrote, contrasted positively with New York's: "The subdued, low growl of London after the explosive frenzy of New York is wonderful. The very motors make less noise and the motor bicycles seem to purr like kittens."[19]

As impressive as the surroundings was the warm welcome from Curzon. According to Rives, in her honor "the blue drawing room [has been] re-dedicated 'Amy's room' isn't it lovely to be welcomed like this?" She found the room "too charming with pictures by Andrea del Sarto, etc. etc. & a sofa made out of a lovely little Indian bed of Mirror work from the Palace of

Theoban, king of Burmah!!! Doesn't it sound fairy-booky?" She was particular ecstatic about the social whirl that confronted her: "English people are *so* dear! I found a letter from Violet Rutland waiting for me, & we go to a dance at her house tomorrow evening. Then lots more engagements waiting from other old friends & George giving me a dinner to meet more."[20]

After a visit to Curzon's country home at the end of May, Rives and Troubetzkoy moved to a luxury hotel, the Cavendish, in the St. James section of London. There they further joined the social and intellectual whirl by contacting old acquaintances. The British author George Moore, well known for his naturalism, thanked Rives for a "marvellous letter" which "was most wonderful & very like you." Telling her that he had ordered *Virginia of Virginia,* he proposed tea together. The upshot was his wish to read *Shadows of Flames,* still in typescript. Rives confided to her sister: "George Moore who never reads modern things, asked me so often for the typed copy of 'Shadows of Flames' that I *had* to lend it to him or seem affected. Heaven knows whether he will like it at all! It makes me so nervous I almost wish he hadn't asked for it. But that's cowardly."[21]

This summer continued to reprise past visits to England, and Rives described it as "a wonderful & delightful time." Margot Tennant, a friend from the days of the Souls, had married H. H. Asquith, who had become prime minister in 1908. In June the Asquiths threw a dinner honoring Pierre and Amélie. The Asquiths were Liberals, and after dinner Rives mused, "It was strange seeing both sides of the question in that way, as all my old time friends are such ultra Conservatives!"[22]

Pierre worked on numerous commissions that July. Rives lightheartedly described his work: "Pierre is painting many portraits—Lady Diana Manners, Mrs. Maguire, who was Miss Peel the speaker's daughter. Lady Salisbury's daughter Nancy Cunard, the child of a Lady Something (I forget her name) and another Lady Somebody. Also I believe he is to paint Lord Ribblesdales nephew & Lady Churston & her little girl." After almost two months in England, they journeyed to Italy to visit Ada Troubetzkoy at Lake Maggiore.[23] They could not know that this would be their last trip to Europe; the aristocratic society in which they moved would soon be shattered by World War I, which began just a month later, and their world would be far more contained within the United States.

During the decade before the outbreak of war, Rives had begun to turn to the genre of the play, and after 1914 she spent more time writing for the theater than on stories or novels. Drama had been her first love; as a fledgling writer in her teens, enthralled by the stage, she had tried her hand at plays. Back in the mid-1880s, one of the pieces that she kept polishing was a dramatic version of the story of Robin Hood.

Even before Rives's blank verse publications, *Seléné* and *Augustine the Man,* some critics had seen dramatic possibilities in her work. A review of *Athelwold,* one of her historical dramas, had argued: "We are half inclined to think that Amélie Rives—the name Mrs. Chanler still keeps in her title-pages—is more of a dramatist than poet or novelist; . . . her genius, for she has genius, lends itself more kindly to the playwright's methods than to the lyrical or narrative modes of expression." Criticizing her for "gross overstatement" and excesses of verbiage, the critic speculated: "It may be that the necessary unavoidable limitations of dramatic composition, the impersonality it imposes, the rigid demand of its unity of effect, bring just the bridle to curb and render tractable her luxuriant and rather reckless imagination."[24]

After 1900 the growing popularity of plays that stressed poetic or historical qualities perhaps further inclined Rives toward drama. One critic in 1901, after praising Stephen Phillips's *Herod,* for the lavishness of its production and "its literary quality," compared it to "Herod and Mariamne," a long blank verse piece that Rives had published in *Lippincott's Magazine* in 1888. "Miss Rives's work strikes me as having more fire and force than Mr. Phillips's," he exclaimed, "and although she has not had the stage experience that has been his, I think it might be a better acting play." The critic pointed out that because *Herod* had been commissioned by the famed English actor and theater manager Herbert Beerbohm Tree, the character of "Herod is 'centre stage' all the time." By contrast, "Miss Rives wrote her play to please herself, without any thought of the stage, and Mariamne is just as striking a part as Herod's. Salome, who is a very insignificant personage in Mr. Phillips's drama[,] is a striking part in Miss Rives's."[25]

After she had returned to blank verse in 1904–5, Rives apparently pondered becoming a playwright. In a 1906 interview with the *New York Times,* she refused to discuss her new publication, *Augustine the Man,* "except to give her impressions of its dramatic uses for the theatre." Rives then "spoke of its adaptability to Richard Mansfield, who had often tried to commission her to write a play for him." Here she was name-dropping: not only was the British actor-producer Richard Mansfield a leading Shakespearean actor but he had also been managing and producing plays in the United States for twenty years. The *Times* article concluded with an aside about Rives's independence: "But no one will ever be quite able to commission Amélie Rives to do anything."[26]

Despite such hints in the press, only in 1911 did Rives take her first steps toward putting her scripts into production. That February, as she and Pierre were staying in New York City, *The Kid Faun,* apparently a one-act play Rives had written, was at Daly's Theater. Later that month, *The Kid Faun* was presented again, along with another by Rives entitled *The King's Garden,* at the Maxine Elliott Theater, as a benefit to support the Downtown Nursery in Cedar Street and the Art Students' Club.[27] Rives was beginning with small productions, yet her ambitions and achievements soon loomed larger.

Rives was joining other women of her day who found playwriting to be financially rewarding. Since the 1890s women had increasingly taken a larger role in creating the shows, both dramatic and musical, appearing on Broadway. That decade Martha Morton had led the way, writing numerous successful plays. Some popular authors fared particularly well. Frances Hodgson Burnett, whose novels included *The Secret Garden* and *Little Lord Fauntleroy,* had eleven different scripts produced between 1890 and 1920. When in 1914, facing a question about the recent "irruption of women dramatists," writer Eleanor Gates replied, "Women are beginning to do their own work in the world. . . . Instead of some man reading a play to them while they criticised, suggested changes, and helped him lick it into shape, they are writing their own plays."[28] Rives too would test the possibilities of playwriting.

While in England in 1914, Rives informed her sister: "I see that I didn't get the Ames prize but Mr. Ames wrote me a letter congratulating me on being one of the last few out of 1,500 plays, that were considered and balanced for 8 months." Rives was referring to the ten-thousand-dollar prize that Winthrop Ames had offered for the best new play each year. Six years earlier, Ames, a Harvard graduate from a wealthy family, had become managing director of the large New Theatre, which failed after only two years. In the following years he financed, built, and managed the Little Theatre and the Booth Theatre, both in midtown Manhattan. In 1913 he issued his challenge in search of the best new play. According to one account, over 2,600 plays were submitted for the prize, the most lucrative ever funded in the United States.[29]

Although it is unclear what play Rives had submitted to the contest, she was taking bolder steps to enter the theatrical world, including the rental of

Well-known photographer Frances Benjamin Johnston took this picture of Pierre's studio in the New York city apartment that he and Rives rented near Central Park. (Library of Congress)

an apartment in New York City. In 1914 she told her sister Landon, "I think with continued joy about the studio that we're going to have next winter with a lovely, cheery bedroom for you." Rives and Troubetzkoy leased this apartment at 15 West 67th Street, less than one block from Central Park, for at least the next six years. She also started working with a theatrical agent, Hungarian-born Alice Kauser, one of the most innovative play brokers then at work. Having noticed that plays, after a Broadway run and perhaps a touring company, tended to disappear, Kauser devised a method to keep such plays in circulation. She bought the rights to them, leased them to interested parties, and paid the playwright a royalty while retaining a commission fee. In 1914 Kauser, who represented numerous playwrights, tried to interest Elsie Ferguson, a successful stage actress from a privileged background, in appearing in a play by Rives.[30]

During World War I, Rives began to achieve success in the New York theater world. She drew upon her knowledge of Italy in her play *Blackmail*, which opened in January 1916, in Boston at the Wilbur, where the theater apparently envisioned only a week's run for it. *Blackmail*'s plot revolves around a privileged young American woman, Sylvia, who finds that her innocent involvement with an Italian opera singer has exposed her to demands from a blackmail organization, working in tandem with a society newspaper devoted to scandal. The twist in the plot is the heroine's discovery that her father heads the group. In a mixed review, the *Boston Daily Globe* praised the production for its "exceedingly interesting narrative, clever in character portraiture and delightful in brightness of dialogue," but also noted "the action often halts because of faulty dramatic construction and the climaxes are not always expertly brought about. In its present form the play is much too long."[31]

A less positive review in the *Christian Science Monitor* suggested that defects in the play sprang from Rives stepping outside her expertise as a novelist. "Some novelists, like [J. M.] Barrie have succeeded in the theater, but like him they have taken the trouble to learn the craft of playwrighting," the critic asserted. "Analysis of the fabric would be futile, for the much that could be said in fault-finding would all come under the head of the author's ignorance of the idiom of the theater." This reviewer also complained that, rather than concentrating on her theme, the author "presents it only episodically, devoting most of the tediously long evening to embroidery of amusing anecdotes about the minor personages." Moreover, "the structure is loosely articulated with preposterous coincidences. Though individual episodes are put together in workmanlike manner, the parts are not designed in relation to the whole, and the whole is not designed in terms of the theater." The review ended with the scathing observation that two scenes designed by the author "may please persons with a taste for hectic amour amid bizarre color."[32]

As *Blackmail* moved from Boston to New York, its name changed to *The Fear Market*. It also gained a well-known producer, Harrison Grey Fiske, husband of the celebrated stage actress Minnie Maddern Fiske and producer of over 140 plays on Broadway. The Fiskes were most famous for having successfully defied the "Syndicate," a booking cartel composed of four men who controlled the leasing of theaters nationwide and thus dictated which shows and actors were able to mount road tours.[33]

On January 24, 1916, *The Fear Market* opened on Broadway at the Booth Theater, and the following month it moved to the Comedy Theater. Rives did her part to promote the play; in an interview, she declared that the craving for gossip in American life had given rise to "scandal sheets" like the

The Princess of Albemarle

This photograph of Amélie Rives, which she autographed in 1916, uses a fur muff and scarf to advertise her sophistication and elite status. (Amélie Rives Troubetzkoy Collection, The Valentine)

society paper in her play. Avowing that the fear of scandal did not make people more moral, Rives argued that fear of capital punishment did not prevent murder. She rather tartly commented, "Men are just as great gossips as women; greater sometimes." The renamed and revamped play met a more favorable reception in New York. The magazine *Puck* half-heartedly endorsed the play as proving "that it is still possible to write for the stage with a tinge of literary value." *The Fear Market* ran for 116 performances that spring. In May, Rives thanked an autograph seeker: "I think it is so very kind of you to write and tell me that you enjoyed 'the Fear Market.'" And she added: "The managers tell me that they expect it to live for two years 'on the Road' as theatrical slang puts it, and that's very nice I think."[34]

The Fear Market also opened up the new medium of motion pictures to Rives. In 1919 she sold the film rights to Realart Corporation and received "a first installment of forty-five hundred dollars." Filmed in 1920, the movie, also titled *The Fear Market*, featured Alice Brady, daughter of a successful

Broadway producer. A cinema trade periodical advised its subscribers to "play up Miss Brady, but remember that Amélie Rives is still a name to conjure with." Rives apparently was also among nine authors of "stage successes" whose movie rights Vitagraph acquired in the fall of 1919.[35]

In 1918 Rives may have been at the height of her creative prowess and earning power. At this point, Grosset and Dunlap published her thriller, *The Ghost Garden*, perhaps her most compelling novel. Set in the contemporary Shenandoah Valley, the protagonist, Evan Radford, a visiting northerner, discovers a lovely but deserted eighteenth-century mansion, "Her Wish," which had been built for Melany Horsemanden, a willful young woman. Visiting the descendants of the Horsemanden family, Radford learns the entire story of how Melany broke her engagement rather than leave her beloved home and died unmarried of a heart attack at age thirty-four. As Radford falls in love with and becomes engaged to Melany Warrenger, the haunted kinswoman of the first Melany, the modern couple find themselves grappling with the past. Warrenger, a talented vocalist, has lost her singing voice—and she fears this has resulted from the antipathy of her long-dead relative, now buried in the garden at Her Wish. As Radford tries to dispel this anxiety, he becomes increasingly obsessed with the house and its past owner, even as he remains convinced of his ability to fend off any spectral powers. Rives's own respect for the supernatural gives her story ambiguity and makes it spellbinding. *The Ghost Garden* combines suspense and character development.

The novel was well received. According to one critic, "The tale is told very skillfully." In particular, he praised the rising "increment of horror" from "when we first hear of 'Her Wish,' . . . to the hour when its substance passes in flame and its baleful influence from the past is no more." Similarly, the *New York Times* called it "a very good story, perhaps . . . the best that she has ever written." Its success, the reviewer suggested, was partly "due to the skill with which she has invested the whole story with beauty."[36]

Rives's steady output of novels and stories for more than a decade had gained her acceptance as a legitimate author, but her overall literary reputation apparently improved little. Creatively and professionally, she may have hit a wall. In contrast, the lure of both fame and fortune from stage productions increasingly attracted her and by 1918 she had found a new producer for her plays, William Faversham, an English-born actor-director and producer who had achieved success on the American stage. That year, she consulted with Faversham about the scripting and staging of two plays, *Allegiance* and a version of Mark Twain's *The Prince and the Pauper*. Rives and Troubetzkoy jointly wrote *Allegiance*, originally called "A House Divided," which seems to have survived only as a typescript in Rives's papers. Set in New York in 1915 after the outbreak of war in Europe, the play treats the problem of wartime immigrant loyalty. In a summary of "war plays" slated to open in the autumn of 1918, one critic called *Allegiance* "a drama of German intrigue in America, of gripping interest, perfectly acted—a classic in play writing." Emphasizing the "spy intrigue that preceded the United States's declaration of war," the critic declared: "The story portrays the conflict of blood—the German American torn with conflicting emotions, the call of blood and the duty of allegiance to America." The play also emphasized the importance of "Americanization" of foreign-born citizens. *Allegiance* played forty-four times in August and September 1918 at Maxine Elliott's Theatre; the two other war plays opening at the same time enjoyed longer runs.[37]

More important was Rives's working partnership with Faversham and his wife, Julie Opp, to produce a new stage version of Mark Twain's *The Prince and the Pauper*. In July 1918 Rives and Faversham signed an agreement to award her royalties according to a sliding scale based on weekly box office sales: she would receive 5 percent for weekly receipts up to $6,000, 7.5 percent on the next $4,000, and 10 percent over $10,000.[38]

The Prince and the Pauper took some time to come together before it opened in 1920. A visit that Pierre and Amélie made to California, most likely regarding her sale of the rights for *The Fear Market*, may have created delays. Rives also became ill in 1918; her letters from that time brim with references to severe colds and attacks of influenza, as an epidemic was washing over the United States. Her continued weakness in the summer of 1920 may have compounded the problems. As the script and show developed, disagreements about compensation arose between the Favershams and Rives. Apparently, Julie Opp Faversham rewrote parts of Rives's version of the script and then demanded half of the royalties due Rives. "My artistic pride as a writer is both hurt and offended by this claim put forward by Mr. Faversham for his wife," Rives complained to her agent, Alice Kauser, in August 1920. "I must ask that it be withdrawn in the letter that Mr. Faversham will write to me." Rives portrayed herself as taking the high road, but she refused to compromise: "At all events, and at whatever cost (because to me money comes second to many things) I am firm as to the conditions that I have laid down in this letter and shall not withdraw a jot from any of them." Rives's confidence in both her abilities and her drawing power show through in these remonstrations. Kauser, Rives insisted, should have more closely consulted with her. Amélie rather loftily justified her actions by asserting that authors "certainly do not expect those agents to close a 'deal' without one word to them beforehand of the nature of that deal, nor to take for granted such a claim against a well-known writer as that put forward by Mr. Faversham for Mrs. Faversham against me."[39]

As the argument over royalties dragged on, Rives held her ground while asserting that she remained above the fray. Determinedly, she informed Julie Opp Faversham: "I can not go over point by point your letter of August 16th with you, dear Julie, as I am not a business woman, but in regard to our friendship—yours, Willie's, Pierre's and mine—friendship is always better safeguarded, when business matters are arranged in a purely business manner." From her perch of fifty-seven years, she further opined: "Experience and life have taught me that." She resolutely held on to the movie rights to the script, as she continued to negotiate, not only with the Favershams but also with her own agents and lawyers.[40]

Indeed, Rives remained unhappy enough with the outcome that she gave herself the final word in her papers. Looking over the drafts, she appended a note on the front of the envelope containing one draft: "This envelope contains a great part of my version of 'The Prince and The Pauper,' *re-written* by me during rehearsals, my version having been much tampered with & injured—(given me by Mr. Kitteridge) and Mr. Chapel the stage manager."[41]

Before opening in New York, *The Prince and the Pauper* previewed in Montreal. There a reviewer observed that "Amelie Rives has preserved much of the whimsical humor of Mark Twain's story—much of its wistful charm and not a little of its subtle philosophy." After its New York run, the show went on the road, playing in Washington, D.C., in November 1920, where a reviewer praised its "especially elaborate production, historically correct and colorful."[42]

Despite several Broadway shows, Rives never wrote a blockbuster. Her modest success in drama may well have stemmed from her delayed entry as well as her lack of experience in the show business world. By the time she had gained the necessary connections to the stage, a younger generation of dramatists, some with college degrees as well as dramatic experience or training, were addressing new themes in a snappier manner that seemed more sophisticated than Rives's examination of wartime loyalty or her re-working of Mark Twain.[43] This was especially true of the younger female playwrights, who were pushing the barriers. Rachel Crothers, generally considered the most successful of the early twentieth-century female play-wrights, often dealt with topics related to gender, and her plays such as *A Man's World* (1909) and *Young Wisdom* (1914) explored modern issues such as sexual discrimination and trial marriage.[44]

In these first decades of the twentieth century, Rives showed a height-ened interest in reform, professional, and charitable activities, with a greater emphasis on benevolence and individual freedoms than on other more egali-tarian, progressive reforms. Long a supporter of enhanced rights for women, she was one of the many signers in the writers' section of the woman suffrage petition that the New York chapter of the National American Woman Suf-frage Association circulated in 1909. When the Equal Suffrage League was established in Virginia, she became a member, though she never took as prominent a role as did her fellow writers Mary Johnston and Ellen Glasgow, who served as officers of the Virginia League for Woman Suffrage. From her residence in Albemarle County, Amélie was more a sympathizer than an activist. Nonetheless, one newspaper article in 1911 mentioned Glasgow and Rives as among the "best people in Virginia" supporting woman suffrage.[45]

In publicizing her books, Rives also voiced her support for the "saner and broader aspects" of feminism. In an April 1914 interview, she stressed the moderate aspects of her advocacy. Declaring her opposition "by instinct and reason to militancy and the extremists," she advocated "sex cooperation" rather than "sex antagonism." She elaborated: "Some of the manifestations that we are having are disheartening, such as the doings of the militants, and the prattle of the people who would leave men out of their scheme of things." A recent incident in which a British suffragette had slashed the painting known as the *Rokeby Venus* by Diego Velázquez particularly appalled Rives, who denounced it as "a horrible thing to have done." The attack was, in her view, "killing a beautiful, living, man-made thing" and seemed "almost like murder." Such acts, she insisted, "did not serve as an index to the character of the movement."[46]

The aspect of feminism that Rives most valued was individual autonomy. Stressing the "inner life," she elaborated: "The sensation of the cage, the prison, has been intolerable to me always." As an aristocrat and an artist, she placed herself above material interests and argued that "political rights or property rights were not the essence of the matter. As for the vote, that does not so much matter; it is relatively unimportant for women to have the right of suffrage."[47] Rives's independence and privilege were particularly apparent in her prizing self-determination over women's suffrage and property rights, both of which she nonetheless supported.

Self-centeredly, perhaps, she showed the greatest interest in the laws of marriage and divorce. "I believe that the marriage contract should be as easy to dissolve as any other civil contract," Rives declared. Indeed, "I have always believed so," she said, and recalled that her father, in response to her questions when she was "fourteen or fifteen" explained the rigor of divorce laws as a way "that if either party to a marriage failed to live up to the bargain, the other might easily force him to do so." Such an answer had not placated the young Amélie: "Even then it seemed absurd to me. How much of the essentials of a true marriage could be left after the law had been evoked to force the return, let us say, of either husband or wife?"[48]

In the political realm, the war raging in Europe further kindled her and Troubetzkoy's concern about Europe. The sinking of the *Lusitania* in 1915 led Rives to lambaste "peace at the price of the highest ideals, at the cost of humanity and civilization." To her, the picture of mothers and children "struggling in the pitiless water" called forth "a vast and noble passion for redress." In addition to writing *Allegiance* with Pierre, a play exploring the motivations of immigrants in America during a time of crisis, Rives supported relief organizations. In 1916 one of her poems, read by renowned actress Minnie Maddern Fiske, was part of the entertainment "for the benefit of the destitute Austro-Hungarian babies" held at the Lyric Theatre on April 11. During the war Rives and Troubetzkoy also produced a broadside, "What the Victory or Defeat of Germany Means to Every American," in support of the Patriotism Through Education program of the National Security League, which claimed that Germany had undertaken a program of extermination through "its systematic destruction of civilians in Belgium, northern France, Poland, Serbia."[49]

While part of this patriotic movement, Rives and Troubetzkoy did not share the anti-immigrant aspect of the National Security League's agenda. In 1921 Rives wrote a foreword to *Aspects of Americanization*, by Edward Hale Bierstadt, a young author and playwright who later became well known for his crime novels and radio scripts. Rives argued that the Great War had awakened Americans to how "so called 'aliens'" could be either a strength or menace. Arguing that all Americans descended from earlier immigrants, she denounced nativism, even while calling for assimilation: "How splendidly the various 'alien' groups responded to the national appeal in time of danger, Mr. Bierstadt shows with facts; but he also shows how, when the war was over, the descendants of the earlier immigrants turned on these more recent immigrants with the furious hysteria of Chauvinism, and how, later, this hysteria passed into the pre-war indifference and neglect of the so-called 'alien' who, whatever name men may impose upon him, is still a part of the American nation, though through that nation's own fault, an unassimilated part." While Rives's reference to aliens had defined them as "people coming from the same hemisphere whence had come those who founded the nation," and seemed to exclude those from Africa and Asia, she asserted: "I like to remind myself, and if I may without offense, to remind others that in its literal sense 'one hundred per cent American' only applies to the Red Indian whom we dispossessed of the land which we call America."[50]

Among other causes in this period, Rives actively supported other authors. The Authors League of America, headquartered in New York City, was incorporated in 1912 to safeguard authors' rights and procure better national and international copyright protections. Rives apparently became an early member but was most involved in social functions. In 1914 the league made a montage film featuring well-known authors to show at its first annual benefit and perhaps circulate nationally. Along with authors such as Booth Tarkington and muckraker Ida Tarbell, Rives was chosen to participate in the film, which combined a scene from a book with a cameo of its author. The opening scene of "The Quick or the Dead?," in which the heroine returns to her Virginia plantation, was Rives's literary contribution. An article in the *New York Times* archly indicated, "Many have hinted the story is more biography than fiction, but as the Princess looks out of her long window over the roofs of New York, or at her husband busy working at the end of the studio, she will tell you the story is purely imaginary."[51]

Evidence of Rives's activity with the Authors League mostly shows her listed among supporters and designated as a princess. In 1916 the Executive Council appointed a committee of "prominent women authors who have taken upon themselves the task of promoting good fellowship among the thousand members of the league." That February the Social Committee, with Rives presiding, gave its first reception at the Colony Club on Park

Avenue and 62nd Street to allow younger writers to meet those more experienced in publishing.[52]

When the *New York Sun* in 1916 published a forum with reactions from numerous authors to Ellen Glasgow's assertion that British novels were superior to American ones because of the latter's evasive idealism, Rives was among those asked to respond. Strongly supporting Glasgow's statements, Rives maintained that Americans "wanted to shut their eyes to everything unpleasant." Writing that "Truth is a terrible God," she found America awash in "false sentimentality" which called for the "happy ending." Rives also wandered into the question of freedom of self-expression by pointing to a current controversy: the vice crusader Anthony Comstock had orchestrated the arrest in 1915 of William Sanger for fulfilling the request of a Comstock agent for a pamphlet on birth control produced by Margaret Sanger, then a nurse in New York City. Rives declared: "When men like Anthony Comstock can agitate against real freedom, the situation is awful . . . to say a woman hasn't the freedom to discuss it [birth control] is, or should be, intolerable."[53]

Rives and Troubetzkoy strongly attested to their belief in freedom of thought and their opposition to censorship in 1920, when the novel *Jurgen: A Comedy of Justice,* by James Branch Cabell, Rives's cousin and a fellow Virginia author, raised the ire of the New York Society for the Suppression of Vice. In his novel, Cabell parodied picaresque adventures, including the amatory ones of his title character. The society, which had been founded by Anthony Comstock in 1873, fought what it considered immorality in different forms ranging from contraceptive advice to pornography. It cited numerous pages of *Jurgen* as lewd, lascivious, and indecent and convinced a magistrate to indict the book, allowing the seizure of the printed copies and the printing plates.

A lawsuit followed, and an emergency committee was organized on Cabell's behalf. Rives was among the numerous authors who supported Cabell "without reservations." Given Amélie's poor health in February 1920, Troubetzkoy penned the endorsement himself, adding, "My wife is only too glad to sign the enclosed paper, and only regrets that her illness prevents her from adding a personal expression of her feelings and opinion in regard to the treatment of *Jurgen,* which we read as it came out and consider a masterpiece honoring American literature." Pierre and Amélie also sent a letter to Cabell's publisher in support of *Jurgen,* which they deemed "a book which rises to the height of permanent achievement above the stream of mediocre literature flooding our times." Cabell and his publisher, Guy Henry, prevailed in the lawsuit in 1922. Rives continued to stand up for fellow authors. In August 1927 she signed a formal statement that condemned censorship after *Circus Parade,* a novel by Jim Tully, was banned in Boston.[54]

In addition to her professional and reform activities, Rives increasingly became a muse of sorts, encouraging literary aspirants. This role was not new; during her visits in Europe she had enjoyed meeting the literary elite and introducing younger authors such as Ellen Glasgow to European authors and social luminaries. Spending time in New York gave also her opportunities to meet fledgling writers. For example, Sinclair Lewis in 1914 sent her *Our Mr. Wrenn,* his first novel published under his own name. Telling him that she was "looking forward to delightful jaunts" with his eponymous hero, Rives offered: "I peeped into his life and I'm anxious to know him better." Thanking Lewis for bringing his fiancée to meet her, Rives closed: "Au revoir. I hope you'll both come soon again."[55]

Rives also offered the same friendship to younger writers in the South. For some, her past associations with European and American authors, as well as her notorious career, symbolized a South that was changing intellectually as well as socially. One can gauge her standing among the younger intellectual set in Richmond in her connection with the literary magazine the *Reviewer,* which was published in Richmond but appealed to literary audiences both North and South.[56]

According to Emily Tapscott Clark, one of the journal's founders and editors, she, along with Mary Street and Margaret Freeman, decided to start the *Reviewer* as a "little magazine" after a Richmond newspaper discontinued its book review section. Such "little magazines," a genre that featured experimental poetry, essays, short stories, and reviews, had since the nineteenth century been posing an alternative to larger commercially oriented periodicals. The twenty-six-year-old Clark, who had worked on the Richmond *Evening Journal,* corresponded with northern novelists such as Joseph Hergesheimer and the newspaperman and critic H. L. Mencken for advice about launching and guiding the *Reviewer,* which was published in Richmond for two years. Soon after the early issues of the magazine appeared in 1921, Clark sought Rives's support. In a note to Hergesheimer that June, Clark wrote: "Princess Troubetzkoy (Amélie Rives) wants me to come to Castle Hill for a week-end soon, and I think I'll go. I'd like for her and Prince Troubetzkoy to be really interested in the Reviewer."[57]

Rives and Castle Hill immediately captivated Emily Clark, and she included long sections about both in a letter to Hergesheimer: "Castle Hill, you know, is one of the two or three loveliest places in Virginia, and to me it is the most lovable. . . . It has the air of quite unattainable aristocracy and seclusion that you like, can't be seen at all from the road, and there is a placard up outside warning the public when the family is at home, so that nobody will come near!" Gushing over the age of the estate, Clark also praised the driveway, bordered by boxwood so old "that it makes the way dark, with the nicest sharp clean scent." Both the house and its owners—past and present—were entrancing.[58]

A clear portrait of Amélie Rives, then approaching the age of sixty, emerges from Clark's letters. The novelist's background—both her acceptance by the Souls in late Victorian England and her past career as a beauty—fascinated Clark. Rives attained a near mythical status for her, only slightly marred by a few flaws of age: "she is charming and has obviously been lovely. She's frightfully made up now. All my life I've heard of her because she's a legend with the men of Father's generation—most of them were in love with her. But she hasn't been in Richmond for fifteen years and I didn't know her till now. She is said to have had more beaux than any woman in Virginia, even Nancy Astor. And that makes her tremendously interesting to me." Compared to Lady Astor (also of Virginian birth), "Amélie Rives [is] more picturesque."[59]

Both Rives and Troubetzkoy seemed to enthrall Clark. "They've both lived everywhere and know nearly everybody," Clark rhapsodized. Rives "just read me a play of hers that Ethel Barrymore is considering, and she and the Prince had such a funny letter from John Barrymore the other day, signed 'Mad love, Jack.'" Despite this frothiness, Rives and Troubetzkoy were intellectually stimulating and "delightful" and generally insightful about art, literature, and culture. As Clark put it, "They knew right away that my new dress looked exactly like a certain kind of sherbet." By October 1921, as she began to refer to Rives as "Amélie," Clark offered this assessment: "I really like her more than ever—she's a darling. She's less made up than in the summer, and sometimes at moments, she's lovely—and always very much of a real person. I believe she's quite crazy about Prince Troubetzkoy too, which is interesting, at her age. And wonderfully honest in every way."[60]

Over time, the Troubetzkoys acted as a sort of intellectual godparents for Clark. When Pierre was in Richmond for a portrait commission, during the spring of 1922, he sometimes visited Clark. "He is nice—almost like a

In this early twentieth-century painting of Amélie Rives, Pierre Troubetzkoy portrays her as a thoughtful, somewhat wistful beauty. (Virginia Historical Society, Virginia Museum of History and Culture)

father," she wrote. "I have had so many troubles about The Reviewer and he is always sympathetic—old like a father but more intelligent than most people's fathers." One Sunday afternoon when Pierre dropped by while Clark was feeling unwell, "he went back in the kitchen and cooked, because he had been painting all day and I don't know how to cook. He is wonderfully efficient." Clark found that Pierre and Amélie gave her entrée into a sophisticated world. Rives shared a box of her cigarettes; Pierre told her about a place in New York's midtown where, even during Prohibition, "you can get both cocktails and wine and wonderful food."[61]

Rives, however, took a limited—and mainly social—role with the *Reviewer*. Both her name—as "Amélie Troubetzkoy (Amélie Rives)"—and that of Pierre graced the masthead as contributors, and Rives published a few pieces in the magazine, which did not pay for content. In an early issue, Rives struck a light note as she gave the journal a small poem on beauty.

In another, perhaps drawing on her own experience with reviewers, she parodied a modern critic's "take" on Shakespeare's *Othello*. (Clark rather dismissively mentioned it: "She has something in the next issue, with John Powell, but it isn't worth anything.")[62]

A realization that Clark's admiration did not extend to her writings may have influenced Rives's self-presentation. Clark confided in a friend, "Of course the Princess's books have been just popular ones, but she knows that and doesn't take herself seriously." Even so, a few months later Clark encountered evidence that Rives did care about her writings. For the October 1921 issue, Amélie contributed a note showing how the American actress Adah Isaacs Menken's poetry about Salomé had prefigured Oscar Wilde's treatment of that temptress. Rives became angry when James Branch Cabell edited her piece, and Clark described the denouement: "She stamped her foot and said 'Damn,' and said the editor of the Fortnightly Review cabled her before he changed a word of her last contribution."[63]

Like other small literary magazines, the *Reviewer* struggled. Its editors wrestled with different visions of what such a journal could do. Joseph Hergesheimer advised publishing the best of the new writers, while Mencken wanted an emphasis on the magazine's southern orientation that would draw stories from those who were intellectually invigorating the region. By the autumn of 1921 Emily Clark was depending for editorial expertise on James Branch Cabell, who was far more experienced in publishing.[64]

Over time Rives took more interest in Clark's career and in autumn 1921 reproved her for "playing too much." By February 1923 Rives was trying to advise Clark about the New York literary and social scene. "Amélie said that I had great talent and great charm," Clark wrote, "but that my head was being turned and I did things that weren't me at all. . . . She said that she was the same at my age, but that I must get straight. My head is straight now." Later that spring Rives asked Clark to stay with her and Pierre in New York City the following winter. Emily, though, was moving in a different direction. That year she became acquainted with Edwin Balch, a wealthy Philadelphian over thirty years her senior. Although at first unimpressed by Balch and what she called the "fearfully erudite books he publishes for geographical, philosophical and historical societies," Clark came to appreciate him and his generosity toward her magazine. In the fall of 1923 she left the *Reviewer* (which soon moved to Chapel Hill) and married Balch a year later.[65]

The Princess of Albemarle

In 1923 Clark offered her frankest description of Rives: "I think Amélie is wonderful, even if her books are trash. She is one of the few women I've ever seen that I'd want to be like. Sometimes I think it is almost better to be a personality than to write remarkable books, because even if the books do live you aren't here to care about it." Clark asserted: "Sometimes I think is more desirable to be Amélie than Willa Cather, though Mencken says Miss Cather is the most wonderful woman in America." Clark also had come to realize that, beneath her candor and kindness, Rives was a person rigidly in control and perhaps quite difficult with her sister and husband: "Amélie is so thoroughly polite that nothing can break it. . . . But I have an idea that Amélie can be rather terrible, alone with Landon or Pierre. I've never seen her off guard, any more than I've seen her without her makeup."[66]

Rives greatly enjoyed the kind of social and intellectual interaction that she garnered from aiding the *Reviewer*. At Clark's behest, Castle Hill hosted the intellectual advisers of the magazine, Hergesheimer and Mencken.[67] This, in fact, introduced Rives to Mencken, whose scathing critique of the South as the "Sahara of the Bozart" had become widely known. Rives, in a letter to Hergesheimer in 1921, indicated that "I believe that Mr. Mencken loves the poor old South at heart, or he wouldn't take so much trouble about it. I hope he'll have a pleasant visit to Richmond, but not such a soften-ing one that it will make him stay his hand one whit from trouncing us for our good and his delight." That autumn, Mencken sent Pierre a bottle of burgundy wine, which (in the midst of Prohibition) Rives and Troubetzkoy seem to have thoroughly enjoyed.[68]

Mencken, perhaps responding to Rives's recent story in the *Reviewer* about Adah Isaacs Menken, included an anti-Semitic comment in writing to her: "La Menken, it appears, was both loose and Yiddish hence she is never mentioned in my house. I specifically deny her talents." In her long reply, Rives espoused tolerance and pointed toward her European ties: "But I must say also, that while I detest certain types of Jews as heartily as I do certain types of Christians, I can't have the same prejudice against them as I might have, if I hadn't spent twenty years off & on in Italy." Earlier, Rives had admonished Mencken that he was mistaken about meeting "*coal black*" Washingtons and Lees in Virginia, but appended: "I don't doubt that there were beige and tan and cafe-au-lait scions of those families." She then linked her own family to race mixing by recounting her meeting with a "beautiful" man "with wavy black hair, dark blue eyes and a skin the color of a faded beech-leaf dipped in cream" and pointedly ended: "his likeness to a 4th cousin of mine told me plainly that that he was a 5th cousin of mine."[69]

In the 1920s Rives continued to write—most likely because she and Pierre needed the money—but success for both plays and novels was becoming more elusive. When *The Prince and the Pauper* ran in Washington, the local paper suggested that she had "under consideration the dramatization of Mark Twain's other whimsical tale, 'A Yankee in King Arthur's Court.'" In 1923 she published a slim volume of two plays, *The Sea-Woman's Cloak* and *November Eve,* which drew on the love of gods and folklore that long had been important in her fiction. A news squib announced them as "the first ever published by this author although others by her have been produced" and called them "highly fanciful, not to say a trifle fantastic productions, a combination of Irish folklore and Amelie Rives' vivid imagination."[70]

In November 1925 the American Laboratory Theatre, under the direction of Richard Boleslavsky, opened Rives's *The Sea Woman's Cloak* in New York as one of its first productions. Polish-born, Boleslavsky had trained as an actor in prerevolutionary Russia and immigrated to the United States in 1922, where he taught method acting and created the American Laboratory Theatre. He told Rives that he greatly regretted that she had not been able to be in the audience opening night to receive "a large bouquet of flowers appropriate to the author." The *New York Sun* critic called the production "utterly entrancing" and a "fine, successful fantasy," noting that it was "the first play I had ever seen by this author, well known in other fields." The *New York Evening World* similarly pronounced *The Sea-Woman's Cloak* "vivid, colorful, moving and highly to be recommended."[71]

Later in the 1920s, Rives moved to romantic comedy. *Love in a Mist,* a three-act play that she wrote with Gilbert Emery, opened at the Gaiety Theater in New York City on April 12, 1926, and ran for 118 performances. The story was slight, although a favorable review called the dialogue "clever." The plot centers on the misadventures of the heroine, who, as one critic put it, "raises myriad kinds of havoc through her penchant for becoming engaged to every man who says he will die if she does not marry him." Once again, Rives had devised a heroine likely to remind the audience of her image in the 1880s. In April 1926 Robert Benchley reviewed the comedy, which included a highly regarded cast, saying, "You may be certain of one thing" about a play with that title, author, and cast members: "It isn't going to be rowdy." Damning with faint praise, he continued, "What merits the performance may have are brought to it by the actors themselves in their own little hand-bags, and, as the evening wears on, these serve to keep the audience moderately satisfied." In Benchley's view, the leading lady, Madge Kennedy, "with practically nothing to work with in the way of lines, performs her customary miracles" and thus cements her reputation as "the subtlest and most effective of our comediennes," while Tom Powers, as the Italian love interest, "plays at least one scene so well that you forget that he is part of a thin, artificial little comedy." *Love in a Mist* traveled to other cities, including Boston, and had a short afterlife as the basis for a musical called *Say When,* which ran for fifteen performances at the Morosco Theatre in June and July 1928.[72]

Rives meanwhile had encountered problems in placing one of her historical plays. Sometime in the early 1920s, she wrote a drama about the early life of Elizabeth I of England. Then called "Crown of Flame," the play certainly existed in 1922 when Rives shared it with her friend Edward Hale Bierstadt. For the *Reviewer,* Bierstadt composed an essay that traced the evolution of drama from its basis in antiquity. He argued for more biographical and historical productions, not "the modern pseudo-biographical play, which is at present neither chronicle nor historical nor anything very definite at all." At the very end of his piece, Bierstadt praised a "manuscript, not yet produced or published, a biographical play that supplies a raison d'être for the whole genus. . . . This play is The Crown of Flame, a drama of Queen Elizabeth by Amélie Rives, the Princess Pierre Troubetzkoy." Lauding the script as doing "for the biographical drama what [Alexandre] Dumas did for the historical novel," Bierstadt claimed that it "combines all that is best of both the historical and the biographical drama. It deals with real persons and real events, but it is not 'realistic' for its actuality is vitalized with romantic feeling. It is romance which comprehends, while realism only narrates."[73]

Despite Bierstadt's extravagant praise, Rives's agent Alice Kauser could not find a taker for this play in 1925. Even while asserting that theater owners claimed that dramas were more attractive to audiences than comedies, Kauser indicated that she was having trouble locating a producer for the play. "Oh my dear, it is fine and beautifully written," Kauser reassured Rives, but tellingly added, "Somehow dramatically it does not quite impress me." Rives admitted that her literary agent had also found the same story difficult to sell as a novel and now argued for moving on. "You must just not worry over it a second longer," Rives counseled her, "for I would much rather submit to you a new, modern drama, and so will keep this in my own hands and for a particular occasion."[74]

Rives rewrote this play, which she renamed *The Young Elizabeth,* sometime in the 1930s. As she was finishing act 4 in December 1937, she told Ellen Glasgow that she was waiting to hear what her agents had to say about it, adding: "But I'm *so* [double underline] tired Ellen. I can't help wishing that I was free from it all, though I am very thankful for such things as I have and most of all for the few friends that I really love and that love me." When the play was produced by the Little Theater of St. Louis in 1938 as its "prize play," a local reviewer called it "in every way worthy of being distinguished as a prize play. It was strongly, symmetrically conceived." The critic added: "Written in blank verse, the lines were of apt beauty."[75]

By the late 1920s monetary problems increasingly beset Rives and Troubetzkoy. Their financial situation was deteriorating, most likely because their artistic talents were less in demand. In 1925, when recruited by Glasgow to join the Richmond chapter of the Society for the Prevention of Cruelty to Animals, Rives responded: "I want to become a Life Member, but being *very* poor at present, I can only pay *half* [double underline] this time viz: $25.00." In addition, Rives continued to battle poor health, which she described to Glasgow in 1928: "My ill health of the past *nine* years is better now, after that severe hacking at scientific hands, but I'm not really strong yet—or I would have run down to Richmond to see you & those that I love there."[76]

In 1929, as Rives encountered rejections of one of her short stories, she sought Mencken's advice. Complaining that her agent had told her that readers would have little sympathy for her heroine, who seemed "a pretty rotten little girl," Rives asked whether he thought "the story is a pretty rotten little story as well as its 'heroine' a pretty rotten little girl." Perhaps disingenuously, she added that because she thought the piece too long for Mencken's *American Mercury:* "I want your opinion only for my private enlightenment. I have no idea at the back of my mind that you might like to publish it." Mencken apparently intimated that she might submit the story to *Cosmopolitan,* perhaps an unkind suggestion, given the magazine's failing status at that time. In her reply Rives thanked him and indicated: "I can see now that the trees of the story hide the wood, but I was trying very hard to get a good deal of story into a short space—telling myself that what popular magazines want is 'a story' and reminding myself that what I wanted was to make the pot boil a bit."[77]

The Princess of Albemarle

As Rives's comment about wanting to produce a "potboiler" indicates, by the beginning of the Depression in 1929, her income was further plummeting. That autumn, Pierre gave up his studio in New York, undertaking "the horrid job of closing & packing all the furniture and canvasses in his studio." Over the next few years, the Castle Hill household encountered ever greater financial problems, but Rives and Troubetzkoy continued to entertain. Julian R. Meade, an aspiring young writer born in Danville and educated at the Virginia Military Institute and the University of Virginia, described visits to Castle Hill in his 1935 travelogue, *I Live in Virginia*.[78]

Castle Hill awed him, as it had Emily Clark: "It was hard to say which entrance of this house was more inviting: the North Front, which faced a nearby mountain and which had been built by Thomas Walker in 1765, or the South Front, which faced the boxwood wall and which had been added by Mr. and Mrs. William Cabell Rives in 1824." Even more impressive than Castle Hill's architecture was the culture of its inhabitants. Describing an evening's entertainment, Meade remembered: "After supper we sat in the comfortable chintz-covered chairs in the living-room and Prince Troubetzkoy read aloud in English and French but, in deference to my ignorance, omitted Italian and German." Marveling at the bibliophilia of Castle Hill's residents, Meade noted that "bookcases lined the walls of the living-room, the halls, the dining-room, the bedrooms, everywhere in the house except the formal French drawing-room which was a souvenir of William Cabell Rives's days as minister to France. And even this gold and shining room had Parisian gift books on the polished tables."[79]

Presenting Rives as a celebrity, Meade divulged that "guests never ceased to knock at the door of Castle Hill," though many of them were tourists who wished to see the scandalous author and famous beauty. "People often asked me," Meade continued, "what the Princess Troubetzkoy really looked like and how she talked and what she said." His view was that "of all the older persons I have known, Amélie Rives as a woman appealed most strongly to youth," adding that "I did not feel that her own work really expressed the charm of her personality." Meade summarized: she "was forever doing something to astound the people of Virginia. . . . All I could say was that the Princess was an amazingly lovely and learned lady whose life had been adventurous and varied and who was tired now and glad to stay at Castle Hill."[80]

Rives also continued to lend her support to authors' causes. When, in October 1931, Glasgow served on the planning committee for a meeting of southern authors in Charlottesville, she looked to sixty-eight-year-old Rives for help with a social event. The two-day conference included such rising stars as William Faulkner, Sherwood Anderson, and Allan Tate and his wife, Caroline Gordon. Glasgow delivered the opening address to the conference but depended on Rives and her husband Pierre to host a reception at Castle Hill. Amélie, still in poor health, received guests in her boudoir. (In what may well be an apocryphal story, she allegedly found the inebriated Faulkner roaming the upper floors of the house and told him, "I have seen how you have walked through my house and looked through my rooms, but I've forgiven you because you were accompanied by genius.")[81]

Rives also took a stand against mob violence against African Americans. In 1931 she joined Glasgow, Mary Johnston, and the activist Lucy Randolph Mason in signing "a strong pronouncement against lynching" that had been endorsed by women in seven southern states. The petition, originating from a women's meeting in Richmond, noted the alarming recent increase in incidents of lynching in the South, while praising Virginia for having had none since 1926. "We repudiate the statement that lynching is done in the defense of Southern Womanhood," the petition stated.

While endorsing freedom of expression and women's rights and denouncing racist violence, Rives seems to have taken little interest in electoral politics (as her tepid support for woman suffrage suggested). In notes for a biographical sketch in 1925 she declared that her political philosophy was that of the French king Henri de Navarre (Henri IV), who wished everyone "to have a chicken in the pot." She also believed "the same justice should exist for the poor and the rich." Observing that was not the case "in any land!" she continued that she "sadly doubt[ed]" that such justice would ever prevail.[82]

Sometime after World War I, Rives had abandoned her aspirations to the literary fame she had once desired. She told Joseph Hergesheimer in July of 1921, "I can spin a rather good yarn sometimes but I have no illusions whatever about myself as a novelist." And Rives was even more dismissive of any claims to literary significance in a letter to Glasgow in 1926: "I've amused myself writing a light little novel called 'The Queerness of Celia' this autumn. I don't know *how* to write novels, but this story was great fun to do."[83] In 1930 Rives published her last book, *Firedamp*.

In 1932 Rives provided the most thorough evaluation of her career as a writer. Replying to Kenneth Magruder, who had undertaken a biography of her, she counseled against publication, positively forbidding it before her death. She argued that if she allowed him to proceed, she would be viewed as endorsing his "all too high praise." She confided: "The simple truth is that I do not consider my writing worthy of such an exhaustive treatise. I have never accomplished in what I have written the thing at which I aimed." She had not created a masterpiece, she wrote, "though I do think that some, few things are better than the rest."[84]

Summing up, Rives declared: "In plain words, I am much disappointed with my work, and if I keep on at it, even now, it is only in the hope that I may do something really worth while before I die—if it be only one sonnet—and also to take my share as a bread winner." This spate of rumination over her literary career also led her to muse about roads not taken: "I often think that if I could have devoted my whole time to writing plays and poetry, I might have accomplished better things. Short stories I had a gift for, but I am not naturally a novel writer, and therefore my novels have been very faulty, not good in fact." She included the self-deprecatory phrases that she earlier used with others: "You see, I haven't any illusions about myself as to my writing. Even my thought about plays and poetry comes from the fact that I like so much to write in those forms—not that I am at all sure of what I might have been able to do with them."[85]

Almost three decades after her return to writing, Rives gave a highly critical view of her literary career. Overlooked in this self-assessment of 1932 was her successful reinvigoration of her career as novelist and playwright and her rebirth as a symbol of European culture. In her attempt to evade unwanted and undeserved attention, she also omitted her efforts to cheer on fledgling writers such as Ellen Glasgow, Emily Clark, and Julian Meade. Rives's life was her own; she would not encourage its interpretation by others.

"Winter for [the Heart] All the Time"

In August 1936 Rives experienced an enormous, wrenching change, the death of her husband Pierre. Four months later, in answer to a letter of sympathy, Rives detailed her reaction to the loss: "I would have written long ago, [if] I could have, you must know that, but it is only during the past three weeks that I have gained any strength, clearness of mind. The shock of his going was as if I had been struck down by a flaming sword. I could not eat or sleep for nearly two months. I have only vague memories of all but anguish of soul & body." Rives depicted the close of a great love as she detailed her last two days with Pierre. "He was never a man of words," she confided, "but he stopped by my bed that morning & said: 'I love you a thousand times better than when we were young together.' Then the night before he died, he turned to me suddenly & said, as if compelled: 'I want to go *quickly* and to go *soon.*' It was like a knife through my heart & yet somehow I knew he didn't mean to hurt me." Rives was suggesting that Pierre's premonitions showed his acceptance of the heart attack that felled him.[1]

Rives in another letter described her agonies after Pierre's death and concluded: "But never for one moment would I give up the anguish if it meant the giving up of the memory of that love. No, not even though I believed that death ended all,—which I do not, which I really *cannot* believe." For a year after Pierre's demise, she often contemplated suicide. Dramatically, she recounted to her friend Ellen Glasgow the discovery of not one, but two revolvers and even a full bottle of phenobarbital. These weapons of self-destruction tempted Rives, but she discarded them. Gaining weight, strength, and the will to live, she resolved: "I see today that I have to stay on this terrible, beautiful earth for a time still."[2]

Lonely and increasingly impoverished (a condition intensified by Archie's death in 1935, which deprived her of his payments), Rives looked to friends and to poetry, which underlay some of her most deeply felt letters in the 1930s. She had already begun to share her verses with James Southall Wilson, who taught at the University of Virginia and edited the *Virginia Quarterly Review*. Asking him to read and critique her poetry as a friend rather than an editor, she entreated him: "What I *do* need and hunger for, is a friend like you, to whom I can show what I write, and know that [I] shall receive a frank opinion. At present, as for the past year the sonnet holds me. I am not strong enough to take more than a short flight at a time & the sonnet-form is a lovely cage to try short flights in." Rives also cautioned Wilson about her poems: "But, please, *don't* think that I want you to take the trouble to send me careful criticisms of them. I only want you to let me know how they appeal to you."[3] The upshot was the publication of some of her poetry over the next few years in the *Virginia Quarterly Review*.

Rives's surviving friends reached out to her. Ellen Glasgow sent questions about beauty hints, and Rives, then in her seventies, responded with a detailed account of her own beauty routine at great length, with knowledge, as she put it, from "a garnered experience of about sixty years, about the *best* and simplest cosmetics to use."[4] In other words, she had begun to learn about beauty aids back in the 1880s, when respectable women were expected to neither know nor use cosmetics.

Rives shared her experience with different brands and her own strong views about proper skincare. She included a step-by-step tutorial on how to apply cosmetics. In a subsequent letter she discussed facials (of which she disapproved), nail care, and other favorite cosmetics, including Endocreme, a face cream later banned from the market because it contained an estrogenic hormone. Showing that she had lost neither her sense of humor nor her sensuality, she counseled Glasgow, "By the way, if your Rouge en crème, from Helena Rubenstein proves too *stiff*, just slip the little box between your thighs as you sit at your toilet table putting on the Harriet Hubbard Ayres cream after washing your face well with Soap, and the rouge will soon get warm & very easy to apply. You should *never* heat it by artificial heat!"[5]

Rives confidently delivered advice and injunctions, sometimes with double underlinings to make her point. On face powder: "I have tried & tried for a perfect powder all my vain little life & feel that I succeeded about four years ago when I tried 'Lady Esther.'" Further demonstrating her familiarity with the beauty business, Rives recounted how, twenty years earlier, a "remarkable skin & hair specialist in New York" had recommended never to "use anything but *cold* water for washing your face, not only in summer but in winter too!" Rives expected the cosmetics manufacturers to recognize her by name, as when she instructed Glasgow in regard to a rouge produced by Helena Rubinstein: "If you send for a box, tell her you need Princess Pierre Troubetzkoy's *special* [double underline]—a mixture of geranium and raspberry."[6]

In these sad years, Rives formed an important new friendship, with young Louis Auchincloss, then a law student at the University of Virginia. Auchincloss later recalled that a friend of his father had asked him to call on "the venerable Princess Pierre Troubetzkoy who lived in romantic, impoverished isolation in a decaying manor house, Castle Hill, near Charlottesville." Having put thoughts of a literary career behind him, Auchincloss delayed but accepted an invitation for tea on "a cool cloudless November afternoon in 1938." Both Castle Hill and Rives made an enormous impression; entranced by the house, Auchincloss was even more delighted with his seventy-five-year-old hostess: "She was small and straight with white hair, carefully waved, and with delicately penciled, dark eyebrows. Her features were very fine and regular, her cheekbones high; her face had few wrinkles. Her eyes were large and blue-gray; they were probingly curious and seemed to hide reserves of laughter." Auchincloss also sensed hauteur, or at least great self-possession: "One felt that she had been a great beauty in a day when great beauties had been made much of." Moreover, she had no doubts why a young law student might wish to spend the afternoon with her: "The Princess knew well what she was worth." By the time he rose to leave, "she asked me to stay for supper," but acknowledged her reduced circumstances with the warning, "you must pray for the miracle of the loaves and fishes!" Auchincloss announced: "So our friendship began."[7]

As had been the case with Emily Clark, Auchincloss, though he read "all of her novels," was not a fan of Rives's writings, calling them "heady stuff, superromantic, at times even 'slushy'" (he did consider *Shadows of Flames* her best novel). At their first meeting, Rives discussed the university and members of the law school whom she knew "and was very funny about them." Auchincloss, however, most wanted to discuss her past. As he put it: "After all she had known Henry James!" Their visits gave Rives a chance to relive the past and the people she had encountered. "She would mimic the long dead with wonderful facial contortions, and her constant, high-pitched laughter seemed to clear away all the ghosts of pretension. She described the naiveté and pomposity of New York society in the nineties, the long, dull, sumptuous dinners and the childish self-importance of the hostesses. She made that life as vivid as the Charles Dana Gibson cartoons of it, and indeed it was easy to visualize her in the center of one of the latter, a Gibson girl, sitting, beautiful but detached in a gilded salon with a balloon over her head showing the Virginia plantation of which she was dreaming."[8]

Conversations with Rives also inspired Auchincloss. Almost forty years later he mused: "I think my greatest regret when I finally began not only to write but publish novels was that I could not show them to Amélie. She had asked to see my work but, rather churlishly, I would never give it to her. While I was at law school I had locked it all away. But she was emphatic that I should not give it up." This he remembered as her greatest contribution to his future. In a letter in 1938, Rives recounted to Auchincloss her recent three-hour conversation with Leslie Buckler, who was her close friend and also a law professor. To her query about how her young friend was faring, Buckler replied that Auchincloss was doing very well but that his "whole heart" did not seem to be in the study of law. When Rives probed further, Buckler said, "He will come out all right. It's only that one's heart must be in it—to devote one's whole life to the law." Rives then responded, as she later reported to Auchincloss: "The truth is, Leslie, that the chief thing in his heart is to be a writer. I think, though he has never even hinted anything of the kind to me, that he is devoted to his father, and is studying law to please him. I know when I asked to see some of his manuscripts he replied that he had locked them all away in New York when he decided to come to the University of Virginia and study law. So you see, though his 'heart' mayn't be in it his will and mind and determination *are* in it." Rives then repeated Buckler's final remark: "He will come out [all right]—I'm quite sure."[9]

At various times in the 1930s Rives contemplated the trajectory of her life and her career. Even before 1932, as she noted to Kenneth Magruder, she had already begun to burn her past correspondence. After Archie's death in 1935, a man attending an estate sale at Merrie Mills retrieved a bundle of Rives's past letters and, through James Southall Wilson, returned them to her; she then apparently trashed the letters. Even as Rives destroyed evidence of her private activities, she retained her writings. In May 1937, as she looked over some of her manuscripts, Rives scribbled on "Herod and Mariamne" (published back in 1888), "very early writing & full of faults." Almost sixty years earlier she had called her writings her children—whether she continued to consider them in that light, they formed a link to her past and to the future, and she did not discard them.[10]

As fascism flourished in Europe, Rives became increasingly worried about the state of the world. When Melville Cane, a lawyer and poet in New York City, sent her a poem about the Anschluss, the annexation of Austria by Nazi Germany in 1938, she replied, "I cannot read of the horrors in Austria," and sighed, "'How it is night for the world indeed." Cane sent her more verses—denunciations of fascism abroad as well as some lyrical observations. Rives reassured him in 1939 how meaningful his writings were to her and contrasted his poems to others she had received: "Many poets send me some of their verses. I read them, half heartedly often, finding them often admirable . . ." Here Rives was interrupted, and when she returned to the letter two days later, she elucidated: "What I was going to say in the unfinished sentence is this: that 'admirable' is not the word I use for poetry like yours that is born of water and of the spirit. Not for a long, long time have poems so reached the core of my being like arrows of light." After pointing out specific verses that she found particularly compelling, she finished, "Forgive me dear Mr. Cane if I write brokenly. Your poetry moves me to such depths of heart and spirit. I thank you with heart and spirit for sending them to me. When I am in a calmer mood I know that I shall enjoy those written in lighter vein." The correspondence with Cane continued. "Thank you for remembering me with the moving poem, 'Climate of the Heart,'" Rives wrote in November 1939, and sadly remarked: "Sometimes, though, the heart does not choose the season, and there is winter for it all the time."[11]

Rives and her never-married sister Landon continued to eke out a living with help from various sources, including guests who paid to stay at Castle Hill. As a friend privy to her daily life, Louis Auchincloss described Rives's "arrangement with two former servants, who were allowed to farm the land in return for cooking and cleaning." He noted, "Checks came in occasionally from old New York friends. . . . Repairs were dispensed with."[12] Ellen Glasgow, along with the customary birthday and Christmas gifts, gave Rives books from her publisher.[13] In 1940 Amélie and Landon received $2,500 each from Bishop Philip Rhinelander and his wife, who were among her

Rives cousins. Thanking them for "the most generous cheques," Amélie remarked: "I know it will make your kind heart glad to be told as I tell you very simply here, that it seemed to us both a beautiful miracle." Rives further assured the Rhinelanders: "We are living here in our old house by practising the strictest economy and sometimes 'the ends' seem just about *not* to 'meet.'" Rives stoically held on to Castle Hill—in response to a suggestion of selling the estate, she retorted: "I should never be able to breathe away from Castle Hill. It is the only life I have left." Louis Auchincloss summed it up: "Castle Hill remained hers till her death."[14]

In 1941 Rives showed some of her old spark as she was compiling an autobiographical account. She wrote, "Until this winter of 1941, I did not know that all those who married foreigners before September 22nd 1922, lost their American citizenship. I shall soon take steps to regain mine." Here Rives was misinterpreting how twentieth-century U.S. legislation regarding the citizenship of married American women applied to her. Her wedding to Pierre had preceded the 1907 Law of Expatriation, which stripped citizenship from U.S. women who married foreign citizens. This challenge to her status, however, led Rives to voice her strongest nationalist and democratic statement: "To me, Democracy is a religion, a great faith, which like all religions has to be ever renewed. And the United States of America is a living growing Democracy. I hope to grow with it until I die."[15]

By 1942 Rives's health was badly deteriorating. In January she informed Ellen Glasgow that "I have been stricken suddenly with illness, a most painful one—rheumatic fever. I can scarcely hold my pencil in my hand, but I *will* do it—to send you my love." That August, Auchincloss, then serving in the U.S. Navy, told his mother: "The Princess is sick—quite sick. I had a letter."[16]

In addition to poor health, Rives remained extremely low-spirited. The war in Europe led her to fear for the future of civilization. In 1942 she wrote Glasgow: "Ah, Ellen, how you must suffer as I do in this awful, mad cruelty of war. . . . As for man becoming civilized—My doubt of that is one of my worst sufferings." Rives mournfully confessed that she had little to live for: "The glow that you speak of lived only in my heart & spirit now I am so old & so worn out with this dreary illness." She confided a growing wish for death: "except for duty I long for it as one famished for water." When late in 1943 Melville Cane again sent Rives a poem, she was too ill to respond. Her attendant Frances Shepherd, who identified herself as "Princess Nurse," replied: "The Princess asked me to write to you as she is very ill.

She appreciated so much you sending her your poem. She sends her best regards."[17]

On June 16, 1945, Rives died. A relative who had visited her in the hospital later recalled that "in her last illness, in the Martha Jefferson Hospital, she insisted upon keeping her face covered with a chiffon scarf, because she wanted no one to see that she had lost her beauty."[18] Although Rives had made peace with not becoming a renowned writer, she perhaps never became reconciled to the loss of the beauty that many years earlier she had called the one gift from providence that she most wished to retain.

What was Rives's contribution to her time and to literature? Early in her career, she was a precursor of the southern writers who pictured plain folks—Black and white—with greater appreciation. Though at times she veered close to minstrelsy and burlesqued these ordinary people, she still saw some of their complexity. Indeed, her common white women—India, Virginia, Tanis—were real people with admirable, even noble aspects. More important, Rives challenged the Victorian conventions that treated women as sexual pawns who could be defiled and abused but seldom tried to take control of their own lives. If her heroines were improbably beautiful and talented, they were also flesh-and-blood women who felt desire and who acted, even if they transgressed norms while doing so.

As one of the first southern women writers to leave the bounds of the "domestic plot" and to publish in top magazines, Rives had a dazzling entrance as an author. Yet, through a lack of mentoring and her own many missteps, she never matured into the acclaimed writer that she wished to be. Instead, she became a celebrity, contributing both for good and bad to the stereotypes that later grew up about beautiful, talented southern women—that they were heartless belles who married for advantage instead of love, or wild flappers who trampled social norms underfoot. Ironically enough, the young unmarried Rives had not been one of the reigning belles in Virginia, but as a beautiful fledgling author, she saw her picture posted in magazines, even in store windows, and became that era's equivalent of a "pinup."

Rives's life also gives us insight into the problems that women, even privileged white women, might face in fin-de-siècle America. Her financially advantageous marriage soon turned deeply unhappy; her recourse to morphine and cocaine saddled her with all the hazards of addiction and temporarily silenced her literary voice. She turned to divorce, and a second marriage helped her begin to solve her many problems.

While Rives had always been involved in crafting an image in the press, that persona careened out of her control during the 1890s. After she married Pierre Troubetzkoy, she constructed for herself a new cosmopolitan identity as a European princess, most at home in Europe, or at the family plantation of Castle Hill. As she fought drug dependency and regained her health, she again found her creativity. Some of her blank verse still aimed high, and her book-length poem *Seléné* was a lush account of the search for love and beauty. Most of her fiction and playwriting during the twentieth century sought a popular audience. Her realism was not the modernism associated with the Southern Renaissance, but her insistence on the passion, insouciance, and capabilities of her female protagonists helped lay the foundations for a new southern literature.

In 1932, when Rives had forbidden a biographer from publishing his book before her death, she had declared, underlining her sentence to emphasize her point: "*I am wholly convinced that you are mistaken in thinking that the public or any publisher would take any interest in a life of me, and an account of my writings.*" To back up her analysis, she continued: "At one time, many years ago, there might have been a demand for such a thing, but there would be none at present, I am quite quite sure. Then I was a 'romantic figure,' so it was said." Rives did try to make some amends to this would-be biographer, remarking that after her death "there may be a momentary interest about me, as that figure of a somewhat romantic past, and then you might use some of your material." And she wryly ended: "You see I know the public better than it knows me—thank God!"[19]

Over time Amélie was best remembered in her native Virginia. There, one might argue, the press coverage she received helped to pave the way for other southern beauties, notably Irene Langhorne Gibson and her sister Nancy, Lady Astor. Echoes of that same treatment of Rives may also be detected in the visibility of such privileged female southern flappers and iconoclasts of the early twentieth century as Zelda Sayre Fitzgerald and Tallulah Bankhead. Closer to home, Rives continued to symbolize and promote a cultured and literary life for young people such as Emily Clark, Julian Meade, and Louis Auchincloss, as she relived her past with them.

Through her lifetime, Rives remained in America's memory; at her death in 1945, the *New York Times* ran a long obituary which, after recalling her popularity as a novelist, celebrated her as "a successful playwright, poet and essayist . . . [who] in addition won fame as a beauty." Detailing her family and marriages, the story mentioned by title all her books.[20]

Because Rives neither produced a great work nor wrote consistently in one genre, she did not create a following. Although she revived her career in the early twentieth century, she did not embrace the modernism then beginning to flower and never figured in the Southern Renaissance. Thus, some of her stronger work—the haunting, supernatural aspects of *The Ghost Garden,* the poignant scenes of drug addiction in *Shadows of Flames*—never passed into popular imagery. Instead, insofar as Rives has remained known, she has lingered in the Albemarle Piedmont as a shadowy wraith of the "romantic figure" that she once somewhat ruefully had called herself.

Notes

Introduction

1. "Amelie Rives," *Atlanta Constitution,* Apr. 21, 1888, 9.
2. Thomas Nelson Page, "Literature in the South Since the War," *Lippincott's Magazine* 48 (December 1891): 753.
3. "Amelie Rives Dies," *New York Times,* June 17, 1945, 26.
4. Welford Dunaway Taylor, *Amélie Rives (Princess Troubetzkoy)* (New York, 1973); George Calvin Longest, "Amélie Rives Troubetzkoy: A Biography" (Ph.D. diss., University of Georgia, 1969); George C. Longest, *Three Virginia Writers: Mary Johnston, Thomas Nelson Page, and Amelie Rives Troubetzkoy: A Reference Guide* (Boston, 1978); Donna M. Lucey, *Archie and Amélie: Love and Madness in the Gilded Age* (New York, 2006); Wayne Mixon, "New Woman, Old Family: Passion, Gender, and Place in the Virginia Fiction of Amélie Rives," in *The Adaptable South: Essays in Honor of George Brown Tindall,* ed. Elizabeth Jacoway et al. (Baton Rouge, 1991); Helen Lojek, "The Southern Lady Gets a Divorce: 'Saner Feminism' in the Novels of Amélie Rives," *Southern Literary Journal* 12 (Fall 1979): 47–69.

1. "There May Be Something Yet for Me to Do in This Big World"

1. Judith P. Rives to Alfred L. Rives, Aug. 25, 1863, Alfred Landon Rives Papers, David M. Rubenstein Rare Book and Manuscript Library, Duke University.
2. Many thanks to Leila Christenbury for sharing with me baptism records, which list Rives's sponsors, at St. Paul's Episcopal Church during the Civil War. These records, which list the sponsors, have been deposited in the Virginia Historical Society .
3. William C. Rives Jr. to Alfred L. Rives, Oct. 11, 1865, William C. Rives Papers, Library of Congress; AR, autobiographical acct, [ca. 1941], Rives Family Papers, Mss 2532, Albert and Shirley Small Special Collections Library, University of Virginia.
4. Ella Rives to S. C. Rives, July 31 [1866?], William C. Rives Papers, LC.
5. Judith P. Rives to S. C. Rives, Dec. 21, 1865, ibid.
6. S. C. Rives to Alfred L. Rives, Mar. 10, 1870, ibid.

7. S. C. Rives to Judith P. Rives, May 14, 1866; S. C. Rives to Judith P. Rives, Aug. 18, 1866, ibid.; AR, autobiographical notes, [Apr. 1, 1925]; and AR, autobiographical acct, [ca. 1941], in Rives Family Papers, Mss 2532, UVA.

8. Judith P. Rives to Grace Rives, Dec. 20, 1868, Rives, Sears and Rhinelander Families Papers, Mss 10596, Albert and Shirley Small Special Collections Library, UVA; MS Census of 1860, Virginia, Albemarle Co., Sch. II, p. 25, accessed Ancestry .com.

9. Louis Auchincloss, *A Writer's Capital* (Minneapolis, 1974), 134.

10. *Boston Daily Globe,* Sept. 30, 1888, 12.

11. Judith Page Rives to S. C. Rives, Mar. 29, 1867, Alfred Landon Rives Papers, Duke University; Judith P. Rives to Grace Rives, Dec. 20, 1868, Rives, Sears and Rhinelander Families Papers, Mss 10596, UVA.

12. Judith P. Rives to William C. Rives Jr., Sept. 24, 1874, and Judith P. Rives to [Grace Rives], Oct. 4, 1874, both in William C. Rives Papers, LC.

13. Judith Rives to [W. C. Rives], Jan. 1, 1871, ibid..

14. AR to Judith Rives, n.d. [c. 1870–74], Rives Family Papers, Mss 1 R5247 a416, VHS.

15. *Chicago Daily Tribune,* May 10, 1896, 43; Alfred L. Rives to William C. Rives, June 12, 1873, William C. Rives Papers, LC.

16. AR Journal, [July 1874], Box 2, Rives Family Papers, Mss 2532, UVA.

17. AR, autobiographical notes, [Apr. 1, 1925], ibid.

18. AR, autobiographical notes, [Apr. 1, 1925], and AR, autobiographical acct, [ca. 1941], both in ibid.

19. AR, autobiographical notes, [Apr. 1, 1925], ibid.; *Boston Daily Globe,* Feb. 11, 1894, 29.

20. AR Journal, [July 1874], Box 2, Rives Family Papers, Mss 2532, UVA. In 1870 Collin Byrd had been a farmhand in the neighborhood of Castle Hill; in 1880 his profession was listed as a "coachman." MS Census of 1870, Virginia, Albemarle Co., p.170; MS Census of 1880, Virginia, Albemarle Co., p. 20, both accessed Ancestry.com.

21. AR Journal, July 22, 1874, and undated [ca. July 1874], ibid.

22. Judith P. Rives to Will Rives, Aug. 15, 1875, William C. Rives Papers, LC.

23. Albert and Shirley Small Special Collections Library, UVA.

24. These volumes are in Albert and Shirley Small Special Collections Library, UVA. The songbook has the inscription, "Amelie L. Rives from her Mamma. 1866." The book of sermons has a presentation date of July 15, 1876, and the quotation is from p. 40.

25. Small Special Collections Library, UVA. This book carries the inscription to "Amélie L Rives from her loving Papa 11 Nov. 1875."

26. AR, autobiographical notes, [Apr. 1, 1925], Rives Family Papers, Mss2532, UVA; S. C. Rives to Grace Rives, Sept. 21, 1877, William C. Rives Papers, LC.

27. Alfred L. Rives to William C. Rives Jr., Mar.14, 1876, William C. Rives Papers, LC.

28. AR, autobiographical notes, [Apr. 1, 1925], Rives Family Papers, Mss 2532, UVA; AR to Margaret Chanler, Jan. 22, 1889, Rokeby Papers; Alfred L. Rives to William Rives Jr., May 4, 1880, William C. Rives Papers, LC.

29. Jane H. Hunter, *How Young Ladies Became Girls: The Victorian Origins of American Girlhood* (New Haven, 2002), 11–22 (quotation on 22).

30. AR Diary, Oct. 7, 1879, Rives Family Papers, Mss 2532, UVA. On Bullock's age, see MS Census of 1870, Virginia, Nelson Co., p. 22, accessed Ancestry.com.

31. Ibid.

32. Oct. 10, 1879, ibid.

33. AR to William C. Rives Jr., Aug. 17, 1886, William C. Rives Papers, LC; AR, autobiographical acct, [ca. 1941] Rives Family Papers, Mss 2532, UVA.

34. Judith Rives to S. C. Rives, Dec. 21, 1865, and Dec. 14, 1865, and Judith Rives to William C. Rives Jr., Mar. 15, 1869, all in William C. Rives Papers, LC.

35. AR Diary, Oct. 7, 1879, and Oct. 8, 1879, Rives Family Papers, Mss 2532, UVA.

36. Oct. 10, 1879, ibid.

37. Nov. 16, 1879, and Nov. 1879, ibid. On Christ Church and Rev. Drysdale, see *Journal of the Thirty-Sixth Annual Convention of the Protestant Episcopal Church in the Diocese of Alabama* (Mobile, 1867), 38; *Savannah Morning News,* Aug. 31, 1886, 1.

38. AR Diary, Oct. 7, 1879, Rives Family Papers, Mss 2532, UVA.

39. Ibid.

40. Ibid.

41. Ibid.

42. Ibid. Leila Graham Page, daughter of Carter Henry and Leila Page, was born Dec. 21, 1858, and died on Nov. 4, 1894, at age thirty-six. Richard Channing Moore Page, *Genealogy of the Page Family in Virginia . . .* , 2nd ed. (New York, 1893), 126. Her tombstone can be seen at https://www.findagrave.com/memorial/15441361/leila -graham-page.

43. AR Diary, Oct. 7, 1879, Rives Family Papers, Mss 2532, UVA.

44. Ibid.

45. Nov. 30, 1879, ibid.; AR, *Athelwold* (New York, 1893), n.p.

46. AR Diary, Nov. 17, 1879, Rives Family Papers, Mss 2532, UVA.

47. Ibid.

48. Ibid.

49. Oct. 8, 1879, ibid.

50. AR, autobiographical notes, [April 1, 1925], and AR Diary, Nov. 17, 1879, both in ibid.

51. AR Diary, Oct. 8, 1879, ibid.

52. Ca. Oct. 30, 1879, ibid.

53. Margaret Chanler, *Roman Spring: Memoirs* (Boston, 1934), 31, 34–35.

54. AR Diary, Oct. 8, 1879, and Nov. 30, 1879, Rives Family Papers, Mss 2532, UVA. On Sherwood Bonner, consult Hubert Horton McWilliams, *The Prodigal Daughter: A Biography of Sherwood Bonner* (Baton Rouge, 1981); and Kathryn B.

McKee, *Reading Reconstruction: Sherwood Bonner and the Literature of the Post-Civil War South* (Baton Rouge, 2019).

55. AR Diary, Oct. 8, 1879, Rives Family Papers, Mss 2532, UVA.

56. Ibid.

57. Ibid.

58. Joan Marie Johnson, *Southern Women at the Seven Sister Colleges: Feminist Values and Social Activism, 1875–1915* (Athens, Ga., 2008), 3; Jane H. Hunter, *How Young Ladies Became Girls: The Victorian Origins of American Girlhood* (New Haven, 2002), 210–15.

59. Barbara Sicherman, *Well-Read Lives: How Books Inspired a Generation of American Women* (Chapel Hill, 2010), 135–54; *Washington Post,* May 21, 1911, M9.

60. AR Diary, Oct. 9, 1879, Rives Family Papers, Mss 2532, UVA.

61. Andrew Wilson, *The Abode of Snow: Observations on a journey from Chinese Tibet to the Indian Caucasus, through the upper valleys of the Himalaya* (1876), in Albert and Shirley Small Special Collections Library, UVA. With a bookplate, marginalia, and the signature Amélie Rives, dated 1879, the book also includes George Gambier's account of replicating Wilson's trek.

62. AR Diary, Nov. 7 and 17, 1879, and n.d. [Nov. 1879], Rives Family Papers, Mss 2532, UVA.

63. Nov. 17, 1879, ibid.

64. Oct. 8, 1879, ibid.

65. Nov. 11, 1879, ibid.

66. Ibid. On postwar Mobile, see Don H. Doyle, *New Men, New Cities, New South: Atlanta, Nashville, Charleston, Mobile, 1860–1910* (Chapel Hill, 1990), esp. chap. 3. A literary history of Mobile, compiled in 1914, included only a brief listing of Rives. See Erwin Craighead, *The Literary History of Mobile* (Mobile, 1914), 15.

67. AR Diary, Nov. 7 and 17, 1879, and n.d. [Nov. 1879], Rives Family Papers, Mss 2532, UVA.

68. Oct. 8, 1879, ibid.

2. "A Gifted and Promising Young Authoress"

1. AR, handwritten notes, [Apr. 1, 1925], Rives Family Papers, Mss 2532, Albert and Shirley Small Special Collections Library, UVA.

2. AR, *The Witness of the Sun* (Philadelphia: J. B Lippincott, 1889), 10.

3. AR to TNP, n.d., Monday [Sept. 28, 1885], Thomas Nelson Page Papers, Mss 7581 K, Albert and Shirley Small Special Collections Library, UVA.

4. *Sumter* (S.C.) *Watchman and Southron,* Aug. 29, 1882, 1. See also *Austin* (Tex.) *Weekly Democratic Statesman,* Aug. 24, 1882, 4, for the same item. Grace Sears Rives Diary, [listing of dates], Sept. 1883, Papers of the Rives, Sears and Rhinelander Families, Mss 10596, Albert and Shirley Small Special Collections Library, UVA.

5. The offer of a reward for the bag's return suggests that it was valuable. Richmond *Daily Dispatch,* Apr. 6, 1884, 2.

6. "Minister to Persia," *National Republican* (Washington, D.C.), July 29, 1886, 3; *New Orleans Daily Picayune,* Aug. 8, 1887.

7. AR to TNP, [Sept. 11, 1884], Thomas Nelson Page Papers, Mss 7581 K, UVA; J. D. Hurrell, "Some Days with Amélie Rives," *Lippincott's Monthly Magazine* 41 (April 1888): 534.

8. See "Prof. A. C. Coolidge of Harvard Dead," *Boston Daily Globe,* Jan. 15, 1928, B1, 16. John Gardner Coolidge's travels may be followed in a book of his letters: *Random Letters from Many Countries* (Boston, 1924), foreword. Many thanks to Lisa Francavilla for her assistance on biographical information on the Coolidges.

9. *Richmond Daily Times,* June 14, 1888, 1.

10. Lois W. Banner, *American Beauty* (Chicago, 1983), 112–46; *Washington Post,* Sept. 30, 1888, 10; AR to TNP, July 9, 1884, Thomas Nelson Page Papers, Mss 7581 K, UVA.

11. AR to TNP, July 20, 1884, and Jan. 11, 1885, Thomas Nelson Page Papers, Mss 7581 K, UVA; Burne-Jones, Sir Edward in Oxfordartonline, https://oxfordartonline .com; *Oxford Dictionary of National Biography,* s.v. Hugessen, Edward Hugessen Knatchbull-; AR Diary, Nov. 17 and Nov. 30, 1879, Rives Family Papers, Mss 2532, UVA. On the medieval revival, see Alice Chandler, *A Dream of Order: The Medieval Ideal in Nineteenth-Century English Literature* (Lincoln, Neb., 1970); an argument that medievalism could be used by Victorians of other political persuasions can be found in Rosemary Jann, "Myths in Victorian Medievalism," *Browning Institute Studies* 8 (1980): 129–49.

12. AR, "On the Lack of Humor in Great Heroines," *Harper's Bazaar,* Sept. 10, 1887, 626. On the seriousness that Woolson and other female authors such as Louisa May Alcott, Elizabeth Stoddard, and Elizabeth Stuart Phelps brought to their authorship, see Anne E. Boyd, *Writing for Immortality: Women and the Emergence of High Literary Culture in America* (Baltimore, 2004). On Woolson's *East Angels,* consult Anne Boyd Rioux, *Constance Fenimore Woolson: Portrait of a Lady Novelist* (New York, 2016), 174–79.

13. See Alison Lurie, *The Language of Clothes,* 2nd ed. (New York, 2000), 218–22; and Stella Mary Newton, *Health, Art and Reason: Dress Reformers of the 19th Century* (London, 1974), 24–31, on corsets and aesthetic dress among the Pre-Raphaelites.

14. Welford Dunaway Taylor, "A 'Soul' Remembers Oscar Wilde," *English Literature in Transition* 14 (1971): 43, 44–45; David M. Friedman, *Wilde in America: Oscar Wilde and the Invention of Modern Celebrity* (New York, 2014), 226–27, 257; AR, *Shadows of Flames* (London, 1915), 48–49. Taylor's article notes Tyne's resemblance to Wilde.

15. Friedman, *Wilde in America.*

16. *Boston Daily Globe,* Sept. 25, 1888, 2.

17. John Tebbel, *The Expansion of an Industry, 1865–1919.* Vol. 2 of *A History of Book Publishing in the United States* (New York, 1975), 253; AR to Houghton Mifflin & Co., Jan. 2, [1885], [misdated Jan. 2, 1884, stamped Jan. 7, 1885], (1799), Houghton Mifflin Company Papers, Houghton Library, Harvard University.

18. AR to Houghton Mifflin & Co., Jan. 2, [1885], [misdated Jan. 2, 1884, stamped Jan. 7, 1885], (1799), Houghton Mifflin Company Papers, Houghton Library, Harvard University.

19. AR to Houghton Mifflin & Co, n.d. [stamped Jan. 15, 1885], ibid.

20. See Boyd, *Writing for Immortality*, 184-233; Shirley Marchalonis, ed., *Patrons and Protégées: Gender, Friendship, and Writing in Nineteenth-Century America* (New Brunswick, N.J., 1988); and Jane Turner Censer, *The Reconstruction of White Southern Womanhood, 1865-1895* (Baton Rouge, 2003), 230-33.

21. Lucey, *Archie and Amélie*, 65-70, argues that the correspondence was "a series of love letters" in which Rives "rather shamelessly pursued" Page. Only Page, not Rives, retained the letters they exchanged; thus, only her side of the correspondence can be known. Twenty-five letters that she wrote over a two-year period survive; this number, averaging around one letter per month, suggests that the flirtation never developed into a serious courtship. In fact, only twelve letters by Amélie pre-dated the announcement of Page's engagement to Anne Seddon Bruce in the fall of 1885. Instead of an intense emotional relationship, this correspondence seems a foray to gain Page's attention and aid.

22. J. J. White to TNP, July 20, 1872, Thomas Nelson Page Papers, David M. Rubenstein Rare Book and Manuscript Library, Duke University. On Page's life and career, see Theodore L. Gross, *Thomas Nelson Page* (New York, 1967); Harriet Holman, "The Literary Career of Thomas Nelson Page" (Ph.D. diss., Duke University, 1947); K. Stephen Prince, "Marse Chan, New Southerner: Or Taking Thomas Nelson Page Seriously," in *Storytelling, History, and the Postmodern South*, ed. Jason Phillips (Baton Rouge, 2013), 88-104; and K. Stephen Prince, *Stories of the South: Race and the Reconstruction of Southern Identity, 1865-1915* (Chapel Hill, 2014), 135-52. See also Douglas L. Mitchell, "'It Will Be as I Now Remember It': Thomas Nelson Page and the Old South," in *A Disturbing and Alien Memory: Southern Novelists Writing History* (Baton Rouge, 2008), 54-92; and Brook Thomas, *The Literature of Reconstruction: Not in Plain Black and White* (Baltimore, 2017), esp. 76-103.

23. TNP to "My dearest Aunt," Apr. 19, 1883, Page Papers, Duke.

24. AR to TNP, n.d. [Mar. 3, 1884], Thomas Nelson Page Papers, Mss 7581 K, UVA.

25. Ibid.

26. Ibid.; AR to TNP, "Xmas night" [Dec. 25, 1885], ibid.

27. AR to TNP, n.d. [Mar. 3, 1884], ibid.

28. AR to TNP, Mar. 16, 1884, ibid.

29. Ibid.

30. AR to TNP, n.d. [Mar. 3, 1884], ibid.

31. AR to TNP, Mar. 16, 1884, ibid.

32. AR to TNP, Feb. 16, 1885, Ibid.

33. Ibid.

34. AR to TNP, July 20, and July 9, 1884, ibid.. Isobel Grundy, *Lady Mary Wortley Montagu* (Oxford, 1999), 331, 350-51, 391.

35. AR to TNP, July 9, 1884, Page Papers, Mss 7581 K, UVA.

36. AR to TNP, Mar. 16, 1884, ibid.

37. AR to TNP, n.d. [1884], ibid.

38. Ibid.

39. AR to TNP, Mar. 16, 1884, and July 9, 1884, ibid.

40. AR to TNP, July 20, 1884, ibid.

41. Ibid.

42. AR to TNP, Sept. 11, 1884, and [Sept. 22, 1884], ibid.

43. AR to TNP, [Jan. 11, 1885], ibid.

44. AR to TNP, July 31, 1885, and Monday morning n.d. [ca. September 28, 1885], ibid.; C. S. Buel to TNP, Sept. 9, 1885, Page Papers, Duke University.

45. AR to TNP, Monday morning n.d. [ca. Sept. 28,1885], Thomas Nelson Page Papers, Mss 7581 K, UVA.

46. Harvard College, *Class of 1878 Secretary's Report* (Boston, 1901), 87–88; Taylor, *Amélie Rives*, 20.

47. Harvard College, *Class of 1878 Secretary's Report*, 87–88.

48. AR to TNP, Sunday morning, n.d. [Oct. 25, 1885], Page Papers, Mss 7581 K, UVA.

49. JAC to Julia Magruder, June 3, 1892, John A. Chaloner Papers, David M. Rubenstein Rare Book and Manuscript Library, Duke University.

50. AR to TNP, Oct. 25, 1885, Page Papers, Mss 7581 K, UVA.

51. Susan Goodman, *Republic of Words: The Atlantic Monthly and Its Writers, 1857–1925* (Hanover, N.H., 2011), 144, 146; Ellery Sedgwick, *A History of the "Atlantic Monthly," 1857–1909: Yankee Humanism at High Tide and Ebb* (Amherst, 1994), 161–99.

52. AR to TNP, [Oct. 25, 1885], Page Papers, Mss 7581 K, UVA; AR to TBA, Oct. 25, 1885, (4407), Thomas Bailey Aldrich Papers, Houghton Library, Harvard University.

53. [AR], "A Brother to Dragons," *Atlantic Monthly* 17 (Mar. 1886); Taylor, *Amélie Rives*, 29.

54. AR to TBA, Nov. 23, 1885, (4408), Aldrich Papers, Harvard University.

55. AR to TBA, Dec. 7, 1885, (4410), ibid. "Yolaunt" was eventually published as *A Damsel Errant* in 1898.

56. AR to TBA, Dec. 6, 1885, (4409), and Dec. 31, 1885, (4404), Aldrich Papers, Harvard University.

57. Envelope [at beginning of file of Rives letters], (4408), ibid.

58. AR, "A Sonnet," *Century Illustrated Magazine* 37 (June 1886): 236.

59. AR to TBA, Oct. 25, 1885, (4407), Aldrich Papers, Harvard University.

60. AR to TNP, 3 Nov. [1885], Page Papers, Mss 7581 K, UVA.

61. AR to TBA, Nov. 23, 1885, (4408), Dec. 6, 1885, (4409), and n.d., [ca. Jan. 1886], (4406), all in Aldrich Papers, Harvard University. See also AR to TNP, "Xmas night," n.d. [Dec. 25, 1885], Page Papers, Mss 7581 K, UVA.

62. AR to TBA, n.d., [ca. Feb. 1886], (4403), Aldrich Papers, Harvard University; AR to TNP, Jan. 29 n.d. [1886], Page Papers, Mss 7581 K, UVA.

63. AR to TBA, Feb. 4, 1886, (4412), and Feb. 4, 1886, (4413), both in Aldrich Papers, Harvard University.

64. AR to TBA, Feb. 4, 1886, (4412), AR to TBA, Feb. 4, 1886, (4413), and AR to TBA, Feb. 5, 1886, (4414), all in ibid.

65. AR to TNP, n.d. [Feb. 5, 1886], Page Papers, Mss 7581 K, UVA.

66. AR to RWG, Feb. 15, 1886, Amélie Rives Papers, David M. Rubenstein Rare Book and Manuscript Library, Duke University.

67. AR to TNP, n.d. [Feb. 5, 1886], and n.d. [Mar. 15, 1886], Page Papers, Mss 7581 K, UVA; AR to RWG, Feb. 15, 1886, Amélie Rives Papers, David M. Rubenstein Rare Book and Manuscript Library, Duke University.

68. AR to TBA, n.d., [ca. Feb. 1886], (4403), Aldrich Papers, Harvard University.

69. [Judith Page Rives], *Tales and Souvenirs of a Residence in Europe* (Philadelphia, 1842).

70. "Autobiography of Judith Page Rives" (typescript), Rives Family Papers, VHS.

71. AR to TBA, Feb. 5, 1886, (4414), Aldrich Papers, Harvard University.

72. AR to Messrs Houghton Mifflin & Co, n.d [stamped Jan. 15, 1885], Houghton Mifflin Papers, Harvard University.

73. AR to TNP, Nov. 3 n.d. [1885], Thomas Nelson Page Papers, Mss 7581 K, UVA.

74. AR to Messrs Houghton Mifflin & Co., Jan. 2, 1885, [misdated Jan. 2, 1884, stamped Jan 7, 1885 by HM], (1799), Houghton Mifflin Papers, Harvard University; AR to TNP, Wednesday night [ca. Dec. 16, 1885], Thomas Nelson Page Papers, Mss 7581 K, UVA; AR to RWG, Apr. 3, 1886, Walter Pforzheimer Collection of Frank Stockton, Yale Documents MSS 560, box 8, Beinecke Library, Yale University.

75. AR to TNP, Mar. 4, 1884, and July 20, 1884, Page Papers, Mss 7581 K, UVA; AR to TBA, New Year's Eve, n.d. [Dec. 31, 1885], (4404), Aldrich Papers, Harvard University.

76. AR to TBA, [Dec. 6, 1885], (4404), Aldrich Papers, Harvard University.

77. AR, "The Story of Arnon," *Harper's New Monthly Magazine* 75 (Nov. 1887): 856–57.

78. AR to TBA, Dec. 7, 1885, (4410), Aldrich Papers, Harvard University.

79. AR to TNP, Jan. 25, n.d. [1886], Page Papers, Mss 7581 K, UVA; AR to TBA, Apr. 12, 1888, (4415), Aldrich Papers, Harvard University.

80. Mark J. Noonan, *Reading the Century Illustrated Monthly Magazine: American Literature and Culture, 1870–1893* (Kent, Ohio, 2010); AR to RWG, Feb. 15, 1886, and Mar. 22, 1886, Amélie Rives Papers, Duke University; AR to RWG, Apr. 3, 1886, Walter Pforzheimer Collection of Frank Stockton, Yale Documents MSS 560, box 8, Beinecke Library, Yale University.

81. AR to RWG, Apr. 3, 1886, Amélie Rives Papers, Duke University; AR to RWG, Apr. 4, 1886, Richard Watson Gilder Papers, Mss 7135, UVA. Amélie's father told her uncle that the *Century* had accepted one of her stories but when it would appear "is not known" (Alfred L. Rives to William C. Rives, Apr. 26, 1886, William C. Rives Papers, LC).

82. Alfred L. Rives to William C. Rives, June 17, 1886, William C. Rives Papers, LC; AR to RWG, July 20, 1886, Amélie Rives Papers, Duke University. A postscript that Rives appended to the letter—"By the way, I haven't received [back] 'Virginia of V.' yet,"—indicates that "the scribble" was "Virginia of Virginia."

83. For positive reception, see, for example, *Current Literature* 1 (Sept. 1888): 272; and *The Literary World: A Monthly Review of Current Literature,* Oct. 13, 1888, 19–21; Taylor, *Amélie Rives,* 34.

84. Noonan, *Reading the Century,* 110; Arthur John, *The Best Years of the* Century: *Richard Watson Gilder,* Scribner's Monthly, *and the* Century Magazine, *1870–1909* (Urbana, 1981), 153.

85. Robert Bush, *Grace King: A Southern Destiny* (Baton Rouge, 1983), 56–59; Noonan, *Reading the Century,* 90–108, 124–53.

86. For the repurchase of the story, see Julia Magruder to the Editor of the Century, Mar. 29, 1889, and JAC to the Editor of the Century, Aug. 28, 1890, Century Company Records, Box 84, Series I, NYPL.

87. AR to TNP, Wednesday night n.d. [ca. Dec. 16, 1885], and Xmas night n.d. [Dec. 25, 1885], Thomas Nelson Page Papers, Mss 7581 K, UVA.

88. Alfred L. Rives to TNP, Mar. 3, 1886, and July 7, 1886, ibid. The following year Amélie in a short note thanked Page "so much for all the charming things you say to me in your last letter" about the recent publication of her second story, "The Farrier Lass o' Piping Pebworth" in *Lippincott's Monthly Magazine.* AR to TNP, July 4, 1887, Page Papers, Duke.

89. AR to TNP, Xmas night n.d. [Dec. 25, 1885], Thomas Nelson Page Papers, Mss 7581 K, UVA.

90. Sarah Bruce to Morelle Bruce, Mar. 16, 1886, Bruce Family Papers, Mss 1 B8306, Virginia Historical Society; *Richmond Dispatch,* Apr. 25, 1886, 8; *New York Daily Tribune,* June 18, 1886, 6. In actuality, Rives was only twenty-two.

3. "The Most Noted of the Younger Writers"

1. Alfred L. Rives to William C. Rives, Dec. 14, 1878, William C. Rives Papers, Library of Congress.

2. Alfred L Rives to S. C. Rives, Aug. 20, 1885, Rives Family Papers, Mss 2532, Albert and Shirley Small Special Collections Library, UVA.

3. Alfred Landon Rives, autobiographical sketch, n.d. [ca. 1895], Rives Family Papers, Mss 1 R5247b7, VHS; AR to William C. Rives Jr., July 18, 1886, William C. Rives Papers, LC.

4. Alfred L. Rives to William C. Rives Jr., June 17, 1886; William C. Endicott to William C. Rives [Jr.], William C. Rives Papers, LC.

5. AR to William C. Rives Jr., July 18, 1886, ibid.

6. Ibid.

7. William C. Rives, Jr. to AR, July 26, 1886, ibid.

8. Ibid.

9. AR to William Cabell Rives Jr., Aug. 17, 1886, ibid.

10. AR to "General Fry," Aug. 13, 1886, Amélie Rives Papers, Mss 7208, Albert and Shirley Small Special Collections Library, UVA.

11. Alfred Rives to William Cabell Rives Jr., Aug. 9, 1886, William C. Rives Papers, LC.

12. The story was "The Farrier Lass o' Piping Pebworth," in *Lippincott's Monthly*, July 1887, 127–57; and the poems were "Love Song," *Century Illustrated Magazine* 33 (Apr. 1887): 839; "Grief and Faith" and "June," both in *Harper's New Monthly Magazine* 74 (May 1887): 867–68, and 75 (June 1887): 151. The essay was "On the Lack of Humor in Great Heroines," *Harper's Bazaar* (Sept. 10, 1887), 626.

13. Nina Silber, *The Romance of Reunion: Northerners and the South, 1865–1900* (Chapel Hill, 1993).

14. Henry M. Alden to TNP, July 23, 1886, Thomas Nelson Page Papers, David M. Rubenstein Rare Book and Manuscript Library, Duke University.

15. John R. Procter to TNP, June 4, 1886, ibid.

16. Robert Burns Wilson to TNP, n.d. [ca. Aug. 1886], ibid.

17. *Staunton Spectator*, July 28, 1886, 2.

18. Charles W. Coleman Jr., "The Recent Movement in Southern Literature," *Harper's New Monthly Magazine* 74 (May 1887): 838. A month earlier *The Critic: A Weekly Review of Literature and the Arts,* Apr. 16, 1887, 34, had announced the forthcoming article.

19. Coleman, "The Recent Movement in Southern Literature," 853.

20. *The Critic,* Apr. 30, 1887.

21. *Chicago Daily Inter-Ocean,* June 18, 1887, 10.

22. *Morning Oregonian,* June 19, 1887, 3.

23. AR, "Grief and Faith," *Harper's New Monthly Magazine* 74 (May 1887): 867–68.

24. Edward L. Tucker, "Thomas Nelson Page's Sonnet to Amélie Rives," *Mississippi Quarterly* 54 (Winter 2000/2001): 69–72.

25. Ibid. Tucker points out that Page's fourteen-line reply gives a fourteenth stanza to Rives's verse.

26. In November 1885, Rives had told Page that she wished to send Richard Watson Gilder "something thro' you someday which he thinks a man wrote"—possibly that "something" was this sonnet with its male narrator. AR to TNP, Nov. 3, [1885], Page Papers, Mss 7581 K, UVA.

27. AR, "Love Song," *Century Illustrated Magazine* 33 (Apr. 1887): 839. Lassiter returned to his native Petersburg the following year to practice law. He later entered politics and served as city attorney and then U.S. attorney for Virginia's eastern district. He was elected to four terms in the U.S. House of Representatives. *Biographical Dictionary of the United States Congress.*

28. Rosalie Rives to Francis R. Lassiter, Apr. 25, 1887, Francis R. Lassiter Papers, David M. Rubenstein Rare Book and Manuscript Library, Duke University.

29. AR to Francis R. Lassiter, May 21, 1887, ibid.

30. *Richmond Daily Times,* Mar. 22, 1887, 4.

31. *Richmond Dispatch,* Apr. 16, 1887, 1.

32. Ibid.

33. *Atlanta Constitution,* Feb. 25, 1888, 3, and Apr. 21, 1888, 9; *Alexandria Gazette,* Dec. 5, 1887, 2.

34. Grace Sears Rives Diary, [listing of dates], Oct. 1, 1887, Papers of the Rives, Sears and Rhinelander Families, Mss 10596, Albert and Shirley Small Special Collections Library, UVA; *Thomas County Catalogue* (Colby, Kans.), Aug. 4, 1887, 6; see also *Savannah Courier,* Aug. 18, 1887, 1.

35. Lucey, *Archie and Amélie,* 60–63.

36. These stories set in the past were "The Farrier Lass o' Piping Pebworth," *Lippincott's Monthly,* July 1887, 127–57; "Nurse Crumpet Tells the Story," *Harper's New Monthly Magazine* 75 (Sept. 1887): 620–33; and "The Story of Arnon," *Harper's New Monthly Magazine* 75 (Nov. 1887): 853–87.

37. AR, "Inja," *Harper's New Monthly Magazine* 76 (Dec. 1887): 31–48.

38. Ibid., 32.

39. Ibid., 33, 36–37, 39.

40. Ibid., 40; 41–42.

41. Ibid., 48.

42. Ibid., 37.

43. Catherine Cole, "Some Southern Writers," *New Orleans Daily Picayune,* Dec. 18, 1887, 10.

44. AR, "Virginia of Virginia," *Harper's New Monthly Magazine* 76 (Jan. 1888): 190, 200.

45. Ibid., 201, 203, 208.

46. Ibid., 207, 206, 209.

47. Ibid., 207, 211.

48. Ibid., 217.

49. Ibid., 222–23.

50. Ibid., 235.

51. Ibid., 210.

52. Ibid, 199.

53. Ibid., 199, 204.

54. Ibid., 200.

55. Ibid., 223.

56. Henry W. Grady to TNP, Apr. 25, 1888, Page Papers, Duke; *Chicago Daily Inter-Ocean* 109 (July 1888).

57. TNP, "Literature in the South since the War," *Lippincott's Magazine* 48 (Dec. 1891): 741, 745.

58. William L. Andrews, *The Literary Career of Charles W. Chesnutt* (Baton Rouge, 1980). For an excellent comparison of the plantation stories of Chesnutt and

Page, see Matthew R. Martin, "The Two-Faced New South: The Plantation Tales of Thomas Nelson Page and Charles W. Chesnutt," *Southern Literary Journal* 30 (Spring 1998): 17–36.

59. Page, "Literature in the South," 747–48.

60. Ibid., 753.

4. "A Hot, Tempestuous Story"

1. Alfred L. Rives to Landon Rives, Aug. 24, 1889, Rives Family Papers, Mss 1 R5247a, Virginia Historical Society.

2. See Jane Turner Censer, "Re-imagining the North-South Reunion: Southern Women Novelists and the Intersectional Romance, 1876–1900," *Southern Cultures* 5 (Summer 1999): 64–91; Elizabeth Varon, *We Mean to Be Counted: White Women and Politics in Antebellum Virginia* (Chapel Hill, 1998).

3. Gross, *Thomas Nelson Page*, 31, 32.

4. Censer, "Re-imagining the North-South Reunion."

5. "Society Topics of the Week," *New York Times,* June 10, 1888, 16; *Richmond Times-Dispatch,* Oct. 18, 1908, 7.

6. AR, "The Quick or the Dead?," *Lippincott's Monthly Magazine* 41 (April 1888): 433–522; and J. D. Hurrell, "Some Days with Amélie Rives," ibid., 531–36.

7. AR, "The Quick or the Dead?," 438.

8. Ibid., 452, 464.

9. Ibid., 510–11.

10. Ibid., 514.

11. Ibid., 453, 462–63.

12. Ibid., 456.

13. Ibid., 457.

14. Ellen Gruber Garvey, *The Adman in the Parlor: Magazines and the Gendering of Consumer Culture, 1880s to 1910s* (New York, 1996), 87, 87–88. Garvey sees Rives as addressing the question of the distinctiveness of the individual: Barbara Pomfret decides that her husband is not reproducible and cannot be replaced.

15. AR, "The Quick or the Dead?," 512–13. See Kristin L. Hoganson, *Consumers' Imperium: The Global Production of American Domesticity, 1865–1920* (Chapel Hill, 2007), 9, 57–104.

16. AR, "The Quick or the Dead?," 439.

17. Ibid., 514–15, 516, 518

18. Ibid., 435, 445, 473.

19. Ibid., 438.

20. Ibid., 477, 479.

21. "Miss Amelie Rives," *Atlanta Constitution,* Feb. 25, 1888, 3

22. AR, "The Quick or the Dead?," 433–34.

23. Ibid., 439–40, 419. On Martha Jane, see Lucey, *Archie and Amélie,* 134, 152.

24. AR, "The Quick or the Dead?," 446–47.

25. Ibid., 446.

26. Hurrell, "Some Days with Amélie Rives," 533, 536.

27. AR, "The Quick or the Dead?," 449.

28. "Amelie Rives Visited," *Chicago Daily Tribune,* 1, 5.

29. Lucey, *Archie and Amélie,* 95.

30. AR, "The Quick or the Dead?," 458.

31. Ibid., 520, 521–22.

32. *Chicago Daily Inter-Ocean,* Mar. 17, 1888, 10; *Boston Daily Globe,* Mar. 26, 1888, 3.

33. "Miss Amélie Rives's Short Stories," *The Critic: A Weekly Review of Literature and the Arts,* May 12, 1888, 228; "Bookishness," *Life,* Apr. 5, 1888, 194.

34. "Fashionable Gossip," *North American,* June 9, 1888.

35. Francis Rives to William Rives Jr., May 12, 1888, Rives Family Papers compiled by Elizabeth Langhorne, Mss 10596-d, UVA.

36. *Chicago Daily Inter-Ocean* 109 (July 8, 1888): 12.

37. "The Dead or the Quick," *Milwaukee Sentinel,* May 13, 1888, 11.

38. *New Orleans Daily Picayune,* Apr. 30, 1888, 4; *Atchison Daily Globe,* Sept. 1, 1888; *Milwaukee Sentinel,* Apr. 29, 1888, 4. The latter critic argued that the South had produced writers of "real merit, such as Sidney Lanier, Joel Chandler Harris, G.W. Cable, and Miss Murfree."

39. "A Talented Young Lady," *Atchison Globe,* Apr. 26, 1888; *Richmond Dispatch,* June 3, 1888, 6.

40. *Richmond Dispatch,* June 3, 1888, 6; *New York Mall,* as reprinted in *Atlanta Constitution,* May 27, 1888, 10; AR to Alice V. Broadus, Apr. 27, 1888, Samuel C. Mitchell Papers, Southern Historical Collection, University of North Carolina at Chapel Hill.

41. *Bangor Daily Whig and Courier,* May 30, 1888.

42. *New-York Daily Tribune,* June 6, 1888, 8.

43. AR to Miss Dickinson, Apr. 13, 1888, Yale Collection of American Literature, YCAL MSS 446, Box 25; and AR to "Judge Ambler," Apr. 13, 1888, Walter L. Pforzheimer Collection of Frank Stockton, YCAL MSS 560, box 8, both in Archives, Beinecke Library, Yale University.

44. Reprinted in *Atlanta Constitution,* May 27, 1888, 10.

45. Ibid.; AR to Alice V. Broadus, Apr. 27, 1888, Mitchell Papers, UNC. For a discussion of writers and reputation, see Susan M. Ryan, *The Moral Economies of American Authorship: Reputation, Scandal, and the Nineteenth-Century Marketplace* (New York, 2016), 127–35. On Broadus, see https://archives.sbts.edu/the-history-of-the-sbts/our-presidents/john-a-broadus-1889-1895/.

46. AR to Alice V. Broadus, Apr. 27, 1888, Mitchell Papers, UNC. In the preface to the book version of *The Quick or the Dead? A Study* (printed in 1889), she closed with the two sentences about books as mirrors.

47. Reprinted in *Atlanta Constitution,* July 5, 1888, 4.

48. Margaret Terry Chanler to "Dear Mama," May 12, 1888, Margaret Terry Chanler Family Papers, MS Am 1595, Houghton Library, Harvard University.

49. Margaret Terry Chanler to "Dear Mama," May 30, 1888, ibid.

50. Lucey, *Archie and Amélie*, 98.

51. AR to Frank Stockton, July 16, 1888, Pforzheimer Collection, YCAL Mss 560, Box 12, Yale University; Alfred L. Rives to Daisy Rives, Aug. 24, 1889, Rives Family Papers, VHS.

52. AR to Messrs Houghton Mifflin & Co., Jan. 2, [1885], item 1799 [misdated Jan. 2, 1884, stamped Jan. 7, 1885, by HM], Houghton Mifflin Company Papers, Harvard University; AR to TNP, Wednesday night [ca. Dec. 16, 1885], Thomas Nelson Page Papers, Mss 7581 K, UVA.

53. *Atlanta Constitution,* Jan. 7, 1889, 2; *New York Times,* Jan. 24, 1889, 2.

54. Reprinted in *Atlanta Constitution,* May 27, 1888, 10.

55. Elizabeth Chanler to JAC, June 2, 1888, John Armstrong Chaloner Papers, David M. Rubenstein Rare Book and Manuscript Library, Duke University.

56. AR to Alice V. Broadus, June 6, 1888, Mitchell Papers, UNC.

57. Lucey, *Archie and Amélie,* 98–99. Van Alen's deceased wife had been Drayton's sister-in-law.

58. "Society Topics of the Week," *New York Times,* June 10, 1888, 16.

59. *Chicago Daily Tribune,* June 6, 1888, 1.

60. *Richmond Daily Times,* June 14, 1888, 1.

61. "Amelie Rives Married," *Raleigh News and Observer,* June 17, 1888.

62. Margaret Terry Chanler to "Dear Mama," May 30, 1888, Chanler Family Papers, MS Am 1595, Harvard University; *Washington Post,* Oct. 17, 1908, 2.

63. Margaret Terry Chanler to "Dear Mama," June 17, 1888, Chanler Family Papers, MS Am 1595, Harvard University; Margaret Terry Chanler to JAC [copy], June 23, 1888, Chaloner Papers, Duke University.

64. Lucey, *Archie and Amélie,* 107; JAC to Winty Chanler [copy], June 27, 1888, Chaloner Papers, Duke University.

65. Alfred L. Rives to William C. Rives Jr., June 25, 1888, and William C. Rives to Sara Pryor, Aug. 8, 1888, both in William C. Rives Papers, LC.

66. *Sunday Herald and Weekly National Intelligencer,* Sept. 20, 1891, 5; *Richmond Times-Dispatch,* Sept. 28, 1904, 1; *Richmond Times,* Nov. 8, 1895, 1. For depictions of the Langhornes as southern or Virginia belles, see, for example, *Rocky Ford* (Col.) *Enterprise,* Jan. 9, 1896, 4, and *Wichita Daily Eagle,* Jan. 7, 1900, 13.

5. "My Life Is Ruined for Me"

1. Lucey, *Archie and Amélie,* 112–14.

2. AR to [Elizabeth Chanler], June 25, 1888, Rokeby Papers.

3. AR to Margaret Chanler, June 30, 1888, as quoted in Lucey, *Archie and Amélie,* 108–9; AR to [Margaret Chanler], July 2, 1888, Rokeby Papers.

4. AR to [Margaret Chanler], July 15, 1888, Rokeby Papers.

5. Lucey, *Archie and Amélie*, 110–11.

6. Nancy F. Cott, "Passionlessness: An Interpretation of Victorian Sexual Ideology, 1790–1850," *Signs: Journal of Women in Culture and Society* 4 (Winter 1978): 219–36; AR to TNP, July 9, 1884, Thomas Nelson Page Papers, Mss 7581 K, UVA.

7. AR to Alice V. Broadus, April 27, 1888, Mitchell Papers, UNC.

8. AR to TNP, [Oct. 10, 1885], Thomas Nelson Page Papers, Mss 7581 K, UVA; Maude Andrews, "Some Women and Then Some Others," *Atlanta Constitution*, Aug. 2, 1891, 6.

9. See, for example, https://www.womenshealth.gov/a-z-topics/endometriosis.

10. On the rise of gynecology in the 1870s and 1880s, see Judith A. Houck, *Hot and Bothered: Women, Medicine, and Menopause in Modern America* (Cambridge, Mass., 2006), 151. In the late nineteenth century, European physicians were beginning to explore the problems that came to be considered forms of endometriosis, though at first only through pathological studies. See Ronald E. Batt, *A History of Endometriosis* (London, 2011), esp. chaps. 2–4.

11. AR to [Margaret Chanler], July 2, 1888, and July 15, 1888, both in Rokeby Papers.

12. AR to Margaret Chanler, n.d. [summer 1888], Rokeby Papers.

13. AR to Mrs. Holloway, Amélie Rives Papers, David M. Rubenstein Rare Book and Manuscript Library, Duke University.

14. Lucey, *Archie and Amélie*, 113.

15. *New-York Daily Tribune*, Sept. 9, 1888, 5.

16. *Chicago Daily Tribune*, Sept. 9, 1888, 25, and Sept. 16, 1888, 9; JAC to [Margaret Chanler], Oct. 1, 1888, Rokeby Papers.

17. "Pretty Amelie Rives," *Boston Daily Globe*, Sept. 25, 1888, 2.

18. *New York Times*, Sept. 9, 1888, 12, and May 14, 1905, SM1.

19. Reprinted in *Atlanta Constitution*, Feb. 18, 1889, 4.

20. AR to Margaret Chanler, Nov. 15, 1888, Rokeby Papers.

21. Reprinted in *Atlanta Constitution*, Feb. 18, 1889, 4.

22. William S. Walsh to AR, Oct. 31, 1888, John Armstrong Chaloner Papers, David M. Rubenstein Rare Book and Manuscript Library, Duke University.

23. AR to Margaret Chanler, Feb. 15, 1889, and JAC to Elizabeth Chanler, Mar. 4, 1889, both in Rokeby Papers.

24. "The Dissenter," *The Critic: A Weekly Review of Literature and the Arts*, no. 253 (Nov. 3, 1888): 223; *Current Literature* 1 (Dec. 1888): 467; Andrew Lang, reprinted in *Atlanta Constitution*, Feb. 28, 1889, 4.

25. The novel contains two stories, an anecdote comparing marriage to champagne and an account of a bird that killed itself in Rives's bedroom, which she recounted as part of her early life in an unpublished autobiographical fragment.

26. AR, *The Witness of the Sun*, 95, 196; Taylor, *Amélie Rives*, 51.

27. AR, *The Witness of the Sun*, 105.

28. Ibid., 235; Taylor, *Amélie Rives*, 50; JAC to Elizabeth Chanler, Mar. 4, 1889, Rokeby Papers.

29. *Milwaukee Daily Journal,* Mar. 29, 1889; *Morning Oregonian,* Apr. 21, 1889.

30. Susy Clemens to Grace King, Apr. 1889, in *A New Orleans Author in Mark Twain's Court: Letters from Grace King's New England Sojourns,* ed. Miki Pfeffer (Baton Rouge, 2019), 165; *Raleigh News and Observer,* May 26, 1889; *State Press* [Galveston, Tex.], Apr. 26, 1889.

31. *Washington Post,* Mar. 22, 1889, 5. The item referred to the host as Rives's cousin, "Professor Cabell." See the biography of William D. Cabell at https://small .library.virginia.edu/collections/featured/the-cabell-family-papers-2/biographies /additional-biographies/william-d-cabell/; *Washington Post,* Mar. 23, 1889, 6.

32. As quoted in the *Atlanta Constitution,* Sept. 29, 1889, 17; Allan Nevins, *Henry White: Thirty Years of American Diplomacy* (New York, 1930), 9–31, 33–36, 45, 50–62.

33. Nevins, *Henry White,* 77.

34. Lucey, *Archie and Amélie,* 126.

35. Richard Davenport-Hines, *Ettie: The Intimate Life and Dauntless Spirit of Lady Desborough* (London: 2008), 93. See also Jane Abdy and Charlotte Gere, eds., *The Souls: An Exhibition . . .* (London, 1982).

36. Kenneth Rose, *Superior Person: A Portrait of Curzon and His Circle in Late Victorian England* (New York, 1969), 190; Davenport-Hines, *Ettie,* 48–50.

37. Davenport-Hines, *Ettie,* 46–51; 56–60, 71; AR, *Shadows of Flames,* 9.

38. Angela Lambert, *Unquiet Souls: A Social History of the Illustrious, Irreverent, Intimate Group of British Aristocrats Known as "The Souls"* (New York, 1984), 73.

39. AR to Kenneth Magruder, June 8, 1932, Rives Family Papers, Mss 2532, UVA.

40. David Gilmour, *Curzon: Imperial Statesman* (New York, 1994), 48–49.

41. Margot Asquith, *The Autobiography of Margot Asquith,* 2 vols. (London, 1920), 175.

42. Ibid., 177, 181.

43. Lucey, *Archie and Amélie,* 141–42.

44. For a particularly interesting account of Curzon's talents, see David Cannadine, *Aspects of Aristocracy: Grandeur and Decline in Modern Britain* (New Haven, 1994), 77–108.

45. AR to My dear Mr. Houghton, Feb. 22, 1889, Houghton Mifflin Company Papers, Harvard University.

46. AR to Messrs Houghton, Mifflin & Co., Mar. 30, 1889, ibid.

47. Ibid.

48. Ibid.; *Current Literature* 2 (June 1889): 543; Lawrence, Marquis of Zetland, *The Life of Lord Curzon . . . ,* 3 vols. (New York, [1927]), 1:172. The author may be incorrect about timing; the decision most likely took place in 1889, since Rives was in Paris most of 1890.

49. Zetland, *The Life of Lord Curzon,* 1:172.

50. Ibid., 1:194–95.

51. AR to Elizabeth Chanler, Oct. 15, 1892, as quoted in Lucey, *Archie and Amélie,* 142.

52. Nevins, *Henry White,* 82–84; Oscar Wilde to Amelie Rives Chanler, [Jan. 1889], in *The Complete Letters of Oscar Wilde,* ed. Merlin Holland and Rupert Hart-Davis (New York, 2000), 388. A subsequent note indicated that Wilde intended to call upon her at three o'clock after a scheduled lunch. Oscar Wilde to Amelie Rives Chanler, [Jan. 1889], ibid., 388. Although the editors indicate that this second letter (in private hands) was postmarked Jan. 15, 1889, both letters must date from June or July, given Rives's arrival in England in April.

53. *Washington Post,* Apr. 7, 1889, 12; *Current Literature 3* (Aug. 1889): 177.

54. *Washington Post,* June 12, 1889, 4; Walter Wellman, "Amelie Rives Visited," *Chicago Daily Tribune,* Feb. 25, 1889, 1.

6. "I Would Teach Her That Passion . . . Is a Great, Pure Fire"

1. Untitled Memo, Aug. 26, 1889, John Armstrong Chaloner Papers, David M. Rubenstein Rare Book and Manuscript Library, Duke University; Lucey, *Archie and Amélie,* 132–33.

2. AR to Margaret Chanler, Aug. 27, 1889, Rokeby Papers.

3. Lutie Pleasants to JAC, Nov. 6, 1889 (emphasis in original), Chaloner Papers, Duke.

4. AR to Margaret Chanler, Dec. 1, 1889, and Dec. 30, 1889 (emphasis in original), Rokeby Papers.

5. AR to Margaret Chanler, Dec. 1, 1889, ibid.; "Love Drove Him Mad," *Atlanta Constitution,* Mar. 30, 1890, 3.

6. See, for example, Lutie Pleasants to Elizabeth Chanler, June 8, 1891, and AR to Margaret Chanler, [Apr. 4, 1890], Rokeby Papers; and [Julia Magruder] to JAC, June 30, 1892, Chaloner Papers, Duke.

7. "The Fine Arts," *The Critic: A Weekly Review of Literature and the Arts* 15 (Feb. 14, 1891): 88.

8. Julia Magruder, "The House of Madame de Pompadour,"158, in Rives Family Papers, Mss 2532, Albert and Shirley Small Special Collections Library, UVA.

9. Ibid.

10. Ibid., 160–61; AR to Margaret Chanler, July 16, 1890 (emphasis in original), as quoted in Lucey, *Archie and Amélie,* 138.

11. AR, "Biographical Notes," [Ap. 1, 1925] (emphasis in original), Rives Family Papers, Mss 2532, UVA.

12. *Chicago Daily Inter Ocean,* Sept. 4, 1890, 5.

13. In this period, morphine use often began through an introduction by physicians. See David T. Courtwright, "The Hidden Epidemic: Opiate Addiction and Cocaine Use in the South, 1860–1920," *Journal of Southern History* 44 (Feb. 1983): 57–72.

14. AR, "To All Women," *Lippincott's Monthly Magazine* (Dec. 1888): 862.

15. *The Critic: A Weekly Review of Literature and the Arts* 15 (Feb. 14, 1891): 89.

16. AR, *According to St. John* (New York, 1891), 347–48.

17. Ibid., 351.

18. AR, *Shadows of Flames*, 87, 90.

19. *Southern Cultivator*, July 1891, 375.

20. *New-York Daily Tribune*, Aug. 7, 1891, 8; *Current Literature* 8 (Sept. 1891): 16.

21. *The Critic: A Weekly Review of Literature and the Arts* 16 (Nov. 14, 1891): 260; *Milwaukee Sentinel*, Nov. 4, 1891, 8.

22. Taylor, *Amélie Rives; Daily Picayune* (New Orleans), Oct. 18, 1891, 16; *Boston Daily Globe*, Oct. 11, 1891, 28.

23. Margaret Chanler Aldrich, "John Armstrong Chanler," as quoted in Lucey, *Archie and Amélie*, 141; *Boston Globe*, Jan. 14, 1891, 6; *Chicago Daily Tribune*, Jan. 18, 1891, 4.

24. Lutie Pleasants to JAC, Jan. 29, 1891, Chaloner Papers, Duke University.

25. Daisy White to Elizabeth Chanler, June 27, 1891, as quoted in Lucey, *Archie and Amélie*, 148. See also Lately Thomas, *The Astor Orphans: A Pride of Lions; The Chanler Chronicle* (New York, 1971), 130–35.

26. JAC to Elizabeth Chanler, July 10, 1891, as quoted in Lucey, *Archie and Amélie*, 149. On Robert Winthrop Chanler's career as an artist, see Gina Wouters and Andrea Gollin, eds., *Robert Winthrop Chanler: Discovering the Fantastic* (Miami, 2016).

27. *Boston Daily Globe*, Aug. 24, 1891, 1.

28. Ibid.; "Amelie Rives Chanler's Return," *Chicago Daily Tribune*, Aug. 24, 1891, 2; "Memo on alimony," Feb. 1, 1915, Chaloner Papers, Duke University.

29. *Milwaukee Sentinel*, Nov. 1, 1891, 11; JAC to Julia Magruder, June 3, 1892, Chaloner Papers, Duke University.

30. Lucey, *Archie and Amélie*, 155; JAC to Julia Magruder, June 3, 1892, Chaloner Papers, Duke University.

31. JAC to Julia Magruder, June 3, 1892, Chaloner Papers, Duke University.

32. Ibid.

33. Ibid.

34. Ibid. Much of Archie's long missive dealt with his fears about his marriage, but he also alluded to his problems earlier in life, especially those in communication. "My internal life, since the death of my dear Mother has been so lonely, so absolutely soul starved," he told Magruder, "that from self defense & common sense for the first ten years thereafter & from mere mental habit for the following years I have become quite Sphinx-like in my hiding the throbs of my really soft, tender heart."

35. Auchincloss, *A Writer's Capital*, 137.

36. AR to "Dr. Bleyer," June 26, 1892, Walter L. Pforzheimer Collection of Frank Stockton, YCAL MSS 560, box 8, Archives, Beinecke Library, Yale University; *New York Times*, Apr. 5, 1915, 11.

37. Gilmour, *Curzon*, 112, 108–14, 116–20; AR to Kenneth Magruder, June 8, 1932, Rives Family Papers, Mss 2532, UVA.

38. Lucey, *Archie and Amélie*, 161.

39. AR, "Innocence versus Ignorance," *North American Review* 155 (Sept. 1892): 287. This essay was excerpted in *Current Literature* 11 (Oct. 1892): 149.

40. Bertha Monroe Rickoff, "A Reply to Amélie Rives," *North American Review* 156 (Mar. 1893): 377.

41. Lucey, *Archie and Amélie*, 162.

42. AR, *Barbara Dering: A Sequel to "The Quick or the Dead?,"* 101, 45.

43. Taylor, *Amélie Rives*, 58–59; AR, *Barbara Dering*, 75.

44. Carroll Smith-Rosenberg, "The Female World of Love and Ritual: Relations between Women in Nineteenth-Century America," *Signs: Journal of Women in Culture and Society* 1 (Autumn 1975): 1–29; AR, *Barbara Dering*, 93, 133, 135.

45. AR, *Barbara Dering*, 106.

46. Ibid., 107.

47. Ibid., 135, 281.

48. *Chicago Daily Tribune*, Nov. 27, 1892, 39; *Atlanta Constitution*, Dec. 4, 1892, 21; *Godey's Lady's Book* 123 (Dec 1892): 544.

49. AR to Joseph M. Stoddart, Sept. 2, 1892 (emphasis in original as double underlinings), YCAL MSS 446, Box 25, Beinecke Library, Yale University.

50. AR, *Tanis, the Sang Digger* (New York, 1893), 183.

51. AR, *Shadows of Flames*, 2.

52. Ibid., 38, 71–72.

53. Jill Jonnes, in *Hep-Cats, Narcs, and Pipe Dreams: A History of America's Romance with Illegal Drugs* (Baltimore, 1996), 17–19, argues that genteel women made up a large group of American addicts in the late nineteenth century. AR, *Shadows of Flames*, 84, 85.

54. AR, *Shadows of Flames*, 90, 123.

55. Ibid., chaps. 25–30.

56. Lutie Pleasants to JAC, Dec. 14, 1892, Chaloner Papers, Duke University; Helen Lefkowitz Horowitz, *Wild Unrest: Charlotte Perkins Gilman and the Making of the Yellow Wall-Paper* (New York, 2010), 121–38, 189; David G. Schuster, "Personalizing Illness and Modernity: S. Weir Mitchell, Literary Women, and Neurasthenia, 1870–1914," *Bulletin of the History of Medicine* 79 (Winter 2005): 695–722.

57. Schuster, "Personalizing Illness and Modernity." Mitchell's *Characteristics* was among the books that Widener Library of Harvard University acquired from Rives's estate.

58. Winthrop Chanler to Elizabeth Chanler, May 14, 1893, Rokeby Papers; Edward W. Bok, "Some Literary Notes," *Milwaukee Sentinel*, May 21, 1893, 19; John Madison Taylor to JAC, Dec. 30, 1905, Chaloner Papers, Duke University. In this letter Dr. Taylor recounted the times that he had treated Amélie from his first meeting her in March or May of 1893.

59. AR to JAC, June 12, 1893, Chaloner Papers, Duke University; *Boston Daily Globe*, Sept. 4, 1893, 3.

60. AR to JAC, Jan. 7, 1894, Chaloner Papers, Duke University (emphasis in original).

61. Dr. John Madison Taylor to JAC, Dec. 30, 1905; AR to JAC, July 5, 1894, both in ibid.

62. AR to JAC, July 3, 1894, ibid. (emphasis in original).

63. AR to Louise Chandler Moulton, July 1, 1894, Louise Chandler Moulton Papers, Library of Congress; Diary of Hope Clement, July 6, 1894, Albert and Shirley Small Special Collections Library, UVA. Some idea of the circles in which Moulton moved can be found in the diary of Clement, who noted that Mrs. Moulton had introduced her to Frances Hodgson Burnett (author of *Little Lord Fauntleroy* and later *The Secret Garden*).

64. Emily Clark, *Innocence Abroad* (New York, 1931), 78.

65. Different sources place Pierre's height somewhere between six feet, two inches and six feet, seven inches. For information on him and his family, see Diane Dallal, "Anthony Arsdale Winans: New York Merchant and His Daughter—*The Canary of Lago Maggiore*," in *Tales of Gotham: Historical Archaeology, Ethnohistory, and Microhistory of New York City*, ed. Meta Janowitz and Diane Dallal (New York, 2013), 327–44; Jesse Willis Jefferis, "Paul and Pierre Troubetzkoy," *International Studio* 68 (July–Oct 1919): 10–15.

66. AR to Louise Chandler Moulton, Tuesday night, n.d. [summer 1894], Moulton Papers, LC.

67. Oscar Wilde to Lord Alfred Douglas, (May 1893?), in *The Complete Letters of Oscar Wilde*, 565. Given the reference to the portrait of Rives, the actual date of this letter must be late July or August 1894.

68. Ibid.

69. Ibid.; Constance, Lady Battersea, *Reminiscences* (London, 1922), 388–89. https://archive.org/details/reminiscences00battgoog.

7. "The Most Beautiful Woman in Literature"

1. See, for example, *Richmond Dispatch*, Apr. 25, 1886, 8; *New York Daily Tribune*, June 18, 1886, 6; *Staunton Spectator*, July 28, 1886, 2.

2. "Howard's Letter," *Boston Daily Globe*, Oct. 21, 1888, 8.

3. On celebrity, see Leo Braudy, *The Frenzy of Renown: Fame and Its History* (New York, 1986), 380–485. Charlene M. Boyer Lewis, in *Elizabeth Patterson Bonaparte: An American Aristocrat in the Early Republic* (Philadelphia, 2012), follows the career of an early nineteenth-century well-to-do woman who builds celebrity on her marriage and international connections. Elizabeth Patterson Bonaparte gave a politically antidemocratic cast to her celebrity that Rives never seems to have considered.

4. On the evolution of the woman's section, see Julie A. Golia, "Courting Women, Courting Advertisers: The Woman's Page and the Transformation of the American Newspaper, 1895–1935," *Journal of American History* 103 (Dec. 2016): 606–28.

5. Hurrell, "Some Days with Amélie Rives," 531; *Bangor Daily Whig & Courier*, Mar. 23, 1888; *Richmond Dispatch*, Oct. 11, 1895, 7.

6. AR to [Alice W.] Rollins, June 9, 1887, Amélie Rives Papers, Mss 214f, Albert and Shirley Small Special Collections Library, UVA.

7. "Miss Amelie Rives," *Atlanta Constitution,* Feb. 25, 1888, 3; "Miss Rives Explains Her Method," *Atlanta Constitution,* May 27, 1888, 10; "Miss Rives Speeds the Day," *Chicago Daily Tribune,* June 14, 1888, 1.

8. *Richmond Daily Times,* June 14, 1888, 1.

9. "Miss Amelie Rives," *Atlanta Constitution,* Feb. 25, 1888, 3; *Richmond Daily Times,* May 18, 1888, 2; Catherine Cole, "Some Southern Writers," *New Orleans Daily Picayune,* Dec. 18, 1887, 10.

10. "Miss Amelie Rives," *Atlanta Constitution,* Feb. 25, 1888, 3; "Miss Rives," *Chicago Daily Inter-Ocean,* Jan. 28, 1888, 5; "Pretty Amelia Rives," *Boston Daily Globe,* Sept. 25, 1888, 2; *Rocky Mountain News,* June 21, 1888, 9.

11. *San Francisco Daily Evening Bulletin,* Feb. 11, 1888; "A Talented Young Woman," *Atchison Daily Globe,* Apr. 26, 1888; "Miss Rives Explains Her Method," *Atlanta Constitution,* May 27, 1888, 10.

12. "Fair Ones in the Saddle," *Chicago Daily Tribune,* May 13, 1888, 26; *Atlanta Constitution,* Feb. 25, 1888, 3, and Jan. 7, 1889, 2.

13. *Atlanta Constitution,* May 27, 1888, 10; AR, *Barbara Dering: A Sequel to "The Quick or the Dead?"* (Philadelphia, 1893), 74.

14. *Staunton Spectator,* July 28, 1886, 2; "Amelie Rives," *Atlanta Constitution,* Apr. 21, 1888, 9; "Amelie Rives's Callers," *New York Times,* Mar. 23, 1889, 1; *Raleigh News and Observer,* Jan. 22, 1888. See also *Atchison Daily Champion,* Jan. 26, 6.

15. *Atlanta Constitution,* Feb. 25, 1888, 3, and June 16, 1888, 10.

16. "Of Interest to the Women," *Washington Post,* July 15, 1888, 12; *Chicago Daily Inter-Ocean,* May 14, 1892, 4.

17. *Washington Post,* Sept. 16, 1888, 9; "Amelie Rives," *Atlanta Constitution,* Jan. 12, 1889, 4.

18. "How Some Women Write," *Morning Oregonian* Apr. 29, 1888; *Atchison Daily Globe,* May 19, 1888; "Women and Their Ways," *Milwaukee Daily Journal,* May 31, 1888.

19. Catherine Cole, "Some Southern Writers," *New Orleans Daily Picayune,* Dec. 18, 1887, 10.

20. *Current Literature* 3 (Sept. 1888): 272; *Yenowine's Illustrated News* (Milwaukee), Dec. 23, 1893, 2.

21. *Belmont Chronicle,* Aug. 25, 1887, 2; *Milwaukee Journal,* July 31, 1891, 8; *Washington Post,* Apr. 7, 1889, 12. See also *News and Observer* (Raleigh, N.C.), Aug. 4, 1891, indicating that a "charming portrait of Miss Rives" is the magazine frontispiece.

22. Walter Wellman, "Amelie Rives Visited," *Chicago Daily Tribune,* Feb. 25, 1889, 1. Part of the interview was published in *Boston Daily Advertiser,* Mar. 1, 1889.

23. Walter Wellman to JAC, Mar. 6, 1889, John Armstrong Chaloner Papers, David M. Rubenstein Rare Book and Manuscript Library, Duke University.

24. "Amelie Rives," *Atlanta Constitution,* Apr. 21, 1888, 9; *Morning Oregonian,* Nov. 18, 1889, 7, and Jan. 18, 1892, 4.

25. *Washington Post,* Apr. 7, 1889, 12.

26. Ibid., Dec. 13, 1891, 10.

27. *Chicago Daily Inter-Ocean,* Sept. 4, 1890, 5; *Raleigh News and Observer,* Aug. 27, 1891.

28. Michael Ayers Trotti, *The Body in the Reservoir: Murder & Sensationalism in the South* (Chapel Hill, 2008), 33–34, 45, 61–65; "Finger-Toed Boots," *Washington Post,* Nov. 25, 1888, 11; "For the Ladies," *National Tribune* (Washington, D.C.), Nov. 29, 1888, 3. The same column declared that, according to a female observer, "the habit of cigaret-smoking by women" has grown in recent years.

29. Newspaper clipping, "Mrs. Amelie Rives's Digitated Boots," ca. Dec. 1888, Amélie Rives Papers, Duke University.

30. *Washington Post,* Aug. 6, 1888, 7.

31. *Chicago Daily Tribune,* Sept. 20, 1888, 1.

32. *Chicago Daily Tribune,* Sept. 25, 1888, 3.

33. *Yenowine's News* (Milwaukee), May 19, 1889, 7; *St. Paul Daily Globe,* Aug. 26, 1888, 4.

34. *Washington Post,* Nov. 5, 1888, 5.

35. "Defends Amelie Rives," *Boston Daily Globe,* Sept. 14, 1890, 21.

36. *New York Times,* Mar. 25, 1890, 3.

37. *Raleigh News and Courier,* Nov. 29, 1888; Maude Andrews, "Some Women and Then Some Others," *Atlanta Constitution,* Aug. 2, 1891, 6.

38. *Washington Post,* Sept. 29, 1889, 14.

39. "Authors' Wives: Vagaries of Genius," *Current Literature* 9 (Jan. 1892): 37; *San Francisco Daily Evening Bulletin,* June 11, 1891, 4.

40. Reprinted in *Atlanta Constitution,* Jan. 12, 1889, 4; *Bangor Daily Whig and Courier,* Apr. 12, 1889.

41. *Washington Post,* July 15, 1888, 12; Sept. 3, 1889, 2; and Sept. 30, 1888, 10.

42. "Crazy to See Amelie Rives," *Chicago Daily Tribune,* Sept. 16, 1888, 9; *Yenowine's News* (Milwaukee), May 5, 1889, 2.

43. *Milwaukee Daily Journal,* Sept. 21, 1889.

44. Banner, *American Beauty,* 112–46; *Washington Post,* Sept. 30, 1888, 10, and Sept. 3, 1888, 2.

45. *Washington Post,* July 15, 1888, 12. In recent years, the corset has drawn increasing attention from historians and those pursuing cultural studies. See Marianne Thesander, *The Feminine Ideal,* trans. Nicholas Hills (London, 1997), 81–105; Lurie, *The Language of Clothes,* 218–24; David Kunzle, *Fashion & Fetishism: Corsets, Tight-Lacing & Other Forms of Body-Sculpture* (Phoenix Mill, U.K, 2004).

46. *Washington Post,* Sept. 16, 1888, 9, and Sept. 8, 1889, 14; *Atchison Champion,* Feb. 3, 1892, 8.

47. Chanler, *Roman Spring.*

48. *Washington Post,* Jan. 11, 1889, 4; *Milwaukee Sentinel,* Aug. 31, 1889; *Morning Oregonian,* Oct. 6, 1889, 11.

49. *New Orleans Daily Picayune,* Nov. 2, 1892, 4; *Atchison Globe,* Aug. 31, 1894; Unidentified newspaper clipping, Feb. 15, 1895, Rives Family Papers, Mss 2532, UVA.

50. Chicago *Daily Inter-Ocean*, July 8, 1888, 12; "Amelie Rives's Callers," *New York Times*, Mar. 23, 1889, 1.

51. *Chicago Daily Inter-Ocean*, May 31, 1896, 17; "Feminine Footwear," *Richmond Dispatch*, Sept. 7, 1902, 3.

52. "Amelie Rives-Chanler," *Chicago Daily Inter-Ocean*, Sept. 4, 1890, 5; *Raleigh News and Observer*, Aug. 27, 1891.

53. *Current Literature* 7 (May 1891): 16.

54. Ibid.; "Plans of Amelie Rives," *Chicago Daily Tribune*, Aug. 1, 1891, 5.

55. *Chicago Daily Tribune*, Jan. 11, 1891, 4, and Jan. 14, 1891, 5; *Sacramento Record-Union*, Feb. 2, 1891, 1; *Galveston Daily News*, April 6, 1891, 4. See also *Atlanta Constitution*, Jan. 14, 1891, 1.

56. *Boston Daily Globe*, Aug. 24, 1891, 1; *Milwaukee Sentinel*, Aug. 8, 1891, 5; *Milwaukee Journal*, Oct. 15, 1892, 4.

57. *Boston Daily Globe*, Sept. 4, 1893, 3. On ill health, see, for example, *Yenowine's Illustrated News* (Milwaukee), Jan. 23, 1892, 2; and *Atchison Daily Globe*, Apr. 7, 1892.

58. *Milwaukee Sentinel*, Nov. 1, 1891, 11; *New York Times*, July 21, 1894, 3; *New-York Daily Tribune*, July 29, 1894, 14; *Charleston Weekly News and Courier*, Apr. 14, 1897, 16.

59. *Milwaukee Sentinel*, July 30, 1893, 10.

60. Ibid., and June 21, 1896, 19; *Boston Daily Globe*, Aug. 24, 1891, 1; *Rocky Mountain News*, Oct. 3, 1891, 4; Unidentified newspaper clipping, Feb. 15, 1895, Rives Family Papers, Mss 2532, UVA.

61. *St. Paul Daily News*, April 4, 1891, 8.

62. *The Bookman; a Review of Books and Life* (April 1895): 1; "Fiction Is Reviving," *Washington Post*, Oct. 25, 1896, 21.

63. *Fayetteville Observer*, Mar. 21, 1896.

64. *Atlanta Constitution*, Mar. 4, 1894, 11.

65. *Boston Daily Globe*, Sept. 4, 1893, 3; *New York Times*, Jan. 10, 1895, 14; Charles Hartnett to JAC, Oct. 14, 1895, Chaloner Papers, Duke.

8. "All That I Ever Dreamed of Love Is Mine, Mine, Mine"

1. Clark, *Innocence Abroad*, 82.

2. AR to [Louise Chandler Moulton], Feb. 6, 1896, Louise Chandler Moulton Papers, Library of Congress; Michael McGerr, in *A Fierce Discontent: The Rise and Fall of the Progressive Movement in America, 1870–1920* (New York, 2003), 77, argues that divorce rates in this period were rising among the very wealthy.

3. AR to JAC, Aug. 10, 1894, John Armstrong Chaloner Papers, David M. Rubenstein Rare Book and Manuscript Library, Duke University.

4. AR, "The Quick or the Dead?," 434.

5. Ibid., 508; AR, *Barbara Dering: A Sequel to "The Quick or the Dead?"*

6. Charles Hartnett to JAC, Oct. 15, 1895, Chaloner Papers, Duke.

7. AR to JAC, July 12, 1896, Chaloner Papers, Duke.

8. Lucey, *Archie and Amélie*, 172–80.

9. Ibid.

10. April White, "The Divorce Colony: The Strange Tale of the Socialites Who Shaped Modern Marriage on the American Frontier," *The Atavist Magazine,* no. 55, https://magazine.atavist.com/the-divorce-colony/. For a general account of the Dakotas as "divorce colonies," see Nelson Manfred Blake, *The Road to Reno: A History of Divorce in the United States* (New York, 1962), 122–29; AR to JAC, Apr. 24, 1895, Chaloner Papers, Duke University.

11. Taylor, *Amélie Rives,* 70. JAC memo, "Isis Unveiled," Feb. 1, 1915, Box 5, Chaloner Papers, Duke University. That the grounds for the divorce were cruelty can be found in an interview with Archie's law partner, William G. Maxwell, in the *New York World,* of Sept. 29, 1901, "clippings," Box 8, Chaloner Papers.

12. Charles Hartnett to JAC, Oct. 14, 1895, and Oct. 15, 1895, Chaloner Papers, Duke University.

13. Charles Hartnett to JAC, Oct. 14, 1895, ibid.; Lucey, *Archie and Amélie,* 187–89.

14. *Raleigh News and Courier,* Oct. 11, 1895, 2; Walter Wellman in *Chicago Times-Herald,* reprinted in *Denver Evening Post,* Oct. 14, 1895, 6; *Chicago Daily Inter-Ocean,* Oct. 27, 1895, 34.

15. *Milwaukee Journal,* Nov. 26, 1895, 5; *Atchison Daily Globe,* Oct. 19, 1895, 4; *Chicago Daily Inter-Ocean,* Feb. 9, 1896, 5.

16. *Morning Oregonian,* Oct. 11, 1895, 4.

17. Ibid., Oct. 11, 1895, and Oct. 21, 1895, 4; *Memphis Commercial Appeal,* Oct. 13, 1895, and Oct.18, 1895, 4.

18. *Milwaukee Journal,* Oct. 23, 1895, 4.

19. AR to Elizabeth Chanler, Dec. 4, 1895, in Lucey, *Archie and Amélie,* 189.

20. Julia Magruder to JAC, Jan. 4, 1896, Chaloner Papers, Duke University.

21. Alfred L. Rives to Grace Rives, Mar. 27, 1896, Rives, Sears and Rhinelander Families Papers, Mss 10596, UVA; AR to [Louise Chandler Moulton], Feb. 6, 1896, Moulton Papers, LC.

22. "Mrs. Chanler Becomes a Countess," *Chicago Daily Tribune,* Feb. 19, 1896, 2.

23. *Raleigh News and Observer,* Feb. 20, 1896, 4; *Atchison Daily Globe,* Mar. 31, 1896, 2; *Denver Evening Post,* Feb. 20, 1896, 4; *Washington Post,* Aug. 23, 1913, 5; *Fayetteville Observer,* Mar. 27, 1896, n.p. The misspellings of Troubetzkoy occurred in part because the transliteration from the Russian alphabet varied according to language (with the French and English versions different) and in part because Americans at that time dealt poorly with names not of British or German derivation. See *Bismarck Daily Tribune,* Feb. 18, 1896; *Memphis Commercial Appeal,* Feb. 18, 1896, 7.

24. *Macon Telegraph,* July 4, 1897.

25. Review in *Nebraska State Journal,* Mar. 8, 1896, reprinted in Willa Cather, *The Kingdom of Art: Willa Cather's First Principles and Critical Statements, 1893–1896,* ed. Bernice Slote (Lincoln, Neb., 1966), 334–35.

26. Ibid.

27. AR to Elizabeth Chanler, Dec. 4, 1895, in Lucey, *Archie and Amélie*,189; Alfred L. Rives to Grace Rives, Mar. 27, 1896, Rives, Sears and Rhinelander Families Papers, Mss 10596, UVA.

28. *Morning Oregonian,* Mar. 10, 1896; AR to JAC, Sept. 24, 1896, Chaloner Papers, Duke University.

29. AR to JAC, Sept. 24, 1896, and July 12, 1896, Chaloner Papers, Duke University.

30. Ibid.

31. Ibid.

32. Grace Rives to William C. Rives (III), Oct 21, [1896], Rives Family Papers compiled by Elizabeth Langhorne, Mss 10596-d, UVA; Clippings from *Charlottesville Daily Progress* and *Richmond Times,* ca. Oct. 17, 1896, Amélie Rives Troubetzkoy Papers, Mss 2495a, UVA.

33. *Milwaukee Journal,* Dec. 29, 1896, 6; Lucey, *Archie and Amélie,* 204-40, 257-58; Steele, DeFriese & Frothingham to Ernle G. Money, Nov. 26, 1907, Chaloner Papers, Duke University; *Washington Post,* Apr. 22, 1911, 5.

34. *Chicago Daily Inter-Ocean,* Mar. 8, 1896.

35. *Chicago Daily Tribune,* June 2, 1897, 1; *New York Journal,* July 18, 1897, in clippings, Rives Family Papers, Mss 2532, UVA; "New Book by Rives," *Chicago Daily Tribune,* July 19, 1897, 5.

36. See, for example, the account of the decision by Justice Thayer of the Philadelphia Court of Common Pleas ruling that the book was not obscene and could be sold there. *New York Times,* Sept. 25, 1890.

37. *New York Journal,* July 18, 1897, in clippings, Rives Family Papers, Mss 2532, UVA.

38. Ibid. Among the additional newspapers running parts of the interview in 1897 were the *New Orleans Times-Democrat* (July 21), the *Chicago Daily Tribune* (July 19), the *Charlotte Observer* (Aug. 14), and the *Milwaukee Journal* (July 20).

39. *Macon Telegraph,* July 4, 1897; *Chicago Daily Tribune,* June 2, 1897, 1.

40. *Raleigh News and Observer,* May 30, 1897, 5; *Chicago Daily Tribune,* June 2, 1897, 1.

41. Lippincott began advertising *A Damsel Errant* in 1897. For the repurchase of the story from the *Century,* see Julia Magruder to the Editor of the Century, Mar. 29, 1889, and JAC to the Editor of the Century, Aug. 28, 1890, Box 84, Series I, Century Company Records, NYPL. Rives mentions Meriel and its possible illustration in AR to Joseph M. Stoddart, Sept. 2, 1892, Yale Collection of American Literature, YCAL MSS 446, Box 25, Beinecke Library, Yale University. "Meriel. A Love Story," *Lippincott's Magazine,* Apr. 1898, 435-94.

42. AR to Louise Chandler Moulton, Dec. 26, n.d. [ca. 1897], Louise Chandler Moulton Papers, LC.

43. *New York Journal,* Feb. 27, 1898, in clippings, Rives Family Papers, Mss 2532, UVA.

44. Ibid. Other papers summarized the interview or advertised his fame; on Mar. 4, 1898, the *Milwaukee Journal* depicted him as "the social lion of the hour in Washington."

45. AR to [Louise Chandler Moulton], n.d., Moulton Papers, LC. This letter, written on stationery with a coronet, dates from a visit by Rives and Troubetzkoy to London, possibly either in 1896, 1901, 1904 or 1905. Pierre Troubetzkoy, *The Passer-by: An Episode* (New York, 1908); *Washington Post*, June 3, 1912, 7.

46. *San Francisco Call*, July 10, 1898, 27; *Washington Morning Times*, Mar. 23, 1896, 5.

47. *Pacific Commercial Advertiser* (Honolulu), Nov. 29, 1899, 14; *Milwaukee Journal*, Nov. 20, 1899.

48. *Washington Post*, July 1, 1900, 26; "The News of the World," *Harper's Bazaar*, July 14, 1900, 28; *Alexandria Gazette and Virginia Advertiser*, July 31, 1900, 2.

49. *Richmond Times*, Aug. 17, 1900, 6, and Aug. 24, 1900, 2.

50. *San Francisco Call*, Aug. 12, 1900, 12; "Amelie Rives Going South," *New York Times*, Nov. 24, 1900, 1; "Women Here and There," *New York Times*, Aug. 23, 1903, SM11.

51. *The Literary World: A Monthly Review of Current Literature*, Oct. 3, 1896, 20; J. P. Mowbray, "The Higher Hysterics," *The Critic*, Sept. 1902, 213.

52. Auchincloss, *A Writer's Capital*, 137.

53. AR to Anne Squire, Apr. 6, 1903, Anne Squire Papers, Firestone Library, Princeton University.

54. AR to Anne Squire, Apr. 6, and June 30, 1903, ibid.

55. AR, "A Hymn to the Sea," *North American Review* 174 (May 1902): 654–57.

56. AR to JAC, Apr. 24, 1895, and Julia Magruder to JAC, Oct. 27, 1895, both in Chaloner Papers, Duke University; AR to Elizabeth Chanler, Aug. 25, 1893, Rokeby Papers.

57. AR to Elizabeth Chanler, Aug. 25, 1893, Rokeby Papers; Taylor, *Amélie Rives*, 74–77; AR, *Sélené* (New York, 1905), 11.

58. AR, *Sélené*, 2, 55, 50.

59. Ibid., 58, 82.

60. Ibid., 8.

61. Ibid., 42.

62. See the discussion of the editorial that Rives published in 1892 in the *North American Review* in chap. 6, above.

63. *Reader* 6 (1905): 474; Louise Collier Willcox, "Some Recent Poetry," *North American Review* 182 (1906): 754.

64. C. H. Gaines, "Amélie Rives as Poet," *Harper's Weekly*, Apr. 15, 1905, 540.

65. Taylor, *Amélie Rives*, 78; AR, *Augustine the Man* (New York, 1906), 16.

66. *Richmond Times*, Aug. 24, 1900, 2.

67. [William Dean Howells], "Editor's Study," *Harper's Monthly*, Mar. 1901, 645–46. In this article Howells also discussed the work of the well-known writer Mary Wilkins (Freeman).

68. *New York Times,* May 10, 1901, 9; Nov. 5, 1901, 14; and Nov. 14, 1904, 7.

69. *The Critic,* n.s., 36 (Aug. 1901): 133; *San Francisco Call,* Sept. 13, 1903, 10, and Nov. 2, 1908, 7.

70. "Celebrate Mark Twain's Seventieth Birthday," *New York Times,* Dec. 6, 1905, 1; Louise Chandler Moulton. "Her Magic," *New Peterson Magazine* 2 (July 1893): 655. Among Rives's papers is an engraved invitation to the American memorial to the poet John Keats in Hampstead, England, on Monday, July 16, 1894. Invitation to AR and friend, July 16, 1894, Amélie Rives Papers, Mss 214, UVA.

71. Taylor, *Amélie Rives,* 70–73; Susan Goodman, *Ellen Glasgow: A Biography* (Baltimore, 1998). A proposed visit to Rives is mentioned in a letter from Ellen Glasgow to Arthur Graham Glasgow, Mar. 27, 1905, in *Letters of Ellen Glasgow,* ed. Blair Rouse (New York, 1958), 47; AR to Louise Chandler Moulton, Sept. 30, 1905, and Sunday, n.d. [ca. Oct. 1, 1905], Moulton Papers. LC.

72. "Amelie Rives: An Impressionistic Interview," *New York Times,* May 14, 1905, SM1.

73. Ibid.

74. Ibid.

75. Ibid.

76. "A Week's End Visit with Amelie Rives," *New York Times,* Apr. 15, 1906, SM3.

77. Ibid.

78. Ibid.

79. "'Americans Slaves to Convention'—Amelie Rives," *New York Times,* May 19, 1907, SM5.

80. "Society in Richmond," *Washington Post,* Jan. 28, 1906, E8.

81. "Deposition of Amélie Rives Troubetzkoy," [Apr. 2, 1906], Chaloner Papers, Duke University.

9. "A Legend with the Men of Father's Age"

1. See *New York Times,* Feb. 1, 1916, 7, indicating that the annual report of Archie's estate included a $3,600 payment to Rives.

2. Taylor, *Amélie Rives,* 81.

3. AR, *Hidden House* (Philadelphia and London, 1912), 24.

4. AR to Ellen Glasgow, Oct. 27, 1913, Ellen Glasgow Papers, Albert and Shirley Small Special Collections Library, Mss 5060, UVA.

5. J. B. Lippincott to AR, Jan. 3, 1913, Box 8, pp. 173–74, J. B. Lippincott Papers, Mss #3104, Historical Society of Pennsylvania; AR to Barclay Rives, May 24, 1914, Rives Family Papers compiled by Elizabeth Langhorne, Mss 10596-d, UVA.

6. Ibid., 416,

7. AR, *World's-End,* 24, 30–34.

8. *New York Times,* Apr. 26, 1914, 18; *The Bookman,* Aug. 1914, 225.

9. *New York Times,* Apr. 19, 1914, SM4.

10. Ibid.

11. Ibid.

12. AR, *Shadows of Flames: A Novel* (New York, 1915), 299, 286.

13. Ibid., 16.

14. Ibid., 349.

15. *New-York Tribune,* Sept. 3, 1915, 9.

16. Robert Hichens, *Felix: A Novel* (New York, 1902), 289, 290, 293–95.

17. *New-York Tribune,* Sept. 3, 1915, 9.

18. *Evening Star* (Washington, D.C.), Sept. 5, 1915, 6.

19. AR to Landon Rives, May 18, 1914, Rives Family Papers, Mss 2532, UVA .

20. Ibid.

21. Ibid., and June 15, 1914; George Moore to AR, n.d., George Moore Papers, GEN MSS 300, Series III, Box 2, folder 54, Beinecke Library, Yale University.

22. AR to Landon Rives, June 15, 1914, Rives Family Papers, Mss 2532, UVA.

23. Ibid.

24. *The Independent,* May 11, 1893, 16.

25. "The Lounger," *The Critic,* Jan. 1901, 3.

26. "A Week's End Visit with Amelie Rives," *New York Times,* Apr. 15, 1906, SM3; *Washington Post,* Feb. 12, 1911, 42.

27. *New York Times,* Feb. 3, 1911, 9; Feb. 12, 1911, BR69; and Feb. 17, 1911, 9.

28. Engle, "An 'Irruption of Women Dramatists.'"

29. AR to Landon Rives, June 15, 1914, Rives Family Papers, Mss 2532, UVA; Edward Foles Coward, "The $10,000 Prize Play," *The Theatre: The Magazine for Playgoers* 20 (July 1914): 11, 48.

30. AR to Landon Rives, May 18, 1914, and June 15, 1914, Rives Family Papers, Mss 2532, UVA; AR to Raphael Link, July 29, 1920, Amélie Rives Troubetzkoy Papers, Mss 24951, Albert and Shirley Small Special Collections Library, UVA; *Los Angeles Herald,* Feb. 8, 1903, 7.

31. *Christian Science Monitor,* Jan. 8, 1916, 18; *Boston Daily Globe,* Jan. 9, 1916, 11.

32. *Christian Science Monitor,* Jan. 10, 1916, 4.

33. James Fisher and Felicia Hardison Londré, *Historical Dictionary of American Theater: Modernism,* 2nd ed. (Lanham, MD, 2018), 238–39, 655.

34. *Washington Post,* Jan. 30, 1916, ES12; *Puck,* Apr. 1, 1916, 21; https://www.ibdb .com/broadway-production/the-fear-market-8262/#0pennightcredit.

35. AR to Mr. Millman, May 7, 1916, Amélie Rives Papers, David M. Rubenstein Rare Book and Manuscript Library, Duke University. Taylor, *Amélie Rives,* 108; *Moving Picture World* 43 (Jan. 1920): 465–66; "Coming Pictures," *New York Times,* Sept. 14, 1919, 52.

36. H. W. Boynton, "Yarns of Sea and Land," *The Bookman: A Review of Books and Life* 48 (Nov. 1918), 353–54; *New York Times,* Sept. 1, 1918, 370, 374.

37. On Faversham, see Fisher and Londré, *Historical Dictionary of American Theater,* 230; Troubetzkoy Papers, Mss 24951, UVA; C. Courtenay Savage, "The

Theatre in Review: The First of the War Plays," *Forum,* Sept. 1918, 361–63; https://www.ibdb.com/broadway-production/allegiance-8317 (accessed July 22, 2019).

38. *Boston Globe,* July 14, 1918, 42; Agreement between Amélie Rives and William Faversham, July 6, 1918, Amélie Rives Troubetzkoy Papers, Mss 2495a, UVA.

39. AR to Alice Kauser (carbon copy), July 31, 1920, Amélie Rives Troubetzkoy Papers, Mss 2495a at UVA. On Rives's poor health, see, for example, Raphael Link to AR and Pierre Troubetzkoy, July 29, 1920, Amélie Rives Troubetzkoy Papers, Mss 2495a, UVA; AR to Joseph Hergesheimer, Oct. 30, 1922, Joseph Hergesheimer Papers, Mss 4046, UVA; AR to Ellen Glasgow, Jan. 4, 1926, Glasgow Papers, Mss 5060, UVA.

40. AR to Julie Opp, Aug. 17, 1920, and AR to Raphael Link, Aug. 26, 1920, both in Amélie Rives Troubetzkoy Papers, Mss 2495a, UVA.

41. Ms. in Box 4, ibid.

42. As quoted in *New York Times,* Oct. 17, 1920, X1; *Washington Post,* Nov. 14, 1920, 62; and Oct. 12, 1920, 48. See also *Boston Daily Globe,* Apr. 17, 1921, 53.

43. Engle, "An 'Irruption of Women Dramatists.'" See also her study of five important female dramatists, *New Women Dramatists in America, 1890–1920,* 1–11, which finds that these women writers came from working-class backgrounds.

44. See Lois C. Gottlieb, *Rachel Crothers* (Boston, 1979), chaps. 2–4, for a nuanced discussion of how Crothers dealt with feminist themes.

45. *Washington Post,* Apr. 18, 1909, M9; *New York Times,* June 11, 1911, 8.

46. *New York Times,* Apr. 19, 1914, SM4.

47. Ibid.

48. Ibid.

49. *Washington Post,* May 24, 1915, 4; *New York Times,* Apr. 2, 1916, 19; AR and Pierre Troubetzkoy, "What the Victory or Defeat of Germany Means to Every American," n.p., n.d. (ca. 1915–18), Hathi Trust.

50. AR, foreword to Edward Hale Bierstadt's *Aspects of Americanization* (Cincinnati, 1922), 9–10.

51. *New York Times,* Dec. 17, 1912, 12, and Feb. 8, 1914, SM5.

52. Ibid., and Feb. 4, 1916, 20.

53. *New York Sun,* Apr. 15, 1916, Special Literary Section, 9. See David M. Kennedy, *Birth Control in America: The Career of Margaret Sanger* (New Haven, 1970), 23–32, 72–76.

54. *Jurgen and the Censor: Report of the Emergency Committee Organized to Protest Against the Suppression of James Branch Cabell's Jurgen* (New York, 1920), 37, 45, 57–58, 44; *New York Times,* Aug. 16, 1927, 44.

55. AR to Sinclair Lewis, n.d. [spring 1914], Sinclair Lewis Papers, YCAL MSS 268, Ser. II, Beinecke Library, Yale University. The references to *Our Mr. Wrenn: The Romantic Adventures of a Gentle Man,* published in 1914, and to "Miss Hegger," Grace Hegger, whom Lewis married in 1914, date this letter to that year. Rives had possibly become acquainted with Lewis when he worked for her new publisher,

Frederick A. Stokes, from 1910 to 1912. Richard Lingeman, *Sinclair Lewis: Rebel from Main Street* (New York, 2002), 39–65.

56. On the *Reviewer,* see Benjamin E. Wise, "'An Experiment in Southern Letters': Reconsidering the Role of *The Reviewer* in the Southern Renaissance," *Virginia Magazine of History and Biography* 113 (2005): 144–78.

57. Emily Clark to Joseph Hergesheimer, June 7, 1921, in *Ingenue among the Lions: The Letters of Emily Clark to Joseph Hergesheimer,* ed. Gerald Austin Langford (Austin, Tex., 1965), 7.

58. Emily Clark to Joseph Hergesheimer, [July 4, 1921], ibid.

59. Ibid., 12, 13.

60. Emily Clark to Joseph Hergesheimer, [July 4, 1921] and [Oct. 1921], ibid. 12, 14, 26.

61. Emily Clark to Joseph Hergesheimer, [Apr. 22, 1922] and [Feb. 1923], ibid., 58–59, 121.

62. *The Reviewer* 1 (Apr. 1, 1921): 119, and 1 (June 15, 1921): 276–78; Emily Clark to Joseph Hergesheimer, June 7, 1921, in *Ingenue among the Lions,* 7.

63. Emily Clark to Joseph Hergesheimer, [July 4, 1921], and Oct. 1921, in *Ingenue among the Lions,* 12, 14, 26–27.

64. Wise, "'An Experiment in Southern Letters.'"

65. Emily Clark to Joseph Hergesheimer, Dec. 21, 1921, [Feb. 1923], and [Apr. 1923], in *Ingenue among the Lions,* 40, 121–22, 137; Leanne E. Smith, "Emily Tapscott Clark (ca. 1890–1953)," *Encyclopedia Virginia,* https://www.encyclopediavirginia.org/Clark_Emily_Tapscott_ca_1890–1953.

66. Emily Clark to Joseph Hergesheimer, [Apr. 1923], in *Ingenue among the Lions,* 137–38.

67. AR to Joseph Hergesheimer, Jan. 9, 1922, Joseph Hergesheimer Letters, Mss 4046, UVA; Emily Clark to Joseph Hergesheimer, [Feb. 1923], in *Ingenue among the Lions,* 27–30.

68. AR to Joseph Hergesheimer, Nov. 25, 1921, Hergesheimer Letters, Mss 4046, UVA.

69. H. L. Mencken to AR, Nov. 21 [1921], H. L Mencken Papers, YCAL MSS 974, Acc. 1, Box 11, Beinecke Library, Yale University; AR to H. L. Mencken, Nov. 25, 1921, and Nov. 21, 1921, H. L. Mencken Papers, New York Public Library.

70. *Washington Post,* Nov. 7, 1920, 43; *Boston Daily Globe,* Dec. 15, 1923, 7.

71. See https://www.ibdb.com/broadway-organization/the-american-laboratory -theatre-company-20059; Fisher and Londré, *Historical Dictionary of American Theater,* 92–93. Richard Boleslavsky to AR, Nov. 4, 1925, Clipping from *New York Sun,* Nov. 6, 1925, 34, and Clipping from *New York Evening World,* Nov. 5, 1925, all in A. R. Troubetzkoy Papers, Mss 2495a, UVA. Although the length of the play's run is unclear, it received favorable reviews.

72. See https://www.ibdb.com/broadway-production/love-in-a-mist-10042; *Washington Post,* Dec. 28, 1926, 5; Robert Benchley, "Drama This Week," *Life,*

Apr. 29, 1926, 21; *Christian Science Monitor,* Nov. 2, 1926, 5B; and https://www.ibdb .com/broadway-production/say-when-10396.

73. Emily Clark to Joseph Hergesheimer, [July 4, 1921], in *Ingenue among the Lions,* 12; Edward Hale Bierstadt, "Creative Evolution in Plays," *The Reviewer* 2 (Jan. 1922): 192–97. On Bierstadt's career, see *New York Times,* Aug. 16, 1916, 9, and July 30, 1934, 11; and *Boston Daily Globe,* Oct. 20, 1929, B11.

74. Alice Kauser to AR, Oct 19, 1925, and AR to Alice Kauser, Dec. 5, 1925, in Amélie Rives Troubetzkoy Papers, Mss 2495a, UVA.

75. AR to Ellen Glasgow, Dec. 26, 1937, Ellen Glasgow Papers, Mss 5060, UVA; *Christian Science Monitor,* May 24, 1938, 12.

76. AR to Ellen Glasgow, Jan. 21, 1925, and Dec. 25, 1928, Glasgow Papers, Mss 5060, UVA.

77. AR to Henry L. Mencken, Sept. 15, 1929, and Sept. 23, 1929, H. L. Mencken Papers, NYPL.

78. AR to Henry L. Mencken, Sept. 23, 1929, ibid.; Julian R. Meade, *I Live in Virginia* (Danville, Va., 1935), 143–53. On Meade, consult Jennifer Leigh Smith, "Julian R. Meade (1909–1940)." *Encyclopedia Virginia,* Virginia Humanities, Mar. 3, 2014.

79. Meade, *I Live in Virginia,* 144, 150–51.

80. Ibid.

81. Goodman, *Ellen Glasgow,* 184–89, describes the conference, as does Joseph Blotner, *Faulkner: A Biography,* 2 vols. (New York, 1974), 1:705–22, quotation on 712.

82. *Recorder,* June 19, 1931; AR, autobiographical notes, [Apr. 1, 1925], Rives Family Papers, Mss 2532, UVA. Several years after Rives penned these reflections, the Republican Party used the adage in the 1928 presidential campaign. Thanks to Jennifer Ritterhouse for the reference to the petition.

83. AR to Joseph Hergesheimer, July 27, 1921, Hergesheimer Papers, Mss 4046, UVA; AR to Ellen Glasgow, Jan. 21, 1925, Glasgow Papers, Mss 5060, UVA.

84. AR to Kenneth Magruder, June 8, 1932, Rives Family Papers, Mss 2532, UVA.

85. Ibid.

Epilogue

1. AR to Ellen Glasgow, Dec. 15, 1936, in Ellen Glasgow Papers, Mss 5060, Albert and Shirley Small Special Collections Library, UVA.

2. AR to Ellen Glasgow, Aug. 25, 1937, ibid.

3. AR to James Southall Wilson, Jan. 13, 1932, and Jan. 1, 1932, both in James Southall Wilson Papers, Mss 6453a, Albert and Shirley Small Special Collections Library, UVA.

4. AR to Ellen Glasgow, Sept. 9, 1937, Glasgow Papers, Mss 5060, UVA.

5. AR to Ellen Glasgow, Oct. 6, 1937, Glasgow Papers, Mss 5060, UVA. On Endocreme, consult Morris Fishbein, *Morris Fishbein, M.D.: An Autobiography* (New York, 1969), 50.

6. AR to Ellen Glasgow, Sept. 9, 1937, Glasgow Papers, Mss 5060, UVA.

7. Auchincloss, *A Writer's Capital,* 134-35.

8. Ibid., 139.

9. Carol Gelderman quotes this letter in *Louis Auchincloss: A Writer's Life,* rev. ed. (Columbia, S.C., 1993), 68-69. See also Auchincloss, *A Writer's Capital,* 141-42.

10. AR to Kenneth Magruder, June 8, 1932, Rives Family Papers, Mss 2532, UVA; AR to James Southall Wilson, June 17, 1936, Amélie Rives Papers, Mss 214, UVA; Ms. "Herod and Mariamne," Amélie Rives Troubetzkoy Papers, Mss 2495a, UVA; AR Diary, Oct. 8, 1879, Rives Family Papers, Mss 2532, UVA.

11. AR to Melville Cane, June 18, 1938, July 22, 1938, and Nov. 8, 1939, all in Melville Cane Papers, Special Collections, Butler Library, Columbia University.

12. Auchincloss, *A Writer's Capital,* 138.

13. Ellen Glasgow to AR, Sept. 18, 1937, Glasgow Papers, Mss 5060, UVA. See also Louis Auchincloss Papers, Mss 9121-F, UVA.

14. Auchincloss, *A Writer's Capital,* 138; Ellen Glasgow to AR, Sept. 18, 1937, Glasgow Papers, Mss 5060, UVA; AR to Mrs. Rhinelander, Oct. 10, 1940, Rives Family Papers compiled by Elizabeth Langhorne, Mss 10596-d, UVA.

15. AR, autobiographical acct, [ca. 1941], in Rives Family Papers, Mss 2532, UVA. The question of married women's citizenship was a fraught one. The Cable Act of 1922 had allowed women in Rives's situation (marrying a European national) to retain their U.S. citizenship. See Linda K. Kerber, *No Constitutional Right to Be Ladies: Women and the Obligations of Citizenship* (New York, 1998), 38-43; Martha Mabie Gardner, *The Qualities of a Citizen: Women, Immigration, and Citizenship, 1870-1965* (Princeton, 2005), 123-27.

16. AR to Ellen Glasgow, Jan. 4, 1942, Glasgow Papers, Mss 5060, UVA; Louis Auchincloss to Priscilla Auchincloss, Aug. 4, 1942, Louis Auchincloss Papers, Mss 9121-F, UVA.

17. AR to Ellen Glasgow, Dec. 24, 1942, Glasgow Papers, Mss 5060, UVA; "Princess Nurse" to Melville Cane, Nov. 30, 1943, Cane Papers, Columbia University.

18. Constance Page Daniel to Elizabeth Langhorne, Mar. 7, 1990, Rives Family Papers compiled by Elizabeth Langhorne, Mss 10596-d, UVA.

19. AR to Kenneth Magruder, June 8, 1932, Rives Family Papers, Mss 2532, UVA.

20. "Amelie Rives Dies," *New York Times,* June 17, 1945, 26.

Novels, Essays, and Stories by Amélie Rives

1886
"A Brother to Dragons." *Atlantic Monthly* 57 (Mar.): 289–308.

1887
"The Farrier Lass o' Piping Pebworth." *Lippincott's Monthly*, July, 127–57.

"On the Lack of Humor in Great Heroines." *Harper's Bazaar*, Sept., 626.

"Nurse Crumpet Tells the Story." *Harper's New Monthly Magazine* 75 (Sept.): 620–45.

"Story of Arnon." *Harper's New Monthly Magazine* 75 (Nov.): 853–87.

"Inja." *Harper's New Monthly Magazine* 76 (Dec.): 31–50.

1888
Virginia of Virginia. New York: Harper and Brothers, 1888. Also in *Harper's New Monthly Magazine* 76 (Jan.): 189–235.

"The Man of the Golden Fillet." *Lippincott's Monthly Magazine* 41 (Feb.): 241–71.

"The Quick or the Dead? A Study." *Lippincott's Monthly Magazine* 41 (Apr.): 433–522. (also in hardcover ed.).

"Herod and Mariamne: A Tragedy." *Lippincott's Monthly Magazine* 42 (Sept.): 305–89.

"Un roman virginien, The quick or the dead." *Revue des deux mondes* 90 (Nov. 15): [368]–95. Translation of "The Quick or the Dead?"

A Brother to Dragons and Other Old-Time Tales. New York: Harper & Brothers.

"My Lady Tongue." *Once a Week* (Dec.).

1889
The Witness of the Sun. Philadelphia: J. B. Lippincott.

1890
"Asmodeus." *Once a Week* (date approximate).

"Was It a Crime?" *Fortnightly* 53 (July): 195–219.

1891
According to St. John. New York: J. W. Lovell.

1892
Barbara Dering: A Sequel to "The Quick or the Dead?," Philadelphia:
    J. B. Lippincott.
"Innocence vs. Ignorance." *North American Review* 156 (Sept.): 287–92.

1893
Tanis the Sang Digger. New York: Town Topics.
Athelwold. New York: Harper and Brothers.

1897
"The Story of a Heart." *The Cosmopolitan: A Monthly Illustrated Magazine* 23
    (July): 331–35.

1898
A Damsel Errant. Philadelphia: J. B. Lippincott.
"Meriel." *Lippincott's Monthly Magazine,* Apr., 433–94.

1902/3
"The Mocking of the Gods," *Harper's Magazine* 106 (Dec. 1902): 122–33; (Jan.
    1903): 282–88.

1905
Sélené. New York and London: Harper & Brothers, 1905.
"The Flittermouse." *Harper's Monthly Magazine* 111 (Nov.): 825–31.

1906
Augustine the Man. New York and London: John Lane.

1907
"The Garden of the King" *Harper's Monthly Magazine,* June, 49–57.

1908
The Golden Rose: The Romance of a Strange Soul. New York and London: Harper
    Brothers.

1909
Trix and Over-the-Moon. New York and London: Harper & Brothers.

1910
"Her Christmas Cabby," *Harper's Monthly Magazine* 122 (Dec.): 94–107.
Pan's Mountain. New York: Harper & Brothers.

1911
"Captain Meg's Son," *Harper's Monthly Magazine* 122 (Jan.): 267–81.

1912
Hidden House. Philadelphia: J. B. Lippincott.

1914
World's-End. New York: Frederick A. Stokes.

1915
Shadows of Flames. New York: Frederick A. Stokes.

1917
"Egeria Unveiled," *Cosmopolitan,* 62 (Apr.): 21–28, 110–14.

1918
The Ghost Garden. New York: Frederick A. Stokes.

1920
As the Wind Blew. New York: Frederick A. Stokes.

1923
The Sea-Woman's Cloak, and November Eve. Cincinnati: Stewart Kidd.

1926
The Queerness of Celia. New York: Frederick A. Stokes.

1927
Love-in-a-mist: A Comedy in Three Acts. New York and London: S. French.

1930
Firedamp. New York: Frederick A. Stokes.

Selected Bibliography

Primary Sources

Manuscript Collections Consulted

Privately Held
  Rokeby Papers

Rare Book and Manuscript Library, Columbia University
  Melville Cane Papers
  Harper & Brothers Papers
  Joseph Margolies Papers

David M. Rubenstein Rare Book and Manuscript Library, Duke University
  John Armstrong Chaloner Papers
  Francis R. Lassiter Papers
  Julia Magruder Papers
  Thomas Nelson Page Papers
  Alfred Landon Rives Papers
  Amélie Rives Papers

Houghton Library, Harvard University
  Thomas Bailey Aldrich Papers, MS Am 1429
  Autograph File, T
  Margaret Terry Chanler Family Papers, MS Am 1595
  Houghton Mifflin Company Papers, MS Am 2516
  Howells Family Papers, MS Am 1784
  Alice Kauser Papers, MS Thr 622
  Story Family Papers, MS Am 1703

Historical Society of Pennsylvania
  J. B. Lippincott Papers

Library of Congress (LC)
  Louise Chandler Moulton Papers
  William C. Rives Papers

Archives and Manuscripts, New York Public Library (NYPL)
  Century Company Records
  Paul Kester Papers
  Macmillan Company Records
  H. L. Mencken Papers
  Miscellaneous Personal Names File
  Alfred Anthony Williams Papers

Special Collections, Firestone Library, Princeton University
  Anne Squire Papers

Southern Historical Collection, University of North Carolina, Chapel Hill (UNC)
  Samuel C. Mitchell Papers

Albert and Shirley Small Special Collections Library, University of Virginia (UVA)
  Louis Auchincloss Papers, Mss 9121-F
  Diary of Hope Clement, Mss 4473e
  Richard Watson Gilder Papers, Mss 7135
  Ellen Glasgow Papers, Mss 5060
  Ellen Glasgow Miscellany, Mss 7225 b
  Louise Imogen Guiney Letter, Mss 7445
  Joseph Hergesheimer Letters, Mss 4046
  Julia Magruder Collection in Clifford Waller Barrett Papers, Mss 8022
  Julia Magruder Papers, Mss 11683
  Magruder Family Papers, Mss 2733-b
  Page Family Papers, Mss 6287g
  Thomas Nelson Page Papers, Mss 7581 K
  Lizette Woodworth Reese Papers, Mss 6550
  Amélie Rives Papers, Mss 214
  Amélie Rives Papers, Mss 7208
  Amélie Rives Letter to Imogene Guiney, Mss 7445
  Amélie Rives Troubetzkoy Papers, Mss 8925
  Amélie Rives Troubetzkoy Papers, Mss 2495a
  Rives Family Papers, Mss 2532
  Rives Family Papers compiled by Elizabeth Langhorne Mss 10596-d
  Rives, Sears and Rhinelander Families Papers, Mss 1059
  James Southall Wilson Papers, Mss 6453a

Virginia Historical Society (VHS)
   Bagby Family Papers, Mss 1 B1463
   Bruce Family Papers, Mss 1 B8306
   Haxall Family Papers, Mss 1 H3203
   Rives Family Papers, Mss 1 R5247

Archives, Beinecke Library, Yale University
   Mary Cadwalader Jones Papers, Yale Collection of American Literature (YCAL)
      MSS 409
   Sinclair Lewis Papers, YCAL MSS 268, Ser. II
   H. L. Mencken Papers, YCAL MSS 974, Acc. 1
   George Moore Papers, GEN MSS 300
   Walter L. Pforzheimer Collection of Frank Stockton, YCAL MSS 560
   Lady St. Helier Papers, GEN MSS 477
   Alfred Stieglitz–Georgia O'Keefe Papers, YCAL MSS 85, ser. 1
   Yale Collection of American Literature, YCAL MSS 446, Letter Collection Sub-
      series, Box 25
   Yale Collection of American Literature, Manuscript Miscellany, "R"

Published Sources

Abdy, Jane, and Charlotte Gere, eds. *The Souls: An Exhibition. . . .* London, 1982.
Andrews, William L. *The Literary Career of Charles W. Chesnutt.* Baton Rouge, 1980.
Asquith, Margot *The Autobiography of Margot Asquith.* 2 vols. London, 1920.
Auchincloss, Louis. *A Writer's Capital.* Minneapolis, 1974.
Banner, Lois W. *American Beauty.* Chicago, 1983.
Batt, Ronald E. *A History of Endometriosis.* London, 2011.
Battersea, Lady Constance. *Reminiscences.* London, 1922.
Bierstadt, Edward Hale. *Aspects of Americanization.* Cincinnati, 1922.
Blake, Nelson Manfred. *The Road to Reno: A History of Divorce in the United States.*
   New York, 1962.
Blight, David W. *Race and Reunion: The Civil War in American Memory.* Cambridge,
   Mass., 2001.
Blotner, Joseph. *Faulkner: A Biography.* 2 vols. New York, 1974.
Boyd, Anne E. *Writing for Immortality: Women and the Emergence of High Literary
   Culture in America.* Baltimore, 2004.
Braudy, Leo. *The Frenzy of Renown: Fame and Its History.* New York, 1986.
Bush, Robert. *Grace King: A Southern Destiny.* Baton Rouge, 1983.
Cannadine, David. *Aspects of Aristocracy: Grandeur and Decline in Modern Britain.*
   New Haven, 1994.
Cather, Willa. *The Kingdom of Art: Willa Cather's First Principles and Critical State-
   ments, 1893–1896.* Ed. Bernice Slote. Lincoln, Neb., 1966.

Censer, Jane Turner. "The Gift of Friendship: Ellen Glasgow and Amélie Rives, Virginia Writers." *Virginia Magazine of History and Biography* 124 (2016): 99–133.

———. *The Reconstruction of White Southern Womanhood, 1865–1895.* Baton Rouge, 2003.

———. "Re-imagining the North-South Reunion: Southern Women Novelists and the Intersectional Romance, 1876–1900." *Southern Cultures* 5 (Summer 1999): 64–91.

———. "The Southern Lady and the Northern Publishers: A Tumultuous Relationship." *Journal of Southern History* 85 (February 2019): 7–32.

Chandler, Alice. *A Dream of Order: The Medieval Ideal in Nineteenth-Century English Literature.* Lincoln, Neb., 1970.

Chanler, Margaret. *Roman Spring: Memoirs.* Boston, 1934.

Clark, Emily. *Ingenue among the Lions: The Letters of Emily Clark to Joseph Hergesheimer.* Ed. Gerald Austin Langford. Austin, Tex., 1965.

———. *Innocence Abroad.* New York, 1931.

Coolidge, John Gardner. *Random Letters from Many Countries.* Boston, 1924.

Cott, Nancy F. "Passionlessness: An Interpretation of Victorian Sexual Ideology, 1790–1850." *Signs: Journal of Women in Culture and Society* 4 (Winter 1978): 219–36.

Courtwright, David T. "The Hidden Epidemic: Opiate Addiction and Cocaine Use in the South, 1860–1920." *Journal of Southern History* 44 (Feb. 1983): 57–72.

Craighead, Erwin. *The Literary History of Mobile.* Mobile, 1914.

Dallal, Diane. "Anthony Arsdale Winans: New York Merchant and His Daughter— *The Canary of Lago Maggiore.*" In *Tales of Gotham: Historical Archaeology, Ethnohistory, and Microhistory of New York City,* ed. Meta Janowitz and Diane Dallal, 327–44. New York, 2013.

Davenport-Hines, Richard. *Ettie: The Intimate Life and Dauntless Spirit of Lady Desborough.* London, 2008.

Doyle, Don H. *New Men, New Cities, New South: Atlanta, Nashville, Charleston, Mobile, 1860–1910.* Chapel Hill, 1990.

Engle, Sherry. "An 'Irruption of Women Dramatists': The Rise of America's Woman Playwright, 1890–1920." *New England Theatre Journal* 12 (2001): 27–50.

———. *New Women Dramatists in America, 1890–1920.* New York, 2007.

Fishbein, Morris. *Morris Fishbein, M.D.: An Autobiography.* New York, 1969.

Fisher, James, and Felicia Hardison Londré. *Historical Dictionary of American Theater: Modernism.* 2nd ed. Lanham, Md., 2018.

Friedman, David M. *Wilde in America: Oscar Wilde and the Invention of Modern Celebrity.* New York, 2014.

Gardner, Martha Mabie. *The Qualities of a Citizen: Women, Immigration, and Citizenship, 1870–1965.* Princeton, 2005.

Gardner, Sarah E. *Blood & Irony: Southern White Women's Narratives of the Civil War, 1861–1937.* Chapel Hill, 2004.

———. *Reviewing the South: The Literary Marketplace and the Southern Renaissance, 1920–1941.* Cambridge, 2017.

Garvey, Ellen Gruber. *The Adman in the Parlor: Magazines and the Gendering of Consumer Culture, 1880s to 1910s.* New York, 1996.

Gelderman, Carol. *Louis Auchincloss: A Writer's Life.* Rev. ed. Columbia, S.C., 1993.

Gilmour, David. *Curzon: Imperial Statesman.* New York, 1994.

Glasgow, Ellen. *Letters of Ellen Glasgow.* Ed. Blair Rouse. New York, 1958.

Golia, Julie A. "Courting Women, Courting Advertisers: The Woman's Page and the Transformation of the American Newspaper, 1895–1935." *Journal of American History* 103 (Dec. 2016): 606–28.

Goodman, Susan. *Ellen Glasgow: A Biography.* Baltimore, 1998.

———. *Republic of Words: The* Atlantic Monthly *and Its Writers, 1857–1925.* Hanover, N.H., 2011.

Gottlieb, Lois C. *Rachel Crothers.* Boston, 1979.

Gross, Theodore L. *Thomas Nelson Page.* New York, 1967.

Grundy, Isobel. *Lady Mary Wortley Montagu.* Oxford, 1999.

Hardwig, Bill. *Upon Provincialism: Southern Literature and National Periodical Culture, 1870–1900.* Charlottesville, 2013.

Harvard College. *Class of 1878 Secretary's Report.* Boston, 1901.

Hichens, Robert. *Felix: A Novel.* New York, 1902.

Hoganson, Kristin L. *Consumers' Imperium: The Global Production of American Domesticity, 1865–1920.* Chapel Hill, 2007.

Holman, Harriet, "The Literary Career of Thomas Nelson Page." Ph.D. diss., Duke University, 1947.

Horowitz, Helen Lefkowitz. *Wild Unrest: Charlotte Perkins Gilman and the Making of the Yellow Wall-Paper.* New York, 2010.

Houck, Judith A. *Hot and Bothered: Women, Medicine, and Menopause in Modern America.* Cambridge, Mass., 2006.

Hunter, Jane H. *How Young Ladies Became Girls: The Victorian Origins of American Girlhood.* New Haven, 2002.

Hurrell, J. D. "Some Days with Amélie Rives." *Lippincott's Monthly Magazine* 41 (April 1888): 531–36.

Jann, Rosemary. "Myths in Victorian Medievalism." *Browning Institute Studies* 8 (1980): 129–49.

Jefferis, Jesse Willis. "Paul and Pierre Troubetzkoy." *International Studio* 68 (July–Oct. 1919): 10–15.

John, Arthur. *The Best Years of the Century: Richard Watson Gilder,* Scribner's Monthly, *and the* Century *Magazine, 1870–1909.* Urbana, 1981.

Johnson, Joan Marie. *Southern Women at the Seven Sister Colleges: Feminist Values and Social Activism, 1875–1915.* Athens, Ga., 2008.

Jones, Anne Goodwyn, and Susan V. Donaldson, eds. *Haunted Bodies: Gender and Southern Texts.* Charlottesville, 1997.

Jonnes, Jill. *Hep-Cats, Narcs, and Pipe Dreams: A History of America's Romance with Illegal Drugs.* Baltimore, 1996.

Jurgen and the Censor: Report of the Emergency Committee Organized to Protest Against the Suppression of James Branch Cabell's Jurgen. New York, 1920.

Kennedy, David M. *Birth Control in America: The Career of Margaret Sanger.* New Haven, 1970.

Kerber, Linda K. *No Constitutional Right to Be Ladies: Women and the Obligations of Citizenship.* New York, 1998.

King, Grace. *A New Orleans Author in Mark Twain's Court: Letters from Grace King's New England Sojourn.* Ed. Miki Pfeffer. Baton Rouge, 2019.

Kunzle, David. *Fashion & Fetishism: Corsets, Tight-Lacing & Other Forms of Body-Sculpture.* Phoenix Mill, U.K, 2004.

Lambert, Angela. *Unquiet Souls: A Social History of the Illustrious, Irreverent, Intimate Group of British Aristocrats Known as "The Souls."* New York, 1984.

Lewis, Charlene M. Boyer. *Elizabeth Patterson Bonaparte: An American Aristocrat in the Early Republic.* Philadelphia, 2012.

Lingeman, Richard. *Sinclair Lewis: Rebel from Main Street.* New York, 2002.

Lojek, Helen. "The Southern Lady Gets a Divorce: 'Saner Feminism' in the Novels of Amélie Rives." *Southern Literary Journal* 12 (Fall 1979): 47–69.

Longest, George Calvin. "Amélie Rives Troubetzkoy: A Biography." Ph.D. diss., University of Georgia, 1969.

———. *Three Virginia Writers: Mary Johnston, Thomas Nelson Page, and Amelie Rives Troubetzkoy: A Reference Guide.* Boston, 1978.

Lucey, Donna M. *Archie and Amélie: Love and Madness in the Gilded Age.* New York, 2006.

Lurie, Alison. *The Language of Clothes.* 2nd ed. New York, 2000.

Marchalonis, Shirley, ed. *Patrons and Protégées: Gender, Friendship, and Writing in Nineteenth-Century America.* New Brunswick, N.J., 1988.

Martin, Matthew R. "The Two-Faced New South: The Plantation Tales of Thomas Nelson Page and Charles W. Chesnutt." *Southern Literary Journal* 30 (Spring 1998): 17–36.

Matthews, Pamela R., ed. *Perfect Companionship: Ellen Glasgow's Selected Correspondence with Women.* Charlottesville, 2005.

McGerr, Michael. *A Fierce Discontent: The Rise and Fall of the Progressive Movement in America, 1870–1920.* New York, 2003.

McKee, Kathryn B. *Reading Reconstruction: Sherwood Bonner and the Literature of the Post–Civil War South.* Baton Rouge, 2019.

McWilliams, Hubert Horton. *The Prodigal Daughter: A Biography of Sherwood Bonner.* Baton Rouge, 1981.

Meade, Julian R. *I Live in Virginia.* Danville, Va., 1935.

Mitchell, Douglas L. *A Disturbing and Alien Memory: Southern Novelists Writing History.* Baton Rouge, 2008,

Mixon, Wayne. "New Woman, Old Family: Passion, Gender, and Place in the Virginia Fiction of Amélie Rives." In *The Adaptable South: Essays in Honor of George Brown Tindall,* ed. Elizabeth Jacoway et al. Baton Rouge, 1991.

Nevins, Allan. *Henry White: Thirty Years of American Diplomacy.* New York, 1930.

Newton, Stella Mary. *Health, Art and Reason: Dress Reformers of the 19th Century.* London, 1974.

Noonan, Mark J. *Reading the* Century Illustrated Monthly Magazine: *American Literature and Culture, 1870–1893.* Kent, Ohio, 2010.

Page, Richard Channing Moore. *Genealogy of the Page Family in Virginia. . . .* 2nd ed. New York, 1893.

Prince, K. Stephen. "Marse Chan, New Southerner: Or Taking Thomas Nelson Page Seriously." In *Storytelling, History, and the Postmodern South,* ed. Jason Phillips, 88–104. Baton Rouge, 2013.

———. *Stories of the South: Race and the Reconstruction of Southern Identity, 1865–1915.* Chapel Hill, 2014.

Rioux, Anne Boyd. *Constance Fenimore Woolson: Portrait of a Lady Novelist.* New York, 2016.

[Rives, Judith Page]. *Tales and Souvenirs of a Residence in Europe.* Philadelphia, 1842.

Rose, Kenneth. *Superior Person: A Portrait of Curzon and His Circle in Late Victorian England.* New York, 1969.

Ryan, Susan M. *The Moral Economies of American Authorship: Reputation, Scandal, and the Nineteenth-Century Literary Marketplace.* New York, 2016.

Schuster, David G. "Personalizing Illness and Modernity: S. Weir Mitchell, Literary Women, and Neurasthenia, 1870–1914." *Bulletin of the History of Medicine* 79 (Winter 2005): 695–722.

Sedgwick, Ellery. *A History of the "Atlantic Monthly," 1857–1909: Yankee Humanism at High Tide and Ebb.* Amherst, 1994.

Sicherman, Barbara. *Well-Read Lives: How Books Inspired a Generation of American Women.* Chapel Hill, 2010.

Silber, Nina. *The Romance of Reunion: Northerners and the South, 1865–1900.* Chapel Hill, 1993.

Smith-Rosenberg, Carroll. "The Female World of Love and Ritual: Relations between Women in Nineteenth-Century America." *Signs: Journal of Women in Culture and Society* 1 (Autumn 1975): 1–29.

Stansell, Christine. *American Moderns: Bohemian New York and the Creation of a New Century.* Princeton, 2010.

Taylor, Welford Dunaway. *Amélie Rives (Princess Troubetzkoy).* New York, 1973.

———. "A 'Soul' Remembers Oscar Wilde." *English Literature in Transition* 14 (1971): 43–45.

Tebbel, John. *The Expansion of an Industry, 1865–1919.* Vol. 2 of *A History of Book Publishing in the United States.* New York, 1975.

Thesander, Marianne. *The Feminine Ideal.* Trans. Nicholas Hills. London, 1997.

Thomas, Brook. *The Literature of Reconstruction: Not in Plain Black and White.* Baltimore, 2017.

Thomas, Lately. *The Astor Orphans: A Pride of Lions; The Chanler Chronicle.* New York, 1971.

Trotti, Michael Ayers. *The Body in the Reservoir: Murder and Sensationalism in the South.* Chapel Hill, 2008.

Tucker, Edward L. "Thomas Nelson Page's Sonnet to Amélie Rives." *Mississippi Quarterly* 54 (Winter 2000/2001): 69–72.

Varon, Elizabeth. *We Mean to Be Counted: White Women and Politics in Antebellum Virginia.* Chapel Hill, 1998.

White, April. "The Divorce Colony: The Strange Tale of the Socialites Who Shaped Modern Marriage on the American Frontier." *The Atavist Magazine,* no. 55, https://magazine.atavist.com/the-divorce-colony/.

Wilde, Oscar. *The Complete Letters of Oscar Wilde.* Ed. Merlin Holland and Rupert Hart-Davis. New York, 2000.

Wise, Benjamin E. "'An Experiment in Southern Letters': Reconsidering the Role of *The Reviewer* in the Southern Renaissance." *Virginia Magazine of History and Biography* 113 (2005): 144–78.

Wouters Gina, and Andrea Gollin, eds. *Robert Winthrop Chanler: Discovering the Fantastic.* Miami, 2016.

Zetland, Lawrence, Marquis of. *The Life of Lord Curzon, . . .* 3 vols. New York and London, [1927].

Index

Note: AR refers to Amélie Rives.

Lee's army, 5; on publications, 58–59; on Troubetzkoy, 191–92

Rives, Amélie (AR): affluence and comfort, 16–17; antilynching petition, 250; art, focus on, 16, 133–37, 142, 180; and authors' causes, 239–42, 249–50; and Authors League of America, 239–42; on beauty, 181–82; as belle and romantic prospects of, 26–28, 33–34, 47–48, 74, 85, 88, 99–100 (*see also* Chanler, John Armstrong "Archie"); on censorship, 240–41; correspondence, burning of, 256; corset, refusal of, 36, 140, 177–78; cosmetics, use of, 176, 216, 245, 254–55; death of, 258–59; education of, 12, 15–16, 25–26; endometriosis, possibility of, 115–16; equestrian and outdoor activities, 15; family expectations for, 25–27; family of origin, financial difficulties, 63–66, 106; and female friendship, importance of, 20–21, 134, 212; finances of, 254, 257–58; ill health and addiction, 43, 65–66, 115–16, 133, 137, 140–41, 152–54, 191, 194–95, 199, 201, 204, 248, 250; on individual autonomy, 237–38; legacy of, 259–61; literature, love of, 9–10; marriage, views on, 31, 42–43, 147–51, 222–23, 238; as mentor and muse, 241–45, 249–50, 256, 257; and Mobile, 11, 27–28, 32–33; mother, relationship with, 17–18; naming of, 5; and philanthropy, 106–7; and physicality, 43–44; reflection on her life, 256–57, 260; on religion and moral instruction, 13–15, 17–19, 214; self portrait of, 146–47; and sexuality, 146–47; theater and drama, 22–24, 27–28, 72–74; Victorian conventions questioning of, 24–25; on women's suffrage, 226, 237

— as author: on ability and self-doubt, 130–31, 250–51; childhood ambitions of, 24–26, 28–29, 31, 34–38; first publication, 48–50; gendered expectations, 55–57; history, fascination with, 40, 50, 89–90, 191, 229, 247–48; income and finances of, 65, 119–20, 191, 217–18, 220, 230, 233, 235–36; and materiality, 93–94; maturing of, 204–9, 218–26; motion pictures, 233–34; poetry, unpublished, 127–30; promotion of works, 167–70, 179–80, 198–99, 212–15, 232–33; publication under own name, 52–55; reception of, 72–74, 82, 107, 139–40, 151; rejection of novella, 197–98; as southern writer, 49–50, 67–70, 74–82, 84; sponsorship, 39–40 (*see also* Otis, William Sigourney; Page, Thomas Nelson); and theater, 72–74, 228–29, 234–37; women authors' experiences, comparison to, 60

— and Chanler: Archie's likeness in AR's writing, 97–101, 148–51, 207–8, 221, 224; AR's addiction, 141, 142–43; death of Archie, 254; divorce, 185–86, 188–90, 195, 197, 216, 217; engagement and wedding, 89, 99, 105–12; in England, 123–31; family relationship, 113–14, 141–42; in France, 132; marital strife, 116–17, 131, 132, 141–46, 155; separation from, 119–20; and sexuality, 114–16; social appearances of, 117–18, 122–23; writing, lack of, 119

— press coverage: AR response to, 172, 173, 179, 183–84; on beauty, 165–70, 175–77, 180–82, 210; on Chanler relationship, 108–9, 117–18, 188–90; on clothing and body, 177–79, 182, 201, 210–11; on deviant behavior and eccentricities, 167, 172–74; on health, 154–55, 180–81, 202; on marriage, 174–75; as princess, 197–98, 201–2, 210–16; on southernness, 170–72; on Troubetzkoy relationship, 192–93; on writing, 98–99, 182–83, 209–10; on youth, 163–65

— and Troubetzkoy: death of Pierre, 253–54; in Europe, 193–96, 226–28; finances, 195, 217, 248–49; introduction, 157–58; relationship, 200, 201, 209, 210–11, 222–23, 242; social gatherings, 249–50; wedding, 191–93

— writings, themes and attributes of: addiction, 152–53, 224–25; autobiographical

Rives, Amélie (AR) (*continued*)
aspects of, 207, 219, 221, 223–25; Black
characters, 80–81, 95–96, 186–87, 221–22;
dialect, use of, 13, 59, 75, 80–81, 219; marriage and courtship, 90–101, 147–51, 152;
poor white characters, 59, 81–82, 96, 151;
self-sacrifice, 137–40, 147–52; sexuality,
150–52, 220–21; unrequited love, 138. *See
also names of individual works*
Rives, Ella (AR's aunt), 13, 19–20, 26–27,
42–43, 97
Rives, Francis (AR's uncle), 101–2, 141
Rives, Gertrude (Potts) (AR's sister), 7,
109, 112, 156, 192, 196, 215, 219; forgery of
letters, question of, 54
Rives, Judith Page (AR's grandmother),
9–11, 13, 17, 22, 54–55
Rives, Rosalie (AR's cousin), 72
Rives, Sarah Landon "Daisy" (AR's sister),
85, 109, 122–23, 153, 156, 192, 196, 257–58;
birth of, 12
Rives, Sarah "Sadie" MacMurdo (AR's
mother), 5–7, 14, 17–18
Rives, William C., Jr. (AR's uncle), 64, 109, 111
Rives, William Cabell (AR's grandfather),
5–6, 9, 249
Robinson, Florence, 179–80
Rollins, Alice W., 163
romance of reunion, 86–88, 112
"Romaunt of Yovanne, The" (AR), 50, 56,
58; published as *A Damsel Errant,* 199
Rotch, Arthur, 112
Rudolf, archduke of Austria, 145

Sanger, Margaret, 240
Sanger, William, 240
Sea-Woman's Cloak, The (AR), 246
Sélené (AR), 205–9; reception of, 208–9
sexuality, 114–15, 124–25, 146–47, 208
Shadows of Flames (AR), 37, 125, 139,
152–53, 223–25; reception of, 225–26, 255
Shakespeare, William, 22
Shaw, Charles Gould, II, 112
Shelley, Percy Bysshe, 35

Shepherd, Frances, 258–59
Sigourney, Amélie Louise Rives (AR's
aunt), 5–7, 10, 47
Silber, Nina, 67
Sinkler, Wharton, 199
Smith, Ellen, 13
Smith-Rosenberg, Carroll, 149
"Sonnet, A" (AR), 51–52
Souls, the, 123–30
southern literary renaissance, 66–70, 77,
82–84
Stockton, Frank, 106
Stoddart, J. M., 119–20, 168
Stokes, Frederick A., 220, 291n55
"Story of Arnon, The" (AR), 50, 56–57, 74
Street, Mary, 241
Swan, Donald, 74

Tanis: The Sang Digger (AR), 151–52
Taylor, J. Madison, 154, 155
Taylor, Welford Dunaway, 36–37, 121, 218,
222
Tennant, Charlotte, 124
Tennant, Laura, 124
Tennant, Lucy, 124
Tennant, Margot (Asquith), 124, 126, 228
"To All Women" (AR), 137–38
Tolstoy, Leo, 197–98
Tree, Herbert Beerbohm, 229
Trix and Over-the-Moon (AR), 219
Trotti, Michael, 172
Troubetzkoy, Ada Winans, 157, 159, 194, 228
Troubetzkoy, Paul, 157
Troubetzkoy, Pierre: AR, introduction and
courtship with, 157–60; career of, 200,
228; on censorship, 240–41; and Curzon,
146; fictionalized in AR's writings, 224;
portrait of AR, 157–58. *See also under*
Rives, Amélie
Troubetzkoy, Pyotr, 157
Tucker, Edward, 70
Tully, Jim, 241
Twain, Mark (pen name of Samuel Clem-
ens), 83, 211

The American South Series

Daniel B. Thorp *In the* True Blue*'s Wake: Slavery and Freedom among the Families of Smithfield Plantation*

Peter Eisenstadt *Against the Hounds of Hell: A Life of Howard Thurman*

Daniel B. Thorp *Facing Freedom: An African American Community in Virginia from Reconstruction to Jim Crow*

Henry Kamerling *Capital and Convict: Race, Region, and Punishment in Post–Civil War America*

Clayton McClure Brooks *The Uplift Generation: Cooperation across the Color Line in Early Twentieth-Century Virginia*

Luis-Alejandro Dinnella-Borrego *The Risen Phoenix: Black Politics in the Post–Civil War South*

Reiko Hillyer *Designing Dixie: Tourism, Memory, and Urban Space in the New South*

Terence Finnegan *A Deed So Accursed: Lynching in Mississippi and South Carolina, 1881–1940*

Deborah Beckel *Radical Reform: Interracial Politics in Post-Emancipation North Carolina*

Randolph Ferguson Scully *Religion and the Making of Nat Turner's Virginia: Baptist Community and Conflict, 1740–1840*

Stephen A. West *From Yeoman to Redneck in the South Carolina Upcountry, 1850–1915*

Bruce E. Baker *What Reconstruction Meant: Historical Memory in the American South*

Andrew H. Myers *Black, White, and Olive Drab: Racial Integration at Fort Jackson, South Carolina, and the Civil Rights Movement*

Richard F. Hamm *Murder, Honor, and Law: Four Virginia Homicides from Reconstruction to the Great Depression*

James David Miller *South by Southwest: Planter Emigration and Identity in the Slave South*

Dianne Swann-Wright *A Way out of No Way: Claiming Family and Freedom in the New South*

Christopher Metress, editor *The Lynching of Emmett Till: A Documentary Narrative*

Charlene M. Boyer Lewis *Ladies and Gentlemen on Display: Planter Society at the Virginia Springs, 1790–1860*

John C. Willis *Forgotten Time: The Yazoo-Mississippi Delta after the Civil War*

Stephen Cushman *Bloody Promenade: Reflections on a Civil War Battle*

M. M. Manring *Slave in a Box: The Strange Career of Aunt Jemima*

Anne Goodwyn Jones and Susan V. Donaldson, editors *Haunted Bodies: Gender and Southern Texts*